Brief Contents

SO-ASU-365

CRIME ANALYSIS

With

CRIME MAPPING

SAGE was founded in 1965 by Sara Miller McCune to support the dissemination of usable knowledge by publishing innovative and high-quality research and teaching content. Today, we publish over 900 journals, including those of more than 400 learned societies, more than 800 new books per year, and a growing range of library products including archives, data, case studies, reports, and video. SAGE remains majority-owned by our founder, and after Sara's lifetime will become owned by a charitable trust that secures our continued independence.

Los Angeles | London | New Delhi | Singapore | Washington DC | Melbourne

CRIME ANALYSIS With CRIME MAPPING

RACHEL BOBA SANTOS

Radford University

Los Angeles | London | New Delhi
Singapore | Washington DC | Melbourne

FOR INFORMATION:

SAGE Publications, Inc.
2455 Teller Road
Thousand Oaks, California 91320
E-mail: order@sagepub.com

SAGE Publications Ltd.
1 Oliver's Yard
55 City Road
London, EC1Y 1SP
United Kingdom

SAGE Publications India Pvt. Ltd.
B 1/I 1 Mohan Cooperative Industrial Area
Mathura Road, New Delhi 110 044
India

SAGE Publications Asia-Pacific Pte. Ltd.
3 Church Street
#10-04 Samsung Hub
Singapore 049483

Printed in the United States of America

Library of Congress Cataloging-in-Publication Data

ISBN: 978-1-5063-3103-4

Acquisitions Editor: Jessica Miller
eLearning Editor: Laura Kirkhuff
Production Editor: Libby Larson
Copy Editor: Amy Harris
Typesetter: C&M Digitals (P) Ltd.
Proofreader: Laura Webb
Indexer: Amy Murphy
Cover Designer: Alexa Turner
Marketing Manager: Amy Lammers

This book is printed on acid-free paper.

SUSTAINABLE FORESTRY INITIATIVE
Certified Chain of Custody
Promoting Sustainable Forestry
www.sfiprogram.org
SFI-01268
SFI label applies to text stock

20 21 22 23 10 9 8 7 6 5 4 3

Detailed Contents

Preface

Crime analysis is a field of study and practice in criminal justice that uses systematic research methods and data, supports the mission of police agencies, and provides information to a range of audiences. Crime mapping is a subset of crime analysis that focuses on understanding the geographic nature of crime and other activity. Crime analysis is a relatively new topic in criminal justice education, and this book is one of the first to bring crime analysis and crime mapping to an undergraduate audience. A class in crime analysis provides students with opportunities to apply theory, research methods, and statistics learned in other courses, as well as presents information on a viable career path for criminal justice majors.

My purpose in this book is to provide an introduction to crime analysis with crime mapping through discussion of the concepts, theories, practices, data, analysis techniques, and the role of crime analysis in policing associated with this field of study. My purpose is not to cover current general or specific crime analysis software products or technology. This is because the rate of change of software products and technology is high, even though the foundations and fundamentals of crime analysis practice have remained the same over time.

In this fourth edition, I have updated and added to the content, so the book reflects current crime analysis practice in the United States and internationally. New to this edition are perspectives from crime analysts from countries outside the United States, from North America, Europe, and South America. These international crime analysts provide insight into crime analysis practices as they are conducted across the world. This book will not serve all purposes for the growing field of undergraduate education in crime analysis, but it is necessary for classes in which an overview of the field and fundamental techniques are taught. The book's website [http://www.sagepub.com/bobasantos4e] provides students with a plethora of practical examples contributed by working crime analysts, as well as opportunities to conduct crime analyses themselves through a variety of exercises.

The book is divided into five parts. Part I covers the foundations of crime analysis, including key definitions, a description of the crime analysis profession and its future, theoretical foundations of crime analysis, and the role of crime analysis in evidence-based policing strategies. Part II addresses the data and processes used in crime analysis, geographic data and crime mapping techniques, and the purpose of crime analysis products. Part III covers the methods and techniques of tactical crime analysis. Part IV looks at the methods and techniques of strategic crime analysis. Part V includes a chapter on crime analysis for crime reduction accountability—an important topic within administrative crime analysis.

The chapters in Part I lay the foundation for the rest of the book. Chapter 1 presents definitions of crime analysis and discusses the history and future of crime analysis and crime mapping; it also includes information on crime analysis career opportunities. In 2014, the International Association of Crime Analysts (IACA) developed a standardized definition of crime analysis as well as its types, so those are new to this edition. Chapter 2 provides an overview of the criminological theories that help to guide the practice of crime analysis. The illustration in Chapter 3 of the policing context in which crime analysis is conducted and the discussion of the role of crime analysis in effective policing strategies has been updated with current research in this edition.

The four chapters that make up Part II are devoted to the topics of the data and processes used in crime analysis, geographic data and crime mapping techniques, and a typology for crime analysis results. Chapter 4 discusses the crime analysis process and the different types of crime analysis (which were standardized by IACA in 2014). Chapter 5 provides a review of key terms, a discussion of the kinds of data commonly used and databases commonly accessed in crime analysis (e.g., crime, arrests, calls for service, traffic crashes, and primary data), information on what analysts must consider when using different kinds of data for analysis, and a brief overview of some of the hardware and software commonly used in crime analysis. Chapter 6 covers, in more detail, geographic data, types of geographic features, geocoding, descriptive crime mapping methods, and density mapping. Chapter 7 outlines a typology that categorizes crime analysis results by type of problem examined, purpose of the analysis, and type of audience for which the analysis results are produced.

The chapters in Part III describe the data, methodologies, techniques, and products of tactical crime analysis. Chapter 8 contains details of data and analysis of repeat incidents as well as data collected specifically for tactical crime analysis and pattern identification. Chapter 9 covers the methodologies analysts employ in identifying and finalizing patterns. Chapter 10 discusses how police respond to patterns and provides current examples of commonly identified patterns of persons and property crime. Chapter 11 highlights specific analytic, temporal, and spatial techniques that analysts use to identify and understand crime patterns. The chapter closes with guidelines for creating pattern bulletins and a bulletin template example.

The chapters in Part IV concentrate on the techniques that analysts use in analyzing long-term crime and disorder problems and provide case examples of how the techniques have been used in practice. Chapter 12 is an overview of the problem-solving process and covers the key statistics used in strategic crime analysis. Chapters 13 and 14 illustrate the strategic analysis of problems by demonstrating various techniques that answer key analysis questions. Chapter 15 discusses the types of strategic crime analysis products and provides guidelines for the substantive and formative development of such products.

Finally, Part V has been significantly changed in this edition. It contains one new chapter that covers one aspect of administrative crime analysis: crime analysis for crime reduction accountability. Chapter 16 focuses on the foundation of and products that support a police department's accountability structure, which ensures that crime reduction activities are taking place and are effective.

By no means does this book cover all facets of crime analysis; however, it does lay a solid foundation for students' understanding of the conceptual nature and practice of crime analysis that assists police in preventing and reducing crime and disorder. It provides an in-depth description of this emerging field and guidelines for the practice of crime analysis that are based on research, practice, and recent innovations, as well as previously available and new information. It also provides opportunities for students to explore possible future careers that support and enhance the effectiveness of modern policing.

Student Study Site

This free student study site provides additional support to students using *Crime Analysis With Crime Mapping, 4th Edition.* Practical crime analysis products, exercises, suggested web resources, and SAGE journal articles with discussion questions are included on this site to provide students with additional information and support and to get students into original research. Visit the study site at **http://www.sagepub.com/bobasantos4c**.

Instructor Teaching Site

This set of instructor's resources provides a number of helpful teaching aids for professors to use *Crime Analysis With Crime Mapping, 4th Edition.* Included on this site are PowerPoint slides, chapter outlines, test questions and answers, a sample syllabus, and suggested web resources for each part of the text.

Acknowledgments

I would like to thank all the reviewers who have helped me make improvements in this fourth edition. Thank you to SAGE reviewers Dr. Stephanie J. Bennett, University of Portsmouth; Don Gardiner, Governors State University; Charles J. Kocher, Cumberland County College, New Jersey; and Jonathan Allen Kringen, University of New Haven. I would also like to show appreciation to the following police agencies and their crime analysts who contributed products and examples used in this edition and/or in the book's resource materials. They include the following:

Detective Dan Benz, Seattle (Washington) Police Department

Mark Bridge, Fredrick (Maryland) Police Department

Rachel Carson, Inspired Acts, Ltd., United Kingdom

Michelle Chitolie, Port St. Lucie (Florida) Police Department

Dawn Clausius, Olathe (Kansas) Police Department

Prof. Dr. João Apolinário da Silva, Presidente da Agência Brasileira de Análise Criminal

Cheryl Davis, Port St. Lucie (Florida) Police Department

Chisen Goto, Royal Canadian Mounted Police

Kendahl Hearn, Salisbury (Maryland) Police Department

Katrine Holt, Oslo (Norway) Police District

Brandon Inscore, Greensboro (North Carolina) Police Department

Ericka Jackson, Gainesville (Florida) Police Department

Carola Jersonsky, Metropolitan Police of Buenos Aires (Argentina)

Jessica LaBlanc, Fairfax County (Virginia) Police Department

April Lee, Fort Pierce (Florida) Police Department

Brian McGrew, Adventos

Mattis Michaelsen, Oslo (Norway) Police District

Tamara Otley, Fullerton, California, Police Department

Daniel Polans, Milwaukee (Wisconsin) Police Department

Karin Schmerler, Chula Vista (California) Police Department

Alex Schneider, Arlington (Texas) Police Department

Tyr Steffensen, Oslo (Norway) Police Department

Dr. Shefali Tripathi, Gainesville (Florida) Police Department

Julie Wartell, on behalf of San Diego (California) District Attorney's office

Michelle Wentz, Port St. Lucie (Florida) Police
   Department

Damien Williams, Rockhill (South Carolina) Police
   Department

Alisha Wilson, Roanoke (Virginia) Police Department

Alyson Yaraskovitch, Ottawa (Ontario) Police Service

I would like to extend my appreciation to members of the SAGE publishing team for their support and assistance—Jerry Westby for his faith in my first edition and encouragement for the next three editions, Amy Harris, Libby Larson, Jessica Miller, and Laura Kirkhuff.

About the Author

Rachel Boba Santos is a professor at Radford University in the Department of Criminal Justice. She works with police departments around the world assisting them in improving their crime reduction efforts, data and crime analysis, accountability, and community partnerships. Her research focuses on environmental criminology, the effectiveness of crime reduction efforts by police, police accountability, and crime analysis.

Foundations of Crime Analysis

Part I contains three chapters that provide a practical and theoretical foundation for the field of crime analysis. Chapter 1 defines *crime analysis* as well as *crime mapping* and *geographic information systems* (GIS), describes the history of the crime analysis profession, and ends with specifics about crime analysis as a career track. Chapter 2 outlines the theoretical concepts that are most relevant for crime analysis by focusing on understanding the opportunities for crime in immediate crime settings. Chapter 3 provides the policing context in which crime analysis is conducted by reviewing the research on effective strategies of policing for preventing and controlling crime, discussing the role of crime analysis in each strategy, and providing a stratified structure for implementing crime analysis, problem solving, and accountability in police departments.

Crime Analysis and the Profession

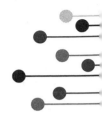

This chapter serves as a foundation for the discipline of crime analysis by providing definitions of crime analysis and crime mapping, along with an overview of the crime analysis profession in the United States. The overview includes the profession's history, the current research findings about crime analysis, descriptions of potential career paths for crime analysts, and ways to develop and improve a crime analysis unit. Finally, the chapter ends with crime analysis profiles and discussion of the future of crime analysis.

Definition of Crime Analysis

In 2011, the International Association of Crime Analysts (IACA) created a series of committees under the umbrella of the Standards, Methods, and Technology Committee (SMT) for the purpose of defining "analytical methodologies, technologies, and core concepts relevant to the profession of crime analysis" ("The SMT Mission," n.d.). This quote comes from the mission statement as written in the initial Standards, Methods, and Technology Strategic Plan completed April 2011. The purpose of the Standards Committee is to produce definitions that are used as the "standard" for the crime analysis profession. The methodology for formulating these standards includes the 1) creation of a draft paper through in-depth meetings and discussions of subject matter experts; 2) review and feedback by the IACA Executive Board; 3) review and feedback from an independent editor with knowledge of crime analysis; and 4) review and feedback by IACA members facilitated through the IACA website. In 2014, I was a member of the subject matter expert committee that produced the white paper titled "Definition and Types of Crime Analysis" (IACA, 2014b). Because of this development, the definitions of crime analysis and the types of crime analysis have been updated in Chapter 1 and Chapter 4 of this edition to the new IACA definitions. The following discussion has been adapted from the white paper (IACA, 2014b).

Foundation of the Definition

It is important to understand that the field of "crime analysis" includes much more than the analysis of crime. That is, crime analysis examines much more than crime, including many types of information that are relevant to police, such as disorder, calls for service, quality-of-life issues, traffic crashes, critical incidents, and, less often, fire and emergency medical incidents. Because the term *crime analysis* has been used historically, IACA has kept it as the standard, but it is important to understand that its processes and types of crime analysis apply to more than just crime.

The discussion of crime analysis throughout this book refers to crime analysts as serving *police agencies*. This term encompasses agencies with general law enforcement authority (i.e., with patrol, investigative, emergency response, prevention, and community service functions). These types of agencies include municipal and local police departments, metropolitan police departments, county police departments, county sheriff offices, state police agencies, and university police agencies within the United States. It also includes national, provincial, and regional police agencies with local-level police responsibilities internationally. While state and federal investigative agencies, intelligence agencies, researchers, statistical analysis centers, and corporate security departments might use aspects of crime analysis, they will not systematically use the majority of types and techniques of crime analysis discussed in this book.

Crime Analysis Definition

According to the IACA (2014b, p. 2), **crime analysis** is defined as the following:

> A profession and process in which a set of quantitative and qualitative techniques are used to analyze data valuable to police agencies and their communities. It includes the analysis of crime and criminals, crime victims, disorder, quality of life issues, traffic issues, and internal police operations, and its results support criminal investigation and prosecution, patrol activities, crime prevention and reduction strategies, problem solving, and the evaluation of police efforts.

In addition, the IACA (2014b) defines crime analysis as all types of analysis performed within a police agency, with the exception of evidence analysis (e.g., DNA, stolen property), human resources–related administrative analysis (e.g., budgeting, overtime, sick and vacation leave, salary), and analysis of supplies and equipment. Importantly, the IACA does not distinguish between crime analysis and crime intelligence analysis performed within a police organization. The term *intelligence* is one that is used in a variety of contexts in the crime analysis profession with some inconsistency. The term is used to describe information about an enemy, typically gathered covertly, resulting in more specific terms such as *military intelligence*, *criminal intelligence*, and *intelligence analysis*. More recently, the term has been used to describe information of operational value—for example, as a product rather than a source of analysis. Thus, the IACA adopts a definition of *crime intelligence analysis* (discussed in Chapter 4) to reflect a focus on criminal offenders as opposed to crime information in general. While certain analysts may specialize in particular functions, the IACA defines crime intelligence analysis as a set of techniques performed by crime analysts.

Crime analysis is not haphazard or anecdotal; rather, it is based in theory and involves the application of social science data collection procedures, analytical methods, and statistical techniques. More specifically, crime analysis employs both qualitative and quantitative data and methods. Crime analysts use **qualitative data and methods** when they examine nonnumerical data for the purpose of discovering underlying causes of crime. The qualitative methods specific to crime analysis include field research (such as observing characteristics of locations and talking to individuals with specific knowledge about a particular type of crime) and content analysis (such as examining police report narratives). Crime analysts use **quantitative data and methods** when they conduct statistical analyses of numerical or categorical data. Although much of the work in crime analysis is quantitative, crime analysts primarily use fundamental statistical methods, such as frequencies, percentages, means, and rates.

The central focus of crime analysis is the study of crime (e.g., rape, robbery, and burglary) and disorder problems (e.g., noise complaints, burglar alarms, and suspicious activity) and information related to the nature of incidents, offenders, and victims or targets (i.e., inanimate objects, such as buildings or property) of these problems. Crime analysts also study other police-related operational issues, such as staffing needs and areas of police service. Although many different characteristics of crime and disorder are relevant in crime analysis, three key types of information that crime analysts use are sociodemographic, spatial, and temporal. Sociodemographic information consists of the personal characteristics of individuals and groups, such as sex, race, income, age, and education. On an individual level, crime analysts use sociodemographic information to search for and identify crime suspects and victims. On a broader level, they use such information to determine the characteristics of groups and how these group characteristics are related to crime. For example, analysts may use sociodemographic information to answer the question "Is there a white, male suspect, 30 to 35 years of age, with brown hair and brown eyes to link to a particular robbery?" or "Can demographic characteristics explain why the people in one group are victimized more often than people in another group in a particular area?"

The spatial nature of crime, disorder, and other police-related issues is central to understanding the nature of a problem. Advanced computer technology and the availability of electronic data have facilitated a large role for spatial analysis in crime analysis. Visual displays of crime and disorder locations (maps) and their relationship to other events and geographic features are essential to understanding the nature of crime and disorder. In addition, results from criminological research within an area called "crime and place" (Eck & Weisburd, 1995) encourage crime analysts to focus on geographic patterns of crime by examining situations in which victims and offenders come together in time and space.

The temporal nature of crime, disorder, and other police-related issues is a major component of crime analysis. Crime analysts conduct several levels of temporal analysis, including examination of long-term trends of crime and disorder over several years, by season, and by day of week and time of day. This book will take a close look at specific analysis techniques used to examine the temporal nature of crime at each of these levels.

The primary purpose of crime analysis is to support redundant the operations of a police department. These functions include criminal investigation, apprehension, and prosecution; patrol activities; crime prevention and reduction strategies; problem solving; and the evaluation and accountability of police efforts. Without police, crime analysis would not exist. Although general, the definition encompasses a wide range of activities in which crime analysts assist police. A publication by the Bureau of Justice Assistance (BJA) provides an overview of how an analytical function benefits law enforcement agencies in nine ways (Bureau of Justice Assistance, 2005, p.1):

1. *Helps solve criminal investigations.* The analytical function develops a variety of intelligence products to assist investigators in detecting, preventing, and responding to criminal and terrorism activities. Analytical personnel initiate inquiries, conduct information searches, and act as a central point for information gathered.

2. *Increases the ability to prosecute criminals.* Personnel assigned to the analytical function develop summary tables, charts, maps, and other graphics for use in a grand jury or trial. Analysts provide factual and expert testimony and organize evidence for presentation in court.

3. *Supports the chief executive and the agency's mission.* By maximizing the analytical function, the chief executive can obtain important information and intelligence to possibly prevent future criminal activities. Personnel can prepare materials to assist in allocating resources; developing budget and resource requests; and preparing departmental reports, investigative briefings, and press releases.

4. *Proactively informs law enforcement officers of crime trends and develops threat, vulnerability, and risk assessments.* The analytical function provides support to tactical and strategic operations. Personnel analyze crime reports, identify crime hot spots, develop crime bulletins and summaries, study serial crime data, and forecast future crime. The analytical function develops proactive intelligence products that assess the potential threats of crime groups or criminal activities and recommends methods to intervene in these threats.

5. *Trains law enforcement and other intelligence personnel.* Staff develop course modules on intelligence and analytic methods and provide awareness and methodology training to agency members, executives, and managers.

6. *Assists in the development of computerized databases to organize information and intelligence.* Personnel within the analytical function help in the development and maintenance of systems that collect, collate, retrieve, and disseminate information. Analytical staff participate in departmental testing and acquisition of investigative, intelligence, and analytical software.

7. *Fosters meaningful relationships with other law enforcement personnel.* Analytical staff interact with other law enforcement agencies and build relationships with peers, allowing them to quickly obtain information and efficiently assist in multijurisdictional or complex cases. Through contact with national programs and professional associations, personnel are able to ascertain national issues that may affect local agencies.

8. *Ensures compliance with local, state, tribal, and federal laws and regulations.* Analytical personnel provide expertise and knowledge in the development of protocols to ensure compliance with local, state, tribal, and federal laws and rules that govern intelligence sharing, privacy, and civil liberties.

9. *Provides support to fusion centers.* Personnel provide support to local, state, or regional fusion centers by performing intelligence services such as crime pattern, association, telephone toll, and financial analysis. They create intelligence reports, briefs, threat assessments, and other intelligence products to aid in the prevention and deterrence of crime, including terrorism.

Definitions of GIS and Crime Mapping

Ever since maps have been available that depict the geographic features of communities, such as streets and city boundaries, police departments have used such maps to determine patrol areas and emergency routes and to assist patrol officers in finding specific addresses. Police and crime analysts also use maps as a key tool for crime analysis, a process that, historically, involved the manual placement of pins on hand-drawn wall maps. Since the 1990s, significant improvements in technology, software, electronic databases, and the Internet along with police innovation have made crime mapping by police departments extremely common. Every crime analyst uses a mapping program to visualize the spatial nature of crime. Because of this, crime mapping plays a key role in this book as an important tool used in crime analysis; thus, it is important to define key terms before proceeding.

A **geographic information system (GIS)** is a combination of software tools that allow the crime analyst to map crime in many different ways, from a simple point map to a three-dimensional visualization of spatial or temporal data. For the purposes of this book, the definition of a *GIS* is as follows:

> A GIS is a set of computer-based tools that allows the user to modify, visualize, query, and analyze geographic and tabular data.

A GIS is similar to a spreadsheet or word processing program in that the software provides a framework and templates for data collection, collation, and analysis. It is up to the user to decide what parts of the system to use and how to use them. A GIS does more than enable users to produce paper maps; it also allows them to view the data behind geographic features, combine various features, manipulate the data and maps, and perform statistical functions.

Crime mapping is a term used in policing to refer to the process of conducting spatial analysis within crime analysis. For the purposes of this book, the definition of *crime mapping* is as follows:

> Crime mapping is the process of using a geographic information system to conduct spatial analysis of crime and disorder problems as well as other police-related issues.

Clarifying where different types of crime and other types of incidents occur is one of the many important functions of crime analysis. Because of the unique nature of the software used and the prominence of geographic data in crime mapping, many people often discuss this type of analysis as though it is distinct from crime analysis; in reality, however, crime mapping is a technique used along with other techniques in crime analysis. Crime mapping serves three main functions within crime analysis:

1. It facilitates visual and statistical analyses of the spatial nature of crime and other types of events.

2. It allows analysts to link unlike data sources based on common geographic variables (e.g., linking census information, school information, and crime data for a common area).

3. It provides maps that help to communicate analysis results.

History of Crime Analysis

Human beings have analyzed crime and criminal behavior throughout history. That is, humans have always made observations about crime and other problematic events (i.e., collected data) and have identified relationships among those observations (i.e., conducted analysis). For example, in the old American West, a rancher may have noticed that he was losing one or two head of cattle from his grazing land every week. He also may have noticed that the cattle went missing only at night and only from a certain field. These observations and his analysis of them may have led him to respond either by sitting and watching the cattle in that field overnight or by moving the cattle to another field. The rancher's thoughts and actions constitute a simple form of crime analysis. Similarly, police officers have historically conducted crime analysis by using memory to link key suspects and property to specific relationships among crime incidents.

The present-day discipline of crime analysis represents an evolution of the kinds of crime analysis illustrated by this example. It is a systematic process in which data about crime and other related factors are collected and stored for long periods of time. Where earlier "crime analysts" relied mostly on their own observations and their own memories of crime incidents, modern crime analysts use complex computer systems to apply various analytic techniques, ranging from simple pattern analysis to complex statistical analysis.

Beginnings of Crime Analysis

The history of the analysis of crime is long, but the history of crime analysis as a discipline begins with the first modern police force, which was created in London in the early 19th century. This makes sense, given that the main purpose of crime analysis is to assist the police. Through the Metropolitan Police Act, passed in the 1820s, England organized about a thousand men to form a London police force. In 1842, this force created a detective bureau, which was given the responsibility of identifying crime patterns to help solve crimes. According to London's Metropolitan Police Service (2016), by 1844 the detective bureau's officers were collecting, collating, and analyzing police information. An example follows:

> 1844: Richard Mayne, Commissioner [was] called to give evidence to the Select Committee on Dogs. He stated that in the Metropolis there were a rising number of lost or stolen dogs. In the preceding year over 600 dogs were lost and 60 stolen. He declared the law to be in a very unsatisfactory state as people paid money for restoration of dogs. "People pay monies to parties whom they have reason to believe have either stolen or enticed them away in order to get the reward. . . ." Mayne believed it to be organised crime. (para. 17)

Additionally, the Metropolitan Police Service (2016) notes that aggregate crime statistics were available for the city of London as early as 1847; that year there were "14,091 robberies; 62,181 people taken in charge, 24,689 of these were summarily dealt with; 5,920 stood trial and 4,551 were convicted and sentenced; 31,572 people were discharged by the magistrates."

United States: 1900 to 1970

Although many large cities in the United States began to create police departments in the mid-1850s, corruption within these departments as well as a lack of organization and technology prevented them from conducting crime analysis systematically. The first indication of an instance of formal crime analysis in the United States is found in the early 1900s. August Vollmer, the most famous police reformer, in addition to instituting the innovations of vehicle patrol, radio communication, and fingerprinting, encouraged the use of pin mapping, the regular review of police reports, and the formation of patrol districts based on crime volume (Reiner, Greenlee, & Gibbens, 1976).

O. W. Wilson, who worked with Vollmer and created an advanced training program for officers, was the first to mention and define the term *crime analysis* in the second edition of his book *Police Administration* in 1963. In the fourth edition of that book, Wilson and McLaren (1977) distinguish between "operations" analysis and "crime" analysis, asserting that crime analysis is the "process of the identification of crime trends and patterns through statistical treatment of information and through examination of actual investigative reports" (p. 175).

From Wilson's writings, it appears that crime analysis was being conducted in (or at least was recommended to) police departments in the 1950s and 1960s; however, no evidence of crime analysis is available from that period. In his lesser-known book, *Police Planning*, which was first published in 1952, Wilson discusses crime mapping and crime analysis, although he does not use those terms. In the second edition of that volume, he outlines the structure of police planning to include a "cartography unit," which among other things "provides technical advice . . . in depicting crime trends or occurrences . . . in located places of arrest" and a "statistics unit," which includes many of the functions of crime analysis that are still practiced today, such as "interpreting and disseminating crime statistics and other related material to be used as aids for more effective and efficient operation of the department; preparing statistical charts, graphs, and artwork as needed by other department units" and "maintaining and operating the modus operandi files" (Wilson, 1957, p. 10).

United States: 1970 to 2000

The 1968 Omnibus Crime Control and Safe Streets Act brought about increased awareness of the use of analysis and evaluation in policing throughout the 1970s. The act allowed the allocation of federal grants to assist state and local police agencies with any purpose associated with reducing crime. The U.S. Bureau of Justice Administration, established by the act for the general purpose of supporting police agencies, provided extensive assistance, helping police departments establish evaluation programs and providing training, technical assistance, and information to support the work funded by the grants (Omnibus Crime Control and Safe Streets Act of 1968; Pomrenke, 1969).

As a result, publications from the 1970s about crime analysis techniques as well as evaluations of crime analysis functions indicate that police departments had begun to take Vollmer's and Wilson's advice to formalize crime analysis. In an annotated bibliography prepared for the National Institute of Justice, Emig, Heck, and Kravitz (1980) provide information on crime analysis publications and products of the 1970s. The bibliography includes entries for many handbooks devoted to the techniques of tactical and strategic crime analysis that were produced by various nonprofit organizations and funded by the U.S. government (e.g., *Police Crime Analysis Unit Handbook* [Austin et al., 1973]; "Management Function of a Crime Analysis Unit" [Booth, 1979]; *Crime Analysis System Support: Descriptive Report of Manual and Automated Crime Analysis Functions* [Chang, Simms, Makres, & Bodnar, 1979]).

During the 1970s, the U.S. government held several symposia on crime analysis and brought academics and practitioners together to work on specific technical assistance projects aimed at increasing the crime analysis capabilities of police agencies (Emig et al., 1980). Popular media sources also provide evidence that formal crime analysis units existed during this period. For example, an article from *The New York Times* published in 1972 mentions crime analysis: "Crime analysts at NYC Police Hq say on July 21 that record 57 homicides in 7-day period that ended at midnight July 20 is attributed partly to hot weather in met area" (Pace, 1972).

In the mid- to late 1970s, a small group of academics began to emphasize the importance of the characteristics of criminal events, where they take place (locations), and the geographic analysis of crime (discussed in Chapter 2; Brantingham & Brantingham, 1981). Also in the late 1970s, Herman Goldstein (1979) suggested another focus, which he called problem-oriented policing (discussed in Chapter 3). This shifted the focus of the police from administrative and political concerns to an emphasis on addressing crime and disorder problems. Ideally, *problem solving,* a systematic process within problem-oriented policing, involves the use of formal analysis to provide a comprehensive understanding of crime problems and to develop baseline measures and methodology to enable the evaluation of police responses to problems (Scott, 2000). Goldstein and other scholars who were working with police agencies began to demonstrate the analysis of crime and disorder problems.

Growing recognition of crime analysis in the police practitioner community around this time is evidenced by the creation of the **Commission on Accreditation for Law Enforcement Agencies (CALEA)** in 1979.[1] To receive CALEA accreditation, police agencies were required to have crime analysis capabilities. In fact, CALEA accreditation increased the likelihood of having a formal crime analysis unit (Giblin, 2006) since agencies began to designate personnel to crime analysis and created new positions to meet the CALEA standards.

Crime analysis practitioners began to organize in the 1980s and early 1990s. The Colorado Crime Analysis Association, the first state association on record, was formed in 1982. It consisted of an active group of professionals who benefited from the sharing of tools and techniques, according to Dale Harris (personal communication, November 2, 2003), a founding member of the association and its first president. In 1989, the California Crime Analysis Association was founded; it is currently the largest state crime analysis organization in the United States, with more than 350 members. The **International Association of Crime Analysts (IACA)** was created in 1990 by a small group of established analysts from Colorado, Texas, Oklahoma, Georgia, Missouri, and Ontario.

In the early to mid-1990s, the discipline of crime analysis grew slowly in the United States. In his 1990 book, *Problem-Oriented Policing,* Herman Goldstein further specified the role of crime analysis that he described in his 1979 article, outlining the importance of police agencies using data and research to identify problems, understand their underlying causes, and evaluate crime prevention programs.

A number of other events that occurred in the mid-1990s fostered the expansion of crime analysis. The philosophy of community policing (discussed in Chapter 3), which was being adopted by departments across the country, emphasized problem solving (the process described by Herman Goldstein) as well as partnerships between police departments and the citizens they serve; in many cases, such partnerships involved the sharing of crime analysis information and statistics. The 1994 Violent Crime Control and Safe Streets Act, which amended the 1968 Omnibus Crime Control and Safe Streets Act, provided significant funding for new police officers ("100,000 new cops on the street") and created the Office of Community Oriented Policing Services (known as the COPS Office) to administer the hiring of police officers.

In 1997, the COPS Office included crime analysis and crime mapping in its focus, with grants aimed at providing substantive as well as technological support of crime analysis and community policing. Finally, in 1994 the New York City Police Department's conception and implementation of Compstat (discussed in more detail in Chapter 3), a data-driven and mapping-driven police management strategy also used in other departments in subsequent years, increased both awareness of crime analysis and its incorporation into the everyday functions of the police (Weisburd, Mastrofski, McNally, Greenspan, & Willis, 2003).

Coinciding with and facilitating the events described previously were vast improvements in computer technology. In the 1990s, enormous increases were seen in the speed and memory of computers, and the creation of the Windows operating system had a significant impact on crime analysis practices. These changes made it much easier for police to house official information electronically and analysts to examine large amounts of data using desktop statistical programs and crime mapping software to clean data and to generate reports.

In the 1980s and early 1990s, practitioners focused on providing police agencies with statistical information about long-term trends as well as recommendations for organizational procedures stemming from the work of policing planning units (i.e., strategic crime analysis). Although the identification of short-term crime trends and patterns (i.e., tactical crime analysis) was conducted during this time, it became more widespread in medium- to small-sized agencies during the mid-1990s. This was in part a result of the decentralization of crime analysis units (i.e., the shift toward having individual crime analysts operate in police precincts out in the field rather than together at headquarters), the teaching of specific techniques in crime analysis training at the time, and a renewed emphasis on the police goal of apprehending criminals.[2]

History of Crime Mapping

Even though crime mapping plays a significant role in crime analysis today, conducting spatial analysis and creating crime maps for distribution have become common over the last 2 decades in policing and crime analysis, thanks to advancements in technology. The history of crime mapping is somewhat distinct from that of crime analysis, which is why it is presented separately in this chapter. The history of crime mapping begins not with the establishment of the first police force, but with the work of researchers long before the invention of computers.

Beginnings of Crime Mapping

In the 1800s, European researchers who adhered to the school of thought known as the cartographic school of criminology examined the levels of crime within different areas (regions) and the relationship of these levels to sociological factors, such as socioeconomic status (Groff & La Vigne, 2002). For example, in 1829 Adriano Balbi, an ethnographer and geographer, and André-Michel Guerry, a lawyer, created the first maps of crime using criminal statistics for the years 1825 to 1827 and demographic data from the census. They examined crimes against property, crimes against persons, and levels of education in France and found that areas with high levels of crimes against property had a low incidence of crimes against people and that higher numbers of educated people lived in areas with more property crime (Weisburd & McEwen, 1997). Also during this period, the Belgian astronomer and statistician Quételet used maps to examine correlations between crime and transportation routes, education levels, and ethnic and cultural variations (Weisburd & McEwen, 1997).

United States: 1900 to 1970

In the United States, the use of crime mapping began a little later than it did in Europe. Because the United States was a relatively new country in the 1800s, reliable maps were not readily available and census data were not regularly collected as they were in France and England at that time. The first substantive spatial analysis of crime in the United States was conducted in the 1920s and 1930s by urban sociologists in Chicago (Shaw & McKay, 1969). Their crime research and related crime maps linked crime and delinquency to factors such as social disorganization and poverty. In fact, these scholars' spatial analysis of juvenile delinquency and social conditions in Chicago is considered to be one of the foremost examples of crime mapping in the first half of the 20th century (Groff & La Vigne, 2002).

Crime mapping was a theoretical component in the development of the concentric zone model, which contends that in an urban setting different types of zones (areas with different purposes) form around a central business district and that some of these zones are more prone to crime and disorder than are others. Researchers who analyzed the locations and distribution of gangs in Chicago based on the concentric zone concept found that gangs were concentrated in parts of the city where social control was weak and social disorganization was high (Weisburd & McEwen, 1997). Most of the early crime mapping conducted in both Europe and the United States examined aggregate levels of crime by area. However, evidence exists of a map that was created by hand in 1929 by Chicago school researchers on which the home addresses of more than 9,000 delinquents were clustered in particular areas of Chicago (Weisburd & McEwen, 1997).

Through the 1950s, 1960s, and 1970s, sociologists and others who were interested in crime and its causes continued to examine the sociological factors associated with crime. The explanations and geographic methods of analysis used remained fairly uncomplicated during this period, possibly owing to the researchers' focus on sociological factors and the lack of adequate technology (Groff & La Vigne, 2002). In the late 1960s, scholars began conducting spatial analysis of crime with the help of large computer systems and unsophisticated visualization methods (Weisburd & McEwen, 1997).

United States: 1970 to 2000

From the late 1960s through the early 1980s, a group of researchers in England, Canada, and the United States shifted their focus of the study of crime away from what traditional criminology examined—the criminal offender—and toward the criminal event and its context, including the physical and social environments that create opportunities for crime (Brantingham & Brantingham, 1981; Clarke, 1980, 1983; Cornish & Clarke, 1986). This movement affected crime mapping, as researchers shifted from aggregate analysis of crime and social factors to the analysis of discrete criminal events and their locations (discussed in Chapter 2). Consequently, researchers began to incorporate information about geography and environment into their study of crime problems and related issues, such as rape (LeBeau, 1987) and a host of other crimes (Harries, 1980) as well as distribution of police personnel (Rengert & Wasilchick, 1985).

In the early 1980s, client server technology made geographic information systems more accessible, and this enabled a number of police departments to experiment with crime mapping in their everyday work (Groff & La Vigne, 2002). A project funded by the National Institute of Justice called DMAP (Drug Market Analysis Program) partnered researchers and practitioners in five U.S. cities (Jersey City, New Jersey; Hartford, Connecticut; San Diego, California; Pittsburgh, Pennsylvania; and Kansas City, Missouri) to use innovative analytic techniques in studying drug markets and tracking their movements over time (Groff & La Vigne, 2002). These projects led the way for crime mapping partnerships between practitioners and researchers and demonstrated how communities could use GIS tools as a central part of crime control initiatives. The program focused primarily on the use of geographic police data, but the participants found that examining other geographically based data contributed to their ability to target problem-solving strategies, brought together key partners with different perspectives, and facilitated the assessment of their joint efforts (Taxman & McEwen, 1997).

In the early to mid-1990s, significant improvements in computer technology and police data systems made electronic crime mapping a much more practical tool for police and researchers. GIS software became available for desktop computers as these computers became capable of processing large amounts of data quickly. In addition, police data on crimes, arrests, traffic crashes, and calls for service became available electronically through computer-aided dispatch systems as well as through electronic records management systems (discussed in Chapter 6). Geographic data such as street and census information became widely available in electronic format and were provided free or at minimal cost by a variety of government agencies and commercial organizations. All of these developments helped to advance the field of crime mapping beyond manual methods and the use of large, costly mainframe mapping systems.

In 1993, the Illinois Criminal Justice Information Authority and the Sociology Department of Loyola University Chicago joined forces to present a computer crime mapping workshop in Chicago. In a publication resulting from the workshop titled *Crime Analysis Through Computer Mapping* (Block, Dabdoub, & Fregly, 1995), participants—many of whom are top researchers and analysts in the field today—described spatial analytic techniques and offered practical advice for both police professionals interested in implementing computer mapping in their agencies and students of spatial analysis. This workshop was one of the first efforts to bring practitioners and researchers together to discuss crime mapping.

During the mid-1990s, the federal government, in a movement spearheaded by Vice President Al Gore, provided increased support for crime mapping technology and methods. Police agencies received federal funding to obtain crime mapping technology, and several programs were developed specifically to assist police agencies with the implementation of crime mapping. The COPS Office allocated a significant amount of funding for crime mapping software and equipment through a program called MORE (Making Officer Redeployment Effective). From 1995 to 2002, just over $53 million (90 individual grants) of MORE funding was allocated directly to crime mapping technology and staff (M. Scheider, personal communication, November 10, 2003).

The Crime Mapping Research Center, now called the Mapping and Analysis for Public Safety (MAPS) program, was formed within the Department of Justice's National Institute of Justice in 1997. Its goal is to support research that helps criminal justice agencies by examining how to use maps to analyze crime, how to analyze spatial data, how maps can help researchers evaluate programs and policies, and how to develop mapping, data sharing, and spatial analysis tools. Since its creation, the MAPS program has held annual conferences at which practitioners and researchers come together to discuss research and spatial analytic techniques. Other activities have included funding spatial analysis research and fellowships, a national survey of crime mapping, developing training curricula, publishing books on crime mapping, and bringing together police professionals and researchers in a technical working group to discuss spatial analysis of crime issues. With the program's help, the United States has seen interest in and development of crime mapping and crime analysis techniques increase significantly among police departments and researchers. From 1998 to 2007, the National Institute of Justice also funded the Crime Mapping and Analysis Program (CMAP), the mission of which was to provide technical assistance and introductory and advanced training to local and state agencies in the areas of crime and intelligence analysis and GIS. CMAP has also provided training to a significant number of crime analysts and officers in the field.

An important influence in the use of crime mapping in policing was Compstat, the data- and mapping-driven police management strategy created by the New York City Police Department in 1994 and adopted by other police agencies across the United States (Henry, 2002; Weisburd et al., 2003). A core component of Compstat is police officials' use of crime mapping software and analysis in weekly meetings to understand local patterns of crime and disorder incidents. Crime mapping is such an integral part of the Compstat program that during the 2001 television season, CBS's *The District,* a show based on New York's Compstat experience, highlighted crime mapping in every episode (Theodore, 2001).

David Weisburd, a distinguished professor in the field of crime and place, has examined the rate of adoption of crime mapping in the 1990s through a number of surveys and a pilot study of his own and found that "crime mapping was widely diffused among police agencies, that the diffusion process began in the late 1980s to early 1990s, it gained momentum in the mid-1990s, and that the adoption of crime mapping appears to follow the standard 's' curve of diffusion of innovation" (Weisburd & Lum, 2005).

Research on Crime Analysis and Crime Mapping: 2000 to Present

Since 2000, many researchers have begun examining crime analysis and crime analysts to begin understanding the prevalence and nature of how it is practiced. A national survey conducted by the Police Executive Research Forum focused on the level of integration of crime analysis into patrol work

(Santos & Taylor, 2014; Taylor & Boba, 2011). The study of 600 randomly selected local police agencies stratified by agency size, type, and geography found that 89% either employed a full-time crime analyst or had a staff member whose secondary responsibility was conducting crime analysis, while only 11% of the agencies reported not conducting any crime analysis. Also, of those agencies with crime analysts, most commonly employed two analysts (Taylor & Boba, 2011). An examination of the 2013 Law Enforcement Management and Administrative Statistics (LEMAS) shows that larger agencies are more likely to employ crime analysts (Bureau of Justice Statistics, 2016). Of the 2,528 agencies surveyed that employed civilian staff, 40% (1,130) had civilian employees who performed research, statistics, or crime analysis duties. The overwhelming majority of those agencies with civilian employees performing these duties are agencies with more than 50 officers (847 of 1,130, 75%), whereas 73.4% (1,022 of 1,393) of agencies with fewer than 50 officers did not have civilians performing these duties. Thus, crime analysis is becoming common, particularly in medium and large agencies.

In addition, a systematic study conducted in 2000 by the University of South Alabama's Center for Public Policy (O'Shea & Nicholls, 2003) examined the data collected in two national surveys—one of all U.S. police agencies with more than 100 sworn personnel and a second of a random stratified sample (by size and region) of 800 agencies with fewer than 100 sworn personnel—and conducted site visits of large agencies that were specifically selected for the quality of their crime analysis operations. They found that most crime analysts were being asked by the agencies in which they worked to focus on criminal apprehension (pattern identification) or on identifying areas with high crime levels. These findings suggest that crime analysts as well as police managers place high value on tactical analysis, which supports short-range planning and is primarily interested in activities aimed at crime control. They seem less interested in strategic analysis, which supports long-range planning and is primarily interested in more complex organizational issues (such as departmental strengths, weaknesses, opportunities, and threats), or even problem analysis (O'Shea & Nicholls, 2003).

Santos and Taylor (2014) found in their examination of who uses crime analysis (i.e., officers, first-line supervisors, and management) and what they use crime analysis for (i.e., directed patrol, arresting offenders, information, and crime prevention) that even though three quarters of the agencies surveyed had a crime analysis capacity, the level of integration of crime analysis in patrol work was fairly low overall. When crime analysis was used in agencies, managers used it the most for tactical purposes, and directed patrol was the main response informed by all types of analysis.

Studies on crime analysis with a smaller focus include research by Chamard (2003) and Sever, Garcia, and Tsiandi (2008), who conducted statewide surveys in New Jersey at different times examining the use and implementation of crime analysis in the local police agencies. Chamard examined 347 agencies and their adoption of crime analysis (i.e., crime mapping). She found that a small number of agencies used crime analysis and that adoption and continued use of crime analysis was a function of agency size in that larger agencies were more likely to adopt and maintain a crime analysis function. Further evidence of sporadic use of crime analysis in police agencies was seen in a survey conducted by Sever et al. (2008), who found that although crime analysis strategies were used in New Jersey police agencies, the level was varied and most agencies did not use advanced methods.

Giblin (2006), who examined the structural incorporation of crime analysis into the police organization, found in a small sample of departments (160) that larger agencies are more likely to have structures established for crime analysis and that accreditation standards (i.e., CALEA) played an important role in implementation. Two other studies examined the corresponding perspectives of police and crime analysis on the police/analyst relationship and analysis products (Cope, 2004; Taylor, Kowalyk, & Boba, 2007). Nina Cope (2004) found through interviews with crime analysts and sworn supervisors in the United Kingdom that a self-fulfilling prophecy existed in the relationship. She found that the requests for analysis made by police managers were not meaningful or action-oriented, so when they received the product, developed to their specifications, it was not helpful for directing police crime reduction efforts. Importantly, the managers in the study subsequently blamed the irrelevance of the analysis and the crime analyst for the results not being helpful. In an exploratory survey, Taylor et al. (2007) found that analysts had very positive attitudes toward sworn personnel, but they felt as though the sworn personnel, particularly the police officers, were not as supportive of them and crime analysis. These two studies conclude that there appears to be a cultural disconnect between crime analysts and the sworn personnel they are attempting to assist.

The discipline of crime analysis with crime mapping is recognized today as important by government, policing, and academic communities; however, it is still being developed. Although these findings may not be surprising, given that short-term pattern analysis and real-time data analysis support a core function of police agencies, they indicate that most U.S. police agencies are not using crime analysis to its full potential. Crime analysts and police leaders alike are focusing crime analysis efforts on short-term pattern and long-term hot spot identification and have not yet expanded the focus to long-term, in-depth analysis of crime and disorder problems to seek solutions for these problems. This may be due partly to a lack of communication and knowledge of the capabilities and usefulness of crime analysis. Notably, research has sought to understand the prevalence and nature of crime analysis implementation. Most of the research is descriptive and exploratory, which is likely due to the relative newness and the need to understand the basic characteristics of crime analysis in policing. None of these studies examines the direct relationship between crime analysis and crime reduction, and their findings suggest that there are many issues still to resolve in the implementation and use of crime analysis in policing.

INTERNATIONAL CRIME ANALYST PERSPECTIVE

Chisen Goto

Crime Analyst

Royal Canadian Mounted Police

Canada

My role as a crime analyst in an urban detachment requires me to be comfortable in various types of analysis. Strategic analysis, including trend analysis and problem area analysis, indicated that my jurisdiction was experiencing an above-average increase in incidents of property crime in an area generally not associated to high incidents of crime. Tactical crime analysis techniques were used in order to assist with identifying potential individual(s) responsible for the incidents in the area. I used the intelligence cycle to develop an actionable report. Since known individuals were being examined by investigators as potential suspects, it was my job as the analyst to explore and identify any other individuals who might be responsible for the increase.

Planning/Collection: In consultation with the investigators, keeping in mind the feasibility and timeliness of the required analysis, a determination was made that information will be collected and analyzed from the records management system (RMS). The collection process included obtaining information on location, time, and the modus operandi (MO) from files, as well as gathering information from police checks in the area of concern. Sourced photos that could be used to enhance the analytical product were also collected during this process.

Analysis/Reporting/Dissemination: A detailed analysis of the files and street checks for patterns, trends, and other relationships of within and between dates, start times, and MO of the incidents and known offenders were conducted using geospatial and analytical software. Link analysis of associates and any suspicious persons from the information of the file was completed. In addition, specific individuals were linked (or tentatively linked) to various property crimes. Through analysis, I was able to identify potential suspects who were previously unknown to the enforcement units. I prepared a summary report of the analysis with an association link chart, complete with photographs of the individuals of interest. The report was disseminated in a very timely manner, included incidents as recent as the previous evening, and was presented in a concise, comprehensive, and actionable format. Through targeted enforcement action, the individuals, as identified through analysis, were observed and apprehended while committing a residential break and enter. The individuals admitted to committing numerous property crimes in the area and were subsequently charged and sentenced accordingly. Their arrest restored the number of property crimes in the area within the normal range.

Crime Analysis as a Career Track

Opinions differ somewhat concerning what makes a "good" crime analyst, and usually the opinions that people hold on this subject mirror their own experiences. That is, a crime analyst who is a police officer is likely to believe that all crime analysts should be police officers, and a crime analyst with an advanced degree is likely to feel that all crime analysts should have such degrees. Although this is a simplification, debate continues about what experience and education crime analysts need in order to do their jobs. Is it necessary for a crime analyst to have been an officer so that he or she knows the ins and outs of a police department, or is an advanced degree in statistics more valuable? In addition, because so much of modern crime analysis relies on computers and software technology, some argue that crime analysts should be computer experts as well.

Ideally, a crime analyst should have police knowledge, research skills, and technological capabilities. One person is not likely to have all of these qualifications at the beginning of a career in crime analysis; rather, he or she may have a particular strength in one of these areas and will need to cultivate the others over time. A crime analyst's capabilities should represent a balance of knowledge and skills in these three areas. One individual may have a relatively academic slant but be able to relate to the everyday work of policing and effectively explain crime analysis information. Another person who is lacking in formal education may have street-level knowledge of crime and police activity as well as skills in technology and statistical analysis.

The current trend in police agencies is to hire civilian crime analysts. Officers tend to change positions every few years, and agencies do not want to risk losing the investment that intensive crime analysis training represents when officers move. In addition, civilians are less expensive than officers (in terms of salary and retirement benefits) for police agencies to employ. Although this makes the position of crime analyst a good entry-level job, the position lacks opportunity for career track advancement. In many police agencies, especially small to medium-sized police departments, the crime analyst is one of only a few professional support positions, and the only way an analyst can advance is to go to a larger department or move to a different position in the city government.

That being said, police agencies vary greatly in how they fill crime analyst positions with both civilians and sworn officers. Generally, successful analysts are experts in data collection, data manipulation, statistics, theory, and research methods. The analyst is the authority in examination, research, and assisting other police personnel in doing their jobs more effectively. Successful crime analysts also have knowledge about policing in general, about police culture, and about the characteristics of the community in which they work. Crime analysts have their own style of dealing with people, but to be successful, an analyst must be able to explain complex ideas clearly to many different types of individuals (e.g., police officers, managers, city officials, citizens) in a way that is not condescending. In addition, crime analysts must be able to relate to police officers (even if they have never been one), work within police culture, think clearly under pressure, defend their views on important issues, and keep a sense of humor. At the end of this chapter, several profiles of current crime analysts are presented to illustrate the varying degree of experience, skill, education, and responsibilities that different analysts have.

Crime Analyst Qualifications and Job Descriptions

Police departments have many different types of crime analysis positions. Some employ only one crime analyst, whereas others have several who function in what is typically called a **crime analysis unit**, or **CAU**. The following text provides general descriptions of several crime analysis–related positions and their roles within CAUs to show the range of levels and activities in the profession of crime analysis as well as the qualifications necessary for employment at various levels.

Interns/Volunteers Police agencies have used volunteers to conduct crime analysis for many years. During the 1970s and 1980s, many police departments employed volunteers for this purpose because few crime analysis professionals were available or because they lacked the resources to hire professionals. Today, police departments typically use volunteers and interns to support and/or enhance their crime analysis resources and productivity. **Volunteers** are people who work for the police department without pay; they tend to be students or retired persons. **Interns** are undergraduate or graduate students who work in a police department to obtain practical work experience and college credit. An internship can often serve as a proverbial foot in the door, gaining the intern access to future career opportunities.

Internship programs can be extremely beneficial to both police departments and their interns. Interns not only help departments by performing crime analysis duties, but they also learn the skills they need to become crime analysts and gain practical experience. Police departments recruit student interns from many disciplines, including criminal justice, sociology, political science, geography, English, psychology, and computer science, depending on the needs of their crime analysis units and the availability of students. For example, a police department that is instituting a geographic information system might recruit geography students, whereas a department looking to conduct tactical analysis might recruit students majoring in criminal justice.

Individual academic programs typically administer the internship programs through which student interns are placed. These programs usually require that students work as an intern for a minimum of one semester (the number of hours per week varies with the number of course credits given), document their experiences through field notes, and write a final paper for a grade. Internships can be paid or unpaid, depending on the resources of the police agency. Volunteers and interns handle many different tasks within CAUs, including tactical data entry, data analysis, production of monthly strategic reports, and the writing of requests to participate in complex analysis projects.

One note of caution about internships: Even though student interns are not becoming police officers, some police departments put applicants for internships through a screening process similar to that used for applicants for police officer training and other police department personnel (e.g., lie detector test, extensive background checks, drug testing) because interns have the same access officers have to department areas and records. Students applying for police department internships should be aware that any illegal behavior in which they have taken part might have a significant impact on their being accepted and, subsequently, on their ability to work in a police agency as a volunteer, an intern, or at all.

Crime Analysis Assistant/Technician A **crime analysis assistant** or **technician** is an administrative support person who answers the phone, conducts data entry, makes copies, keeps files, produces simple standardized reports, and does anything else that arises administratively in the CAU. This position normally requires a high school diploma and 1 to 2 years of secretarial/data entry experience. It is typically filled by someone who has been a secretary or by an individual just beginning in the profession of crime analysis (e.g., a student). In some cases, crime analysis assistants are able to move up in the CAU as they obtain additional education and experience.

Entry-Level Crime Analyst When a police agency has multiple levels of crime analysis positions, one of these is often described as **entry-level crime analyst.** Analysts in this position usually conduct relatively routine crime analysis duties, as they are likely to be new to the field, have limited experience, and obtain a significant amount of training in their first years on the job. Typically, this position requires an undergraduate degree in criminal justice, political science, sociology, or a related field that includes statistics and research methodology in its curriculum and 1 year of analytic experience, although not necessarily crime analysis experience (a master's degree is often seen as the equivalent of a year of experience). Some police departments require that applicants for the position of entry-level crime analyst have crime analysis certification (offered in several states) when they are hired or that they obtain such certification within a specific period after they begin working in the position.

Experienced Crime Analyst An **experienced crime analyst** may be part of the structure of a CAU or may be a solo practitioner of crime analysis in a police agency. In departments that employ a number of analysts, this level exists to create career advancement opportunities for analysts. Compared with the entry-level crime analyst, the experienced crime analyst holds more responsibility and is expected to conduct more advanced analyses. An individual in this position may also have the duty of supervising lower-level personnel, such as crime analysis assistants/technicians, volunteers, and interns. Typically, the position of experienced crime analyst requires at minimum a bachelor's degree in criminal justice, political science, sociology, or other related field that includes statistics and research methodology in its curriculum and 2 years of crime analysis experience.

Specialty Crime Analyst A **specialty crime analyst** is an analyst who is hired to conduct a particular type of crime analysis. An agency with a relatively large CAU may prefer to employ crime analysts who are specialists (i.e., who have their own individual sets of specialized skills and knowledge) rather than generalists (i.e., who are cross-trained so that all members of the unit have similar skills and knowledge). In some cases, agencies may receive grant funding that requires crime analysts to analyze particular types of crime or other activity. For police agencies, the advantage of having specialty crime analysts available is that these individuals have substantial skills and knowledge in their particular areas of crime analysis; the disadvantage is that their work cannot be shared easily with other analysts, so if a specialty analyst resigns, no one else can conduct the work until another analyst with the same specialty is hired.

There are numerous types of specialty crime analysts, and the education and experience required for these positions varies by specialty. In general, however, the position of specialty crime analyst is typically considered to be equivalent to the experienced crime analyst level, as both positions require proficiencies in particular areas. The following are some examples of types of specialty crime analysts:

- *Tactical crime analyst:* This type of analyst conducts only tactical crime analysis and does not produce long-term reports or statistics.

- *Problem analyst:* This type of analyst conducts analysis within the context of understanding long-term problems only.

- *Sex crime analyst:* This type of analyst conducts tactical, strategic, and administrative crime analysis having to do with sex crimes and is likely to work closely with detectives. The position of sex crime analyst might exist in a large agency that has developed a long-term task force to address sex crimes. (Other types of crime analysts also specialize in particular kinds of crime; these include violent crime analysts, property crime analysts, and robbery crime analysts.)

- *School safety analyst:* This type of analyst conducts analysis on the safety in and around schools, working directly with school administrators and school resource officers.

- *Repeat offender analyst:* This type of analyst would focus on analyzing arrest and offender data to produce repeat/ chronic offender lists and in-depth analysis of chronic offenders' criminal histories. These analysts often work with the criminal investigations division and/or support repeat offender or intelligence-led policing (see Chapter 3) units.

- *Geographic information systems analyst:* This type of analyst specializes in the use of geographic information systems and conducts spatial analysis of crime and various types of police activity. Salaries for GIS analysts are typically higher than those for crime analysts because of the specialized technical skills required and because police agencies must compete for qualified analysts with private companies offering high salaries. Compared with crime analyst positions, significantly fewer GIS analyst positions are available, for a number of reasons: (a) Smaller departments that conduct crime analysis typically have only one crime analyst position, and that is not a specialist position; (b) many police officials do not feel that filling a position with a person who works only on spatial analysis of crime is warranted; and (c) the number of potential applicants for GIS analyst positions (i.e., individuals who have both geography and criminal justice backgrounds) is relatively small.

Crime Analysis Supervisor The **crime analysis supervisor** is a person with substantial crime analysis knowledge and experience who supervises a crime analysis unit. This job title is not applied to police managers (sworn personnel) who supervise the crime analysis function as part of their other duties. The position of crime analysis supervisor is considered to be a "working" position because it involves hands-on crime analysis work. The key responsibilities of a crime analysis supervisor are to represent the interests of the CAU at high-level organizational meetings (such as command staff and patrol or investigations operations meetings), to lead the development of CAU goals and objectives, and to be knowledgeable about the crime analysis discipline regionally, nationally, and internationally. Typically, this position requires a master's degree in criminal justice, political science, sociology, or other related field, 2 years of crime analysis experience, and at least 1 year of supervisory experience.

Embedded Criminologist The **embedded criminologist** is a person with a doctorate degree and/or who is a researcher who is not working *with* the police agency but is working *within* the police agency as an independent, unbiased full-time employee with expertise in criminology, criminal justice practices, analysis, statistics, research methodology, and evaluation (Braga, 2013; Petersilia, 2008). Embedded criminologists carry out independent research and analysis that support a police agency's mission as well as collaborate on the development of programs by introducing and implementing evidence-based practices. While embedded criminologists are not crime analysts, they might assist with large-level crime analysis projects and work closely with the agency's crime analyst personnel.

CAU Organizational Chart

Figure 1.1 depicts a hypothetical CAU organizational chart, including the positions discussed in the previous section and their minimum requirements. The arrows in the figure indicate potential routes for career advancement.

Developing and Improving a Crime Analysis Unit

A **strategic plan** for any type of organization, division, or unit outlines strategies and direction, lays out expectations, and helps guide decisions about how work is done and how to allocate resources. When developing a new crime analysis unit or improving the capabilities of an existing CAU, the formulation of a strategic plan is important because it is a formal mechanism that describes the function and purpose of the CAU within the specific agency. Therefore, this section of the book is a brief discussion of how a strategic plan might be developed either for a new or an existing CAU. Although this information may not be immediately relevant for college students, it provides a foundation for understanding how crime analysis units are developed and the role they serve within a police agency. For practitioners, the section provides information that can be used to guide the development of their own strategic plans. In general, the strategic plan for a CAU should be developed in line with the agency's strategic goals, should include specific short- and long-term goals for the CAU itself, should be realistic in terms of allocating resources (e.g., funding, time, personnel capabilities), and should describe the future needs as well as discuss the substantive areas of work of the CAU.

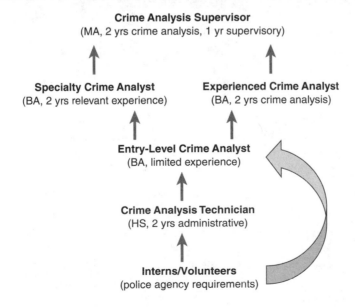

Figure 1.1 Sample Crime Analysis Unit Organizational Chart

Crime Analysis Supervisor
(MA, 2 yrs crime analysis, 1 yr supervisory)

Specialty Crime Analyst
(BA, 2 yrs relevant experience)

Experienced Crime Analyst
(BA, 2 yrs crime analysis)

Entry-Level Crime Analyst
(BA, limited experience)

Crime Analysis Technician
(HS, 2 yrs administrative)

Interns/Volunteers
(police agency requirements)

The first step in developing a strategic plan for a CAU is to understand the current state of the agency and its crime analysis capabilities. For agencies without a crime analysis function, one would consider the strategic goals of the agency, available data sources and their accessibility, and available hardware and software that might be used for crime analysis. For agencies with an existing CAU, the previous issues would be considered in addition to the number of current crime analysis personnel, their capabilities, and how their time is spent, as well as the types of crime analysis products that are produced and their uses.

The second step in developing a strategic plan for a CAU is to determine the crime analysis "needs" of the agency. This would be accomplished through a triangulation of methods. A review of literature on crime analysis (which would include this book and others) would provide an overview of what the field's standards are and what is effective. Specific to each agency, information would be gathered informally from personnel by talking to individuals in the agency, conducting "ride-alongs," and attending departmental meetings. Formal methods of inquiry would include conducting a departmental survey and creating a committee that is brought together to specifically discuss crime analysis needs. Questions that might be asked in interviews and in the survey might include the following: How might current products be improved? What additional information is needed? What new products are needed? Observation conducted on ride-alongs and in meetings would focus on determining the level of understanding of crime analysis by sworn personnel in the agency and on what type of crime reduction/prevention strategies are being employed.

Once this information is gathered and analyzed, the third step is to write the strategic plan. Overall, the plan would describe the current state of the CAU or of the agency (based on information collected in the first two steps), prioritize the needs of the CAU, and list both short- (1 year) and long-term (5 years) goals. More specifically, the plan might include the following parts:

- *Structure:* This part would detail the number and type (e.g., civilian, officer, volunteer, student) of personnel conducting crime analysis full or part time and their positions (e.g., crime analysis technician, entry-level crime analyst, specialty analyst, crime analysis supervisor). It would also include job duties and responsibilities for each position and the location of the unit within the organizational chart (i.e., within the chain of command), as well as whether the unit is centralized or decentralized.

- *Functions/products:* The function (i.e., what type of analyses are conducted) would be determined through collaboration with agency executives who would help prioritize the type of analysis. This part would also describe any standardized products such as reports and bulletins and would lay out the dissemination strategy for each.

- *Data issues:* This part would describe the quality of current data in terms of timeliness, accuracy, and completeness and would include any limitations imposed by the current data. It would also specify what improvements would be needed to conduct the analysis needed by the agency and identify any new data sources that the agency might pursue.

- *Technology:* This part would describe the hardware and software used for crime analysis, detail replacement and update plans, and list any additional needs.

- *Training and promotion:* In terms of training, this part would discuss the local and national training opportunities for the analysts and develop a schedule based on the current budget and personnel needs. In terms of promotion, this part would lay out a structure for advancement (e.g., from crime analysis technician to crime analyst to supervisor) and provide suggestions for realizing the structure if it was not already in place.

- *Policies and procedures:* Because it is important to have formal policies that are not only followed by crime analysts but also are adhered to by customers of crime analysis, this part of the plan would contain each policy and procedure (i.e., methodology). Examples of policies include a citizen request policy, an internal-personnel request policy, and a media request policy. Examples of procedures include standardizing product format, methodology for data entry and cleaning, conducting a staffing analysis, and disseminating crime analysis products. Importantly, policies should be developed in collaboration with sworn personnel and approved by the chief or the command staff.

- *Goals:* This section would indicate the achievements the CAU will work toward and would summarize the suggestions for improvements made in each of the previous parts categorized by short-term (e.g., 1 year) and long-term (e.g., 3 to 5 years) goals. It would also include goals focused on the substantive work of the CAU that would include improving the quality and usefulness of crime analysis for crime reduction, prevention, and evaluation.

- *Placement in the organizational structure:* An important consideration for crime analysis is the placement of the crime analysis function in the organizational structure of the agency. When an agency uses analysis to enact crime reduction strategies and hold personnel responsible for these activities, the crime analysts become vulnerable to undue influence by commanding officers who may seek to manage their own workload and success. For this reason, the crime analysis function should be housed in an "accountability-neutral" division (i.e., administrative bureau), where it is supervised by personnel outside the accountability structure for crime reduction activities that occur in the patrol and criminal investigations bureaus. The crime analysts will, of course, provide products for patrol, criminal investigations, and other operational divisions, but their priorities must be set by supervision outside the operational structure and accountable to the chief of police.

Obviously, the detailed information for each of the parts described would be tailored to the agency for which the plan was developed. In addition, there are many different ways to prepare the written strategic plan, but by using this information as a guide, a strategic plan provides a CAU with a formal set of guidelines for the operation and improvement of the crime analysis capabilities, functions, and personnel.

Crime Analysis Profiles

Analysts from around the country have provided information on their own backgrounds, skills, responsibilities, and thoughts about their careers as analysts. These are provided for students to get a sense of who crime analysts are and what they do. For definitions of tactical, strategic, and administrative crime analysis, refer to the glossary or see Chapter 4.

Detective Dan Benz

Seattle (Washington) Police Department

Crime Analyst

Education and Crime Analysis Experience

- Bachelor of science, criminal justice studies

- 7 years as a crime analyst

- 20 years as a sworn police officer/detective

Previous Related Work Experience

- 3 years as an all-source intelligence officer, U.S. Army

Breakdown of Responsibilities

70% tactical analysis

20% strategic analysis

10% investigative analysis

Dan's Thoughts on Being a Crime Analyst

I believe that an effective crime analyst is a pivotal component to the crime fighting mission. You can *truly* have an impact on your community by providing timely, accurate, and actionable information to patrol resources on a regular basis. It is very rewarding to see crime numbers drop as a result of series bulletins, hot-spot maps, or other products you have provided to the officers out there. I particularly enjoy "putting the pieces together" in terms of digging through data and reports and discovering patterns and series. This job also provides the ability to be creative in many ways and to continually be learning new skills. It is especially rewarding to be actively involved with the command staff and have an impact on the decision-making process in your organization. I was a patrol officer in my organization for many years prior to becoming an analyst. From that experience, I discovered a greater appreciation for the importance of accurate data and thorough report writing. The quality you put in will likely yield better products coming back out that will benefit everybody.

Michelle Wentz

Port St. Lucie (Florida) Police Department

Crime and Intelligence Analyst

Education and Crime Analysis Experience

- Bachelor of applied science, organizational management

- 5 years as crime analyst, Florida Department of Law Enforcement

- 1 year and 4 months as crime analyst, Palm Beach Regional Fusion Center

- Law Enforcement Analyst certification, Florida Department of Law Enforcement

Previous Related Work Experience

- 8 years as education coordinator, Healthy Start of St. Lucie County

Breakdown of Responsibilities

30% investigative analysis (support criminal investigations)

50% tactical analysis

15% strategic analysis

5% administrative analysis

Michelle's Thoughts on Being a Crime Analyst

I have found crime analysis to be a perfect career choice for me. I enjoy the challenges that are presented by the ever-changing landscape of this profession. While each day there are tasks to be met and a regiment to the work, you truly never know exactly what new challenge you will face to help your department and community stay safe. Working with the Port St. Lucie (Florida) Police Department on the research grant and continuing to work and develop our repeat offender program is some of the most interesting work I have done in my career. This work has enriched my skills and tradecraft greatly as I collaborate with experts in the field of crime analysis and strategic policy. The professionalism and dedication of the individuals I work with makes my job rewarding and enjoyable while we take pride in the keeping our city safe.

Brandon Inscore, GISP

Greensboro (North Carolina) Police Department

Crime Analysis Supervisor

Education and Crime Analysis Experience

- Bachelor of arts, secondary social science education, Elon University

- Master of arts, applied geography, University of North Carolina at Greensboro

- Master of business administration, Liberty University

- 2 years as crime analysis supervisor, Greensboro Police Department

Previous Related Work Experience

- 4 years as social studies teacher, Guilford County Schools

- 6 months as GIS technician, City of Greensboro Water Resources Department

- 7 years as GIS analyst, City of Greensboro Field Operations Department

Breakdown of Responsibilities

25% investigative crime analysis

25% tactical crime analysis

25% strategic crime analysis

25% administrative crime analysis

Brandon's Thoughts on Being a Crime Analyst

Crime analysts have the ability to help command staff and front-line supervisors to make smarter decisions about the deployment of resources. While technology helps to make our identification of trends and patterns more efficient, I never cease to be amazed by the human intelligence factor our analysts bring to the table. Our analysts connect seemingly disparate pieces of information to create actionable intelligence on a regular basis. Crime analysts make a huge difference to our internal response and serve to improve the quality of life of our residents.

Dawn Clausius

Olathe (Kansas) Police Department

Police Intelligence Analyst

Education and Crime Analysis Experience

- Master of science, criminal justice from Boston University
- Bachelor of general science, psychology, from University of Kansas
- 10 years as a police intelligence analyst
- 8 years as a police officer

Previous Related Work Experience

- 6 years as secretary on the executive board for the International Association of Crime Analysts (IACA)
- 2 years as president on the executive board for the Mid-America Regional Crime Analysis Network (MARCAN)

Breakdown of Responsibilities

80% criminal intelligence analysis

10% tactical analysis

10% strategic and administrative analysis

Dawn's Thoughts on Being a Crime Analyst

I was introduced to the profession of crime analysis while I was a crime prevention officer for a small Midwest police agency. At that time, crime analysts were primarily seen in larger police agencies around the area and not in small agencies such as the one I worked in. When an opportunity to pursue the profession of crime analysis at the Olathe Police Department opened up, I jumped at it and moved to a larger, more progressive department to develop their crime analysis program. Pursuing the profession of crime analysis was a great decision and to this day continues to be. The profession has changed and developed from being considered a luxury item to a necessity item in law enforcement. Through tactical, strategic, administrative, and criminal intelligence analysis, a crime analyst has the opportunity to impact every area of the department and city. If implemented and used appropriately, crime analysis is a powerful tool for any size of department to leverage to be more efficient and effective. Simply stated: I loved being a police officer, but I love being a crime analyst even more!

Challenges and the Future of Crime Analysis

There are a number of challenges facing the crime analysis discipline, many of which are a result of the discipline's relative infancy. They include the following:

- The availability of relevant training and education
- The availability of data that are adequate in both quantity and quality
- The effective use of crime analysis products by police
- The ability to communicate with other crime analysts in neighboring jurisdictions

From a broader standpoint, the challenge for the field of crime analysis is developing a cadre of qualified individuals to assume crime analyst positions and providing individuals with adequate career advancement once they are hired within a police agency. Once a person is hired as an analyst, there is often little opportunity for promotion and for lateral movement (O'Shea & Nicholls, 2003) in the majority of agencies. Some police agencies create a new crime analysis position without a clear sense of what the qualifications and responsibilities should be. Many analysts have obtained their positions more through chance than through standardized training and education because there is not a clear path to becoming a crime analyst (i.e., college degree or standardized certification).

In terms of crime analysis practice itself, the discipline is continually challenged with proving its usefulness to police personnel. Although research has shown that crime analysis is worthwhile and important for effective policing, line-level police and supervisors who work alongside crime analysts are harder to convince. Analysts often produce reports and statistics that support the essentially reactive nature of the police because that is what is asked of them, and the data on which analysis is based is often subpar (i.e., police officers do not write acceptable crime reports). However, the primary challenge of crime analysis may not rest on the training of analysts or on enabling them to provide better products but rather on the actual structure and operations of the police organization. That is, accountability for the quality and use of crime analysis must be focused on police managers, who must, in turn, hold others accountable to produce better data and implement strategies based on the crime analysis they are provided.

Crime analysis has existed as long as police have existed, but it is only in the last 25 years that crime analysis with crime mapping has become common practice in mid-sized to large police departments in the United States. The discipline can still be considered to be "young," but the future of crime analysis seems extremely bright, especially with the results of the comprehensive policing research that indicates analysis is the key to understanding and preventing crime. In response to the challenges already discussed, the major areas of future growth and development for crime analysis are in the areas of crime analysis education, regional initiatives, and improvements in policing.

As noted, the central challenge is creating a pool of potential crime analysts who are specifically trained and educated for this career, as well as standards for crime analysis knowledge and skills. The best way to address the issue of creating a pool of crime analysts is to provide undergraduate and graduate education and training in crime analysis. College courses and degree programs (e.g., certification programs and area concentrations at both the undergraduate and graduate levels) provide instruction in crime analysis techniques to encourage the pursuit of the profession of crime analysis. The field is also challenged in the areas of compensation and career development. One purpose of this book is to help create standards in analysis definitions and techniques as well as in job descriptions and qualifications. The International Association of Crime Analysts has and continues to work to develop standards for crime analysis as a career and its practice. They have developed a national certification process and a handbook that provides basic crime analysis knowledge needed for certification, as well as a certification training (IACA, 2011a). The IACA has initiated a standards, methods, and technology committee with the purpose of defining analytical methodologies, technologies, and core concepts relevant to the profession of crime analysis from which the new definition for crime analysis in this chapter has resulted.

An effort to overcome the challenge of standardization of skills and knowledge is the development of a body of crime analysis literature. Academic journals such as *Police Practice and Research, Policing: An International Journal of Police Strategies and Management, Security Journal, Crime Science,* and *Crime Mapping Research and Practice* as well as others include articles about crime analysis written by practitioners and researchers. An increasing number of books about crime analysis and crime mapping are being published, and formal communication networks for crime analysts, such as Listservs, have been established.

If we look outside the borders of the United States into the international policing community, we find evidence that standardization and development of crime analysis as a profession is also growing in other countries. Most European countries have formal crime analysis functions within their national or state police agencies, as do Japan, Australia, Brazil, South Africa, and other nations. Police agencies in the United Kingdom also have seen a significant push for crime analysis, both within the problem-solving process and tactically. The concerns of crime analysts in the United Kingdom mirror those of their counterparts in the United States, revolving around issues of data integrity, effectiveness of techniques, usefulness of crime analysis products, and staffing and resources.

Another area of growth in crime analysis is related to regional data sharing and analysis. Over the last decade or so and with the increased focus on counterterrorism, police agencies are discovering that analysis of data within their own agency's borders is not sufficient. They are beginning to share data with neighboring police agencies as well as nonpolice agencies, such as probation/parole offices, health and social services, and educational institutions. Fusion centers, as they are called, enable the police agencies to collaborate and widen their scope of knowledge to provide a more comprehensive picture of local problems and a better foundation for effective cross-jurisdiction. Specifically, geographic information systems and the Internet have become important tools within law enforcement for sharing data and facilitating analysis across disciplines and agencies (Hollywood & Winkelman, 2015).

Lastly, the future of crime analysis sits squarely on the shoulders of policing. Crime analysis exists to support police, so it follows that its usefulness will depend on its acceptance and inclusion into the police organization and its practices. It will not be enough for academics, researchers, and crime analysts themselves to help improve the tools and techniques of crime analysts. Police leaders will have to understand and appreciate the value of crime analysis and incorporate it into their standard operational practices.

The discipline of crime analysis is fairly young, even internationally, and is steadily being incorporated into police practice. Current research results support crime analysis and its importance in focused and effective police approaches. The future of crime analysis lies in its increased adoption and effective integration to police practice. By developing training programs, providing education, creating a body of literature, testing analytic techniques, and evaluating their effectiveness, scholars and practitioners also contribute to the future of crime analysis. As a dynamic and growing profession, crime analysis offers significant opportunities to individuals who enter the field.

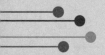

SUMMARY POINTS

This chapter defines crime analysis, crime mapping, and GIS; describes the history of the profession; and discusses crime analysis as a career track. The following are the key points addressed in this chapter:

- Crime analysis is a profession and process in which a set of quantitative and qualitative techniques are used to analyze data valuable to police agencies and their communities. It includes the analysis of crime and criminals, crime victims, disorder, quality of life issues, traffic issues, and internal police operations, and its results support criminal investigation and prosecution, patrol activities, crime prevention and reduction strategies, problem solving, and the evaluation of police efforts.

- Temporal, spatial (crime mapping), and sociodemographic factors are key areas of focus in crime analysts' examinations of crime, disorder, and other police-related issues.

- The goals of crime analysis are to assist police in criminal apprehension, crime and disorder reduction, crime prevention, and evaluation.

- The federal government outlines nine ways an analytical function benefits law enforcement agencies: (1) helps solve criminal investigations, (2) increases the ability to prosecute criminals, (3) supports the chief executive and the agency's mission, (4) proactively informs law enforcement officers of crime trends and develops threat, vulnerability, and risk assessments, (5) trains law enforcement and other intelligence personnel, (6) assists in the development of computerized databases to organize information and intelligence, (7) fosters meaningful relationships with other law enforcement personnel, (8) ensures compliance with local, state, tribal, and federal laws and regulations, and (9) provides support to fusion centers.

- A geographic information system (GIS) is a set of computer-based tools that allows the user to modify, visualize, query, and analyze geographic and tabular data.

- Crime mapping is the process of using a GIS to conduct spatial analysis of crime problems and other police-related issues.

- The three main functions of crime mapping are (a) to facilitate visual and statistical analyses of the spatial nature of crime and other types of events, (b) to enable analysts to link unlike data sources based on common geographic variables, and (c) to provide maps that help to communicate analysis results.

- Citizens and police have conducted informal crime analysis throughout history, but formal crime analysis did not begin until the first formal police department was established in England in the early 19th century.

- Crime analysis did not begin to develop in the United States until the 20th century.

- In the early 1900s, August Vollmer, the most famous police reformer, was the first police practitioner to write about crime analysis and the mapping of police reports in the United States.

- O. W. Wilson, a student of Vollmer, developed recommendations for analysis and "crime mapping" units in police departments in the 1950s and 1960s.

- The 1968 Omnibus Crime Control and Safe Streets Act helped to fund police agencies' crime analysis endeavors throughout the 1970s.

- A number of publications—including manuals, media articles, and conference proceedings—provide evidence of the use of crime analysis in police agencies in the 1970s.

- Scholars' focus on the geographic analysis of crime and problem-oriented policing increased attention to crime analysis in the 1970s and 1980s.

- The first professional associations concerned with crime analysis were established in the 1980s, and an international association was formed in 1990.

- In the mid-1990s, the U.S. government's emphasis on community policing and problem solving led to the availability of federal grants that enabled police agencies to implement crime analysis. In addition, improvements in computer technology encouraged the use of crime mapping and crime analysis in everyday policing.

- The beginnings of crime mapping are different from the beginnings of crime analysis in that crime mapping began through the work of researchers (vs. police) in the 1800s and the early 1900s.

- The first substantive spatial analysis of crime in the United States was conducted in the 1920s and 1930s by urban sociologists in Chicago. This research focused on linking crime and delinquency to factors such as social disorganization and poverty.

- In the 1970s and 1980s, improvements in technology and academic developments encouraged the use of crime mapping in police agencies. However, the use of crime mapping did not increase dramatically until the 1990s.

- Federal funding in the form of grants and the establishment of crime mapping centers, improvements in technology and data collection, and the implementation of Compstat in police agencies across the United States fueled the rapid adoption of crime mapping in the mid- to late 1990s.

- Ideally, a crime analyst should have police knowledge, research skills, and technological capabilities. . . . One person is not likely to have all of these qualifications at the beginning of a career in crime analysis; rather, that individual may have a particular strength in one of these areas and will need to cultivate the others over time.

- Although many police agencies employ only one or two crime analysts, the crime analysis discipline includes a range of potential careers, from assistant positions to specialty and supervisory positions.

- Students who are interested in pursuing careers in crime analysis may gain a "foot in the door" through internships or volunteer positions.

- Crime mapping positions in police departments are sometimes separate from crime analysis positions and in many cases have higher salaries because of the high level of training and expertise required. Crime mapping positions are much rarer than general crime analysis positions.

- In general, the strategic plan for a crime analysis unit (CAU) should be developed in line with the agency's goals, should include specific short- and long-term goals for the CAU itself, should be realistic in terms of allocating resources, and should describe the future needs as well as discuss the substantive areas of work of the CAU.

- The first step in developing a strategic plan for a CAU is to understand the current state of the agency and its crime analysis capabilities. The second step is to determine the crime analysis "needs" of the agency. The third step is to write the strategic plan.

- The CAU strategic plan might include sections describing the following: (1) the structure of the unit, (2) its functions and products, (3) any data issues, (4) technology, (5) policing and procedures, and (6) short- and long-term goals.

- Crime analysis is now a recognized profession within the policing community. As a profession, it is still in the process of being developed.

- Most large and many medium-sized police agencies in the United States conduct some form of crime analysis.

- Most crime analysts today focus on tactical crime analysis and/or on providing statistical information directly to police management.

- Recent efforts by the International Association of Crime Analysts, crime analysis scholars, and police practitioners have addressed the development of crime analysis literature as well as research, training, and practical assistance for crime analysts.

- Anecdotal information from crime analysts in countries around the world indicates that they share the same concerns about development, training, data, and management support issues that crime analysts in the United States have.

- Current challenges for crime analysis include developing a cadre of qualified individuals to assume crime analyst positions and providing individuals with adequate career advancement once they are hired, proving its usefulness to police personnel, and making improvements in training and education.

- The future of crime analysis is bright, and continued developments in crime analysis education, regional initiatives, and improvements in policing will help this fairly young profession.

DISCUSSION EXERCISES

Exercise 1

Using the crime analyst profiles in this chapter, compare and contrast the analysts' (1) education and experience, (2) previous related work experience, (3) breakdown of analysis responsibilities, and (4) overall impressions of being a crime analyst. What would it take for you to become qualified to be a crime analyst?

Exercise 2

Compare and contrast the history of crime analysis with the history of crime mapping. Why do you think their histories are different? What roles do research, technology, and recent innovations in policing play?

Exercise 3

Based on the research being conducted on crime analysis and the information in this chapter, develop and explain the reasoning behind three research questions that would be important to answer about the crime analysis profession and its practice in police agencies.

Exercise 4

Search the Internet and identify a website with crime analysis information. Include the web address in your response, and answer the following questions: What type of organization is publishing the information? What types of information is provided? Does the website represent crime analysis similar to how the book describes it?

NOTES ———————————————————————————

1. CALEA is an independent accrediting authority whose purpose is "to improve delivery of law enforcement service by offering a body of standards, developed by law enforcement practitioners, covering a wide range of up-to-date law enforcement topics" (CALEA, 2016). Chapter 15 of CALEA's *Standards for Law Enforcement Agencies* specifies requirements for police agencies concerning crime analysis; this information has been included in every edition of that manual since it was first published in August 1983.

2. These conclusions are based on my own observations and experience during the 1990s, as no study has been conducted to date concerning the evolution of crime analysis in the 1990s.

Theoretical Foundations of Crime Analysis

H istorically, the everyday practice of crime analysis has involved only limited use of criminological and criminal justice theory. Crime analysts tend to spend substantial amounts of time obtaining and cleaning data, counting incidents, and finding short-term patterns; they spend considerably less time using theory to guide analysis. As the discipline develops, however, it is becoming more important and common for analysts to apply certain relevant criminological theories in their work.

The primary objective of crime analysis is to assist the police in addressing everyday crime and disorder. Sociological and psychological theories that explain the root causes of criminal activity, pointing to factors such as social disorganization, personality disorders, and inadequate parenting, are not relevant for crime analysis because police have little influence over these root causes. Police agencies, and crime analysts in particular, deal with individuals who have already chosen to commit crime, and police personnel must focus on how and why crimes are occurring in particular situations in order to seek solutions for those immediate problems. Consequently, crime analysis, as well as the police, require theories that assume a motivated offender instead of those that try to explain why the individuals have become offenders in the first place. These latter theories are considered *criminal justice theories* and the former, *criminology theories*.

Over the past 30 years, significant developments have taken place in scholars' efforts to define and make sense of crime events as they happen in everyday life (Felson & Boba, 2010). These theories, together called **environmental criminology** (even though the word *criminology* is used here, these theories are considered criminal justice theories), contain important concepts that guide crime analysis and crime prevention efforts as well as evaluation of those efforts. This chapter provides a concise introduction to this theoretical framework. Although this chapter's discussion refers primarily to crime, the concepts presented here can also be applied to disorder and other types of activity that concern crime analysts and the police.

Environmental Criminology

Environmental criminology is different from traditional criminological theories because it does not attempt to explain root causes of crime and why people become criminals. Instead, it focuses on the various aspects of "settings" in which crime occurs. A setting is "a location for recurrent use, for a particular activity, at known times" (Felson, 2006, p. 102). Every city, town, and even rural area can be divided into settings in which particular behavior occurs. Think of a public park with picnic tables and a basketball court versus a major retail store and its parking lot. Distinct types of people and behaviors are present in these different settings. It is within these specific settings that routine behavior creates opportunities for crimes to occur in a systematic way.

Importantly, a crime occurs only when the opportunity exists for that crime (e.g., a theft cannot occur if there is nothing to steal; an assault cannot occur if there is only one person in the room). Some settings contain more opportunities for crime than others, and the theories of environmental criminology help us understand how these opportunities are created and subsequently cluster together (Felson & Boba, 2010). The goal of environmental criminology is not to explain why a specific offender commits a specific crime but to understand the various aspects of a criminal event in order to identify patterns of behavior and environmental factors that create opportunities for crime and other unwanted activity (Brantingham & Brantingham, 1990).

For example, Jane Doe's wallet was stolen while she was working out at the gym; it was taken from her purse, which was in her car in the gym's parking lot. To prevent this crime from happening again, it is not helpful to explain why the offender took Jane's wallet by examining factors in the offender's background (e.g., bad parenting, poor education). Rather, it is important to focus on how Jane's leaving a wallet in a parked car for several hours creates an opportunity for crime (i.e., no wallet, no crime) and on how knowledge of routine behaviors of individuals within that setting facilitates crime (e.g., all women avoid taking their purses with them into the gym while they work out, and everyone, including potential offenders, knows this).

The crime analyst would examine the crime data, gym patron behavior, and the parking lot itself (i.e., the potential crime setting) to understand the crime opportunities in this setting and would subsequently recommend ways in which the environment and victim behavior could be altered to reduce or eliminate opportunities for this type of crime. In this case, simply removing the personal belongings from the vehicle could eliminate this particular crime. Before this discussion proceeds any further, several more important concepts require explanation.

Problem Analysis Triangle

The core of the theories that assist crime analysis and policing in understanding crime settings is the concept of the **problem analysis triangle** (Center for Problem-Oriented Policing, 2016; also called the *crime triangle*), which is illustrated in Figure 2.1. The small triangle in the center of the figure represents a particular type of problematic activity, either criminal or a form of disorder such as unruly juveniles, loud music, and the like. On each of the three sides

Figure 2.1   The Problem Analysis Triangle

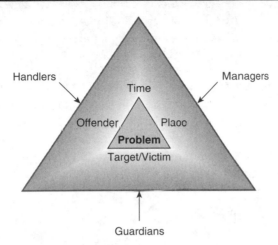

and on top of the smaller triangle are the four necessary components of a crime (we will use "crime" in this discussion for simplicity's sake, even though the triangle can be applied to any problematic activity). That is, a crime event occurs when an offender and a victim or target (a target is an inanimate object, such as property, a vehicle, or a building) come together at a particular place at a particular time (at the top of the triangle). However, even though these are necessary elements of a crime, this does not mean that crime occurs every time these elements are present together.

Consequently, the larger triangle helps us understand how opportunities are influenced within the crime setting; that is, opportunities are not static and do change. On each side of the larger triangle are the types of people or mechanisms that can exhibit control over victims/targets, places, and offenders. *Guardians* are people who have the ability to protect victims/targets by watching over them or removing them from particular settings. For example, neighbors watch over other people's homes, and security guards watch over both people and property, oftentimes in semipublic areas such as stores or downtown areas. Parents remove their children from particular settings—for example, from a park known for fighting—and individuals conceal or remove property by placing items in the trunk of a car or taking a purse out of a car altogether.

Managers are people who are responsible for places, such as hotels, retail stores, apartment buildings, and homes. They set rules and manage the places. The actual rules, how they are enforced, and the physical environment of the place all affect crime opportunities. Place managers (e.g., the manager of a mall or school) are extremely important when examining opportunities for crime because they normally have a span of control that affects a large number of people. For example, a bar owner with lax policies on underage drinking and overserving is increasing the opportunities for drunk driving, fights, and sexual assaults.

Finally, *handlers* are people who know the potential offenders and are in positions that allow them to monitor and/or control potential offenders' actions. Parents and parole officers are examples of handlers who might discourage offenders from committing a crime by establishing a curfew; a friend is an example of a handler who might encourage potential offenders by egging them on to fight in a bar or get drunk and rowdy at a sporting event.

An important aspect of the effect of guardians, managers, and handlers is that they have the ability to *both* discourage or reduce opportunities and encourage or increase the opportunities for crime. Not only is it important to understand what is currently happening in a particular crime setting that creates crime opportunities, but it is also important to understand how things can be changed to reduce the opportunities.

Returning to the example of Jane Doe's stolen wallet: Jane, as a guardian of herself and her property, has left her purse unprotected by leaving it in her vehicle. The place is the parking lot, and the place manager is the gym owner who controls the lighting in the parking lot, the number of security guards, and the location of the parking spaces (e.g., in front of the gym vs. behind the gym where no one can see them). Finally, the offender is someone who may be alone or with a friend (a handler) who evaluates the situation and decides to steal the purse. This example illustrates a central concept that opportunities for crime are highly specific and that crime does not always occur when opportunities are present. If the offender had walked through the parking lot while Jane Doe or another gym patron was there or if there had been a security camera in the parking lot (guardianship), the offender may have decided not to take the wallet because it appeared too risky.

These ideas have important implications for crime analysis. They suggest that analysts can use specific techniques to identify and understand patterns of events and that understanding, in turn, can inform police efforts to address or prevent crime and disorder. For instance, analysis of thefts from autos by location and time of day may show that cars are being victimized in a certain area of a shopping mall parking lot in the evening hours. Further examination may reveal that the affected area of the lot is near a movie theater and that people often leave the merchandise they have just purchased at mall stores in their cars while they go to the movies. Measures designed to facilitate protection of the targets (e.g., hiding the property in the trunk) or manage the parking lot better (e.g., have security guards patrol that particular part of the parking lot during the most frequent theft times) would help to reduce the opportunity for this crime. However, only a detailed analysis of the crime incidents and behavior within that setting can lead to specific crime prevention responses.

The problem analysis triangle explains the basic idea of how opportunities for crime are influenced. What follows are three related theories that are useful for helping crime analysts understand and anticipate how offenders make choices about committing crimes and how victims and offenders come together at particular times in particular places through their routine behavior. They provide insights into patterns of behavior at the individual level (rational choice theory), the social interaction level (crime pattern theory), and the societal level (routine activities theory).

Rational Choice Theory

According to **rational choice theory**, offenders make choices about committing crimes based on anticipated risks and rewards. The theory suggests that, if given a chance or the right "opportunity," any person will commit a crime (Felson & Clarke, 1998). The motivation that a drug abuser with no money has to commit a robbery might be obvious, but it is more difficult to understand why seemingly noncriminal people commit crimes in certain circumstances; rational choice theory explains their motivation.

A person who would normally not steal may decide to steal in a situation where the reward outweighs the risk of getting caught. For example, a person puts 10 bags of garden soil on a cart at a home improvement store. When the clerk counts only 8 bags, the individual does not say anything and walks out of the store with 10 bags, having paid for only 8. Technically, this is not theft when the clerk miscounted, but it becomes a crime when the individual makes a choice not to tell the clerk about the error. The individual weighs the reward (getting two bags for free) with the risk of getting caught (whether the clerk or the store manager will notice before the customer gets the soil to the car).

It is also important that rational choice theory suggests that individuals will decide *not* to commit crimes when the risks are too high or the rewards are not adequate enough—an idea that differs from some criminological theories that imply that criminal behavior is inevitable. For example, a group of teenagers may want to hang out and drink alcohol. They might spend a Saturday night looking through their parents' liquor cabinets or finding a fake ID to purchase alcohol. But in the end, if these opportunities are blocked (parents lock their alcohol) or the risk is too great (they hear the police are cracking down on underage buying of alcohol), they may not drink at all that night. Understanding how individuals choose to commit crimes or choose *not* to commit crimes in particular circumstances can lead to developing strategies to prevent these crimes in the future.

Rational choice theory is useful for crime analysis and policing because of the importance of determining why groups of offenders choose to commit particular crimes systematically. For crime analysis and police, it is more important to understand patterns of behavior rather than only one or two individual events in order to have a more widespread impact on crime. If offenders choose to offend based on the perceived risks and anticipated rewards of their actions, an understanding of offenders' perceptions can help police agencies and communities take measures that can change the opportunities for crime and deter offending. For instance, again using the gym parking lot example, analysis may show that over time offenders are targeting cars in the back row of the parking lot, farthest away from the gym's front doors. The multiple offenders seem to be choosing these cars because of the lack of guardianship in this area—that is, because of the relatively low risk of their being seen while committing the crimes. Based on this finding, police might advise the gym's owners to take measures such as increasing lighting or installing video security cameras in the area to increase any potential offenders' perceived risk of being caught.

Crime Pattern Theory

Crime pattern theory seeks to understand how people come together in space and time within crime settings. According to this theory, criminal events will most likely occur in areas where the activity space of potential offenders overlaps with the activity space of potential victims/targets (Brantingham & Brantingham, 1993; Felson & Clarke, 1998). An individual's activity space is that area that becomes familiar through everyday activities, such as where the individual lives, works, commutes, and goes shopping. The activity space of a place is, simply stated, its location.

Figure 2.2 illustrates a simple example of how certain areas within the activity space of an offender intersect with those of a victim—for example, work, movies, and shopping areas. Crime pattern theory asserts that a crime event involving this offender and this victim can only occur within or stem from the intersection of their activity spaces. This is a relatively simple example, given that individuals' actual activity spaces are vast. More broadly, crime pattern theory would suggest that a downtown area with retail stores, restaurants, and a movie theater would be worthy of analysis since it may have a considerable amount of crime because many people frequent the area, including victims and potential offenders.

A crime analyst examining this area would break down the data into specifics about the various types of victims/targets and potential offenders who frequent the area to understand why they are there and how they come together. Such an area may have a problem with thefts from vehicles and auto theft from parking lots because of the high volume of vehicle traffic. It may also have a problem with purse snatching because of the high number of potential victims in the area carrying their purses while shopping.

Also, crime pattern theory suggests and research has found that offenders commit crimes in places they know or frequent. A study by Bernasco (2010) found that offenders are more than 22 times more likely to commit crimes in an area where they currently live or formerly lived than in a comparable area where they have never lived, and this effect is similar for burglary, robbery, and theft from auto. The implications of this research are that when analysts are looking for suspects for a particular crime series, they may begin with

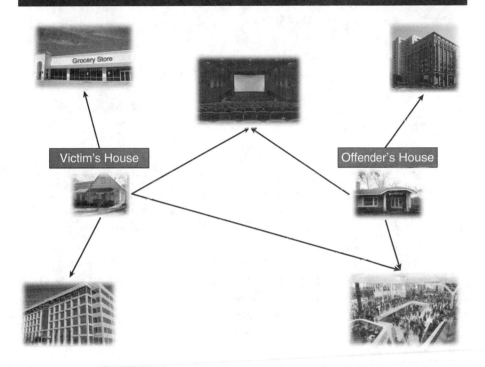

Figure 2.2 Offender and Victim Activity Space Example

Grocery Store

Victim's House

Offender's House

individuals who live in the area and/or frequent that place during their routine activities. Additionally, this means that offenders who are not familiar with a particular area may spend some time "casing" it to become familiar with the behavior or people in that setting. The movie *Home Alone* has a good example of this, as one burglar shows the other he knows exactly when each home's Christmas lights will turn on because he has surveilled the area for several days. Based on this idea, a crime analyst might look for previous contacts with suspicious people in an area of a burglary pattern to identify possible suspects. Hence, crime pattern theory provides a structured way for crime analysts to view and investigate patterns of behavior.

Routine Activities Theory

Routine activities theory focuses on how opportunities for crime change based on changes in behavior on a societal level. For example, Felson and Boba (2010) discuss how significant changes in Americans' routine activities were responsible for increases in crime rates in the United States in the mid- to late 19th century. They note that the number of Americans who routinely left their homes on a daily basis to go to workplaces increased significantly during that time period. The behavior in the home (setting) changed because guardianship over homes decreased, increasing opportunities for crimes such as residential burglary. In addition, with more people out in the working world, increasing the numbers of potential victims (individuals) and targets (cars and other personal property), opportunities for crime such as robbery, rape, and vehicle crime also increased.

Looking again at the example of Jane Doe's stolen wallet, routine activities theory would argue that new opportunity for crime was created when working out at a gym became popular in Jane's community and when many gym patrons developed the habit of leaving their wallets and/or purses in their cars while they worked out for several hours. What is also important about the gym setting is that offenders gain knowledge about victims' behaviors because going to the gym is also part of their own routine activities.

In recent years, the most significant example of a change in routine activity on a societal level is the use of smartphones. The fact that almost every person in the United States and many countries uses a smartphone has created many more opportunities for certain types of crimes. Smartphones are like mini computers with much of the same functionality. Because people carry them around and use them nearly all day, every day, there are more opportunities for computer-related crimes such as identity theft, dissemination of computer viruses, cyber bullying, distribution of pornographic material, and theft of the phone. Routine activities theory also suggests that societal changes in behavior can decrease opportunities for crime. For example, many states have made wearing a helmet mandatory when riding a motorcycle to reduce injuries, which has also reduced the opportunities for motorcycle theft. That is, a thief has to have his own helmet when stealing a motorcycle or risk being stopped, not for the theft but for the helmet violation.

Crime analysts working from the perspective of this theory ask questions about general patterns of behavior and the impacts of those patterns on crime opportunities. Local patterns of behavior, such as the prevalence of a particular type of drug in a community or the tendency of teenagers in an area to use drinking and driving as their primary form of entertainment on weekends, are particularly important because crime analysis usually focuses on smaller subsets of society, such as one city or a specific region.

Law of Crime Concentration

A very important aspect of environmental criminology for crime analysts is the "place" side of the problem analysis triangle. Research over the last 30 years has established that crime reduction strategies that focus on "place" are more effective than those that focus on people (Telep & Weisburd, 2012). Thus, out of policing and criminology of place research, a new criminological law has been developed. A criminological law refers to a conclusion we make about the "way the world works" based on facts and research findings. Criminological laws do not apply to individual situations, but because criminology is a social science, a criminological law refers to broader patterns of crime and behavior. One such law that has been established through many years of research is the age-crime curve in that offenders' criminality is not consistent and stable throughout their lives, but that most individuals "age out" of crime (Laub & Sampson, 2003). There are only a few "laws" in criminology since much of the research lacks consistent and definitive answers to criminological questions.

In 2014, Professor David Weisburd established a new criminological law called the "law of crime concentration." He defines it as follows: "For a defined measure of crime at a specific microgeographic unit, the concentration of crime will fall within a narrow bandwidth of percentages for a defined cumulative proportion of crime" (Weisburd, 2015, p. 138). What this means is that not only do we know that crime clusters by place but that these clusters can be narrowly defined and are stable and predictable over time. This law fully supports the discussion thus far of the importance of place in the problem analysis triangle, opportunities for crime, activity space, and routine activities of individuals.

What does this mean for crime analysts? It means that crime analysts should spend a majority of time using the theories discussed here as well as focus their analysis on understanding crime at places. While understanding offenders and their choices for committing crime in the immediate situation are important, this law and the research imply that places are much more reliable units of analysis. The simplest way to understand why this makes sense is that offenders are mobile and move around to commit their crimes, but places do not move around and the routine behaviors and purpose of the places are stable as well. Thus, analyzing, understanding, and responding to crime at place is the most promising strategy for police departments and, by extension, crime analysts.

Repeat Victimization, Near Repeats, and the 80/20 Rule

Repeat victimization is the recurrence of crime in the same places or against the same people. A major finding of the research on repeat victimization is that people and places that have been victimized in the past have a higher likelihood of being victimized again than do people and places that have never been victimized (Farrell & Pease, 1993). In fact, the best predictor for victimization is that the person or place has been victimized in the past (Grove, Farrell, Farrington, & Johnson, 2012; Weisel, 2005). Referring to the law of crime concentration, it is through repeat victimization of places that the clusters of crime are established.

This is an important theoretical consideration in crime analysis, not only because repeat victimization is common but also because it facilitates the identification of patterns of opportunity. When the same group of people, location, or type of target is repeatedly victimized in different situations, the crime analyst has an opportunity to identify common characteristics among the crime events and understand why crime is occurring at a specific setting or to a specific group. The phenomenon of repeat victimization also provides a focus for prevention since those who have been victimized in the past should be at the top of the list for the targeting of prevention measures. This is particularly important for police because they have limited resources and have to prioritize their crime prevention efforts. Chapter 3 discusses more about how police have the most impact on crime when they focus their efforts toward particular problems, places, victims, and so on.

Repeat victimization is broken down into the following four types (Weisel, 2005):

1. **True repeat victims:** These are the exact same individuals or places that were previously victimized. For example, the same residents are living in the same house, which is burglarized twice.

2. **Near victims:** These are victims or targets that are physically close to and share characteristics with the original victim. Burglary of several condos in the same community is an example, not only because they are physically close but also because they may have the same door locks and physical design.

3. **Virtual repeats:** These are victims or targets that are virtually identical to the original victim and share some of the same characteristics. For example, electronics retail stores of the same name that are victimized across cities or states are considered virtual repeats because they have similar, if not identical, store layouts, policies, and types of property. Also, new occupants (e.g., owners of a store or residents of a home) in places victimized in the past are considered virtual repeats.

4. **Chronic victims:** These are individuals who are repeatedly victimized over time by various offenders for various types of crimes (e.g., assault, robbery, theft). This is also called *multiple victimization.*

Repeat victimization is also related to other ways in which crime clusters:

- **Repeat offenders:** Individuals or types of individuals who commit multiple crimes. These can be individuals who specialize in one type of crime (e.g., robbery) or commit a variety of crimes (e.g., theft, robbery, assault).

- **Hot spots:** Areas that suffer from proportionately large amounts of crime (Sherman, Gartin, & Buerger, 1989). Areas can be hot spots based on one type of crime or a variety of crimes. The size of the hot spot area depends on both the amount of crime and the relative size of the jurisdiction.

- **Risky facilities:** Individual locations that attract or generate a disproportionate amount of crime (Eck, Clarke, & Guerette, 2007). Examples include a large retail plaza or mall, a low-budget motel, and a high school. Also, these include types of places that are frequently victimized but not necessarily in the same area. Examples include beauty salons, convenience stores, day care centers, bars, and fast-food restaurants.

- **Hot products:** Types of property that are repeatedly targeted or, as Clarke (1999) puts it, "those consumer items that are most attractive to thieves" (p. 23). In order for an item to be a hot product, it must fit the following criteria: It must be "concealable, removable, available, valuable, enjoyable, and disposable" (p. 25). Examples include precious metal (e.g., gold, copper, platinum from catalytic converters), smartphones and tablets, and handguns.

Near repeat victimization is a very specific type of repeat victimization that is particularly important for crime analysis and falls under the concept of repeat victimization and the law of crime concentration. Near repeats are defined as nonvictimized places near places that have been victimized (Bowers & Johnson, 2005). In fact, clusters of near repeat crimes have been identified by police crime analysts for decades as crime patterns to assist police in their tactical responses (Austin et al., 1973; Gwinn, Bruce, Cooper, & Hick, 2008). Because of this, research on near repeats is summarized here to provide a foundation for the later techniques covered in the tactical crime analysis chapters.

- Research has established that near repeats occur regularly and that they have been shown to occur rapidly (i.e., one right after another; Johnson & Bowers, 2004; Johnson, Summers, & Pease, 2007, 2009; Townsley, Homel, & Chaseling, 2003). Most of the research on near repeats has been conducted for residential burglary and theft from vehicle crimes, which are two crime types often analyzed by crime analysts. Thus, these findings from the research have direct relevance for crime analysts (Bernasco, 2010; Coupe & Blake, 2006; Johnson, Lab, & Bowers, 2008):

- Houses next to a burgled home have been found to be at a substantially higher risk of being burglarized.

- Most near repeats occur within 1 week of the initial burglary.

- The increased risk is caused by offenders returning to the area of a prior successful burglary. If the previous house is still vulnerable, a "true repeat" will occur, but if that house has been hardened (e.g., posted alarm signs in the front yard, locked windows and doors), a near repeat will occur.

- Short-term clusters of crime occur within, but also outside of, long-term clusters. One study showed that most 2-week periods had little risk of repeat victimization, but there were 2-week periods here and there with very high risk. Thus, simply examining crime for long-term hot spots can make it seem that a stable hot spot exists when it does not and ignore crime flare-ups that occur in isolation.

- Offenders are tightly coupled to place in that burglars are most likely to commit crimes that require the least amount of effort and energy by choosing targets that are most convenient to them.

The implications of the near repeat research for crime analysis are 1) crime analysts should look for additional incidents in the same area soon after one burglary occurs; 2) crime analysts should look for clusters of short-term crime within long-term clusters but also throughout the rest of the jurisdiction, and 3) crime analysts should consider that the same offender is committing the crimes within a cluster of near repeats.

The **80/20 rule** (also called the *Pareto principle*) is another important concept related to repeat victimization. In general, this concept comes from the observation that 80% of some kinds of outcomes are the result of only 20% of the related causes. This is true in many phenomena in nature; for example, a small proportion of the earthquakes that take place are responsible for a very large proportion of the world's earthquake-related damage. The same is true for many of the phenomena examined in crime analysis: A large proportion of offenders repeatedly target a small proportion of people and places, small numbers of locations account for large numbers of crime events, and a small proportion of offenders accounts for a large proportion of offenses (Clarke & Eck, 2005).

An 80/20 analysis allows us to look more broadly at how repeat victimization or repeat offending is taking place. However, the numbers 80 and 20 are used here only to represent "large" and "small" amounts; the actual proportions change in each analysis, depending on the type of activity and nature of the community in which it occurs. The 80/20 rule suggests that by identifying the small proportion of areas, victims, and offenders where a large amount of activity is concentrated, police can get the most out of their crime prevention efforts (i.e., by addressing crimes in specific areas—say, 20% of the community—they can address 80% of the crime problem). These analytic techniques are discussed in Chapter 14.

Situational Crime Prevention

Situational crime prevention, a practice initiated in England in the 1980s, is based on the concepts of environmental criminology, which addresses why crime occurs in specific settings and seeks solutions that reflect the nature of those settings (Cornish & Clarke, 1986). Situational crime prevention provides specific actions police can take to address crime problems in local settings based on the crime analysis of those problems. In an article published in 1980, Clarke first presented a system for classifying the techniques that people and communities can use to reduce opportunities for crime, based on the problem analysis triangle and the theories discussed so far. Cornish and Clarke updated this classification system in 2003. Table 2.1 is an outline of the classification system, and what follows are examples of each technique. For more examples of each technique, see http://www.popcenter.org/25techniques/

Within the system, the first category of techniques is made up of those that prevent crime by increasing the offender's *perceived effort* to commit the crime. In simple terms, these techniques make it more difficult for the offender to commit the crime, thereby addressing the offender's motivation and anticipated rewards. Prevention techniques are divided into five general types: (a) target hardening (e.g., deadbolts, special locks on sliding glass doors); (b) controlling access to facilities (e.g., reducing numbers of entrances/exits, installing gated barriers); (c) screening exits (e.g., using electronic merchandise tags, requiring a ticket for exit); (d) deflecting offenders (e.g., closing streets, implementing a police beat office); and (e) controlling tools/weapons (e.g., restricting sales of spray paint to adults).

The second category consists of techniques that increase the offender's *perceived risk* in committing a crime. In other words, these techniques make offenders "think twice" because they perceive a possibility of getting caught. Prevention techniques are divided into five general types: (a) extending

Table 2.1 25 Techniques of Situational Prevention

Increase the Effort	Increase the Risks	Reduce the Rewards	Reduce Provocations	Remove Excuses
1. Harden targets	6. Extend guardianship	11. Conceal targets	16. Reduce frustrations and stress	21. Set rules
2. Control access to facilities	7. Assist natural surveillance	12. Remove targets	17. Avoid disputes	22. Post instructions
3. Screen exits	8. Reduce anonymity	13. Identify property	18. Reduce emotional arousal	23. Alert conscience
4. Deflect offenders	9. Use place managers	14. Disrupt markets	19. Neutralize peer pressure	24. Assist compliance
5. Control tools/ weapons	10. Strengthen formal surveillance	15. Deny benefits	20. Discourage imitation	25. Control drugs and alcohol

guardianship (e.g., joining a neighborhood watch group, carrying a phone, not walking alone); (b) assisting natural surveillance (e.g., improving street lighting, maintaining landscaping); (c) reducing anonymity (e.g., requiring school uniforms, requiring taxi drivers to display identification); (d) utilizing place managers (e.g., having two clerks on every shift at convenience stores); and (e) using formal surveillance (e.g., installing video cameras and burglar alarms).

The third category in the classification system comprises techniques that reduce the offender's *anticipated rewards* from committing the crime. In other words, these techniques reduce the value to the offender of the crime itself. These prevention techniques fall into the following five general areas: (a) concealing targets (e.g., parking vehicles in a garage instead of on the street, putting valuables in the trunk instead of the car); (b) removing targets (e.g., keeping a maximum of $50 in cash in a convenience store register); (c) identifying property (e.g., licensing bicycles, etching a car's vehicle identification number on car parts); (d) disrupting markets (e.g., monitoring pawn shops and street vendors for stolen merchandise); and (e) denying benefits (e.g., installing removable faces on car stereos, attaching ink tags to clothing).

The fourth category in the system is made up of techniques that reduce the offender's *provocation* for committing the crime. In other words, these techniques aim to change social and environmental conditions in ways that will diminish stress, conflict, and temptation to offend. These prevention techniques are divided into five general types: (a) reducing frustrations and stress (e.g., managing lines efficiently, providing comfortable seating, music, or other entertainment for people waiting for service); (b) avoiding disputes (e.g., reducing crowding in bars, establishing fixed cab fares); (c) reducing emotional arousal (e.g., eliminating a bikini contest at a bar, controlling the serving of alcohol); (d) neutralizing peer pressure (e.g., dispersing groups at schools and at sporting events); and (e) discouraging imitation (e.g., repairing vandalized property rapidly, censoring details of crimes when providing information to the media).

The final category of the classification system consists of techniques that address the offender's motivation by focusing on *removing excuses* for the crime. In other words, these techniques are intended to change social practices as a way to encourage compliance with the law. These prevention techniques are divided into five types: (a) setting rules (e.g., requiring written rental agreements, requiring registration for admittance to a hotel); (b) posting instructions (e.g., installing signs specifying "No Parking" or "Private Property"); (c) alerting conscience (e.g., installing a roadside speed display, warnings on social networking sites about soliciting sex from children); (d) assisting compliance (e.g., providing trash bins and containers for recyclables in public areas); and (e) controlling drugs and alcohol (e.g., installing Breathalyzers in bars, refusing to serve alcohol to drunk individuals).

Situational crime prevention seeks to provide measures that are directly related to the immediate crime settings, and just as the opportunities that facilitate crime may be unique, unique measures may be needed to prevent those opportunities from occurring. Also, a particular crime prevention action may address more than one opportunity or problematic behavior; thus, the goal is selecting actions that have the most impact. For example, school uniforms reduce anonymity of students in public, but they also increase compliance with rules requiring that students wear appropriate clothing in school, which may reduce provocations for inappropriate behavior. Another example is implementing a curfew for juveniles that both increases the perceived risk of juveniles being caught after curfew but also removes potential victims (e.g., of assault and/or rape) during that time. Even though crime analysts do not implement such crime prevention measures themselves, an important part of crime analysis involves recommending them and evaluating their effectiveness once implemented.

Displacement and Diffusion of Benefits

In addition to using theory to understand opportunities for crime and disorder (problem analysis triangle) and to select and apply specific techniques to prevent crime (situational crime prevention), crime analysts use theory to understand how and why crime phenomena change when crime prevention responses are applied. A crime phenomenon can change by being moved to another time or place or can take on another form; this is called **displacement**. The problem can also change by being eliminated (either partially or fully). In some circumstances, when one type of crime activity is eliminated, the action affects other types of crime as well (e.g., when prostitution is eliminated from an area, traffic problems and assaults on women also decrease). This is called **diffusion of benefits**. It is important for crime analysts to understand how crime phenomena change because they are tasked to examine such changes on a regular basis (e.g., a decrease in burglaries at an apartment community) and to evaluate the outcomes of specific crime prevention programs (e.g., a program that restricts entry into an apartment community).

Displacement of Crime

Displacement occurs when crime or other types of activity shift to other forms, times, and locales instead of being eliminated. Crime analysts need to consider the following four types of displacement (Clarke & Eck, 2005):

1. **Spatial displacement** is the shifting of an activity from targets in one area to those in another area. For example, when the police address prostitution in one area, the activity moves to another area of the city.

2. **Temporal displacement** is the shifting of an activity from one time to another. This can include changes in

the time of day, day of the week, and season of the year. For example, if police routinely patrol a particular area between 8:00 p.m. and 10:00 p.m. looking for gang members hanging out on the street, the gang members may shift their behavior and hang out in the area either later or earlier in the day.

3. **Target displacement** is the shifting of the choice of one victim/target to a more vulnerable victim/target. That is, when place managers harden one type of target, offenders may focus on other types of targets. For instance, if officials change the pay phones in a bus station so they take only credit cards and no coins, they become poor targets for offenders who want to obtain cash. Offenders in the bus station may shift from breaking into pay phones to breaking into coin-operated vending machines.

4. **Tactical displacement** is the shifting of tactics by offenders. This can happen when offenders find that their usual methods are no longer working or if they become more confident and reckless in committing crime. Offenders might shift from conning their way into someone's home to steal valuables to breaking into the home, or an offender who has previously gone no further than exposing himself to women at a bus stop may shift to touching his victims.

Comprehensive reviews of crime reduction studies (Guerette & Bowers, 2009; Hesseling, 1994; Johnson, Guerette, & Bowers, 2014) found that, in the few studies that did find spatial displacement, it was rarely one-for-one. That is, for example, if there were 100 crimes at one location, only 75 or 50 would be displaced to another location. However, because these studies find that displacement of activity is possible, crime analysts should examine the likelihood of displacement when examining the effects of crime reduction strategies to help police agencies understand how crime activity changes and whether any changes seen are the results of their strategies or other factors.

Diffusion of Benefits

Research has shown that crime problems can be eliminated through the application of the principles of situational crime prevention, which aims to reduce/remove the opportunities for crime (Clarke, 1992). In addition, research indicates that when targeted problems are successfully eliminated, other problems are also often eliminated; this is referred to as the *diffusion of benefits* (Clarke & Weisburd, 1994). For example, when police close down a hotel that has served as a hub for prostitution and drug dealing, other negative types of activity that have been taking place in the area of the hotel—such as robbery, theft, assaults, vandalism, and traffic concerns—decrease or even cease. Once opportunities to offend are removed by closing the hotel, offenders leave the vicinity, which eliminates robbery by drug users who have been robbing people nearby to get money to buy drugs at the hotel and eliminates traffic problems caused by men driving slowly past the hotel as they seek prostitutes (Sampson, 2003).

Analysts can use crime mapping to determine whether crime or other activity has been spatially displaced and whether a diffusion of benefits has taken place as the result of a particular crime prevention effort or the change in opportunity for a crime. An analyst examining the outcomes associated with the closure of the hotel in the previous example would identify areas 500 to 1,000 feet around the hotel to determine whether crime and disorder activity had declined in surrounding areas.

Opportunity

Opportunity is the overarching theme of this chapter's discussion of how crime analysts understand and address patterns of crime events. To synthesize the concepts of environmental criminology, situational crime prevention, repeat victimization, the 80/20 rule, displacement, and diffusion of benefits, Felson and Clarke (1998, pp. v and vi), two of the original thinkers in this area, lay out 10 key points related to opportunity and crime:

1. Opportunities play a role in causing all crime.
2. Crime opportunities are highly specific.
3. Crime opportunities are concentrated in time and space.
4. Crime opportunities depend on everyday movements of activity.
5. One crime produces opportunities for another.
6. Some products offer more tempting crime opportunities than do others.
7. Social and technological changes produce new crime opportunities.
8. Crime can be prevented through the reduction of opportunities.
9. Reducing opportunities does not usually result in the displacement of crime.
10. Focused opportunity reduction can produce wider declines in crime.

SUMMARY POINTS

This chapter provides an overview of the role of environmental criminological theory in guiding crime analysis. The following are the key points addressed in this chapter:

- Criminological theories that deal with immediate situational causes of crime are more relevant to crime analysis than theories that seek to explain the underlying sociological and psychological causes of crime or why people become criminals.

- Environmental criminology focuses on patterns of motivation for offenders, opportunities that exist for crime, and levels of protection of victims within the criminal event as well as the environment in which it occurs. The goal of environmental criminology is not to explain why a specific offender commits a specific crime, but to understand the various aspects of a criminal event in order to identify patterns of behavior and environmental factors that create opportunities for crime.

- The problem analysis triangle illustrates the relationships among the elements that create crime opportunities: the offender's motivation, the vulnerability of the target/victim, the time and place of the crime event, and the lack of oversight/protection.

- Guardians are people who have the ability to protect victims/targets by watching over them or removing them from particular settings.

- Managers are people who are responsible for places. They set rules and manage the places.

- Handlers are people who know the potential offenders and are in positions that allow them to monitor and/or control potential offenders' actions.

- Three theoretical perspectives help crime analysts understand and anticipate patterns of behavior that create opportunities for crime: rational choice theory (offender choices), crime pattern theory (activity/space), and routine activities theory (patterns of behavior).

- Rational choice theory states that offenders make choices about committing crimes based on opportunities and anticipated rewards. It suggests that if given a chance or the right "opportunity," any person will commit a crime. It also suggests that a person will decide not to commit crimes when the risks are too high or the rewards are not adequate—an idea that differs from traditional criminological theory, which implies that criminal behavior is inevitable.

- Crime pattern theory helps to explain the nature of the immediate situation in which a crime occurs. According to this theory, criminal events are most likely to occur in areas where the activity spaces of offenders overlap with the activity spaces of potential victims/targets. Offenders tend to commit crimes in areas with which they are familiar.

- Routine activities theory focuses on how opportunities for crime change based on changes in behavior on a societal level. The widespread use of the Internet is an example of a change in society that has created opportunities for crime.

- The law of crime concentration says "For a defined measure of crime at a specific microgeographic unit, the concentration of crime will fall within a narrow bandwidth of percentages for a defined cumulative proportion of crime." This means that not only do we know that crime clusters by place but also that these clusters can be narrowly defined and are stable and predictable over time.

- Repeat victimization is the recurrence of crime in the same places or against the same people. A major finding from the research on repeat victimization is that people and places that have been victimized in the past have a higher likelihood of being victimized again than do people and places that have not been victimized.

- Repeat victimization is broken down into four types: true repeat victims, near victims, virtual repeats, and chronic victims.

- Repeat victimization is also related to other ways in which crime clusters: repeat offenders, hot spots, risky facilities, and hot products.

- Near repeat victimization is a very specific type of repeat victimization. Near repeats are defined as nonvictimized places near places that have been victimized.

- Findings from near repeat research have concluded that 1) houses next to a burgled home have been found to be at a substantially higher risk of being burglarized; 2) most near repeats occur within 1 week of the initial burglary; 3) the increased risk is caused by offenders returning to the area of a prior successful burglary; 4) short-term clusters of crime occur within, but also outside of, long-term clusters, and 5) offenders are tightly coupled to place.

- An important concept related to repeat victimization is that of the 80/20 rule. This concept comes from the observation that 80% of some kinds of outcomes are the result of only 20% of the related causes. This suggests that by focusing their efforts on areas and people who are repeat victims or that account for a large amount of crime activity, police can maximize the impacts of a crime prevention strategy.

- Situational crime prevention is a practice based on the components of the crime triangle. A classification system developed by Ronald V. Clarke specifies five types of crime prevention techniques—increasing the offender's perceived effort, increasing the offender's perceived risk, reducing the offender's anticipated rewards, reducing provocations for committing crime, and removing excuses for committing crime—each of which can be divided into five general kinds of techniques.

- Displacement occurs when crime or other types of activity shift to other forms, times, or locales instead of being eliminated. Crime analysis techniques can identify and describe any displacement of activity to help police agencies understand how crime activity changes and whether any changes seen are the results of crime prevention efforts.

- Research has shown that crime problems can be eliminated through the application of the principles of situational crime prevention, which aims to reduce or remove the opportunities for crime. In addition, the successful elimination of targeted problems may also reduce other problems; this process is called the diffusion of benefits.

DISCUSSION EXERCISES*

Exercise 1

Think of a situation in which a crime has occurred in your own life or in the life of a family member, friend, or acquaintance. Answer the following questions in relation to that crime event:

1. What was (or seemed to be) the offender's motivation to commit the crime?

2. What was the nature of the place where the crime occurred?

3. What was the nature of the target or behavior of the victim during the crime?

4. How might the handlers, the guardians, and the managers have increased the opportunity for the crime to occur?

5. How might the crime have been prevented? (Focus on the opportunities that enabled the crime to occur. For the offender, could anything have increased the perceived effort, increased the perceived risks, or reduced the anticipated rewards?)

Exercise 2

For this exercise, partner up with one other person from class and go into the parking lot; then document the contents and condition of one another's vehicle. Collect information on the following:

- Name of fellow student

- Make, model, year, color of vehicle

- Crime prevention devices available

- Crime prevention devices in use (e.g., locks, alarms, clubs)

- Property in the vehicle in view

- Other observations about the vehicle

Document your observations of your fellow student's vehicle and rate it from 1 to 10 on crime prevention vulnerability/opportunity—1 being not very vulnerable, with few opportunities, and 10 being very vulnerable to crime.

Exercise 3

Select one or more of the following problems and describe how one technique from each of the five general situational crime prevention categories (e.g., increase risk, increase effort, reduce rewards, reduce provocations, and remove excuses) could be implemented to reduce the opportunities for this problematic activity;

- Assaults at high schools

- Robbery at grocery stores

- Graffiti on residential fences along a major roadway

- Shoplifting at a major retailer

- Disorderly youth at a movie theater

- Theft from vehicles in an apartment complex

- Street prostitution in an industrial park

- Theft of purses at a hospital

- Drug sales at a convenience store

*Additional exercises using data and other resources can be found on **http://www.sagepub.com/bobasantos4e.**

3

Evidence-Based Policing and the Role of Crime Analysis

B oth research and practice have shown the most effective methods police employ to prevent and control crime are those in which crime analysis plays a vital role. Thus, the focus of this chapter is on the results of crime analysis research, as well as research on "what works" in policing for preventing and controlling crime. The chapter presents what we know from research to be **evidence-based policing** practices (Sherman, 1998) for crime analysis and crime reduction and highlights the role of crime analysis in assisting with these efforts. It also covers how to "make it work" in a police organization. The "it" is the implementation of evidence-based crime analysis and crime reduction practices. The "how" is a stratified approach that breaks the work of police into immediate, short-term, and long-term activity for which crime analysis and crime reduction practices are focused.

Research on Crime Analysis and Crime Reduction

As discussed in Chapter 1, there is a growing body of knowledge about crime analysis in terms of its prevalence and implementation; however, there is little research on the relationship between crime analysis and crime reduction (Santos, 2014). Only two studies, both doctoral dissertations, have explored the question of whether crime analysis reduces crime by examining crime analysis characteristics of police agencies and their crime and clearance rates.

Demir (2009) used 1997 data from a national survey conducted by the Crime Mapping Research Center (CMRC) of the National Institute of Justice (NIJ) to examine the relationship of more than 2,000 agencies' crime analysis and crime mapping functions and their crime clearance rates to determine if agencies with crime analysis also cleared more crimes than those without crime analysis. The researcher found some evidence that agencies participating in more crime analysis and crime mapping had lower clearance rates. Baltaci (2010) used the national survey data collected by O'Shea and Nicholls in 2000 (O'Shea & Nicholls, 2003) to examine the effect of crime analysis activity on crime and clearance rates of police agencies. The results from a sample of around 800 agencies with more than 100 officers showed that the broader the crime analysis activities of an agency, the lower the violent crime rates and the higher the violent, property, and total clearance rates.

Although these two studies examined crime analysis and crime statistics, they are both correlational studies and not causal studies, thus cannot make conclusions about the "effect" of crime analysis on levels of crime. That is, although the studies showed a relationship between crime analysis and crime clearance rates, they have no evidence that crime analysis, in fact, "caused" a decrease or whether other factors (e.g., police response, evidence gathering, downturn in the economy) explained the difference in crime and clearance rates of the agencies.

Many researchers and practitioners ask the question "Does crime analysis reduce crime?" This question is a difficult one because the link between crime analysis and crime reduction is not direct. As discussed in Chapter 1, crime analysis is the process of examining data and making conclusions; it is not a crime reduction strategy by itself. An analogy to the medical field helps to understand the relationship of crime analysis to crime reduction.

In medicine, a magnetic resonance imaging (MRI) machine is used to conduct an analysis of the entire body or a particular body part to diagnose an injury or illness. The MRI technician uses the machine's software to produce a series of images, which are the data. This data is then given to the radiologist (i.e., a medical doctor) who interprets the images to determine any problems or issues with the patient. The radiologist makes definitive conclusions but also less definitive ones based on what the data show. The radiologist's report is forwarded to the patient's doctor, who is often not the same person. This doctor assesses the radiologist's report and decides upon a medical strategy to address the patient's illness based on the report, best medical practices, and characteristics of the patient. Different strategies might be selected for different patients for the same illness depending on, for example, the age, sex, or degree of illness of the patient. Thus, the final strategy carried out for the patient depends on a multistep process by multiple experts. And while the MRI itself and the analysis reports may be accurate and of high quality, the success of the strategy (i.e., treatment) selected by the patient's doctor depends on the doctor's understanding of the MRI data analysis, the quality of the radiologists report, the treatment's appropriateness, and, importantly, the proper implementation of the treatment.

Based on this explanation, would you say that an MRI analysis cures an illness? Or even whether the radiologist cures an illness? No, probably not. An MRI is important and necessary for doctors as a diagnostic tool, as an MRI can catch an illness in the early stages and point to a particular treatment to cure the illness. However, the MRI technology, data produced, and the radiologist's report only address one aspect of the process. It is an important and oftentimes necessary process to "diagnosis" an illness, but it does not by itself "cure" a patient's illness. Figure 3.1 shows this medical process.

The crime analysis process in crime reduction is analogous to the MRI process in medicine. Like the radiologist, a crime analyst has access to computer software and data (e.g., crime data from a police record management system)

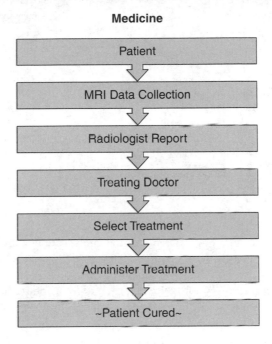

Figure 3.1 Process for Diagnosing and Curing a Patient

Medicine

- Patient
- MRI Data Collection
- Radiologist Report
- Treating Doctor
- Select Treatment
- Administer Treatment
- ~Patient Cured~

and uses specific techniques to analyze and interpret the data to develop a "diagnosis" of a particular crime problem. As with medicine, the report is passed to another doctor—in this case, the sworn police officers—who select an evidence-based response as well as oversee its implementation, just like the doctor administers the treatment. Thus, it is impossible for crime analysis to have a direct relationship with crime reduction and "cause" crime to go down. The relationship is indirect, and the reduction of crime significantly depends on the police taking the results from the crime analyst, selecting an effective strategy, and implementing it effectively. Figure 3.2 depicts a similar flow chart of the crime analysis process in crime reduction.

On the left, the crime analysis results start the process (i.e., the radiologists report). The results are dependent on the quality of the data, the techniques used, and the analyst's interpretation. If any of these aspects is weak or incorrect, the results will also be. This information is provided to sworn police personnel who ideally select an effective, evidence-based response and subsequently oversee and provide resources for the response (i.e., selecting and carrying out the treatment). Only if these two steps are done effectively is there a chance that crime can be impacted. Finally, the outcome of the response in the ideal situation is crime reduction (i.e., curing the illness). This effect, of course, requires close scrutiny and rigorous evaluation methods to determine if, in fact, it was the police response and not other factors that affected crime. The analogy and the figures illustrate how there is not a direct link between

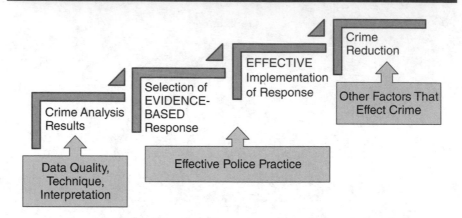

Figure 3.2 Crime Analysis Process in Crime Reduction

crime analysis and crime reduction. Yet crime analysis does play a part in crime reduction just as the MRI plays a part in diagnosing illnesses.

Because crime analysis does not have a direct link to crime reduction, its role in crime reduction is understood by examining effective crime reduction strategies by police (i.e., evidence-based policing) and the role of crime analysis. The following sections discuss the key components of crime reduction policing approaches commonly used today, the research conclusions about whether they are effective in reducing crime, and the role of crime analysis in each. Each section ends with the key takeaways of the discussion. By the end of this section, a clear pattern reveals itself that crime analysis is central to promising strategies, effective approaches, and newer approaches that have not yet been evaluated. This conclusion is important because it promises a significant future for crime analysis practice in policing.

Standard Model of Policing

The standard model of policing encompasses strategies that come to mind when the average person thinks about what police are supposed to do. The central element of the **standard model of policing** involves enforcing the law in a broad and reactive way, primarily using police resources (Weisburd & Eck, 2004). Specifically, the strategies of the standard model of policing include the following (Sherman et al., 1997; Weisburd & Eck, 2004):

- Increased number of police officers (to increase the ability to detect crime and arrest offenders)

- Unfocused, random motorized patrols (to create a perception of a police "omnipresence" to deter crime in public places)

- Rapid response to calls for service (to increase the likelihood of catching offenders)

- Follow-up investigations by detectives (to increase the solvability of the crimes)

- General reactive arrest policies (to deter and punish specific offenders as well as deter the general public from committing crimes)

The general consensus of the research on effectiveness of these strategies is that each one of these generally applied enforcement efforts has been of limited effectiveness (Sherman et al., 1997; Skogan & Frydl, 2004; Telep & Weisburd, 2012; Weisburd & Eck, 2004).

Crime analysis is used within the standard model of policing to help assess how many officers may be needed to staff the requisite number of calls for service and crimes and to determine future optimal staffing levels. The agency assesses its own practices, such as allocation of personnel, money, equipment, and other resources geographically, organizationally, and temporally. This type of analysis does not support crime reduction, but the administration of resources in the agency. Analysis is also used in the standard model of policing to assess and improve the rapid response to calls for service by examining the types of calls, priorities, geographic routes officers take to answer calls, and geographic assignment of officers.

Specifically related to crime, criminal investigation work requires the identification of suspects and individual offenders as well as conducting investigative searches of databases (O'Shea & Nicholls, 2003). While some crime analysts may do this work, it is not technically crime analysis but is investigative support, which is done by a crime analysis or investigative technician (see Chapter 1). Crime statistics that are produced by crime analysis for the standard model of policing are used to determine the overall amount of crime and whether crime has increased or decreased. However, the statistics are not used for directing crime reduction strategies since random patrol and reactive arrests are generally applied. Thus, crime analysis is used primarily as information so that sworn personnel, from patrol officers to the chief, have an idea of when and where crime has occurred and overall how much has occurred, but it does not directly inform their proactive crime reduction strategies because in the standard model proactivity is extremely limited (Weisburd & Eck, 2004). Much of crime analysis in this approach focuses on identifying individual offenders and conducting investigative support (O'Shea & Nicholls, 2003).

Key Takeaways. The standard model of policing has limited effectiveness in reducing crime. Because it generally applies various tactics such as patrol, arrests, and investigation, there is little use for crime analysis beyond resources allocation and providing crime and arrest statistics.

Community Policing

Police scholars have touted community policing as one of the most widely adopted police strategies in the last several decades (Weisburd & Eck, 2004). However, it is difficult to define because its definition has changed over time, and its concepts are vague. According to the U.S. Department of Justice's Office of Community-Oriented Policing (the COPS Office; 2014), **community policing** is defined as the following:

> A philosophy that promotes organizational strategies which support the systematic use of partnerships and problem-solving techniques, to proactively address the immediate conditions that give rise to public safety issues such as crime, social disorder, and fear of crime. (p. 1)

The first key component of community policing is developing partnerships and relationships with the community to understand and respond to problems as well as to engender cooperation and legitimacy of the police so that partnerships are meaningful. The second key component of community policing is the process of problem solving (i.e., scanning, analysis, response, and assessment [SARA]), which is also a process used in problem-oriented policing discussed later in the chapter.

There are specific strategies that fall under the umbrella of community policing that have been evaluated. One strategy is "neighborhood watch" (also called block watch), which is one of the most-implemented community policing programs; it has the goal of increasing surveillance by residents and community members of their own neighborhoods. Other strategies include increasing the flow of information from the community to the police through community meetings, officers walking the "beat" and talking to residents; using storefront beat offices; and providing crime information to the public through the Internet, crime maps, letters, and "reverse 911" phone calls so they can protect themselves (Sherman et al., 1997). However, research shows that neighborhood watch, community meetings, storefront offices, and newsletters do not reduce crime (Weisburd & Eck, 2004). While door-to-door visits by the police have been found to reduce crime, simply providing information about crime to the public has not been shown to prevent crime (Sherman et al., 1997; Weisburd & Eck, 2004).

A review of the research on the effectiveness of community policing shows a variety of results but concludes that overall the results are "ambiguous" (Gill, Weisburd, Telep, Vitter, & Bennett, 2014). The researchers conclude that while there is some impact on reduction of property crime, the most positive and strongest evidence indicates that community policing strategies do increase citizens' satisfaction with police, aspects of police legitimacy, and their perceptions of disorder. That is, when effective community policing strategies are implemented citizens feel more positive about police, that there is less disorder, and that they are more likely to work with police in partnerships.

On the contrary, the researchers find no evidence that community policing reduces citizens' fear of crime or that it reduces levels of officially recorded crime. Gill et al. (2014) conclude that more evidence is necessary to make conclusions about effectiveness and note that the research findings are based on how community policing has been carried out by police, which has not been its ideal implementation. Going back to the medical analogy, this is similar to trying to evaluate the effectiveness of a medicine that was not taken as it was prescribed.

Crime analysis is used for community policing by providing information to citizens as part of a police department's efforts to be transparent and to take collective responsibility for crime problems in the community. Crime analysts have historically played a central role in providing statistical information about crime to community groups, neighborhood and block watch organizations, businesses, and for newsletters with the goal of communicating crime information to the public. Over the last 15 to 20 years, the distribution of crime and disorder information has shifted to the Internet, so the analysis is not necessarily created or distributed by crime analysts, but through public Internet companies to which the police agency provides data that are accessed by citizens to search the data themselves.

Crime analysis methodology is also used by a police agency to solicit and analyze information collected from citizens about satisfaction with police, victimization, and perceptions of crime, fear, and safety. In some cases, crime analysts oversee this process, while in others researchers and survey companies are hired to carry out the work. Again, this information is used to understand relationships with the community as well as identify common problems to be addressed in the community. Although analysts may not play a central role in disseminating and collecting this information, the processes are considered a crime analysis function of a police department.

> **Key Takeaways.** Specific community policing programs are limited in their effectiveness in reducing crime and do not require crime analysis. Overall, research results on community policing are "ambiguous," and better measurement is required to make more definitive conclusions about its effectiveness. However, there is some evidence that community policing can impact property crime, and there is little evidence on its impact on fear of crime. Community policing does affect satisfaction with the police and legitimacy. The role of crime analysis in the overall approach is that it provides information to and solicits information from citizens to support building partnerships and transparency.

Problem-Oriented Policing

First introduced by Herman Goldstein in his seminal 1979 article "Improving Policing: A Problem-Oriented Approach," **problem-oriented policing (POP)** is the idea that police take a proactive role in identifying, understanding, and responding to problems (not just individual incidents) in their communities. Goldstein argued that the police were too focused on the means (i.e., conducting patrols and making arrests) and not enough on the ends of their work (i.e., preventing crime and disorder). He suggested that if police were to take a more "problem-oriented focus" they could be more effective in impacting crime and disorder problems. At the same time, Goldstein argued that to be "problem oriented" the police must take a new, more systematic approach that demands they collect new data, develop new methods of analysis, identify innovative solutions, and apply measures for assessing the success of their efforts (Goldstein, 1990).

John Eck and William Spelman (1987) gave the approach a specific method when they developed the **SARA** model in their application of problem-oriented policing in Newport News, Virginia. The SARA model (discussed in detail in Chapter 12) includes (S)canning and defining specific problems, (A)nalyzing data to understand the opportunities that create the problem, (R)esponding to the problem using both police and nonpolice methods, and (A)ssessing whether the response has worked (Center for Problem-Oriented Policing, 2016). POP is rooted in the theories of environmental criminology and situational crime prevention (as described in Chapter 2). The analysis and strategies of POP are focused on identifying and reducing the opportunities for crime and disorder problems in specific situations.

A systematic meta-analysis of the highest-quality POP research found that in the limited number of studies that it had a modest but significant effect on crime reduction (Weisburd, Telep, Hinkle, & Eck, 2010). In addition, even less rigorous pre-/postevaluations revealed positive results of POP in reducing crime. Researchers concluded that even addressing problems somewhat superficially using the problem-solving process is enough to impact crime and disorder levels (Braga & Weisburd, 2006; Telep & Weisburd, 2012). Although more rigorous research needs to be conducted on POP efforts, the evidence so far shows that it is the most promising of the police strategies (Skogan & Frydl, 2004; Weisburd & Eck, 2004, Weisburd et al., 2010).

Crime analysis has a very clear role in problem solving for crime reduction. Notably, crime analysis plays an integral role in all phases of problem solving, not only in the two As of SARA—analysis and assess—which are obvious, but also in the S and R—scan and respond. That is, scanning requires analysis that helps to identify and prioritize problems for selection. In the response stage of problem solving, the responses are not only selected based on the analysis, but the specific deployment of responses depends on additional analysis. Fundamentally, problem solving cannot occur without crime analysis, which is also called "problem analysis" (Boba, 2003; see Chapter 4 for the definition).

Hot Spots Policing

Hot spots policing is a place-based policing approach in which traditional police strategies, such as increased police presence and arrests, are implemented in areas or "hot spots" that have disproportionately more crime than other areas within a jurisdiction (Braga, Papachristos, & Hureau, 2014; Telep & Weisburd, 2012; Weisburd & Eck, 2004). The research on the effectiveness of hot spots policing is rigorous and plentiful. The results show that police response to hot spots, whether they are individual or clusters of addresses, street segments, or blocks, is effective in reducing crime (Braga et al., 2014; Telep & Weisburd, 2012; Weisburd & Eck, 2004). Although the research shows that displacement of crime does not often occur and more often diffusion of benefits is the result of the interventions, the sustainability of crime reduction is limited in that the results are primarily short term (Braga et al., 2014). However, Braga and Weisburd (2010) asserted that when hot spots policing is coupled with more in-depth problem solving as is used in problem-oriented policing (i.e., not just identifying the hot spots but also understanding why they are "hot"), the strategy can be effective in the long term as well

Crime analysis, particularly the use of crime mapping and spatial analysis, has an important role in identifying the hot spots where the policing strategies are best implemented. Analysis is an important facet of properly identifying hot spots because many researchers have found that police do not accurately identify hot spots or regularly agree on what is a hot spot in their respective areas of responsibility (Bichler & Gaines, 2005; McLaughlin, Johnson, Bowers, Birks, & Pease, 2006; Ratcliffe & McCullagh, 2001). When hot spots policing is coupled with in-depth problem solving, crime analysis plays an even more central role in identifying and understanding the nature of the hot spot to implement appropriate responses, as noted earlier in the discussion of POP. In both hot spots policing with traditional responses and when coupled with problem solving, crime analysis also plays an important role determining whether there is an effect on crime and whether the strategies result in displacement of crime or diffusion of benefits (Braga et al., 2014; Telep & Weisburd, 2012).

Focused Deterrence

Focused deterrence, also called the "pulling levers" strategy, is essentially a specific problem-solving approach to address serious violent offenders in high-crime areas of a city (Braga & Weisburd, 2012). The focus of the responses, based in deterrence theory, is that they be certain, severe, and swift (Braga & Weisburd, 2012). Individual offenders are identified as chronic or high-risk offenders, and responses are tailored for each offender to encourage him or her to stop committing crimes. Police may bring in prosecutors and probation officers as well as family members, community members, and others with the hope of "pulling" whatever "lever" is important to that offender to persuade and convince her or him that committing crime is no longer a preferable way of life. This approach was first implemented as a POP project in Boston in the 1990s but has been implemented in many different communities across the country. In each community, a problem-solving approach is taken in which the specific deterrence strategies are implemented based on the nature of the violent crime and offenses in that community (Braga & Weisburd, 2012; Telep & Weisburd, 2012).

The results of a meta-analysis of the most rigorous research on the focused deterrence approach indicate that the strategies are shown to reduce crime at a significant level (Braga & Weisburd, 2012). Although there is a lack of systematic experimental research to support this conclusion, less rigorous studies showed large effect sizes, which indicate the approach is promising. As with POP, the problem-solving process is central in this approach, thus crime analysis is also central (Telep & Weisburd, 2012). Although the responses within this approach focus on individuals, the process of identifying the appropriate individuals involves identifying areas of disproportionately high crime (i.e., hot spots; Kennedy, Braga, & Piehl, 1998) and understanding the nature of crime and the relationship of the offenders to crime (Kennedy, Braga, & Piehl, 2001), both of which require crime analysis.

> **Key Takeaways.** The focused deterrence strategy is effective and shows promise in reducing crime. Crime analysis is essential as part of the problem-solving approach that is fundamental in this strategy.

Disorder Policing

Disorder policing, also called "broken windows policing," is based on an idea developed in the 1980s (Wilson & Kelling, 1982; Kelling, 2015) that makes a logical connection between disorderly conditions of a neighborhood and crime and disorder. That is, residents, business owners, and workers in neighborhoods with high levels of social incivilities (loitering, public drinking, drug dealing and prostitution) as well as physical decay, such as run-down infrastructure (streets, sidewalks, lighting), buildings either run down or vacant, and vacant, overgrown lots become afraid and either move out or protect themselves through avoiding others and isolating themselves. Once this happens, individuals are not connected to one another, and the community and offenders who commit both low-level and more serious crime begin to move in and operate with little resistance (Welsh, Braga, & Bruinsma, 2015). While Wilson and Kelling (1982) do not lay out specific strategies to employ for disorder policing, more generally they suggest that police should engage in "order maintenance" and address the physical deterioration of the neighborhoods (Welsh et al., 2015). Thus, a policing approach based on this idea employs strategies that seek to "clean up" the social incivilities (e.g., disorderly behavior and minor offenses) to prevent more serious crimes from happening (Sousa & Kelling, 2006).

The research results of the effectiveness of broken windows policing have been mixed (Weisburd & Eck, 2004), but the meta-analysis of 30 randomized and quasi experiments conducted by Welsh and his colleagues (2015) found that the disorder strategies employed by police had a modest effect on crime. They found that strategies that were community-oriented and used the problem-solving process to focus on changing physical and social disorder were the most effective, but aggressive-order maintenance tactics that targeted individuals with little discretion, also called "zero tolerance policing," were not effective at all. In fact, the researchers found that these aggressive strategies appeared to separate the police from the communities in which they worked, resulting in increased complaints against police officers, racial disparities, and criminalization of homeless and mentally ill populations (Welsh et al., 2015). In addition, little evidence has been found that disorder policing reduces fear of crime or enhances community cohesion (Welsh et al., 2015).

The role of crime analysis in disorder policing depends on how the strategies are implemented. If they are applied in an unfocused way in that police conduct order maintenance tactics generally in the jurisdiction, crime analysis is limited to the ex post facto evaluation of the tactics since no analysis is necessary to focus the tactics in any way. On the contrary, if disorder policing strategies are applied to specific neighborhoods using the process of problem solving, then crime analysis plays a central role in determining the nature and cause of the problem as well as when and where strategies are deployed.

Key Takeaways. There is no evidence that disorder policing reduces fear of crime or increases community bonds, but it does have a modest effect on crime overall, with the largest effect occurring when strategies are focused in places and small areas. Aggressive-order maintenance strategies do not result in lower crime and more likely result negatively on police–community relations. The role of crime analysis is important for the effective implementation of disorder policing (i.e., focused on places and areas) but is not as important when the strategies are generally applied.

Compstat

Compstat was created and implemented in the NYPD in 1994 (Silverman, 2006), but its rapid and widespread adoption by police agencies around the United States has moved it beyond being an isolated strategy used by one agency (Police Executive Research Forum, 2013; Weisburd, Mastrofski, McNally, Greenspan, & Willis, 2003). The Compstat model is an attempt to synthesize an accountability structure and strategic problem solving (Weisburd et al., 2003), and many police departments have implemented it because of pressure to appear progressive and successful in reducing crime (Willis, Mastrofski, & Weisburd, 2007).

Ideally, the Compstat process is centered on four principles that are directly correlated to the four steps of the SARA problem-solving process. Compstat's first step of "accurate and timely intelligence" shares its purpose with the scanning and analysis processes of SARA in analyzing crime and disorder data to provide an understanding about when activity is occurring, as well as how, where, to whom, and by whom. Compstat's "effective tactics" and "rapid deployment of personnel and resources" shares a similar purpose with the response stage of SARA. Finally, "relentless follow up and assessment" is akin to the assessment stage of SARA. Although the implementation of Compstat has not been as strategic or as in depth as Goldstein has laid out for problem solving (Boba & Crank, 2008), both the problem-solving and Compstat processes provide a framework for a dynamic process to address problems, with Compstat's contribution and uniqueness being the development of a formal structure of accountability to ensure the process is carried out (Weisburd et al., 2003).

Although many attribute the notable reduction in crime in NYC to Compstat, there has been no systematic evaluation of Compstat's effectiveness. One case study of Compstat implemented in Fort Worth, Texas, showed reductions in property crime but not in violent crime (Jang, Hoover, & Joo, 2010). One might argue that the rapid and comprehensive adoption of "Compstat-like" programs in police agencies in the United States and around the world (Weisburd, Mastrofski, Willis, & Greenspan, 2006) might represent success, but again, this provides no evidence on its effectiveness in crime reduction. Similar to the research on crime analysis, most of the research on Compstat thus far has focused on its prevalence and nature of its implementation (e.g., Dabney, 2010; Willis, 2011; Willis, Mastrofski, & Kochel, 2010).

The role of crime analysis in Compstat is significant. Importantly, not all police agencies have implemented the management model as NYPD has, but in most implementations of "Compstat-like" programs, crime analysis is the core component (Boba & Santos, 2011; Weisburd et al., 2003). In addition to the routine analyses produced by crime analysts that are used to direct resources and hold managers accountable, crime mapping is the central mechanism of communication in Compstat meetings (Ratcliffe, 2004a). In fact, many police agencies today have crime analysis and crime mapping technology simply because they implemented a "Compstat-like" program.

> **Key Takeaways.** Although little can be said about the effectiveness of Compstat in reducing crime directly, crime analysis is central to its components that coincide with the problem-solving process. Routine crime analysis products are used to hold personnel accountable, and crime mapping in particular is a central mechanism of communication in accountability meetings.

Intelligence-Led Policing

Intelligence-led policing (ILP) is a contemporary police management model in which the intelligence or analysis function is central in police agency's crime reduction and prevention efforts (Ratcliffe, 2008). As a top-down management philosophy and business model, the gathering of intelligence and dissemination of analysis products directly inform decision-makers (Ratcliffe, 2008). Focused on prolific and serious offenders, ILP combines traditional intelligence analysis within a problem-solving approach (Ratcliffe, 2008). Many agencies around the United States and around the world have implemented ILP. To date, there have been no systematic evaluations of its effectiveness on crime reduction. Most of the research, as with Compstat, is concerned with aspects of implementation of the business model (Darroch & Mazerolle, 2013; McGarrell, Freilich, & Chermak, 2007; Ratcliffe, & Guidetti, 2008; Schaible & Sheffield, 2012).

As the name of the approach implies, crime analysis, especially of intelligence data, is central to the ILP model. Crime analysts serve a central role in producing and disseminating analysis for crime reduction responses and decision-making (Ratcliffe, 2008). Problem solving is a key component in ILP, thus analysis, in that context, is important as well.

> **Key Takeaways.** Although little can be said about the effectiveness of ILP in reducing crime, crime analysis is central within the offender-based approach as well as in the implementation of problem solving.

Predictive Policing

A recently developed approach, **predictive policing** is defined as "any policing strategy or tactic that develops and uses information and advanced analysis to inform forward-thinking crime prevention" (Beck & McCue, 2009; Uchida, 2010, p. 10) and as "the process of using computer models, supported by prior crime and environmental data, to anticipate risks of crime and inform actions to prevent crime" (Hollywood, Smith, Price, McInnis, & Perry, 2012, Slide 2). Predictive policing is not a specific set of tactics or police responses but is an "advanced" analytical approach used to deploy patrol officers in the immediate and short term.

There is a wide variety of software programs that facilitate predictive policing with different statistical models (Harris, 2014). The goal of most of these software programs is to identify small geographic areas (e.g., several hundred feet square) based on an increased likelihood of crime happening in that area into which patrol officers can be deployed within their shift for that day. The statistics used for predictive policing are nearly as different as the individual software programs, and unfortunately, many of the statistical models and algorithms have not been made available by the software providers, so the exact methods are not discernible (Chammah, n.d.).

Predictive policing is becoming widely implemented in its various forms in the United States as well as internationally—for example, in Canada, Europe, South Korea, countries in the Caribbean, and South America. Because of its relative newness as well as the variety of statistical approaches used and the variety of police tactics that are implemented in the identified areas, there is no systematic evidence that indicates 1) that the predictions of the statistical models are accurate in predicting crime events or 2) that responding to the identified areas reduces crime. However, researchers are beginning to study specific statistical methods and responses implemented in the predicted areas in Los Angeles and by the Kent Police Department in the United Kingdom (Mohler et al., 2015), in Shreveport, Louisiana (Hunt, Saunders, & Hollywood, 2014), and in Philadelphia, Pennsylvania (Haberman & Ratcliffe, 2012). The role of crime analysis in predictive policing is clear and central. In fact, predictive policing is arguably synonymous with crime analysis, as it is more of an analytical approach than it is a police response. Thinking back to the medical analogy, predictive policing is the MRI machine.

> **Key Takeaways.** Conclusions from systematic research cannot be made about the effectiveness of predictive policing because of its newness. Crime analysis is synonymous with predictive policing, as it appears to be an analysis approach instead of a specific police strategy.

Conclusions About Police Effectiveness and Crime Analysis

Consequently, from the last 30 years of policing research, researchers conclude that for policing approaches to be effective, they must be focused and approached in a systematic way through the problem-solving approach (Braga & Weisburd, 2006; Sherman et al., 1997; Telep & Weisburd, 2012; Weisburd & Eck, 2004; Weisburd et al., 2010). This makes sense when we reflect on Chapter 2, understanding that opportunities for crime and crime prevention strategies are localized and specific (i.e., occur in specific crime settings). Researchers conclude that if policing is to have a prevention role, crime reduction strategies must be focused and approached in a systematic way through the problem-solving approach (Sherman et al., 1997; Weisburd & Braga, 2006a; Weisburd & Eck, 2004; Weisburd et al., 2010). Also, recent practice-based research (Boba, 2010; Santos, 2011) goes even further to put forth that accountability, as emphasized in Compstat, is integral in institutionalizing effective crime reduction efforts in police organizations (Santos, 2013; Santos & Santos, 2015a; Taylor & Boba, 2011).

Table 3.1 is a summary of the effectiveness and the role of crime analysis in each policing approach discussed. It is clear from the key takeaways and the summary table that in the most effective strategies (i.e., POP, hot spots, and focused deterrence), crime analysis is essential in the implementation of the approach. Importantly, crime analysis plays a role in all policing approaches to some degree, and even in those approaches that have moderate crime reduction effects, such as community policing and disorder policing, crime analysis is important. The standard model of policing is not effective in reducing crime, but crime analysis plays a role, although a limited one, to support resource allocation and provide information about crime statistics to a variety of audiences. Looking at the three approaches in which there is little research on police effectiveness—Compstat, ILP, and predictive policing—the role of crime analysis is quite clear in that it is a significant and central component to the approach itself.

So going back to the original question: Does crime analysis reduce crime? In other words, is it a cure? No, but it is a necessary diagnosis tool for effective crime reduction. However, the role of crime analysis in policing is not as

Table 3.1 Summary of Crime Analysis Assessment

Policing Approach	Effectiveness	Role of Crime Analysis
Standard model	Not effective	Limited
Community policing	Ambiguous	Limited
Disorder policing	Modest effect	Essential when focused
Problem-oriented policing	Shows promise	Essential
Hot spots policing	Effective	Essential
Focused deterrence	Shows promise	Essential
Compstat	No evidence	Essential
Intelligence-led policing	No evidence	Essential
Predictive policing	No evidence	Synonymous

simple as just "getting a crime analyst" or buying a piece of technology or software (i.e., the MRI). The process by which an agency would begin to reduce crime would be first to select one of the effective policing approaches that best suits the community's problems and then hire a crime analyst to have effective "diagnosis" capacity. Lastly, once the crime analysis was produced, the agency would have to then implement the approach effectively (i.e., administer the medicine) in order for the entire process to work and the sickness to be "cured."

In conclusion, crime analysis plays a role in each police strategy discussed here, although a much greater role in some than in others. The importance of crime analysis in policing cannot be overstated, and unfortunately, since crime analysts have only recently been incorporated into police agencies, the discipline is still struggling with being recognized and used effectively. The remainder of this book will describe and explain a majority of what is needed for crime analysis to assist police in implementing crime reduction. Those crime analysis techniques that are not included focus primarily on operational functions, such as staffing allocation, resource assessment, and performance measures, which are better suited for an advanced crime analysis text.

Stratified Policing: Framework for Crime Analysis

In this last section, a stratification of crime and disorder activity is defined to frame the material covered in Parts III, IV, and V of the book. It is based on an organizational approach to crime reduction called **stratified policing** (Santos & Santos, 2015b). Stratified policing is not a crime reduction strategy like hot spots policing or community-oriented policing, but is a way in which a police department can organize its crime analysis and crime reduction activities. It defines different types of "problems" (i.e., strata) for which a structure of crime analysis techniques and products, police tactics and strategies, and accountability mechanisms are provided to create a structure for the rest of the book. Importantly, it is the only policing approach that seeks to institutionalize crime analysis into the day-to-day operations of the police department and specifically lays out a structure for crime analysis products and how they should be used.

As police departments implement crime analysis along with evidence-based strategies, they require a structure for "how" to do so. For example, as discussed previously in this chapter, police know that hot spots policing is effective, yet there is a lack of guidance on how exactly to implement it. For example, we know hot spots policing is an approach in which hot spots with disproportionate amounts of crime are identified and police respond in those hot spots. But there are organizational and operational questions that must be answered before a police organization can implement hot spots policing: What makes up a hot spot? How often should police identify new hot spots? Who responds to hot spots? Which responses should be implemented—when and how? Who makes sure responses are appropriate and enough? How do we know when to stop responding, and who decides when to stop? Stratified policing is a structure that standardizes the processes that answer these questions in terms of the crime analysis, the crime reduction strategies implemented, and how individuals are held accountable.

INTERNATIONAL CRIME ANALYST PERSPECTIVE

Tyr Steffensen

Law Enforcement Analyst

Oslo Police District

Oslo, Norway

Sentrum Police Station polices the downtown area of Oslo, where the nighttime economy is concentrated. The crime analysis unit (CAU) works closely with the crime intelligence unit (CIU) in their cyclic scanning and analysis of the coming weekend. The CIU in turn briefs command every Wednesday. Command wants to know two things: First, do we need to increase staffing for the coming weekend night shifts? Second, what must the uniformed division know in order to respond correctly to each identified threat and ensure the safety of the public and themselves? As part of the intelligence report the brief is based on, the CAU produces a weekly map that contrasts last weekend's registered assaults and robberies with those registered the previous 3 weekends. This is done to identify emerging, persistent, and diminishing local hot spots of violent crime. The map is not shown to command; it serves as analysis support for the CAU and CIU in their work to prepare the brief.

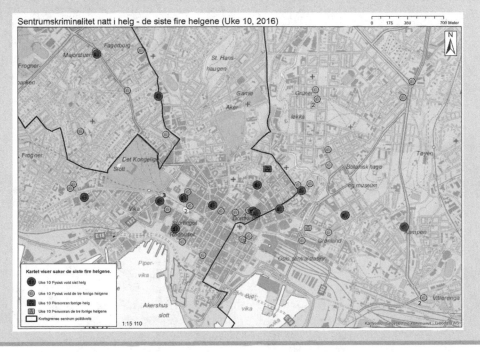

Problem Stratification

Stratified policing begins with the idea that the police address crime, disorder, and quality of life problems at different levels of activity for which evidence-based strategies are implemented. The levels vary by their temporal nature and complexity and generally include immediate incidents, short-term clusters, and long-term problems. The stratified policing structure is fundamentally organized (i.e., stratified) around these types of activities. By breaking down what police do into different levels, a stratified structure for addressing them is defined, organized, and carried out in a standardized way within the organization.

The goal of crime analysis is not to understand and analyze one crime or incident at a time, but to examine problematic activity that occurs at different levels. Thus, the stratification of crime and disorder activity centers on the idea of the "problem," which can be defined in many different ways. According to Herman Goldstein, a problem is either (1) a cluster of similar, related, or recurring incidents rather than a single incident; (2) a substantive community concern; or (3) a unit of police business (1990, p. 66). Clarke and Eck (2005) similarly define a problem as "a recurring set of related harmful events in a community that members of the public expect the police to address" (Step 14). These conceptual definitions have, unfortunately, been difficult to apply in practice, and police researchers have noted that the police have had difficulty clearly defining problems, which subsequently impacts their ability to problem solve and prevent crime (Braga & Weisburd, 2006; Scott, 2000).

The categories of crime and disorder activity are most easily understood in terms of their complexity and the temporal nature of their development. That is, simpler problems, such as combination of several incidents, are typically manifested over a very short period of time, whereas more complex problems, such as long-term problem locations, develop over a longer period of time. Although a particular problem can sit anywhere on this continuum, problems can be broken down into three categories (adapted from Boba & Santos, 2011):

1. **Immediate problems:** Incidents and serious incidents (individual calls for service and crime reports)

2. **Short-term problems:** Repeat incidents and patterns

3. **Long-term problems:** Problem locations, problem areas, problem offenders, problem victims, problem products, and compound problems

Immediate Problems Problems considered "immediate" are isolated incidents that occur and are resolved within minutes, hours, or in some cases, days. They are responded to by patrol officers and detectives who use the investigative skills learned in basic police training and more intensive investigative training. While crime analysts do not typically examine individual immediate problems, this level is the most specific strata of crime and disorder problem. Typically, the analysis for immediate problems is conducted by officers and detectives and is what is commonly referred to as *investigation*. Here, immediate crime and disorder activity is broken down into two types—incidents and serious incidents.

Incidents are individual events that an officer typically responds to or discovers while on patrol. Incidents are citizen- and officer-generated calls for service and include crime, disorder, or service-related tasks such as disturbances, robbery in progress, traffic crashes, subject stops, and traffic citations, all of which usually occur and are resolved within minutes or hours—most of the time within one shift. Police officers typically conduct the preliminary investigation and respond to incidents with the goal of resolving each incident as quickly and effectively as possible in accordance to the laws and policies of the jurisdiction and the police agency.

Serious incidents are individual events that arise from calls for service but are deemed more serious by laws and policies of the police department; thus, they require additional investigation and/or a more extensive immediate response. They include rapes, hostage negotiations, homicides, traffic fatalities, or armed robberies and occur within minutes or hours but may take days, weeks, or in some cases, months to resolve. Typically, detectives or specially trained personnel (e.g., homicide detectives, traffic crash investigators) conduct more comprehensive analysis and respond to these serious incidents with the goals of resolving the event according to the laws and policies of the jurisdiction and police agency and, in particular, apprehending the offender(s).

Short-Term Problems Short-term problems are the next strata and are clusters of incidents and serious incidents. Problems considered "short-term" are those that occur over several days or weeks and typically require short-term versus immediate responses. Here, short-term problems are broken down into two categories—repeat incidents and patterns.

Repeat incidents occur when there are two or more individual incidents that are similar in nature and happen at the same place (typically) or by the same person. Repeat incidents occur less frequently than individual incidents since they represent clusters of incidents. These (usually) common noncriminal or interpersonal criminal incidents may, but do not always, result in a crime report and include domestic violence, neighbor disputes, barking dogs, problem juveniles, traffic crashes, and the like. The individual incidents that make up a repeat incident happen within hours, days, and, in some cases, weeks of one another. A repeat incident is an important strata because it represents a short-term pattern of opportunity that can focus crime analysis and problem-solving techniques. Analysis and problem solving of a repeat incident focuses on identifying an address with multiple calls for service and resolving the immediate underlying issue. For example, two calls for a disturbance and one for loud noise at a particular address may be the result of a neighbor dispute over a barking dog. Once the police have identified and understood the underlying "problem" of the repeat incident, they would develop and implement a response to resolve the overall issue between the neighbors (vs. just addressing the individual calls for service).

Patterns are groups of two or more crimes reported to or discovered by police that are treated as one unit of analysis because (1) the crimes share one or more key commonalities that make them notable and distinct, (2) there is no known relationship between victim and offender, and (3) the criminal activity is typically of limited duration (IACA, 2011b). Examples of crimes examined for patterns include stranger rape, indecent exposure, public sexual indecency, robbery, burglary, theft from vehicle, auto theft, and grand theft. The police, citizens, businesses, the media, and all members of a community consider crime patterns to be vitally important because they perceive them as the most immediate threat to personal safety (i.e., offenders preying on unknown victims).

Importantly, the main difference between patterns and repeat incidents is the types of data that are analyzed. Both concern activity in the short term, but a repeat incident consists of common "quality of life" or interpersonal issues, whereas patterns consist of reported crime committed by strangers. Traditionally, police officers and detectives have linked patterns together on an ad hoc basis through informal communication and the review of police reports. More recently, analysts with specific training have become central police personnel conducting pattern analysis (i.e., tactical crime analysis; O'Shea & Nicholls, 2003). Analysis of and response to patterns are discussed in detail in Part III: Tactical Crime Analysis.

Long-Term Problems A long-term problem represents the next strata and is a set of related activity that occurs over several months, seasons, or years that stems from systematic opportunities created by everyday behavior and environment. Problems can consist of common disorder activity (e.g., loud parties or speeding in residential neighborhoods) as well as serious criminal activity (e.g., bank robbery or date rape). It is important to differentiate problems and patterns for the purposes of this book. The following are three important distinctions (IACA, 2011b):

1. *Scope and length:* Where a long-term problem is chronic in frequency and duration and may be characterized by acute spikes, a crime pattern is acute in its frequency and duration.

2. *Nature of activity:* Where a long-term problem is related to "harmful events" that may include crime, safety, disorder, or quality of life concerns (Clarke & Eck, 2005), a crime pattern is limited to a specific set of reported crimes.

3. *Response:* Where a long-term problem requires specialized strategic responses that often involve multiagency and community collaboration, a crime pattern typically requires routine operational tactics carried out primarily by the police.

Not every repeat incident or pattern is part of a larger problem; however, repeat incidents and patterns may be part of a series of related activity that, over time, becomes a problem. Problems, conversely, will contain numerous patterns or repeat incidents, and by first identifying these short-term issues and determining the effectiveness of the responses to them, more can be learned about the problem (e.g., interviews with offenders about why they commit those crimes, what works to resolve repeat incidents and what does not).

There are several types of long-term problems, distinguishable because oftentimes the type of analysis and police responses are different, based on each type. The types of long-term problems are easily understood because they are based on the three sides of the problem analysis triangle—place, offender, and victim/target.

The first is the **problem location**, which also can be called a "risky place" (Clarke & Eck, 2005; Eck, Clarke, & Guerette, 2007). Problem locations can be an individual address (e.g., one convenience store) or a type of place (e.g., all convenience stores) at which there is a concentration of crime or problematic activity. In the problem location, various victims and offenders are involved in the activity, making the place or the type of place the focus. In this case, the analysis would focus on identifying all the activity, understanding how opportunities are created and acted upon, and understanding how that location or type of place compares to similar, nonproblematic places.

The second is the **problem area**, which also can be called a "hot spot" (Chainey & Ratcliffe, 2005; Eck, Chainey, Cameron, Leitner, & Wilson, 2005). They are relatively small geographic areas with a disproportionate amount of crime or disorder activity of one or several types. The areas can be a block face and entire square block areas, clusters of street segments, or designated police geographic areas such as zones or beats. Importantly, problem areas should be small enough that the opportunities for crime are similar across the area. For example, a problem area of residential burglaries would not include commercial businesses, but primarily residences. Like problem locations, various victims and offenders are involved in the activity in the area. In this case, the analysis would focus on identifying all the activity going on in the problem areas, understanding how opportunities are created and acted upon, and understanding how that area compares to similar, nonproblematic areas.

The third type of long-term problem is the **problem offender**. These can be individual people who commit a disproportionate amount of crime or groups of offenders who share similar characteristics. For the problem offenders, the key component is that one person or a group of people moves through different settings and takes advantage of different victims. For example, a city might have a problem with truancy in its high schools. These students share common characteristics in that they are not attending school, and while not in school, they may be burglarizing homes, hanging out in public places, and buying or selling drugs. Analysis and response would focus on understanding and addressing these offenders and their truancy that has resulted in a wide range of problematic behavior.

The fourth type of long-term problem is the **problem victim**. Similar to problem locations and offenders, these can be individual people (e.g., someone whose car has been stolen three times) or groups of victims who share characteristics (e.g., Hispanic migrant workers who are victims of robbery). For the problem victims, the key component is that one person or a group of people moves through different settings and is victimized by different offenders. Analysis and response focus on why these individuals are victimized and what aspect of their behavior makes them vulnerable. For example, in the case of the Hispanic migrant workers, the fact that they do not have vehicles and walk from place to place, combined with the fact that they do not use banks but carry all their money in cash on their person makes them vulnerable to robbery.

The fifth type of long-term problem is the **problem property**. Usually, problem property is not one piece of property that is stolen repeatedly but is a class of products that share characteristics that make them attractive and vulnerable in various situations to various types of offenders. For example, copper wire is a problem property because many different types of offenders take copper from a variety of places (e.g., construction sites, cell phone towers, old homes, etc.) and turn it in for cash. Analysis and response focus on the settings in which the property is located and the opportunities that exist for crime. In the case of copper wire, often the lax practices of scrap metal buyers who do not require identification and do not ask questions of the scrap metal sellers encourage the thefts (because the metal is easy to turn into cash).

The final and most broad type is the **compound problem**—a problem that encompasses various locations, offenders, and victims and, in most cases, exists throughout an entire jurisdiction. For example, a problem may be initially identified as a theft from vehicle problem, but further analysis determines that the crime predominantly occurs in residential areas; however, no one type of location, small area, victim, or offender can be attributed to this problem. This would make it a compound problem. These types of problems require the most comprehensive analysis and response because a number of factors (e.g., offenders, locations, and victims) may contribute to the problem. However, luckily these tend to be the least frequent types of problems.

Notably, the importance of the stratification is that addressing immediate problems successfully helps to prevent repeat incidents and patterns (short-term problems) from surfacing, and addressing these successfully helps to prevent long-term problems from becoming significant issues. Long-term problems contain numerous incidents, significant incidents, repeat incidents, and patterns, and by systematically identifying these smaller, less complex problems and responding to them effectively, police can prevent long-term problems. This can be easily understood using a fire analogy: Small sparks arise and can be stomped out fairly easily; however, if they are not stomped out, they can merge and grow into small fires. If these small fires are not put out, they too can merge and create even larger fires that are even more complex and difficult to put out. Thus, as firefighters focus on sparks, small fires, and large fires simultaneously, police and crime analysts do the same with different levels of problems.

In this section, the word *problem* is used both generally (e.g., immediate, short-term, and long-term problems) and specifically (e.g., problem location). All types of activity that the police address can be considered "problems," which is most likely why the confusion of the word has been paramount. By creating a stratification of problems with different terms defined by their complexity and temporal nature, it is easier to apply and understand the discussion of crime analysis methods and techniques.

Stratification of Police Responsibility

Simply laying out the types of activity and standardizing the processes for analysis, response, and evaluation for each is not enough to provide a structure for a police agency to sustain its practices, so stratified policing also matches the stratification of activity with the stratification of ranks within the police organization. Police officers and detectives are already given the responsibility of addressing calls for service and investigations, so as the activity becomes more complex, higher ranks are assigned responsibility for addressing them. Organizations with more ranks can spread crime reduction responsibility wider and thinner, while those with fewer ranks must assign more responsibility to each rank. The most important aspect is that every rank in the agency is responsible, actively involved, and held accountable for crime reduction work. Similarly, crime analysis is stratified in that different types of products are necessary at each level to facilitate response and evaluation.

This structure ensures that the entire organization moves in the same direction and individuals play a specific and appropriate role in addressing crime, disorder, and quality of life issues. This is analogous to an offense of a football team. All players have a job to do and have a common goal to score points. The players' roles are based on their abilities, and specific "responses" are expected of them. Just as the team would not have linemen act as wide receivers on a regular basis, in this approach, a police agency does not ask line-level officers to conduct crime reduction work that is not within the scope of their positions. That is not to say that individual officers (or linemen) are not capable of the work, but that the responsibility of each rank within the overall agency is realistic and fits its authority, experience, training, abilities, and scope. This is one of the most important components of stratified policing because it ensures standardization and sustainability since crime reduction and prevention become part of the job—expected and conducted, every day by everyone.

Stratification of Accountability and Evaluation

The accountability process within stratified policing is important since organizational change within a police department does not occur without accountability. Just as officers are inspected by their sergeants for their weapons and equipment to be in compliance with agency policy, individuals in each rank are held accountable for their work by their direct supervisors. The system of accountability centers on creating realistic expectations for evidence-based strategies, reviewing progress of those strategies, documenting the work being done, and evaluating the success of the strategies. In stratified policing, accountability occurs every day, but more generally, it employs a structure of meetings that is also stratified by the levels of activity. They include the following:

- **Daily roll calls** facilitate action-oriented accountability at the line level for evidence-based strategies implemented for immediate and short-term problems.

- **Weekly accountability meetings** facilitate action-oriented accountability because individuals from the various divisions of the organization (e.g., patrol, investigations, crime prevention, and media relations) come together to coordinate, track, and assess responses to short-term activity—repeat incidents and patterns. This meeting does not include a review of any statistics or crime counts since its focus is on "action" (i.e., response).

- **Monthly accountability meetings** facilitate evaluation-oriented accountability. Specifically produced crime analysis products and maps are used to assess whether short-term strategies are effective as well as to identify emerging long-term problems and to monitor ongoing long-term strategies. In addition, every 12 months,

Figure 3.3 Stratified Policing Structure

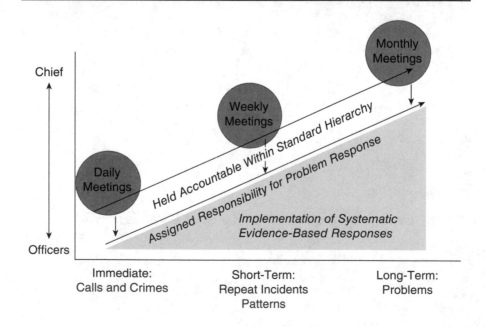

the monthly meeting facilitates evaluation-oriented
accountability for the entire organization, based on the
agency's crime reduction and prevention goals. The results
of this meeting are shared with the agency as well as with
city government to show how the chief is holding the
entire agency accountable for crime reduction.

Chapter 16 illustrates specific crime analysis products that support accountability
and evaluation in these meetings. In summary, Figure 3.3 illustrates all the
components of stratified policing and the idea that more complex problems
are addressed by higher ranks in the organization and that the organizational
structure ensures that people are being held accountable by the rank above them.
The x-axis shows the different levels of problems, and the y-axis indicates the
rank in the organization. The lower black arrow indicates which rank is assigned
responsibility for the problem response (i.e., officers to calls/crimes, sergeants to
repeat incidents, commanders to problems). The upper black line indicates how
those individuals are held accountable (i.e., by the rank above them). The circles
reflect which meetings apply to a particular type of problem and rank.

Conclusion

The purpose of this chapter has been to discuss the role of crime analysis within
what is known about "what works" in policing. Evidence-based approaches
require systematic and meaningful crime analysis. The chapter has also laid out
a structure for organizing the implementation of evidence-based strategies that
help to structure the development of crime analysis products, implement police
responses, and ensure accountability and evaluation.

SUMMARY POINTS

This chapter provides an overview of the role of crime analysis in effective police
approaches for crime reduction as well as a structure for implementing crime analysis into
an agency. The following are the key points addressed in this chapter:

- Both research and practice have shown the most effective methods police employ to
  prevent and control crime are those in which crime analysis plays a vital role.

- Research shows that although the studies showed a relationship between crime
  analysis and crime clearance rates, there is no evidence of the causality of this
  relationship or whether other, more important factors explain the difference in crime
  and clearance rates of the agencies.

- Crime analysis is much like using an MRI to diagnosis a problem. It is not the cure, but
  an important tool for identifying and understanding a problem for police to address.

- Because crime analysis does not have a direct link to crime reduction, its role in crime reduction is understood by examining effective crime reduction strategies by police (i.e., evidence-based policing) and the role of crime analysis.

- The standard model of policing has limited effectiveness in reducing crime. Because it generally applies various tactics such as patrol, arrests, and investigation, there is little use for crime analysis beyond resources allocation and providing crime and arrest statistics.

- Specific community policing programs are limited in their effectiveness in reducing crime and do not require crime analysis. Overall, research on community policing is "ambiguous," and better measurement is required to make more definitive conclusions. However, there is some evidence that community policing can impact property crime, but there is little evidence on the impact on fear of crime. Community policing does affect satisfaction with the police and legitimacy. The role of crime analysis in the overall approach is that it provides information to and solicits information from citizens to support building partnerships and transparency.

- POP shows significant promise for reducing crime. Crime analysis is absolutely essential in this approach as it is necessary in all stages of the problem-solving process.

- Hot spots policing is effective in reducing crime, but the effects of most strategies used today are primarily short term. Crime analysis is central in the implementation of hot spots policing and essential when it is coupled with problem solving.

- The focused deterrence strategy is effective and shows promise in reducing crime. Crime analysis is essential as part of the problem-solving approach that is fundamental in this strategy.

- There is no evidence that disorder policing reduces fear of crime or increases community bonds, but it does have a modest effect on crime overall, with the largest effect occurring when strategies are focused in places and small areas. Aggressive-order maintenance strategies do not result in lower crime and more likely result negatively on police–community relations. The role of crime analysis is important for the effective implementation of disorder policing (i.e., focused on places and areas) but is not as important when the strategies are generally applied.

- Although little can be said about the effectiveness of Compstat in reducing crime directly, crime analysis is central to its components that coincide with the problem-solving process. Routine crime analysis products are used to hold personnel accountable, and crime mapping in particular is a central mechanism of communication in accountability meetings.

- Although little can be said about the effectiveness of ILP in reducing crime, crime analysis is central within the offender-based approach as well as in the implementation of problem solving.

- Conclusions from systematic research cannot be made about the effectiveness of predictive policing because of its newness. Crime analysis is synonymous with predictive policing, as it appears to be an analysis approach instead of a specific police strategy.

- The importance of crime analysis in policing cannot be overstated, and unfortunately, since crime analysts have only recently been incorporated into police agencies, the discipline is still struggling with being recognized and used effectively.

- Stratified policing is a way in which a police department can organize its crime analysis and crime reduction activities. It is the only policing approach that seeks to institutionalize crime analysis into the day-to-day operations of the police department and specifically lays out a structure for crime analysis products and how they should be used.

- Stratified policing begins with the idea that the police address crime, disorder, and quality of life problems at different levels of activity for which evidence-based strategies are implemented. The levels vary by their temporal nature and complexity and generally include immediate incidents, short-term clusters, and long-term problems.

- Problems considered "immediate" are isolated incidents that occur and are resolved within minutes, hours, or, in some cases, days. Incidents are individual events that an officer typically responds to or discovers while on patrol. Serious incidents are individual events that arise from calls for service but are deemed more serious by laws and policies of the police department.

- Short-term problems are the next strata and are clusters of incidents and serious incidents. A repeat incident occurs when there are two or more individual incidents that are similar in nature and happen at the same place (typically) or by the same person. A pattern is a group of two or more crimes reported to or discovered by police that are treated as one unit of analysis because (1) the crimes share one or more key commonalities that make them notable and distinct, (2) there is no known relationship between victim and offender, and (3) the criminal activity is typically of limited duration.

- A long-term problem is a set of related activity that occurs over several months, seasons, or years that stems from systematic opportunities created by everyday behavior and environment.

- The problem location, which also can be called a "risky place," can be an individual address (e.g., one convenience store) or a type of place (e.g., all convenience stores) at which there is a concentration of crime or problematic activity.

- The problem area, which also can be called a "hot spot," is a relatively small geographic area with a disproportionate amount of crime or disorder activity of one or several types.

- The problem offender can be individual people who commit a disproportionate amount of crime or groups of offenders who share similar characteristics.

- The problem victim can be individual people (e.g., someone whose car has been stolen three times) or groups of victims who share characteristics (e.g., Hispanic migrant workers who are victims of robbery).

- The problem property is not one piece of property that is stolen repeatedly but is a class of products that share characteristics that make them attractive and vulnerable in various situations to various types of offenders.

- The most broad type is the compound problem, which is a problem that encompasses various locations, offenders, and victims and, in most cases, exists throughout an entire jurisdiction.

- Stratified policing also matches the stratification of activity with the stratification of ranks within the police organization. Police officers and detectives are already given the responsibility of addressing calls for service and investigations, so as the activity becomes more complex, higher ranks are assigned responsibility for addressing them.

- The accountability process within stratified policing is important since organizational change within a police department does not occur without accountability. Individuals in each rank are held accountable for their work by their direct supervisors.

- In stratified policing, accountability occurs every day, but more generally, it employs a structure of meetings that is also stratified by the levels of activity. They include daily, weekly, and monthly meetings.

DISCUSSION EXERCISES*

Exercise 1

The chapter presents the analogy that the use of crime analysis in policing is similar to the use of the MRI by doctors. Discuss a *different* analogy of the role of analysis in policing as well as the nature of crime analysis, but use your own experience and ideas to relate it to another field. You may not use the medical field.

Exercise 2

Compare and contrast the research results and role of crime analysis in disorder policing, community policing, hot spots policing, focused deterrence, and problem-oriented policing. If you were a crime analyst, under what type of policing would you like to work and why?

Exercise 3

Provide specific examples about how the following types of problematic activity are manifested at different levels (e.g., immediate, short-term, and long-term):

- Robbery at convenience stores

- Disorderly youth at a movie theatre

- Thefts from vehicles at the mall during the holiday season

*Additional exercises using data and other resources can be found on **http://www .sagepub.com/bobasantos4e.**

Crime Analysis Process, Data, and Purpose

Part II contains four chapters that illustrate specific processes, data, purposes, and examples of how crime analysis results are used by different "strata" within the police organization. Chapter 4 describes the crime analysis process that was developed in 1994 and that crime analysts still use today. It is an overview of the steps that analysts take to conduct analysis but does not include the tasks carried out using specific technology. This is because even though the types of hardware and software that crime analysts use change over time, the fundamental processes and critical thinking do not.

More importantly, the second section of Chapter 4 describes the four types of crime analysis that have been updated and refined by the International Association of Crime Analysts (2014b). Chapter 5 provides important information about the types of police data used generally in crime analysis, considerations about data quality and management, and discussion of the types of technology used in crime analysis. Chapter 6 discusses geographic data, types of maps, classifications for thematic map development, and density mapping. Finally, Chapter 7 discusses how the results of crime analysis differ by type of problem (i.e., strata), purpose, and audience. A typology of crime analysis results is presented in this chapter, and practical examples are used to illustrate how the results are used in a variety of contexts. Together, these chapters provide a foundation for the three types of analysis—tactical, strategic, and administrative— that frame the remaining parts of the book.

CHAPTER 4

Crime Analysis Process and Application

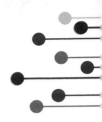

The purpose of this chapter is to describe the crime analysis process that was developed in 1994 and that crime analysts still use today. It is an overview of the steps that analysts take to conduct analysis but does not include the tasks carried out using specific technology. More importantly, the second section of Chapter 4 describes the four types of crime analysis that have been updated and refined by the International Association of Crime Analysts in 2014.

The Crime Analysis Process

This section covers the crime analysis process, which is a method specific to crime analysis that applies to all the work that crime analysts do. However, the crime analysis process is not a defined set of tasks and techniques or hardware and software used by crime analysts, but is an overview of the method and approach that a crime analyst uses to conduct crime analysis and create crime analysis products. No matter what technology an analyst uses now (and even if it changes in the future), the crime analysis process will remain the same.

Figure 4.1 illustrates the **crime analysis process**—the way in which crime analysis is generally conducted and improved upon over time. The steps involved in this process are data collection, data collation, analysis, dissemination of results, and incorporation of feedback from users of the information (Gottlieb, Arenberg, & Singh, 1994). The crime analysis process begins with observations (data). Data come from many sources, including, in most cases, from outside crime analysis. Crime analysts examine data observed and collected by others, such as police officers, 911 dispatchers, community service officers, census workers, and geographers.

Collection

The first step in the crime analysis process is the collection of data; this step is closely connected to data storage. As previously discussed, this step occurs outside the direct control of the crime analysis function. In most police agencies, officers or civilian employees enter crime reports and other data into a computer system. While many agencies have moved to using computers to write police reports, some agencies still have officers write some or all of their reports in longhand or have them call in reports over a phone system to be transcribed by data entry clerks. In nearly all agencies,

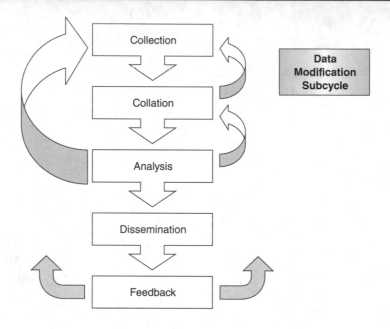

Figure 4.1 The Crime Analysis Process

Collection

Collation

Analysis

Dissemination

Feedback

Data Modification Subcycle

police dispatchers enter details of each call for service directly into the computer system. The policies dictating data entry procedures, as well as the care taken by the individuals who execute the procedures, are crucial to crime analysis because they affect both the quantity and the quality of the data and subsequent analysis.

Some of the data collected by police departments is not directly relevant for crime analysis, so subsets of information are compiled for analysis purposes. For example, police officers draw diagrams of traffic crashes for purposes of insurance claims and other legal concerns. While this information is stored for understanding the nature of each individual crash, crime analysts usually are not concerned with the exact circumstances of each event. Rather, they are concerned with compiling data on the dates, times, locations, and nature of all crashes. So only the relevant information (not each diagram) is made available and downloaded for crime analysis, as this information can help them to understand this type of activity more generally.

In addition, the manner in which data are stored and the amount of data stored are important in crime analysis and can impact the relevance and usefulness of crime analysis results. Data must be in an electronic format, collected regularly (e.g., on a daily or weekly basis), and archived for a significant amount of time (e.g., for several years) to be useful for crime analysis. Paper copies of reports and other information are not efficient for crime analysts to use regularly because data in this form are too time consuming and cumbersome to analyze. Information has to be coded into an electronic database to be useful for crime analysis. Although, in some departments, crime analysts still enter particular data into a computer system themselves, in the last decade or so it has become much more common for police departments to make their reports and other important information available electronically, not only for crime analysis but for all purposes.

The time that elapses between the observation, or data collection, and the availability of data needs to be reasonably short if the data are to be useful for crime analysis—especially for immediate and short-term problems. For example, if electronic crime report data are not available until several weeks after the reports are written by officers, the information is not useful for identifying current crime patterns. The amount of data archived also needs to be adequate (e.g., multiple years' worth) for crime analysts to have enough information to conduct satisfactory analyses—especially for long-term problems. For example, 2 months' worth of data would not provide as comprehensive a picture of a burglary problem as 1 or 2 years' worth would.

Finally, it is also important for crime analysts to have access to large amounts of raw data. Many police computer systems allow only the retrieval of individual records or the creation of statistical reports or lists. Crime analysts must be able to download electronic data and selected variables into a myriad of software programs to conduct analyses using the various techniques discussed in this book.

To summarize, the crime analysis data collection process requires the following:

1. The data must be collected accurately and consistently.
2. Only data relevant for crime analysis are compiled.
3. The data must be collected in a timely manner.
4. The data must be archived for an adequate amount of time to allow for effective analysis.
5. The data must be accessible in electronic raw form to be queried and downloaded.

These requirements apply to any data used in crime analysis, even data obtained from outside the police agency (e.g., probation and parole data, geographic data, and census information).

Collation

The main sources of the data (e.g., crime reports and calls for service) used in crime analysis are general police data collection systems, such as a record management system and a computer-aided dispatch system, which are described in more detail in the next chapter. Even with advancements in technology, many of these systems still are not designed to capture and store data that facilitates effective crime analysis. Because of this, crime analysts often find it necessary to query, reformat, and bring together data before using it for analysis. This can include selecting subsets of data, creating new variables, and performing quality control (i.e., cleaning the data). Data collation entails a number of different tasks, but generally it takes three forms:

1. *Cleaning* is the process of identifying then correcting mistakes and inconsistencies in the data.

2. *Geocoding* is the process of bringing crime analysis data together with geographic data so they can be analyzed spatially (discussed in depth in Chapter 6).

3. *Creating new variables* is the process of recoding or computing new variables from existing variables for more effective analysis. For example, the time it takes for an officer to respond to a call for service after being dispatched (i.e., response time) is computed by subtracting the time the call came in to the call center from when the officer arrived on the scene.

Analysis

Analysis takes place after data are collected and prepared and includes the use of many different statistical and visualization techniques, all of which are described at length in Parts III, IV, and V of this book. Unfortunately, a crime analyst often is unaware of issues with the data (e.g., the data do not measure what needs to be studied or have not been collected correctly) until the analysis process begins. When this occurs, the analyst must often return to the collection and collation steps to improve or change the way data are collected, archived, or collated to be able to complete the analysis and create the crime analysis products. This practice, called the **data modification subcycle**, is intrinsic to the crime analysis process and important for improving the overall process of crime analysis within each police department that practices it.

Data Modification Subcycle

The arrows in Figure 4.1 illustrate how the data modification subcycle operates. In this subprocess of crime analysis, data collection and collation are changed based on the crime analysis process itself. The crime analysis process is not linear; it moves from collection to collation to analysis. Generally, the analyst will find that each of these steps can inform the next step or require revisiting a previous step. For example, in cleaning the data during the collation process, the analyst may gain insight into new ways to collect data; the requirements of the analysis may cause the analyst to recommend changes in both collection and collation of police department data. The following gives some specific examples of this interplay:

- An examination of the nature of loud parties in a particular area reveals that calls-for-service data contain only a "loud noise" call type, so the analyst cannot distinguish reports of loud parties from reports of general loud noises. The analyst must go back to the data collection step and recommend a new call type labeled *loud party* for police officers and dispatchers to use.

- The chief of police requests that an analyst examine crime data for the past 10 years, but there is a departmental policy that requires storage for only 5 years. The analyst examines the existing 5 years of crime data and recommends the adoption of a new policy for data storage that will allow for the preservation of 10 years' worth of data.

- Through analysis, a crime analyst determines that there are inconsistencies in the crime location variable (e.g., addresses are assigned to incorrect police beats); this leads to the development of a more comprehensive data cleaning process.

Although issues such as those described here may not appear in every analysis situation, an undeniable aspect of crime analysis is that the crime analysis process and improvement of data collection and collation requires continuous attention for improvement. Analysts should never assume any database is accurate or that it will immediately serve a crime analysis purpose. Unanticipated complications often arise, and data on new aspects of crime, disorder, and policing may not have yet been collected. (For a more detailed discussion of a variety of these issues, see Chapter 5.) The data modification subcycle is a key component of the crime analysis process and is an important quality control mechanism for the entire police department as some issues with the data are not discovered until the data are analyzed. Thus, crime analysts spend a significant amount of their time and resources addressing such issues.

Dissemination

Once the data analysis is completed, the crime analyst needs to communicate the results to various types of audiences. In fact, information and statistics do not become analysis until they are effectively communicated (Bruce, 2008a). The methods of disseminating crime analysis results include paper and electronic reports and maps, presentations, e-mails, Internet documents, and phone calls. The audiences for crime analysis information include police officers, police management, citizens, students, other analysts, and the news media.

Analysts need to keep two important considerations in mind when communicating crime analysis results. First, the presentation should be tailored to the knowledge of the particular audience. For example, for an audience of citizens, analysts might need to clarify the definitions of various types of crimes (e.g., robbery vs. burglary) before presenting analysis results. Second, the presentation of results should convey only the most necessary information. Much of the work of crime analysis takes place behind the scenes (e.g., collation of data), and the presentation of results need not include information on all that work.

In disseminating their findings, crime analysts should include only information that is relevant to the topic or issue at hand but should keep records of all the work they have conducted. Analysts do not need to present every detail of an analysis project when the project's findings can easily be communicated through one or two key points. Analysts also should document their data collection, collation, and analysis methods to ensure that proper methods have been used and for their own replication purposes, but disseminating results should focus on only the content most appropriate for a particular audience.

In addition to assisting police departments, crime analysts can contribute to the creation of knowledge about crime, disorder issues, and general police practices by disseminating their analysis results to other analysts, researchers, and police practitioners. Such results can inform police practices (e.g., enforcement or prevention efforts) and crime analysis practices (e.g., duplication of successful data collection methods and analytic techniques), as well as add to the general knowledge about crime and other police-related issues (e.g., the nature of prostitution in rural areas). This is not to say that one report from one crime analyst is likely to create a significant amount of knowledge about a given topic; rather, the dissemination of crime analysis results from numerous police agencies over time can begin to form a body of knowledge and enhance the discipline.

Feedback

After disseminating the results of their analyses, crime analysts need to seek and receive feedback from the individuals to whom they provided the information. As in the data modification subcycle, feedback from the use of the products of an analysis can help to inform and improve the entire process. Analysts may receive feedback about the quality of particular analyses or reports, about the nature of the data analyzed, or about the usefulness of their analyses for decision-making.

Summary

In summary, the crime analysis process is not linear; it is cyclical since each step in the process can inform subsequent steps as the analyst gains insight and receives feedback. Crime analysts spend much time and energy on the subcycle of data modification; however, with improved policies, technologies, databases, training, and examples of effective analysis, the tools and techniques to carry out the crime analysis process are constantly evolving.

Types of Crime Analysis

To ensure consistency in the definitions and the discussion of crime analysis types in the discipline, as with the definition of crime analysis generally, this section has been taken from the International Association of Crime Analysts' (IACA) white paper titled *Definition and Types of Crime Analysis* (IACA, 2014b). As a member of the IACA Standards Committee that developed these definitions, I can confirm that at the beginning of this work, the committee members were devoted to starting from scratch, as they were not wedded to the current definition and types already published in the field (for example, the types used in the first three editions of this book). The goal was to break down the factors of crime analysis, including the nature and sources of data used, the techniques applied, the results of the analysis, the regularity and frequency of the analysis, and the intended audience and purpose. After this, the committee then categorized the work into types and constructed the definitions.

It is important that the types of crime analysis provide a structure to the profession, the work of analysts, and crime analysis training and education. They should also provide a framework for job descriptions, roles, and responsibilities. They should assist police agencies that seek to implement or improve their crime analysis functions to ensure the analyst is conducting each type and should help crime analysts organize their work into daily, weekly, monthly, and annual tasks and categorize products for their customers. The IACA (2014b) recognizes four types of crime analysis that are ordered on a continuum, starting with detailed data and analysis for individuals and groups, moving to aggregate data and analysis of locations, areas, and problems: 1) crime intelligence analysis, 2) tactical crime analysis, 3) strategic crime analysis, and 4) administrative crime analysis.

Crime Intelligence Analysis

Crime intelligence analysis is defined by the IACA (2014b, p. 3) as follows:

> Crime intelligence analysis is the analysis of data about people involved in crimes, particularly repeat offenders, repeat victims, and criminal organizations and networks.

Crime intelligence analysis makes conclusions about the context of the lives, jobs, activities, motives, and plans of offenders and their criminal networks. The conclusions are based on offenders' criminal activity but also their social, financial, and routine activity, so a wide range of data is considered in addition to crime and arrests that are known to the police. For example, information might come from an offender's financial records, phone calls, travel plans, social media activity, and interactions with family and friends. Crime intelligence analysis uses police data as a starting point, and the heart of the crime analysis process for this type involves the collection of confidential information—"intelligence." There are unique concerns when conducting this type of analysis that are related to data security, data access, and individual privacy. In many cases, the data obtained requires a court order (e.g., obtaining phone records, a search warrant). Processes and techniques of crime intelligence analysis include:

- **Repeat offender and victim analysis:** This is using data to identify and prioritize (i.e., put in a rank order) individual offenders by the number, type, and seriousness of their crimes, and individual victims by the number, type, and seriousness of their victimizations.

- **Criminal history analysis:** This analytical product is more than just running a person's name in a database and retrieving his or her criminal history; it is a report compiled by an analyst on an individual that includes personal identification information (driver's license, social security number, birthdate, work and home addresses), aliases, financial information, criminal and arrest activity, correctional status, social media activity, and other relevant information. While this is listed here as crime intelligence analysis, this is also produced as part of strategic offender approaches discussed in Chapter 14 where it is called a "criminal résumé."

- **Link analysis:** This is typically done for a criminal network but may also be conducted for one individual with significant criminal activity. It is a visual representation of individuals, their relationships with one another as criminal associates, spouses, friends, and "enemies," as well as relevant addresses (e.g., home, work, hangouts), and other information relevant to a particular person or case. The link analysis is used to visualize the nature and strength of "links" between people (i.e., relationships) and their activity. They are used for investigation to guide intelligence gathering or to "make the case" or to visualize a large criminal case or network for court purposes.

- **Commodity flow analysis:** This is a specific type of link analysis in which the focus is on the "flow" of money and other financial information. This is useful in cases involving individuals and networks of drug trafficking, illicit weapons sales, human trafficking, and money laundering, among others.

- **Communication analysis:** This is a specific type of link analysis in which the focus is on the relationships and "flow" of communication through different types of media, including but not limited to in-person interaction, phone calls, e-mail, Internet, intranet, and social media. For example, in days before the Internet, child pornography sharing networks distributed hard copy photos and videos through stores, in-person delivery, and post office mail. Today, these networks share computerized images and video through e-mail and the Internet. Understanding how this network of communication is carried out is important for apprehending individuals and stopping the activity.

- **Social media analysis:** Many people, especially those who are young, have a presence on social media (e.g., Facebook, Twitter, Snapchat). By the time this book is published, there are likely to be new popular media apps, but overall, social media has become a very large part of communication between and among individuals, including people committing crimes. Thus, crime analysts have begun systematically analyzing social media sources to identify information on suspects, such as where they are staying if they are not at home, who their associates are, and, believe it or not, a description of their actual criminal activity (e.g., some criminals brag about their criminal exploits in public forums!). In addition, crime analysts examine social media to prevent crimes as well, looking for events or activity that have not yet happened. Some examples from city police departments are the advertising of large house parties with a DJ and illegal drugs and discussions by one or more individuals who talk about "shooting up" a school. In addition to local activity, analysis at the FBI and other federal agencies look for patterns and discussions of potential terrorist activity.

Importantly, criminal intelligence analysis as it is defined here is a type of analysis under the umbrella of crime analysis as it is defined in Chapter 1. The IACA makes the following clarification about this distinction (2014b, p. 4):

> "Criminal intelligence analysis" historically developed as a profession parallel to crime analysis, drawing from a tradition of military intelligence and applying its techniques to domestic "enemies" like organized crime enterprises. It has flourished in national, international, and special-purpose organizations such as the U.S. Federal Bureau of Investigation, the U.K. Security Service, and Interpol; in U.S. Fusion Centers; and in very large local police organizations. Aside from the large local police agencies, these other agencies have mandates that generally restrict their analytical needs to analysis of people,

networks, and criminal organizations. This, in turn, justifies the continued development of criminal intelligence analysis as a specialized profession. For those analysts who perform only intelligence analysis, it makes sense for them to classify themselves as a profession distinct from crime analysis. In local-level police organizations, however, which need all types of crime analysis, we [the members of the IACA] regard the separation of intelligence analysis from the overall profession of crime analysis as artificial, even harmful, to a total understanding of the crime dynamic of a jurisdiction.

Tactical Crime Analysis

Tactical crime analysis is defined as follows (IACA, 2014b, p. 4):

> Tactical crime analysis is the analysis of police data directed towards the short-term development of patrol and investigative priorities and deployment of resources. Its subject areas include the analysis of space, time, offender, victim, and modus operandi for individual high-profile crimes, repeat incidents, and crime patterns, with a specific focus on crime series [sic].

In contrast to crime intelligence analysis, the data primarily used for tactical crime analysis comes from police databases and includes calls for service, police crime reports, arrests, and field information. The goal of tactical crime analysis is to identify short-term patterns (of which a series is one type, ergo the use of [sic] in the IACA's definition). Different types of patterns are linked by activity type, place, offender, victim, property, and MO (i.e., modus operandi or method of the crime). Processes and techniques of tactical crime analysis include the following:

- **Repeat incident analysis:** This is using calls-for-service data to identify locations in which similar types of calls have occurred over a short period of time to direct police resources to "repeat call" locations (covered in Chapter 8).

- **Crime pattern analysis:** This is using crime report data to identify groups of crimes that are related in some way to direct police resources to prevent future crime and/or apprehend the offender(s) (covered in Chapters 8–11).

- *Linking known offenders to past crimes*: This is using data of individuals who have been arrested for and/or convicted for a particular crime to link these known offenders to individual crimes or patterns that have occurred recently to direct police resources to apprehend the individual again and/or to clear one or more cases by arrest (covered in Chapters 9–10).

- **Criminal investigative analysis:** In the 1970s and 1980s, this type of analysis was referred to as *criminal profiling*, but overuse by television shows and movies led the FBI to change the term. It entails the process of constructing "profiles" of offenders who have committed serious crimes against strangers, primarily rape and/or murder. Analysis of the elements of the linked crimes (i.e., pattern) infers the characteristics of the unknown offender, such as drug addiction, social habits, and work habits with the purpose of identifying and prioritizing suspects for the crimes. According to the IACA (2014b, p. 7), "To the extent that criminal 'profiling' or criminal investigative analysis occurs within local police agencies, we [IACA members] regard it as inherent in the tactical analysis process, as its focus is almost always on a series of crimes."

- **Geographic profiling:** This is a subset of criminal investigative analysis, thus also falls under the purview of tactical crime analysis. Here, the analyst uses geographic locations of an offender's crimes (such as body dump sites or encounter sites) to identify and prioritize areas where the offender is likely to live (Paulsen, Bair, & Helms, 2009; Rossmo, 2000). Once again, the goal is to identify and capture an unknown offender.

Strategic Crime Analysis

Strategic crime analysis is defined as follows (IACA, 2014b, p. 4):

> Strategic crime analysis is the analysis of data directed towards development and evaluation of long-term strategies, policies, and prevention techniques. Its subjects include long-term statistical trends, hot spots, and problems.

Similar to tactical crime analysis, the data used for strategic crime analysis comes from police databases; however, strategic crime analysis often includes the collection of data from a variety of other sources, such as census data, geographic zoning data, and city data, and can include primary data collected through both quantitative and qualitative methods. Also, strategic crime analysis looks at the same crime data but in aggregate form and over a longer period of time. For example, where tactical crime analysis would find that four of five cars were unlocked in thefts from vehicles occurring in a neighborhood last week, strategic crime analysis would find that 85% of the 1,000 cars were unlocked in thefts from vehicles in the entire city last year. The goal of strategic crime analysis is to identify long-term problems and understand why they are occurring to direct police resources to develop long-term solutions. Processes and techniques of strategic crime analysis include the following:

- **Trend analysis:** This includes the aggregation of data, typically by time period (e.g., month) and by geographic area (e.g., police district) to identify increases or decreases in crime. The statistics are relatively simple and straightforward in this analysis, but the analysis technique is aggregating the data into categories that make sense for crime reduction. Most trend analyses examine many different categories (e.g., robbery by year; street robbery by month; street robbery with a firearm by month for District 4; covered in Chapters 12–15).

- **Hot spot (i.e., problem area) analysis:** This is the identification of areas within a jurisdiction with a disproportionate amount of crime compared to other areas both temporally and spatially. Similar to trend analysis, how the data are aggregated will determine the findings and usefulness of the problem areas identified in the analysis (covered in Chapter 7).

- **Problem analysis:** This is "an approach/method/process conducted within the police agency in which formal criminal justice theory, research methods, and comprehensive data collection and analysis procedures are used in a systematic way to conduct in-depth examination of, develop informed responses to, and evaluate crime and disorder problems" (Boba, 2003, p. 2). It includes identifying and prioritizing long-term problems for police to address; understanding how, when, where, who, and why the problem is occurring; guiding the response to the problem; and assessing the effectives of the response (covered in Chapters 12–15).

INTERNATIONAL CRIME ANALYST PERSPECTIVE

Alyson Yaraskovitch

Crime Intelligence Analyst

Ottawa Police Service

Ottawa, ON, Canada

In 2015, the Ottawa Police Service (OPS) undertook a geographic redistricting project to improve the allocation of frontline resources and enable evidence-based deployment. Central to the redistricting exercise was the alignment of patrol areas with city neighbourhoods, as defined by the Ottawa Neighbourhood Study (ONS). Led by the University of Ottawa and supported by the city and a number of community-based organizations, the ONS aims to better delineate neighbourhoods, with the aim of better understanding the social and environmental determinants of health. Currently, there are 108 neighbourhoods in the city, with 21 defined as rural. These neighbourhoods served as the building blocks of the new patrol areas.

This project had five main objectives: (1) achieve workload parity across patrol areas; (2) achieve service-level goals and standards; (3) preserve neighbourhood integrity; (4) ensure flexibility to adjust for operational considerations; and (5) align with political boundaries (where possible). Through these objectives, the intention for this project was to foster geographic ownership and encourage familiarity with the unique challenges present within each of Ottawa's communities. Through detailed analysis, it was identified that the majority of OPS calls for service require two units, and on average, approximately 32% of a patrol officer's time is spent responding to calls within his or her assigned area. These two factors demonstrated the requirement for a minimum of two officers to be assigned to each deployment area. The second objective was to equalize workload among frontline officers. This was accomplished by reviewing the patrol time allocation model. The OPS model calls for the theoretical time allocation of 40% reactive, 40% proactive, and 20% administrative. Based on continuous coverage (24/7/365), with three overlapping 10.75-hour shifts per 24-hour period, each unit has approximately 4,500 hours of capacity to respond to reactive calls each year.

Using the Esri ArcGIS Business Analyst extension, the sectors were created by clustering ONS neighbourhoods so that the total service effort falls within an optimal range of +/_10% of the annual reactive time capacity (4,500 hours). Workload equalization was completed by assigning units to each sector according to its total level; for each multiple of the optimal range, an additional unit was assigned. The geographic deployment model was academic in its approach, and the design was highly user driven. Focus groups with frontline officers were held in order to identify potential geographic issues, response or backup challenges, officer safety concerns, points of interest, and future development that may have been overlooked. The result was 19 sectors citywide, with 15 in the urban or suburban operating environment and four rural.

Administrative Crime Analysis

Administrative crime analysis is defined as follows (IACA, 2014b, p. 5):

> Administrative crime analysis is analysis directed toward the administrative needs of the police agency, its government, and its community.

This type of crime analysis includes a variety of techniques and products that serve a wide range of purposes and audiences. Where tactical and strategic crime analysis are concerned more with supporting external crime reduction activities of officers, detectives, and supervisors, administrative crime analysis supports the internal operations of the agency, decision-making, efficiency, and accountability (e.g., Compstat). The IACA (2014b) has incorporated *operations analysis*, which is a term used in other texts and is defined by Bruce (2008a) as follows:

The study of a police department's policies and practices—
including its allocation of personnel, money, equipment, and
other resources, geographically, organizationally, and temporally—
and whether these operations and policies have the most effective
influence on crime and disorder in the jurisdiction. (p. 18)

In addition, administrative crime analysis supports the police department's
interactions with the community and other government entities.

Oftentimes, products created for tactical and strategic analysis purposes are
adapted for use by external audiences. Even though it is not focused on crime
reduction activities, administrative crime analysis is a valuable type of crime
analysis, as it supports the agency's decision-making and planning, crime
reduction accountability processes, community engagement, grant work,
and other areas. Note that "administrative" does not include secretarial or
nonanalytical tasks, such as preparing brochures and taking notes in meetings,
nor does it include technological tasks such as performing basic technological
support for police personnel. Processes and techniques of administrative crime
analysis include, but are not limited to the following:

- *Crime analysis for accountability*: This includes creating
  original statistics and regular reports that support an
  agency's crime reduction accountability processes. Several
  products depict statistics and trends about the police
  crime reduction responses (i.e., how much directed patrol
  was conducted in a hot spot) and the amount of crime.
  While this type of analysis may overlap strategic crime
  analysis, its main purpose is to support accountability
  meetings held by agency command staff. The products for
  accountability tend to be slightly different than those used
  for identifying, understanding, and evaluating individual
  problems (covered in Chapter 16, new to this edition).

- **Districting and redistricting analysis**: There are specific
  methods and software that crime analysts use to determine
  the best geographic boundaries of districts and beats within
  a jurisdiction. This analysis is meant to maximize efficiency
  by determining the best size and location of these areas to
  reduce the response time of officers to calls and equalize
  the number of calls and crime across the areas. This type
  of analysis is conducted only rarely (e.g., every 5–10 years)
  because any changes made are resource intensive (e.g., all
  maps used to dispatch officers must change, and officer
  deployment must be adjusted).

- *Patrol staffing analysis*: This includes examining
  calls-for-service and unit history data to conduct

workload calculations by area and shift. That is, based on the data, recommendations for an optimal patrol schedule are made. Unlike districting analysis, this is often conducted each year to ensure that how officers are deployed during the day and during the week is most efficient. Similar to districting analysis, there are relatively sophisticated methods, statistics, and software that analysts use for this process.

- *Community-focused analysis*: Many of the analysis products that are created for tactical and strategic crime analysis might also be useful for community members, community groups, businesses, and other external police entities. However, often those products contain information that cannot be released to the public. So a large part of community-focused analysis is taking what has been produced and "sanitizing" it for the public. In addition, crime analysts also create products specifically for the community and/or individual community or neighborhood groups. This is an important part of transparency and partnerships developed as part of community policing, as discussed in Chapter 3 and Chapter 11.

- *Cost-benefit analysis*: This is an assessment of the relative cost of a particular program or initiative in the police department in comparison with the benefit or impact of that program or initiative. The results are used by police decision-makers to decide whether the particular program was "worth it." Oftentimes, the costs are fairly straightforward to assess, but the benefits are not so clear to estimate. For example, the cost of a police officer assigned to a high school is simple to compute, but how would the benefit of that officer be assessed? This analysis process often involves qualitative data collection and assessment of potential benefits based on research.

- *Support for the agency's grant work*: Analysts often conduct specific trend or other types of analysis to provide statistics and support for requests for grant funding from state or federal organizations. Once the grant is received by the police department, additional crime analysis reports are required for quarterly progress reports and the final grant report.

- *Media requests*: Similar to community-focused analysis, the media is often provided products by crime analysts that have been adapted for the public. Crime analysts typically do not work directly with the media but provide this information to the public information officer within the department.

Not Types of Crime Analysis

The IACA specifically rejects categories of crime analysis that have been used historically or are currently used by others. The discussion of each category comes directly from the white paper (IACA, 2014b, pp. 7–8):

- *Compstat analysis*: Depending on agencies' approaches, Compstat models can be tactical, strategic, administrative, or intelligence-oriented, and thus, analysis for Compstat can take on any or all of these characteristics. Compstat is an outlet for many types of analysis but is not a unique type of analysis itself.

- *Crime mapping*: This is a set of skills and technologies useful to all types of crime analysis, not a unique category of crime analysis.

- *Criminal analysis*: This term has gained favor in some sources (e.g., Baker, 2004; Petersen, 1994) that use it in an attempt to unify crime analysis and criminal intelligence analysis. It has not generally been embraced by practitioners, and we find the term unsatisfying to describe any aspect of crime analysis, which almost always involves more than just the criminal.

- *Criminal investigative analysis*: To the extent that criminal investigative analysis, which is also sometimes called *profiling*, is performed within police agencies by crime analysts, it is almost always part of the tactical crime analysis process. We therefore include it as a technique there and not a separate type.

- *Evidence analysis or crime scene investigation*: There will be no confusion in this area among actual professionals in the field, but for other readers, we must emphasize that crime analysis has nothing to do with the analysis of crime scene evidence, including blood spatters, DNA, fingerprints, and ballistics. Crime analysis is wholly unrelated to forensic science.

- *Investigative, clerical, and administrative support*: Particularly given their computer skills, crime analysts are often called upon to provide various types of support unrelated to analysis, including preparing "wanted" or "BOLO" posters for an investigative unit, creating facial lineups, performing information technology duties, and running basic searches in common databases. Although such tasks might be vital to a police agency (and we don't specifically discourage analysts from helping in these areas when necessary), they are not analysis tasks, and we see no need to codify them under any typology of crime analysis.

- *Operational analysis*: The term appears in some European typologies (e.g., INTERPOL, 2014), almost always synonymous with tactical crime analysis. Between the two terms, we prefer *tactical crime analysis* as holding a more secure historical foothold in the profession. Also, the term is easy to confuse with *operations analysis*, described next.

- *Operations analysis*: Operations analysis is often defined in literature as "the analysis of police operations, including workload distribution by area and shift" (e.g., Gwinn et al., 2008, pp. 18–19). The techniques associated with these processes are too limited and the literature too scant for the practice to merit a separate category of crime analysis. We enfold it in administrative crime analysis for this reason, as well as because it is too easy to confuse with *operational analysis*, which is used by some international agencies.

- *Police planning*: Although aspects of budget, equipment, and personnel analysis are sometimes part of administrative crime analysis, we do not seek to extend the crime analysis profession to encompass all types of research and analysis that go into the profession of police planning.

- *Predictive analysis*: Tactical crime analysis, strategic crime analysis, and crime intelligence analysis are all inherently predictive; the only point in analyzing any of their subjects is the likelihood that they will continue to present a threat in the future. There are techniques within all of these analysis types that help improve the accuracy and precision of predictions, but predictive analysis is not otherwise a unique type of analysis.

Crime Mapping by Type of Analysis

Finally, crime mapping complements all forms of crime analysis and plays an important role in every type of analysis, even if it is not present in every crime analysis product. As noted by IACA in the previous list, crime mapping does not stand alone as its own subcategory of analysis; rather, it is a method that occurs within the larger process of crime analysis that focuses specifically on geography. The following are some examples of how crime mapping is used within the types of crime analysis discussed in this chapter:

- In *crime intelligence analysis,* crime mapping is used to display crime and relationships of individuals within networks in terms of where they live, work, and frequent (i.e., activity space). These maps can be of local communities or of states and regions of the country. One example is a map of gang territories along with gang-related crimes. Another is a map of gang members' home, work, and hangout locations, as well as the same for their associates, which may be used to help identify a gang territory or help build a case by connecting individuals in the gang.

- In *tactical crime analysis,* crime mapping is used to identify patterns that are linked by the proximity of the incidents. Crime mapping is particularly useful in identifying property crime and street robbery patterns. For example, spatial analysis of auto theft incidents may reveal clusters of activity at specific locations that might indicate a crime pattern. Crime mapping is also used to illustrate the locations of crimes in any crime pattern. In the case of geographic profiling, crime mapping and spatial analysis of crime and other locations are central.

- In *strategic crime analysis,* crime mapping is used in long-term applications, such as (a) to analyze the relationship between criminal activity and indicators of disorder, such as a high volume of vacant property or disorder calls for service; (b) to examine patterns of crime at or around specific locations, such as schools, bars, or drug treatment centers; (c) to calculate crime rate information, such as numbers of residential burglaries per household; and (d) to incorporate crime data with qualitative geographic information, such as information on teenage hangouts, student pathways to school, or drug and prostitution markets.

- In *administrative crime analysis,* crime mapping is used in accountability meetings to evaluate the effectiveness of crime reduction activities by area. It is used to examine dispatched calls for service to determine geographic allocation of resources (i.e., patrol scheduling), as well as the best design of patrol beats and locations of beat offices. For example, spatial statistics are used to estimate area boundaries that distribute calls evenly among police beats and determine locations for beat offices that minimize the distance of travel for officers. It is also a valuable tool used by police, researchers, and media organizations to convey criminal activity information to the public. Websites operated by police departments and news organizations routinely post maps that depict areas of crime, along with corresponding tables and definitions. For example, a police agency can reduce citizen requests for neighborhood crime information by placing monthly or weekly crime maps on a website that members of the public can access using computers in their homes or at the local library.

SUMMARY POINTS

This chapter describes the crime analysis process and the five different types of crime analysis. The following are the key points addressed in this chapter:

- The crime analysis process—that is, the general way in which crime analysis is practiced—includes the steps of data collection, data collation, analysis, dissemination of results, and the receipt of feedback from users of the information.

- The crime analysis data collection process requires the following: (a) the data must be collected accurately and consistently; (b) only data appropriate for crime analysis should be compiled; (c) the data must be collected in a timely manner; (d) the data must be archived for an adequate amount of time to allow for effective analysis; and (e) the data must be accessible in electronic raw form to be queried and downloaded.

- Data collation entails a number of different tasks, but it generally takes three forms: (1) cleaning—the process of correcting mistakes and inconsistencies in the data, (2) geocoding—the process of bringing crime analysis data together with geographic data so they can be analyzed spatially, and (3) creating new variables—the process of recoding or computing new variables from existing variables for more effective analysis.

- Analysis, which takes place after data are collected and prepared, includes the use of many different statistical and visualization techniques, all of which are described at length in Parts III, IV, and V of this book.

- The data modification subcycle is a subprocess within the crime analysis process in which the analyst makes changes to data collection and collation procedures based on insights gained during the analysis.

- Dissemination includes communicating and distributing crime analysis results to various types of audiences. The methods of disseminating crime analysis results include paper and electronic reports and maps, presentations, e-mails, Internet documents, and phone calls. The audiences for crime analysis information include police officers, police management, citizens, students, other analysts, and the news media.

- After disseminating the results of their analyses, crime analysts need to seek and receive feedback from the individuals to whom they provided the information.

- Crime intelligence analysis is the analysis of data about people involved in crimes, particularly repeat offenders, repeat victims, and criminal organizations and networks, and includes repeat offender and victim analysis, criminal history analysis, link analysis, commodity flow analysis, communication analysis, and social media analysis.

- Tactical crime analysis is the analysis of police data directed toward the short-term development of patrol and investigative priorities and deployment of resources.

Its subject areas include the analysis of space, time, offender, victim, and modus operandi for individual high-profile crimes, repeat incidents, and crime patterns, with a specific focus on crime series [sic]. It includes repeat incident analysis, crime pattern analysis, linking known offenders to past crimes, criminal investigative analysis, and geographic profiling.

- Strategic crime analysis is the analysis of data directed toward development and evaluation of long-term strategies, policies, and prevention techniques. Its subjects include long-term statistical trends, hot spots, and problems. It includes trend analysis, hot spot (i.e., problem area), and problem analysis.

- Administrative crime analysis is analysis directed toward the administrative needs of the police agency, its government, and its community. It includes crime analysis for accountability, districting and redistricting analysis, patrol staffing analysis, community-focused analysis, cost-benefit analysis, support for the agency's grant work, and media requests.

- The following are *not* types of analysis: Compstat analysis; crime mapping; criminal analysis; criminal investigative analysis; evidence analysis or crime scene investigation; investigative, clerical, and administrative support; operational analysis; operations analysis; police planning; and predictive analysis.

DISCUSSION EXERCISES*

Exercise 1

How is the crime analysis process (data collection, data collation, analysis, dissemination, feedback) different from the scientific process (theory, hypothesis, observation, empirical generalizations) and the problem-solving process (scanning, analysis, response, and assessment)? What might explain the differences among the three processes?

Exercise 2

Compare and contrast the different types of crime analysis and the ways in which they contribute to how police address crime and disorder. If you were a crime analyst, which type of analysis would you like to do? Why?

Exercise 3

Do an Internet search on crime intelligence analysis, criminal investigative analysis, profiling, and intelligence analysis. Compare and contrast what you find with what you know about crime analysis described in this chapter.

Crime Analysis Data and Technology

Data collection and collation are significant components of the crime analysis process, and analysts spend a substantial amount of their time and energy on collecting and preparing data for crime analysis purposes. Using technology is essential for analysts in order to save time and have the capabilities to conduct the necessary techniques and create the necessary products. Police agencies use many different methods and hardware for collecting and managing their data, so analysts must deal with data in many different formats and of varying quality. Analysts also can use a variety of software to work with data and create products. This chapter presents a general overview of the most common data types and technology, and it discusses their use in crime analysis.

Key Terms

To ensure understanding of many of the basic concepts discussed throughout this and the following chapters, brief definitions of some key terms are in order.

Data Matrix

Data refers to a collection of organized information that has been collected or gleaned from experience, observation, or experiment, or a set of ideas. Data may consist of numbers, words, or images that represent values of a *variable* (i.e., a measurable characteristic of an individual or a system that is expected to vary). Examples of variables collected for crime data include the type of crime, time, date, and location. A **data matrix** then is a rectangular table of variables and units from which data have been collected, such as individuals, organizations, and crimes, that are organized into rows and columns. In a data matrix, variables are always depicted in columns (also called *fields*) and units (also called *cases* or *records*) in rows. In crime analysis, a record or case would be a crime report, a traffic crash report, or an arrest report. Matrices can be in paper or electronic form. Table 5.1 depicts a simple data matrix of crimes (cases in rows) and their type, date of report, and location (variables in columns).

Database

A **database** is a data matrix that has been organized for the purposes of searching for, retrieving, and analyzing data through a computer. Databases can contain seemingly infinite numbers of records or cases. Most

Table 5.1	Data Matrix Example		
Incident No.	Type	Date of Report	Location
2017–0001	Residential burglary	01/01/17	15 Exchange Pl
2017–0002	Grand theft	01/01/17	169 York St
2017–0003	Robbery	01/01/17	111 1st St
2017–0004	Commercial burglary	01/01/17	685 Grand St
2017–0005	Robbery	01/05/17	344 Pacific Ave
2017–0006	Rape	01/05/17	49 Fisk St
2017–0007	Auto theft	01/05/17	26 Journal Sq
2017–0008	Theft from vehicle	01/11/17	920 Bergen Ave
2017–0009	Auto theft	01/12/17	438 Summit Ave
2017–0010	Arson	01/13/17	921 Bergen Ave
2017–0011	Robbery	01/13/17	234 16th St

modern databases (e.g., Microsoft Access, SQL Server, Oracle) allow users to examine complex relationships among various tables through what are called **relational databases**.

Geographic Data

Just as police agencies enter crime reports into computer systems, crime analysts enter data about the geographic features associated with crime and other activity into geographic information systems (GIS) for analysis purposes. Chapter 6 introduces the three types of geographic data or features that a GIS uses to represent objects or locations: point, line, and polygon, as well as the features and data associated with them, called *tabular* (or *attribute*) *data*.

Tabular Data

Tabular data describe events that are not inherently geographic but that may contain geographic variables. Crime reports, traffic crashes, and student information are examples of tabular data.

Secondary Data

Secondary data are data that have been collected previously and normally on an ongoing basis; such data are typically housed in electronic databases. The use of secondary data is common in crime analysis because police agencies, city departments, and government entities routinely collect and store data that are relevant to the issues crime analysts examine. For example, police agencies collect and store data from crime reports, crash reports, and arrest reports in an RMS (records management system) as well as collect and store data from

calls for service in a computer-aided dispatch system. City agencies collect and store data on street networks in geographic data systems, keep business registries, compile information on utilities usage, and collect data on taxes and licenses. The U.S. Bureau of the Census collects sociodemographic data, such as information about income, education, age, and race. Secondary data may be either qualitative (i.e., primarily narrative) or quantitative (i.e., numeric).

Primary Data

Because the secondary data that crime analysts use have been collected for purposes other than crime analysis, they are not always adequate to allow analysts to examine a topic fully. When that is the case, the crime analyst needs to collect **primary data**—that is, data collected specifically for the purposes of the analysis at hand. Analysts collect primary data through surveys, interviews, field research, and direct observation; such data may be coded and entered into a database or may be left in narrative form. For primary data to be both accurate and pertinent to the analysis, the crime analyst must invest explicit effort in collecting the data. The final section of this chapter provides details and examples of primary data collection.

Computer-Aided Dispatch System

A **computer-aided dispatch (CAD) system** is a highly specialized system that uses telecommunications and geographic display to support police dispatch response operations as well as those of public safety agencies, such as fire and ambulance services. Police departments use CAD technology to dispatch officers to a "call for service," to keep track of officers' locations and activities, and to track officer-initiated activity (e.g., traffic stops). All activity concerning calls for service is recorded in the CAD. The information includes details about the dispatched or officer-initiated call itself, such as which officers were dispatched to the scene, the call location, when officers arrived, and the disposition of the call (i.e., how it ended). In addition, correspondence is captured in the CAD between officers and dispatchers (e.g., tag and registration searches, officers taking lunch), which is typically called *unit history* as it records the activity of each police unit during a call (vs. about the overall call). It is important to note that a CAD system may not record all phone calls coming into the dispatch center, but only those in which an officer is sent to respond or is initiated by an officer. Because of the vast information contained in a CAD system, information is often purged after a certain amount of time. However, it is standard for police departments to retain a summary or snapshot of a call for service for a longer period of time for crime analysis purposes. Depending on the system, this CAD data may be linked or downloaded into a records management system for retrieval.

Records Management System

A **records management system (RMS)** is the informational heart of any police department's operations. It is a data entry and storage computer hardware and software system designed especially for police activity records. Some police agencies enter information directly into the RMS, whereas others download information to the RMS from other software programs, such as CAD or crime report-writing software. Ideally, the RMS contains all relevant data within the police agency and can include separate databases, such as crime reports, arrest reports, persons information, property and evidence information, vehicle information, crash reports, field information, calls for service, and case investigations. The contents of RMS can vary by agency, but the system's purpose—to store crime incidents data and link them with related data—is consistent across different software products and police departments.

The IACA has a series of recommendations for police agencies to consider to ensure that their RMS system is well suited for crime analysis since this is the central source of crime analysis data. The following is an abbreviated list of the recommendations (for a detailed discussion, see IACA (2013) "RMS Technical Requirements for Crime Analysis"):

1. Analysts should be involved with the procurement and implementation of the RMS.

2. The RMS should allow for third-party technology tools and open architecture for accessing data.

3. The RMS should provide a detailed data dictionary describing all data elements and how they relate.

4. The RMS should provide the ability to see database tables and fields within the system.

5. Analysts should be involved with importing legacy data (i.e., data from a previous system).

6. If not directly linked, CAD data should be imported into the RMS once the CAD event is complete.

7. Data entry should be clear, understandable, and customizable to account for an agency's needs.

8. The RMS should include validation rules to assist with data entry and quality control of the data.

9. To support the quality control, agencies should employ specific personnel to verify the RMS data.

10. The RMS should store historical data in the current data format so those records are accessible.

11. The RMS should include geographic coordinates for every address in the system.

12. The RMS should be flexible to be integrated into external systems.

13. The RMS should allow attachment of files to records in the system with searchable text.

14. The RMS should use a relational database management systems technology.

15. Analysts should have access to data that is not yet finalized in order to have immediate access.

16. The RMS should have a single search function that queries both variables, narratives, and attachments.

17. RMS with reporting functions should provide metadata for the reports.

18. Agencies should consider an RMS vendor that partners with companies specializing in crime analysis.

19. In lieu of a crime analysis module, the RMS should provide replicated data for crime analysis purposes.

Agency Management System

An agency management system (AMS) is an intranet web-based hardware and software system that facilitates communication and transparency within the police agency and streamlines internal police business. At its core, an AMS securely manages official communications, administration, and business functions in an agency. It can include modules that allow employees to review policies and general orders, track internal investigations and use-of-force incidents, disseminate crime analysis products, and facilitate communication about crime reduction and other operational activities. It allows for archiving and searching documents and information contained within the system. Regional sharing of crime analysis and homeland security bulletins and data can be facilitated through an agency management system. In the way the RMS is an agency's core repository of official records, the AMS is an agency's communications, administrative, and business management system. An AMS enables information sharing and collaboration related to crime analysis among departments, partner agencies, and community groups.

Information-Sharing Platforms

According to the International Association of Crime Analysts (2014a), an information-sharing platform "is a centralized computer system that allows authenticated users to collect, manage and share structured and unstructured data sets from a variety of sources" (p. 2). While this is a general category that may cover a wide range of specific hardware and software configurations, the purpose of the information-sharing platform is to have a mechanism to collect, organize, and centralize the vast amount of data generated by modern police departments. Traditional data such as crime and calls for service are contained in information-sharing systems, as well as data collected through new technologies such as body-worn cameras, license plate readers, closed-circuit cameras (CCTVs), and so on. The goal of the platform is to provide specific users with a streamlined process for accessing and searching data with common terms.

Jail Management System (JMS)

A **jail management system (JMS)** is a computer-based system that stores a detention facility's information pertaining to the people that have been booked into the facility, including the current population as well as those already released. The JMS provides the arrestee's current booking photo and personal statistics (e.g., height, weight, eye color, hair color), as well as address, driver's license, identification numbers, employer, and emergency contact information, when available. Identifying characteristics such as tattoos, glasses, scars, gang affiliation, and medical conditions may also be documented. The JMS also contains booking information relating to each arrest, such as offense charge, statute, and warrant information, if applicable. Active warrant information is accessible and searchable, including date of issue, charge(s), and bond amount. A feature of a JMS is the ability to view archived arrest history information as it relates to a suspect. While crime analysts may not use this system every day, they often have access to it directly or to its data through personnel working at the jail.

Criminal Justice Information Services (CJIS)

The **Criminal Justice Information Services (CJIS)** is the largest division of the Federal Bureau of Investigation and serves as the central division of its crime services and programs. Included under CJIS are the National Crime Information Center (NCIC), Uniform Crime Reporting (UCR), Integrated Automated Fingerprint Identification System (IAFIS), NCIC 2000, and the National Incident-Based Reporting System (NIBRS). CJIS also refers to the criminal justice agency within a district, state, territory, or federal agency that has administrative responsibility for the use of NCIC. Because the information is sensitive, records are protected. Access is restricted to users with specific authorization, each log-in to the system and individual search is tracked by the FBI, and periodic audits are conducted of the system so that no unnecessary searches will be conducted (e.g., a father doing a search on his new son-in-law).

National Crime Information Center (NCIC)

The **National Crime Information Center (NCIC)** is a computerized index of criminal justice information pertaining to individual criminal record histories, fugitives, stolen property, and missing persons within the entire United States. It is a centralized repository of law enforcement information brought together and classified by the FBI. The system is operated in cooperation with local, state, and federal law enforcement agencies and the FBI. The database is accessed by federal, state, and local law enforcement personnel at any time and on any day so that they can access the most current information pertaining to crimes and criminals in the system. As a program within CJIS, access to NCIC is restricted, and searches of the system are tracked continually. In addition, most states also have a similar database that contains such information for activity and criminals in their own states (e.g., Florida has FCIC; Arizona has ACIC).

Geographic Data System

A **geographic data system** creates, maintains, and stores geographic data. Typically, city or county agencies use geographic data systems to create and maintain data concerning parcels, buildings, streets, roads, and highways and to store aerial photographs and other geographic information for use by various

INTERNATIONAL CRIME ANALYST PERSPECTIVE

Katrine Holt

Law Enforcement Analyst Oslo Police District

Oslo, Norway

The CAU has analyzed crime in the city center for several years. This work has informed district command as well as station command and has helped clarify the actual extent of violent and other crime in public places in Oslo.

One of several methods we have used is to compute statistically significant hot spots of violent crime, as in this map. On the basis of such analysis of key crime types for the downtown area –assaults,

robberies, disturbances of the peace, and pick pocketing –the CAU started defining an area within which crime appeared to be both homogeneous and concentrated in space and time. Based on a theory of geographically disparate challenges to law and order, this type of analysis has helped increase the efficiency of policing these areas. Note the solid black line, signifying the current boundary between stations, that cuts through the middle of the violent crime hot spot. The solid blue line represents an area that contains a significant percentage of all cases for several crime types. The work of the CAU is now used to inform ongoing redistricting analysis work.

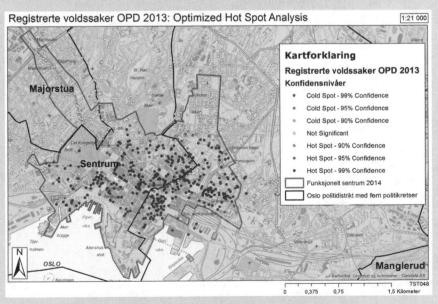

departments and agencies (e.g., planning, utilities). In addition, such agencies often obtain tabular and geographic data from other sources—such as census information, demographic information, and typological information—and store them along with local geographic data. It is important to note that police agencies and crime analysts do not collect or maintain the data housed in geographic data systems; rather, they only borrow and use these data for analyses.

Databases Used in Crime Analysis

Databases are vital for conducting crime analysis because they allow analysts to use computers to analyze large numbers of cases efficiently. Crime analysts use many different databases, but for the sake of brevity, only the most commonly used types are detailed in this section. Crime analysts most frequently use four types of secondary data: data on crime incidents, arrests, calls for service, and traffic crashes.

Crime Incidents

The data about crime incidents used in crime analysis come from crime reports taken by police officers or other police personnel and are, in most cases, stored in an RMS. Crime reports provide information for other types of databases that are linked to a **crime incident database**, also called a *crime report database*. These include suspect, witness, victim, vehicle, and property databases. The crime incident database contains information from each crime report concerning the nature of the crime, such as the type of crime and how, when, and where the crime occurred. The unit of analysis is the criminal incident report, which means that the database contains one case for each criminal incident report. Crime incident databases contain many variables; however, the following variables are typically used in crime analysis:

- *Record number:* A unique number used to identify the crime incident and related information. (Nearly all databases assign a unique number to each case to distinguish it from the other cases.)

- *Date of report:* The date the crime was reported to the police. Crime statistics are tallied based on when crimes were reported to the police rather than when they actually occurred.[1]

- *Type of crime* (state and federal): The type of crime the officer assigned to the event as dictated by the laws of the state and/or the police jurisdiction. Often, there are corresponding federal (Uniform Crime Report or National Incident-Based Report) codes included as well.

- *Location of the crime:* The address where the crime occurred as well as the area, such as police district or beat and census tract. Some databases also include the type of location, such as vacant lot, single-family home, or commercial business.

- *Date and time of occurrence:* The date and time when the crime occurred. This is often different from the date of report and can also be a range of time if the exact time of the crime is not known (e.g., burglary, auto theft). Military time is used in most police agencies when capturing temporal data and is always used in crime analysis (times are converted to military time, if necessary). It is important for analysis and statistical purposes that there is a unique value for each time of the day. (See Chapter 11 for examples of converting, rounding, and analyzing temporal data.)

- *Method of the crime* (also called "MO" or modus operandi): How the crime occurred, such as the point of entry, method of entry, weapon used, and suspect's actions. Numerous variables are used to capture this information. (For further discussion of MO [modus operandi] information, see Chapter 8.)

- *Disposition:* The outcome of the incident (e.g., cleared by arrest, pending). A disposition is assigned when the initial report is written and is then updated if and when an investigation leads to arrest or another status.

Table 5.2 is an example of what a portion of a crime incidents database might look like, with each row representing a crime incident report and each column containing information about a particular characteristic, such as date, address, and disposition.

Arrests

When an arrest is made, an officer completes an arrest report that includes information specific to the arrest of that individual. These data are linked to the original crime report (if applicable). The unit of analysis is the arrest, meaning there is one record for every arrest. If one person is arrested multiple times on different days, there will be multiple arrest records for that person. If three people are arrested for one crime, officers generate three arrest records, one for each person. Consequently, the crime incident database and **arrest database** do not have a one-to-one relationship. Crime analysts typically use the following variables found in arrest databases:

- *Arrest number:* A unique number used to identify the arrest
- *Date and time of arrest:* May vary from both the date of the report and the date and time of the crime occurrence

Table 5.2 Sample Crime Incidents Data Table

Incident No.	Report Date	Crime Type	Address	Beat	First Date	Last Date	Disposition
2017141524	11/15/2017	Burglary	1350 Allesandro Rd	24	11/15/2017	11/15/2017	Arrest
2017142640	11/18/2017	Burglary	1528 Calle Constancia	21	11/17/2017	11/18/2017	Pending
2017142676	11/18/2017	Burglary	953 Mendocino Way	16	11/17/2017	11/18/2017	Pending
2017142509	11/23/2017	Criminal trespass	1065 W Colton Ave	12	11/20/2017	11/21/2017	Pending
2017143275	11/23/2017	Burglary	996 E Colton Ave	16	11/19/2017	11/23/2017	Arrest
2017143496	11/26/2017	Burglary	298 5th St	19	11/15/2017	11/15/2017	Unfounded
2017144169	11/26/2017	Burglary	3235 Greenspot Rd	11	11/23/2017	11/25/2017	Pending
2017142878	11/27/2017	Criminal trespass	857 W Lugonia Ave	13	11/23/2017	11/23/2017	Pending
2017013294	12/20/2017	Burglary	210 Anita Ct	11	12/11/2017	12/19/2017	Pending

- *Charge(s):* The specific crime(s) for which the arrestee is charged for one arrest

- *Location of arrest:* The address and area where the arrestee was at the time of the arrest; may not match the location of the crime

- *Location of residence:* The address of the residence of the arrestee

- *Physical description:* A description of the arrestee's physical characteristics, including height, weight, hair color, and eye color

- *Date of birth:* The arrestee's date of birth; note that date of birth, rather than age, is collected for identification purposes (age often computed from this variable)

Table 5.3 is an example of what a portion of an arrest database might look like, with each row containing a record of one individual's arrest and the columns containing the characteristics of the arrest.

Table 5.3 Sample Arrest Data Table

Arrest No.	Date	Hour	Charge	Address of Arrest	First Name	Last Name	Race	Sex	DOB
20164615	7/20/2016	0235	14-269	254 W 1st St	John	Patters	B	M	02/11/62
20169395	12/11/2016	1400	14-269	988 N Sunset Dr	Robert	Haars	W	M	06/09/44
20165518	10/5/2016	2325	14-269	51 S Martin L King Jr Dr	Kevin	White	B	M	01/02/65
20172213	1/12/2017	2130	14-269	1500 E 1st St	Rodney	Powers	W	M	07/18/82
20176639	3/4/2017	0800	14-269.2	12 S University Dr	Karim	Williams	B	M	11/15/78

Calls for Service

Among the many activities carried out by police are responses to noncriminal activities, such as traffic crashes, neighbor disputes, disturbances, loud parties, and burglar alarm calls, which are housed in a **calls-for-service database**. Citizens call a police department's emergency number (i.e., 911) or a nonemergency number (e.g., the police department's main line) to request police services. Not all phone calls to the department warrant a police officer's response, and some citizens' calls are resolved in other ways. All citizen calls to which an officer responds, whether the reason is criminal or noncriminal, are known as **citizen-generated calls for service**. Police classifications for such calls for service include, but are not limited to, the following:

- Robbery in progress
- Burglary in progress
- Rape in progress
- Theft
- Homicide
- Shoplifting
- Family fight
- Assault
- Suspicious person
- Suspicious vehicle
- Loud noise
- Dog barking
- Collision
- Assist motorist

- 911 hang-up
- Burglar alarm
- Narcotics activity
- Welfare check
- Neighbor dispute
- Loud party
- Shots fired
- Criminal trespassing
- Speeding in neighborhood

Police officers also generate calls for service when they proactively identify problematic activity in the field. An officer records a call for service by reporting it to the dispatcher. The police classifications for these types of calls often vary by agency, but generally they are referred to as **officer-generated calls for service**.

Citizen-generated calls for service are more commonly used in crime analysis than officer-generated calls because citizen calls indicate the community's demand for police services, whereas officer-generated calls indicate officers' self-initiated activity. In addition, the volume of officer-generated calls for service is highly influenced by the volume of citizen-generated calls for service because the number of citizen-generated calls influences the amount of time officers have to generate calls themselves. For example, if during a shift an officer is dispatched from one citizen-generated call to the next, he or she has no time to initiate calls such as traffic stops. Therefore, crime analysts use officer-generated calls to examine officer activity and use citizen-generated calls to examine citizen demand for service by the community and its concerns about crime and disorder. That is, the police department serves the community's concerns first, and when there is time, officers address other issues and problems.

A call for service is the unit of analysis, in that one record represents one call for service in the database. The variables examined in crime analysis are based on a snapshot of the overall call and are similar for both citizen-generated and officer-generated calls for service. The variables include the following:

- *Incident number:* A unique number assigned by the computer system and used to track the call for service. In many cases, this number is the same for any subsequent reports (e.g., crime, traffic crashes, or information reports) written based on a call for service. This is done for tracking purposes, so a call for service and its resulting reports are linked together.

- *Dates and times*: A measurement that displays particular dates and times of importance for a call. They include when the call was received by police call takers, when it was dispatched to an officer, when the first officer arrived at the scene, and when the call was closed or cleared. These variables are used to compute other variables, such as response time (i.e., how much time elapses between a person's call to the police and an officer's arrival at the scene).

- *Type of call:* This is either an arbitrary number (e.g., 459, which signifies burglary) or descriptive term (e.g., burglar alarm call) specifying the type of call.

- *Priority:* A number showing the call's level of importance. To manage the order in which officers respond to calls for service, police assign priorities to calls as they are received. A call's priority is correlated to its seriousness and is dictated by the individual agency's policies. Calls with an "emergency" priority are dispatched first.

- *Disposition:* A description of the outcome of the call (e.g., no action taken, arrest, crime report, collision report, unable to locate). A call can have multiple dispositions.

- *Location of call:* The address and area from which the call came. This is not necessarily the address where the problem is occurring, but only where the call is being made since a citizen may not be able to provide that information (e.g., loud noise coming from the next apartment building).

Table 5.4 is an example of what a portion of a call for service database looks like, with each row representing the summary information from one call for service and the columns containing characteristics of the call.

Traffic Crashes

Traffic crashes, also called *traffic collisions*, are incidents in which vehicles collide with people, property, or other vehicles. Traffic crashes are a cause of concern in most communities, and responding to crashes accounts for a considerable amount of police officers' time, making the data on collisions important in crime analysis. Typically, officers collect and report crash information in the manner dictated by the laws of their states on a state form. Each record in a **traffic crash** or **collision database** contains information about one traffic crash; therefore, a crash is the unit of

Table 5.4 Sample Call for Service Data Table

Event No.	Date	Day	Call Type	Receive Time	Dispatch Time	Arrive Time	Complete Time	Priority	Location
201710621	10/1/2017	Sun	Robbery in progress	0015	0016	0018	0129	1	16 Morton Pl
201703160	10/2/2017	Mon	Suspicious person	0015	0020	0025	0045	2	238 Carbon St
201739616	10/2/2017	Mon	Disturbance	0015	0030	0039	0052	3	253 Stegman St
201714600	10/2/2017	Mon	Domestic dispute	0100	0101	0105	0312	1	48 Lienau Pl
201764094	10/3/2017	Tue	Burglar alarm	0130	0132	0137	0345	1	560 Bramhall Ave
201749640	10/3/2017	Tue	Burglary report	0130	0139	0145	0201	3	608 Bramhall Ave
201731049	10/4/2017	Wed	Traffic crash	0130	0142	0159	0235	3	68 Milk Dr

124

analysis. Crime analysts typically use the following variables from traffic crash databases:

- *Report number:* A unique number used to track the traffic crash, which is often provided to an insurance company as well

- *Date of report:* The date on which the traffic crash was reported to the police

- *Date and time of occurrence:* The date and time when the traffic crash occurred

- *Location of the crash:* The address at which the traffic crash took place (in many cases, at an intersection); this information often is recoded into one variable from two others (e.g., street the traffic crash "occurred on" and street the traffic crash "occurred at")

- *Violation(s):* Description of what traffic law(s) were violated, if any (e.g., speed too fast for conditions or improper left turn); in many cases, multiple violations are listed in the data

Table 5.5 is an example of what a portion of a traffic crash database looks like, with the rows representing individual crash and the columns containing their characteristics.

Table 5.5	Sample Traffic Crash Data Table				
Report No.	Date	Time	Location	Violation 1	Violation 2
2017009877	1/5/2017	0730	E Main Ave & S Center St	Improper left turn	None
2017009878	1/7/2017	1544	W Main Ave & N Cherry Ave	No signal	None
2017009882	1/12/2017	0845	E Elliot Dr & S Apple St	Speed too fast for conditions	No signal
2017009883	1/15/2017	0921	E Main Ave & S Center St	Improper left turn	Speed too fast for conditions
2017009879	1/28/2017	1623	E Main Ave & S Center St	Speed too fast for conditions	None

Other Databases

In addition to the types of databases discussed so far, the following kinds are also used in crime analysis:

- **Persons database:** This database contains information about all individuals involved in criminal incidents, including witnesses, victims, investigative leads, suspects (some police agencies have suspect databases that are separate from their persons and arrest databases), and arrestees. In this database, the unit of analysis is the individual. Each record contains information about the individual (name, birth date, address, physical description, aliases) and the nature of the contact (e.g., suspect, arrestee, witness, or victim). These data are normally linked relationally to the crime incidents database in the RMS.

- **Property database:** This database contains information about individual pieces of property that have been stolen, found, or used in the commission of crimes. The unit of analysis is the piece of property, so multiple records for property can result from one criminal incident. These data are normally linked relationally to the crime incidents database in the RMS, and variables often include a description, type of property (e.g., jewelry, electronics), and value in dollars.

- **Vehicle database:** This database contains information about vehicles stolen, recovered, or used in the commission of crimes. The unit of analysis is the vehicle, and each record includes information about the vehicle (VIN [vehicle identification number], make, model, color, and year) and the nature of the incident (date, time, and location). These data are normally linked relationally to the crime incidents database in the RMS.

- **Field information database:** Many police agencies collect information from the field (also called *field intelligence*) through field interview cards filled out by officers. This information is collected when an officer determines that a crime report is not necessary, but the agency would like to document specific information that may not be able to be captured in a call-for-service record. (For further discussion of field information data, see Chapter 8.) This database is often a part of the RMS, but stands alone (i.e., is not linked to the crime database).

- **Traffic database:** In addition to crash data, police agencies collect data on traffic citations and vehicle stops (one type of officer-generated calls for service). In recent years, because of racial profiling concerns, vehicle stop data have been examined more often by both researchers and crime analysts in order to more thoroughly understand the issue. This database is often a part of the RMS, but stands alone (i.e., is not linked to the crime database).

- **Known-offender database:** This database contains information about individuals who have been convicted, not just arrested, for crimes in the local jurisdiction. Typically, police agencies have their own known-offender databases that are obtained through local jail/prison release records and court/prosecution databases. However, there is a current trend to develop statewide databases with this information for use by crime analysts. Each record contains information about an individual (name, birth date, address, physical description, aliases), the crimes for which she or he has been convicted, and his or her correctional status (e.g., probation, parole, etc.). This database is normally a stand-alone database in that it is not directly linked to an agency's crime database.

- **Pawn database:** In many states, pawnbrokers are required to enter the property they receive along with the person's information into a database, so detectives can search for property that may have been stolen and pawned.

- **Gang database:** This database contains information collected and validated by patrol officers and detectives about individuals who are both members and associates of gangs. Most states have specific guidelines for classifying whether a person is a gang member or an associate that are used for "validation."

- **Registered sex offender database:** This database contains information about sex offenders who live in the local jurisdiction (or surrounding jurisdictions) and have registered as part of their sex offender status. Each record contains information about an individual (name, birth date, address, physical description, aliases), the sex crimes for which he or she has been convicted, her or his correctional status, and sex offender classification that varies by state. This database is normally a stand-alone database in that it is not directly linked to an agency's crime database.

Primary Data Collection

Secondary data, such as crime reports and information on calls for service and arrests, do not always answer important questions about problems of crime, disorder, and other issues analyzed by crime analysts. Because of this, crime analysts often have to collect primary data—that is, information collected for specific analysis purposes directly from individuals or places.

Primary data collected from people are typically gleaned through interviews, focus groups, and surveys. Interviews tend to be more in depth because they are one-on-one and allow the analyst to clarify issues and use follow-up questions with the interviewee. Focus groups are essentially interviews with groups of people. Focus groups are often used when collecting data from a class of people, such as police officers or community members. One consideration is that individuals may not say everything in a focus group forum that they would in a one-on-one interview. On the other hand, individuals may forget information or not "know the whole story," when a focus group would result in more complete data collection. Lastly, surveys are used to collect information from a large number of individuals when resources and time do not allow interviews. The type of data collection used obviously depends on the nature and purpose of the analysis.

Primary data collected from places are typically gleaned through environmental surveys and direct observation. An environmental survey is used to systematically observe the physical features of a place, such as lighting, parking spaces, and number of windows. Direct observation refers to observing a place for a certain amount of time over several days or weeks to determine the social environment of the place—that is, how the space is used, what types of people are present, how they congregate, and so on. Researchers recommend that direct observation be done in 20-minute increments over a series of representative time periods (i.e., to observe a bar with problems, the crime analyst would go on several of the nights of the week when the problem was occurring; Schmerler, Wartell, & Weisel, 2004). Also, the crime analyst should be unobtrusive when conducting observation and develop a standard simple protocol (i.e., things to focus on) to standardize the observations at the same type of place (Schmerler et al., 2004).

The following are some practical examples of primary data collection techniques that crime analysts have used or might use:

- In analyzing a crime problem at local motels, analysts interview the maids who work at the motels to help determine how the rooms were used by patrons staying in them (e.g., determined by the condition of the room and the garbage left behind; Schmerler & Velasco, 2002).

- Crime analysts interview burglary victims to determine what prevention methods they employed before and after they were victimized (Schmerler & Velasco, 2002).

- A crime analyst conducts a focus group with construction site building supervisors to gather data on their building practices, current victimizations, crime prevention, and crime reporting methods (Boba & Santos, 2007).

- A crime analyst annually surveys citizens locally to determine their rates of victimization, attitudes toward police, quality of life, fear of crime, and crime prevention behaviors. The citizens are selected randomly, and the analyst uses the survey results to help determine problems that need attention and to contribute to current crime prevention efforts.

- After a safety problem is identified involving crimes occurring around schools, along pathways to and from schools used by elementary school children, and in areas where children hang out before and after school, crime analysts conduct an environmental survey to determine the exact locations of the children's hangouts and their pathways to and from school. The analysts then enter data about the locations of these pathways and hangouts into a GIS and analyze them in relation to crime in the area (see Figure 5.1). They also use the information to scan for other problems and to identify intersections that are unsafe for children to cross.

- A crime analyst studying the problem of thefts from parking lots conducts an environmental survey to determine how many vehicles in particular parking lots are locked, how many have antitheft devices, how many have valuables left in view, and so on.

- A crime analyst directly observes a downtown area during the evening to determine the level of crowding, clustering of people at particular corners, and general attitude and behavior of individuals walking around.

Even though analysts collect primary data directly from individuals and places, before they can use the data to perform analyses they often quantify their results by creating coding standards, creating databases, and entering the data. The following example illustrates this process:

Problem: You are a crime analyst who has been asked to help assess a chronic problem of thefts from autos and auto theft at several local apartment communities.

Methodology: In order to understand victim behavior, you decide to develop an environmental survey about the security habits of the residents who park at one of the affected communities.

Figure 5.1   Map of Student Pathways to School and Hangouts

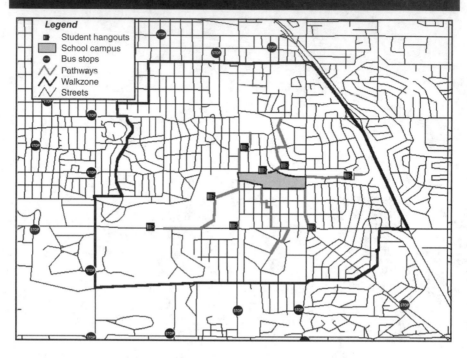

You use the following questions to guide your observation of cars in the parking lot:

1. Are any vehicle doors unlocked?   Yes   No

2. Are any vehicle windows open?   Yes   No

3. Are any valuables in view in the car
    (e.g., cash, smartphone, or purse)?   Yes   No

4. Is there an antitheft device?   Yes   No

    If so, what type (alarm, steering wheel lock, other)?

You then code the results of 250 observations and enter them into a database. Table 5.6 shows several cases and some variables that you might include in the database for analysis.

Analysis: By examining the data, you learn that although most people lock their car doors and close the windows when they park, 60% of the cars you observed had valuables in view, and few drivers used alarms. The results indicate that community residents should be advised not to leave valuables in view in their parked cars and to use their car alarms. You can conduct this same survey again later to determine whether the residents, in fact, changed their behavior.

Table 5.6 Sample Database: Primary Data Collection

Observation No.	Door	Window	Valuables	Anti-Theft	Type of Anti-Theft
1	Yes	No	Yes	No	None
2	No	No	Yes	Yes	Alarm
3	No	Yes	No	No	None
4	No	No	No	Yes	Other
5	Yes	Yes	No	Yes	Alarm

Data Considerations

The data commonly used in crime analysis raise several important issues related to the inherent characteristics of the data produced by all police agencies. These issues include (a) the fact that the data represent "reported" activity, (b) the distinction between local and federal data standards, (c) the appropriateness of the use of call-for-service data to study crime problems, (d) the appropriateness of the use of arrest data to study crime problems and offenders, and (e) the integrity of the data. These issues are addressed in turn in the following sections.

"Reported" Activity

The databases examined in crime analysis represent activity "reported" or "known" to the police (e.g., crime incidents, arrests, traffic crashes, calls for service) rather than all of the crime or other activity that actually occurs. Certain types of activity tend to be reported more consistently or come to the attention of the police more often than others. For example, incidents of rape, assault, and child abuse are vastly underreported, while incidents of prostitution, drunk driving, and gambling are discovered primarily by the police rather than reported by victims. Incidents of auto theft and arson tend to be reported fairly accurately, given victims' need for documentation for insurance purposes.

Crime analysts need to know the limitations of data on reported activity when they are analyzing and interpreting findings. Victimization surveys show that not all crimes are reported to law enforcement (Truman & Langton, 2014) and that different types of crimes are reported at different levels. The Bureau of Justice Statistics estimates from the National Crime Victimization Survey that violent crime was reported to police 45.6% of the time in 2013, 44.2% in 2012, and 50.3% in 2004. Property crime was reported 36.1% of the time in 2013, 33.5% in 2012, and 39.2% in 2014 (Truman & Langton, 2014). For example, it is well known that a very small proportion of the rapes that are committed are reported to police. Analysts should be aware that changes in rape statistics may not represent actual changes in the occurrence of rape; rather, they may simply come from changes in the level of reporting of this crime. This issue is not limited to crime data; call-for-service data, crash data, and other kinds of data, such as arrests and field information, also represent only activity that is known to the police and may not provide the entire picture concerning particular problems.

Local and Federal Crime Data Standards

Historically, data collected by police agencies have been similar, but, in fact, they vary by region, state, and even by police agency. Each agency has its own policies and procedures for recording activity, and this has made it difficult to compare counts, levels, and rates of crime. For this reason, the U.S. government developed a nationally based classification system, the **Uniform Crime Reporting (UCR)** program in 1930 to keep consistent counts of crime across the United States. The purpose of the UCR program has been to develop reliable information about crime reported to law enforcement that can be used by law enforcement as well as by criminologists, sociologists, legislators, municipal planners, and the media for a variety of research and planning purposes. Still today, the UCR program is used to measure crime by providing national standards for the uniform classification of crimes and arrests (for further details, visit the FBI's website at www.fbi.gov/ucr). Notably, UCR crime definitions are distinct and do not conform to definitions in federal or state laws.

There are well-documented criticisms of the UCR data that must be considered when using it for any purpose. But while the nature of the data and their limitations should be understood, they do not preclude researchers, practitioners, and crime analysts from using the data to understand crime and guide policy decisions. While individual law enforcement agencies classify reported crimes based on the laws of their own states and jurisdictions, these agencies reclassify these crimes according to UCR definitions when reporting them and provide aggregate counts of (a) particular crimes (known as Part I crimes: murder, rape, robbery, aggravated assault, burglary, larceny/theft, motor vehicle theft, and arson) and (b) arrests for all crimes. Note that the FBI does not report the aggregate counts of Part II crimes, including simple assault, fraud, prostitution, and DUI; it reports only the arrests that occur. Thus, when statistics about reported violent and property crime are published, they are only based on the eight Part I crimes.

In addition, UCR reporting requires the use of a hierarchical coding system, meaning that if two crimes happen during one incident, only one is counted. For example, if one person is the victim of both rape and robbery, only the rape will be counted, or if a car is stolen out of a locked garage, it is considered a burglary, not a burglary and an auto theft. The UCR program has specific rules for coding that are not detailed here; however, the result is that the actual number of reported crimes might be underestimated in that the number of incidents is counted and not the number of unique crimes that occur.

Compliance with UCR reporting is voluntary, but most police agencies participate; currently, more than 95% of the U.S. population is represented in UCR statistics. Police agencies report their counts monthly to state agencies, which report to the FBI twice a year. Some criticisms of the UCR data include inaccuracy due to inputting errors and handling of missing data (Lynch & Jarvis, 2008; Maltz, 1999), pressure on some law enforcement agencies to "doctor" the numbers, and the use of aggregate numbers that mask other factors such as time of day, location, and circumstance of the crime (e.g., whether the crime is committed by a stranger or family member).

Yet the UCR data are the most comprehensive and consistently collected data on crime in the United States. In most cases, analysis of UCR data begins the conversation, and additional in-depth analysis of crime in local areas is required to really understand the nature and context of crime problems.

UNIFORM CRIME REPORT: CRIME DEFINITIONS

Because various state laws define crimes differently, the definitions provided here are from the FBI's Uniform Crime Report, the U.S. national crime reporting system. As the FBI (2004) states:

> The Uniform Crime Reporting Program classifies offenses into two groups, Part I and Part II crimes. Each month, contributing agencies submit information on the number of Part I offenses (Crime Index) known to law enforcement; those offenses cleared by arrest or exceptional means; and the age, sex, and race of persons arrested. Contributors provide only arrest data for Part II offenses. (Appendix II)

Part I offenses are defined as follows:

Criminal homicide: (a) Murder and nonnegligent manslaughter: the willful (nonnegligent) killing of one human being by another. Excluded: deaths caused by negligence, attempts to kill, assaults to kill, suicides, and accidental deaths. The program classifies justifiable homicides separately and limits the definition to: (1) the killing of a felon by a law enforcement officer in the line of duty; or (2) the killing of a felon during the commission of a felony by a private citizen.
(b) Manslaughter by negligence: the killing of another person through gross negligence. Excluded: traffic fatalities.

Forcible rape (before 2013): The carnal knowledge of a female forcibly and against her will. Rapes by force and attempts or assaults to rape regardless of the victim's age are included. Excluded: statutory offenses (no force used—victim under age of consent).

(Continued)

(Continued)

Forcible rape (after 2013): Penetration, no matter how slight, of the vagina or anus with any body part or object, or oral penetration by a sex organ of another person, without the consent of the victim.

Robbery: The taking or attempting to take anything of value from the care, custody, or control of a person or persons by force or threat of force or violence and by causing the victim fear.

Aggravated assault: An unlawful attack by one person upon another for the purpose of inflicting severe or aggravated bodily injury. This type of assault usually is accompanied by the use of a weapon or by means likely to produce death or great bodily harm. Excluded: simple assaults.

Burglary (breaking or entering): The unlawful entry of a structure to commit a felony or a theft. Attempted forcible entry is included.

Larceny/theft (except motor vehicle theft): The unlawful taking, carrying, leading, or riding away of property from the possession or constructive possession of another. Examples are thefts of bicycles or automobile accessories, shoplifting, pocket-picking, or the stealing of any property or article that is not taken by force and violence or by fraud. Attempted larcenies are included. Excluded: embezzlement, confidence games, forgery, worthless checks, etc.

Motor vehicle theft: The theft or attempted theft of a motor vehicle. A motor vehicle is self-propelled and runs on the surface, not on rails. Excluded: motorboats, construction equipment, airplanes, and farming equipment.

Arson: Any willful or malicious burning or attempt to burn, with or without intent to defraud, a dwelling house, public building, motor vehicle or aircraft, personal property of another, etc.

Part II offenses, for which only arrest data are collected, are defined as follows:

Other assaults (simple): Assaults and attempted assaults where no weapons are used and which do not result in serious or aggravated injury to the victim.

Forgery and counterfeiting: Making, altering, uttering, or possessing, with intent to defraud, anything false in the semblance of that which is true. Attempts are included.

Fraud: Fraudulent conversion and obtaining money or property by false pretenses. Confidence games and bad checks (except forgeries and counterfeiting) are included.

Embezzlement: Misappropriation or misapplication of money or property entrusted to one's care, custody, or control.

Stolen property (buying, receiving, possessing): Buying, receiving, and possessing stolen property, including attempts.

Vandalism: Willful or malicious destruction, injury, disfigurement, or defacement of any public or private property, real or personal, without consent of the owner or persons having custody or control. Attempts are included.

Weapons (carrying, possessing, etc.): All violations of regulations or statutes controlling the carrying, using, possessing, furnishing, and manufacturing of deadly weapons or silencers. Attempts are included.

Prostitution and commercialized vice: Sex offenses of a commercialized nature, such as prostitution, keeping a bawdy house, procuring, or transporting women for immoral purposes. Attempts are included.

Sex offenses (except forcible rape, prostitution, and commercialized vice): Statutory rape and offenses against chastity, common decency, morals, and the like. Attempts are included.

Drug abuse violations: State and local offenses relating to the unlawful possession, sale, use, growing, and manufacturing of narcotic drugs. The following drug categories are specified: opium or cocaine and their derivatives (morphine, heroin, codeine); marijuana; synthetic narcotics—manufactured narcotics that can cause true addiction (Demerol, methadone); and dangerous nonnarcotic drugs (barbiturates, Benzedrine).

Source: FBI (2016).

Gambling: Promoting, permitting, or engaging in illegal gambling.

Offenses against the family and children: Nonsupport, neglect, desertion, or abuse of family and children. Attempts are included.

Driving under the influence: Driving or operating any vehicle or common carrier while drunk or under the influence of liquor or narcotics.

Liquor laws: State and local liquor law violations except drunkenness and driving under the influence. Excluded: federal violations.

Drunkenness: Offenses relating to drunkenness or intoxication. Excluded: driving under the influence.

Disorderly conduct: Breach of the peace.

Vagrancy: Begging, loitering, etc. Prosecutions under the charge of suspicious person are included.

All other offenses: All violations of state and local laws except those listed and traffic offenses.

Suspicion: No specific offense; suspect released without formal charges being placed.

Curfew and loitering laws (persons under age 18): Offenses relating to violations of local curfew or loitering ordinances where such laws exist.

Runaways (persons under age 18): Limited to juveniles taken into protective custody under provisions of local statutes.

More recently, the federal government created the National Incident Based Reporting System (NIBRS) in an attempt to improve on the UCR (see https://www.fbi.gov/about-us/cjis/ucr/nibrs/2012 for more information). This system also requires the uniform classification of crime without regard to local differences and is only used to categorize, not exact charges against individual offenders. Participation in the system is voluntary. In 2012, 33% of law enforcement agencies submitted individual records rather than aggregate counts to the FBI in electronic database form, so the national crime statistics published yearly by the FBI are still based on UCR figures. Agencies report many more categories of crime to the FBI, which include the following:

NATIONAL INCIDENT BASED REPORTING SYSTEM: CRIME DEFINITIONS

Group A Offenses

Arson: To unlawfully and intentionally damage, or attempt to damage, any real or personal property by fire or incendiary device.

Assault offenses: An unlawful attack by one person upon another.

Aggravated Assault: An unlawful attack by one person upon another wherein the offender uses a weapon or displays it in a threatening manner, or the victim suffers obvious severe or aggravated bodily injury involving apparent broken bones, loss of teeth, possible internal injury, severe laceration, or loss of consciousness. This also includes assault with disease (as in cases when the offender is aware that he or she is infected with a deadly disease and deliberately attempts to inflict the disease by biting, spitting, etc.).

Simple Assault: An unlawful physical attack by one person upon another where neither the offender displays a weapon, nor the victim suffers obvious severe or aggravated bodily injury involving apparent broken bones, loss of teeth, possible internal injury, severe laceration, or loss of consciousness.

Intimidation: To unlawfully place another person in reasonable fear of bodily harm through the use of threatening words and/or other conduct, but without displaying a weapon or subjecting the victim to actual physical attack.

Bribery: (Except Sports Bribery) The offering, giving, receiving, or soliciting of anything of value (i.e., a bribe, gratuity, or kickback) to sway the judgment or action of a person in a position of trust or influence.

Burglary/Breaking and Entering: The unlawful entry into a building or other structure with the intent to commit a felony or a theft.

Counterfeiting/Forgery: The altering, copying, or imitation of something, without authority or right, with the intent to deceive or defraud by passing the copy or thing altered or imitated as that which is original or genuine; or the selling, buying, or possession of an altered, copied, or imitated thing with the intent to deceive or defraud.

Destruction/Damage/Vandalism of Property: (Except Arson) To willfully or maliciously destroy, damage, deface, or otherwise injure real or personal property without the consent of the owner or the person having custody or control of it.

Drug/Narcotic Offenses: (Except Driving Under the Influence) The violation of laws prohibiting the production, distribution, and/or use of certain controlled substances and the equipment or devices utilized in their preparation and/or use.

> *Drug/Narcotic Violations*: The unlawful cultivation, manufacture, distribution, sale, purchase, use, possession, transportation, or importation of any controlled drug or narcotic substance.

> *Drug Equipment Violations*: The unlawful manufacture, sale, purchase, possession, or transportation of equipment or devices utilized in preparing and/or using drugs or narcotics.

Embezzlement: The unlawful misappropriation by an offender to his or her own use or purpose of money, property, or some other thing of value entrusted to her or his care, custody, or control.

Extortion/Blackmail: To unlawfully obtain money, property, or any other thing of value, either tangible or intangible, through the use or threat of force, misuse of authority, threat of criminal prosecution, threat of destruction of reputation or social standing, or through other coercive means.

Fraud Offenses: (Except Counterfeiting/ Forgery and Bad Checks) The intentional perversion of the truth for the purpose of inducing another person, or other entity, in reliance upon it to part with something of value or to surrender a legal right.

> *False Pretenses/Swindle/ Confidence Game*: The intentional misrepresentation of existing fact or condition or the use of some other deceptive scheme or device to obtain money, goods, or other things of value.

> *Credit Card/Automated Teller Machine Fraud*: The unlawful use of a credit (or debit) card or automated teller machine for fraudulent purposes.

> *Impersonation*: Falsely representing one's identity or position and acting in the character or position thus unlawfully assumed to deceive others and thereby gain a profit or advantage, enjoy some right or privilege, or subject another person or entity to an expense, charge, or liability which would not have otherwise been incurred.

> *Welfare Fraud*: The use of deceitful statements, practices, or devices to unlawfully obtain welfare benefits.

> *Wire Fraud*: The use of an electric or electronic communications facility to intentionally transmit a false and/or deceptive message in furtherance of a fraudulent activity.

Gambling Offenses: To unlawfully bet or wager money or something else of value; assist, promote, or operate a game of chance for money or some other stake; possess or transmit wagering information; manufacture, sell, purchase, possess, or transport gambling equipment, devices,

(Continued)

(Continued)

or goods; or tamper with the outcome of a sporting event or contest to gain a gambling advantage.

Betting/Wagering: To unlawfully stake money or something else of value on the happening of an uncertain event or on the ascertainment of a fact in dispute.

Operating/Promoting/Assisting Gambling: To unlawfully operate, promote, or assist in the operation of a game of chance, lottery, or other gambling activity.

Gambling Equipment Violations: To unlawfully manufacture, sell, buy, possess, or transport equipment, devices, and/or goods used for gambling purposes.

Sports Tampering: To unlawfully alter, meddle in, or otherwise interfere with a sporting contest or event for the purpose of gaining a gambling advantage.

Homicide Offenses: The killing of one human being by another.

Murder and Nonnegligent Manslaughter: The willful (nonnegligent) killing of one human being by another.

Negligent Manslaughter: The killing of another person through negligence.

Justifiable Homicide: The killing of a perpetrator of a serious criminal offense by a peace officer in the line of duty, or the killing, during the commission of a serious criminal offense, of the perpetrator by a private individual.

Kidnapping/Abduction: The unlawful seizure, transportation, and/or detention of a person against his or her will, or of a minor without the consent of her or his custodial parent(s) or legal guardian.

Larceny/Theft Offenses: The unlawful taking, carrying, leading, or riding away of property from the possession, or constructive possession, of another person.

Pocket-Picking: The theft of articles from another person's physical possession by stealth where the victim usually does not become immediately aware of the theft.

Purse-Snatching: The grabbing or snatching of a purse, handbag, etc., from the physical possession of another person.

Shoplifting: The theft, by someone other than an employee of the victim, of goods or merchandise exposed for sale.

Theft From Building: A theft from within a building that is either open to the general public or where the offender has legal access.

Theft From Coin-Operated Machine or Device: A theft from a machine or device that is operated or activated by the use of coins.

Theft From Motor Vehicle: (Except Theft of Motor Vehicle Parts or Accessories) The theft of articles from a motor vehicle, whether locked or unlocked.

Theft of Motor Vehicle Parts or Accessories: The theft of any part or accessory affixed to the interior or exterior of a motor vehicle in a manner that would make the item an attachment of the vehicle, or necessary for its operation.

All Other Larceny: All thefts that do not fit any of the definitions of the specific subcategories of Larceny/Theft already listed.

Motor Vehicle Theft: The theft of a motor vehicle.

Pornography/Obscene Material: The violation of laws or ordinances prohibiting the manufacture, publishing, sale, purchase, or possession of sexually explicit material (e.g., literature, photographs, etc.).

Prostitution Offenses: To unlawfully engage in or promote sexual activities for anything of value.

 Prostitution: To engage in commercial sex acts for anything of value.

 Assisting or Promoting Prostitution: To solicit customers or transport persons for prostitution purposes; to own, manage, or operate a dwelling or other establishment for the purpose of providing a place where prostitution is performed; or to otherwise assist or promote prostitution.

Robbery: The taking, or attempting to take, anything of value under confrontational circumstances from the control, custody, or care of another person by force or threat of force or violence and/or by putting the victim in fear of immediate harm.

Sex Offenses, Forcible: Any sexual act directed against another person without the consent of the victim, including instances where the victim is incapable of giving consent.

 Forcible Rape: (Except Statutory Rape) The carnal knowledge of a person, forcibly and/or against that person's will, or not forcibly or against the person's will in instances where the victim is incapable of giving consent because of his or her temporary or permanent mental or physical incapacity.

 Forcible Sodomy: Oral or anal sexual intercourse with another person, forcibly and/or against that person's will, or not forcibly or against the person's will in instances where the victim is incapable of giving consent because of her or his youth or because of his or her temporary or permanent mental or physical incapacity.

 Sexual Assault With An Object: To use an object or instrument to unlawfully penetrate, however slightly, the genital or anal opening of the body of another person, forcibly and/or against that person's will, or not forcibly or against the person's will in instances where the victim is incapable of giving consent because of his or her youth or because of her or his temporary or permanent mental or physical incapacity.

 Forcible Fondling: The touching of the private body parts of another person for the purpose of sexual gratification, forcibly and/or against that person's will, or not forcibly or against the person's will in instances where the victim is incapable of giving consent because of her or his youth or because of his or her temporary or permanent mental or physical incapacity.

Sex Offenses, Nonforcible: (Except Prostitution Offenses) Unlawful, nonforcible sexual intercourse.

(Continued)

(Continued)

Incest: Nonforcible sexual intercourse between persons who are related to each other within the degrees wherein marriage is prohibited by law.

Statutory Rape: Nonforcible sexual intercourse with a person who is under the statutory age of consent.

Stolen Property Offenses: Receiving, buying, selling, possessing, concealing, or transporting any property with the knowledge that it has been unlawfully taken, as by Burglary, Embezzlement, Fraud, Larceny, Robbery, etc.

Weapon Law Violations: The violation of laws or ordinances prohibiting the manufacture, sale, purchase, transportation, possession, concealment, or use of firearms, cutting instruments, explosives, incendiary devices, or other deadly weapons.

Group B Offenses

Bad Checks: Knowingly and intentionally writing and/or negotiating checks drawn against insufficient or nonexistent funds.

Curfew/Loitering/Vagrancy Violations: The violation of a court order, regulation, ordinance, or law requiring the withdrawal of persons from the streets or other specified areas; prohibiting persons from remaining in an area or place in an idle or aimless manner; or prohibiting persons from going from place to place without visible means of support.

Disorderly Conduct: Any behavior that tends to disturb the public or decorum, scandalize the community, or shock the public sense of morality.

Driving Under the Influence: Driving or operating a motor vehicle or common carrier while mentally or physically impaired as the result of consuming an alcoholic beverage or using a drug or narcotic.

Drunkenness: (Except Driving Under the Influence) To drink alcoholic beverages to the extent that one's mental faculties and physical coordination are substantially impaired.

Family Offenses, Nonviolent: Unlawful, nonviolent acts by a family member (or legal guardian) that threaten the physical, mental, or economic well-being or morals of another family member and that are not classifiable as other offenses, such as Assault, Incest, Statutory Rape, etc.

Liquor Law Violations: (Except Driving Under the Influence and Drunkenness) The violation of laws or ordinances prohibiting the manufacture, sale, purchase, transportation, possession, or use of alcoholic beverages.

Peeping Tom: To secretly look through a window, doorway, keyhole, or other aperture for the purpose of voyeurism.

Runaway: A person under 18 years of age who has left home without permission of his or her parent(s) or legal guardian.

Trespass of Real Property: To unlawfully enter land, a dwelling, or other real property.

All Other Offenses: All crimes that are not Group A offenses and not included in one of the specifically named Group B offense categories listed previously.

Using Calls-for-Service Data
to Study Crime Problems

Occasionally, crime analysts use call-for-service data rather than crime incident data to study crime problems. In such cases, they use call for service—labeled as *criminal activity that results in police reports*—to represent crime incidents. Analysis of crime based on calls for service can be misleading for several reasons, which also highlight the differences between these two data sources:

- *Crime type:* When a call comes in to a police department, the call taker assigns it a call type. In many cases, once on the scene an officer will discover that the incident is actually a different type. For example, a person calls the police department and says, "I've been robbed!" but the responding officer finds that in reality the person's house has been burgled. In many calls-for-service databases, the original call types noted are never updated by the call takers, so these databases do not accurately represent the types of activities that actually occurred.

- *Date and time:* The date and time variables in calls-for-service databases reflect when each call was received and dispatched to the officer, when the officer arrived, and when the call was cleared. Such databases do not accurately indicate when crimes occurred. For example, a victim can call on Monday morning about her car being stolen on Saturday night.

- *Location:* The location listed in a call-for-service database may not be the location of the crime incident but instead a nearby location or the location from which the call was made. The recording of apartment numbers in call-for-service data is often haphazard and depends on the amount of information available (e.g., "a loud fight coming from the next building") and the diligence of the call taker (e.g., in determining the apartment number at which the incident is occurring, not where the call originates).

Given these limitations, call-for-service databases are more appropriately used in analyses of police disorder activity (e.g., suspicious behavior, disorderly behavior, public drunkenness, noise complaints, and code violations) and officer activity (e.g., officer-generated calls) than in crime incident analyses.

Using Arrest Data to Study
Crime Problems and Offenders

Arrests occur when sufficient evidence (probable cause) exists to indicate that a person has committed a crime. Crime analysts use arrest data to understand certain types of crimes as well as offenders. The use of arrest data in such analysis raises three main issues. The first is that arrests tend to reflect police activity. Police departments document certain types of crime only through arrests (e.g., prostitution, shoplifting, gambling, and driving under the influence of alcohol). For example, if a police crackdown on prostitution occurs in February, analysis of arrests for prostitution will show a dramatic increase in February. This change, however, is the result of police action rather than an actual increase in prostitution activity. For this reason, crime analysts need to be aware of police practices that might influence arrests for certain types of crimes.

The second issue is that arrestees may not be representative of offenders because offenders who are caught may differ (e.g., in intelligence and experience) from those who are not caught.

The third issue is that arrest rates for certain crimes (e.g., property crimes) are extremely low; therefore, analysts' use of a small number of offenders to understand the larger problem may be misleading. For example, an analysis of individuals arrested for auto theft may reveal that 60% are juveniles. Does that mean there is a juvenile auto theft problem? Before analysts can draw any conclusions in this regard, they must know the overall arrest rate for auto theft. Property crimes typically have low arrest rates—between 15% and 20%. As a result, if in the example the arrest rate is only 20%, then juveniles were arrested in 12% of the auto thefts (60% of 20% is 12%). More generally, in this instance we are looking at only 20% of the cases—or we have no information about who is committing auto thefts in 80% of the cases. The answer to the question is that we do not know whether a majority of the thefts are being conducted by juveniles, but we do know that "of the people who are arrested" for auto theft, a majority of offenders are juveniles. These are two very different conclusions.

Data Integrity

Several factors can affect the integrity of police data, which may influence crime analysis results, including the following:

- *Data entry:* Crime analysis relies primarily on secondary data, and the individuals who enter data typically have little understanding of the importance of those data to crime analysis. In police agencies, these individuals include police officers, call takers, dispatchers, and records clerks. Their lack of awareness regarding the need for data accuracy can lead to carelessness and result in unreliable data. Data entry can be improved with technology (e.g., providing variable values, address-cleaning software) and proper training that includes information on the uses and importance of the data.

- *Timeliness:* A primary concern in crime analysis is that the data obtained are current and available in a timely manner. Missing or old data can affect the quality of crime analysis.

For example, it is difficult to analyze and identify immediate crime patterns using data that are several weeks old.

- *Validity:* Valid data accurately reflect the concepts they are meant to measure. Issues of validity include the facts that (a) as previously discussed, crime data do not reflect all crime that occurs, only crime reported to the police; (b) calls for service do not represent crime incidents; and (c) arrests are a better indicator of police activity than of criminal incidents.

- *Reliability:* Reliable data are data that are the same in repeated observations. Two reliability issues related to police data involve changes in policies or laws (e.g., mandatory arrest for domestic violence offenses) and the coding of similar activities in the same way (e.g., theft from building vs. residential burglary).

- *Data transfer process:* In many cases, crime analysts download, clean, and manipulate data before conducting their analyses. This process can affect data quality and integrity since data can be inadvertently or unavoidably lost or reformatted. An issue associated with the data transfer process is data compatibility. Police departments are notorious for having data in many different formats; converting and combining these data is often time-consuming and frustrating.

- *Data confidentiality/privacy:* Crime analysts are managers of police data; they are responsible for protecting the information and individuals represented within the data. Normally, the data used and created in crime analysis adhere to a jurisdiction's policies on privacy and confidentiality. In recent years, new ways of gathering and disseminating information have surfaced that require additional and more detailed policies, such as the use of the Internet and mapping. Consequently, police departments need to include specific crime analysis concerns in their data protection plans.

- *Data management:* Every police department has its own set of procedures outlining how crime analysis data are to be collected and manipulated. However, many details regarding these procedures exist only in the memories of individual analysts. The term *metadata* refers to information about data. In the metadata process, this information is written down to ensure consistency in data handling and cleaning procedures, to provide guidelines for sharing work with others and keeping track of products and files created, and to reduce duplication of effort.

Hardware and Software Considerations

Computer-aided dispatch (CAD), records management (RMS), agency management systems (AMS), and geographic data systems all produce data that are used in crime analysis, but these are not analysis systems since their primary purpose is to produce and store data, not provide analytical tools. Thus, it is necessary to use software for crime analysis activities. Crime analysts use four basic types of general desktop software applications to organize data as well as to conduct analyses: **database management (DBMS) software**, **spreadsheet software**, **statistical software**, and **geographic information system (GIS) software**. Crime analysts use six basic types of software applications, alone or in combination, to create reports, publications, and presentations: **word processing software**, spreadsheet software, **graphics software**, **publication software**, **presentation software**, and software related to the use of the Internet and **intranets**.

These types of software can all be used in crime analysis but have not been created specifically for that purpose. Thus, a number of software applications have been created specifically for crime analysis. These include smaller applications for data entry and creating standardized crime analysis reports as well as more comprehensive programs that provide numerous capabilities and techniques needed for different types of crime analysis. Most of the applications designed specifically for crime analysis have been created to perform functions that are not available in other existing software. In addition to these commercially produced and federally funded programs, many police departments have created their own software to perform crime analysis. For example, one analyst created a data entry module and database in Microsoft Access because his department had not yet acquired a records management system; he simply had no other way of accessing electronic data for analysis. Another analyst with advanced computer programming skills created a program to speed up the process of address cleaning (bringing the time needed down from 4 hours to 30 seconds). In many cases, analysts and police agencies find that off-the-shelf software is not always a good fit with their data, analysis, and presentation needs. As a result, they hire computer experts to customize existing software or create new software themselves that provides the functionality they require.

Lastly, automation of reports and dissemination of information is an important consideration for crime analysts and their use of hardware and software. Crime analysts use software products to automate the creation of crime analysis reports that are nearly identical each day, week, or month and, once created, require little review by an analyst. This saves an inordinate amount of the crime analyst's time that can be used to create original reports. Software for this purpose is becoming more common, and many CAD and RMS systems already have the ability to query data and create automated reports. In addition, crime analysts use technology to automate the dissemination of information to a variety of audiences. Both automated and original crime analysis reports are disseminated to police personnel and others through e-mail, an intranet site, or the Internet, depending on the circumstance.

SUMMARY POINTS

This chapter provides an overview of the common secondary data used in crime analysis as well as a discussion of primary data and the issues associated with the use of these types of data. The following are the key points addressed in this chapter:

- Crime analysis is a discipline that relies heavily on computer technology, both hardware and a variety of software programs.

- Data refers to a collection of organized information that has been collected or gleaned from experience, observation, or experiment, or a set of ideas.

- Data may consist of numbers, words, or images that represent values of a variable (i.e., a measurable characteristic of an individual or a system that is expected to vary).

- A data matrix is a rectangular table of variables and units from which data have been collected. Examples include individuals, organizations, and crimes that are organized into rows and columns.

- A database is a data matrix that has been organized for the purposes of searching for, retrieving, and analyzing data through a computer.

- Geographic data are data used primarily in mapping; in many cases, these data do not make much sense outside of a GIS. Three types of geographic data are used to represent real-world objects and locations: point, line, and polygon.

- Tabular data describe events that are not inherently geographic but may contain geographic variables.

- Secondary data are data that have been collected for purposes other than crime analysis and are housed in databases.

- Primary data are data collected—through surveys, interviews, field research, and direct observation—specifically for use in a particular analysis.

- A computer-aided dispatch system (CAD) is a highly specialized system that uses telecommunications and geographic display to support police dispatch and response functions (as well as those of public safety agencies, such as fire and ambulance services).

- A records management system (RMS) is a specialized data entry and storage system that contains police activity records produced by the police agency.

- An agency management system (AMS) is an intranet web-based hardware and software system that facilitates communication and transparency within the police agency and streamlines internal police business.

- According to the International Association of Crime Analysts (IACA), an information-sharing platform is a centralized computer system that allows authenticated users to collect, manage, and share structured and unstructured data sets from a variety of sources.

- A geographic data system creates, maintains, and stores relevant geographic data. Such a system is usually maintained at the city or county level, and crime analysts "borrow" data from it.

- A jail management system (JMS) is a computer-based system that stores a detention facility's information pertaining to the people who have been booked into the facility, including the current population as well as those already released.

- Criminal Justice Information Services (CJIS) is the largest division of the Federal Bureau of Investigation and serves as the central division of their crime services and programs.

- National Crime Information Center (NCIC) is a computerized index of criminal justice information pertaining to individual criminal record histories, fugitives, stolen property, and missing persons within the entire United States.

- Crime analysts most frequently use four types of secondary data: data on crime incidents, arrests, calls for service, and crashes.

- Data about crime incidents come from crime reports taken by police officers and describe the nature of reported crimes, such as the type of crime and how, when, and where the crime occurred.

- Data about arrests come from arrest reports completed by officers and include information specific to individual arrests.

- Call-for-service data are recorded in the dispatch center of a police agency and may be generated by either citizens or officers. A call for service is defined when officers are dispatched to an incident or discover an incident themselves.

- Traffic crash data are typically recorded in standardized ways dictated by state laws. Crashes are incidents in which vehicles collide with property or other vehicles.

- Other police tabular databases used in crime analysis include property, vehicle, persons, known-offender, gang, field information, and traffic databases.

- Crime analysts typically collect primary data from people through interviews, focus groups, and surveys.

- Interviews tend to be more in depth because they are one-on-one, and they allow the analyst to clarify issues and use follow-up questions with the interviewee.

- Focus groups are essentially interviews with groups of people.

- Surveys are used to collect information from a large number of individuals when resources and time do not allow for interviews.

- Crime analysts also collect primary data from places through environmental surveys and direct observation.

- Direct observation refers to observing a place for a certain amount of time over several days or weeks to determine the social environment of the place—that is, how the space is used, what types of people are present, how they congregate, and so on.

- Important issues related to crime analysts' use of police tabular databases include (a) the fact that the data represent "reported" activity, (b) the distinction between local and federal data standards as well as between UCR and NIBRS, (c) the appropriateness of the use of call-for-service data to study crime problems, (d) the appropriateness of the use of arrest data to study crime problems and offenders, and (e) the integrity of the data.

- Data integrity is affected by the following factors: data entry, timeliness, validity, reliability, the data transfer process, data confidentiality/privacy, and data management.

- Crime analysts use four basic types of general desktop software applications to manipulate data and conduct analyses: spreadsheet software, database management software, statistical software, and geographic information system (GIS) software.

- Crime analysts use six basic types of software applications to create reports, publications, and presentations to communicate their analysis findings: word processing software, spreadsheet software, graphics software, publication software, presentation software, and software related to use of the Internet and intranets.

- Among the software applications that have been created specifically for crime analysis are small applications for data entry and creating reports as well as more comprehensive programs that provide numerous capabilities needed for the crime analysis process.

- Many police agencies often do not find off-the-shelf software to be a good fit with their data, analysis, and presentation needs, so they hire computer experts to customize existing software or create new software that provides the crime analysis functionality they require.

DISCUSSION EXERCISES _____

Exercise 1

You have been asked to collect primary data (observations) about either the problem of theft from vehicles or theft of vehicles in parking lots (to be assigned by the instructor). The purpose of this data collection is to supplement secondary data to help understand why the problem is occurring in particular parking lots as well as to compare the various types of parking lots in the city. To prepare for actually collecting primary data, you will (a) observe the school parking lot, taking notes on information you might want to collect for all parking lots in the city, and (b) develop five specific variables for which data will be collected for each lot (be specific). Even though you will observe the school parking lot for this exercise, you would be observing others as well (commercial lots and apartment lots) for the data collection, so think about including information pertaining to these types of lots as well.

Exercise 2

Determine which type(s) of data would be *best* to examine the following problems. Justify your selection in each case:

1. Street robberies in a residential area

2. College parties at off-campus housing

3. Traffic crashes around schools

4. Sale and buying of drugs around convenience stores and apartment complexes

5. Shootings at and around night clubs

Exercise 3

Why was it important to set up the Uniform Crime Report program and the National Incident Based Reporting System? Discuss the issue of validity versus reliability in the context of the UCR and NIBRS data and their creation. Also discuss what the UCR and NIBRS data tell us and what they *do not* tell us.

NOTE

1. Crime statistics are not based on when crimes occur because crimes can be reported hours, days, weeks, months, and even years after they occur. Using report date is a static, reliable way of counting crime, but it may not provide a completely accurate picture of when crime is occurring (e.g., a high number of burglaries may be reported in January because people who were on vacation in December did not report the crimes until January).

CHAPTER 6

Geographic Data and Crime Mapping

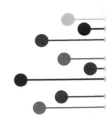

Geographic data and crime maps are particularly relevant in crime analysis and are discussed in their own chapter because of their unique data characteristics and distinct analysis techniques. The purpose of this chapter is to provide an overview of geographic data and its components, types of descriptive maps typically used in crime analysis, and statistical classifications used to categorize and analyze data using maps, as well as the techniques for creating density maps. The data and techniques discussed here are used in examples throughout the rest of the book as they are relevant, so this chapter focuses more on the definitions, descriptions, and analytical techniques and less on practical examples.

Geographic Data

There are a number of unique components and terms that are used in crime mapping to refer to data and their depiction on maps. This section highlights and describes the most important concepts; however, it does not cover the entirety of components, as these are described more appropriately in a specific crime mapping text or an advanced crime analysis course.

Vector Data

In crime analysis, a geographic information system (GIS) translates physical elements in the real world—such as roads, buildings, lakes, and mountains—into forms that can be displayed, manipulated, and analyzed along with police information such as crime, arrest, and traffic crash data. A GIS uses three types of features to represent objects and locations in the real world; these are called **vector data**, for which the basic units of **spatial information** are points, lines, and polygons. In a GIS, these different features are displayed separately and have accompanying attribute (or tabular) data that describe them.

A **point feature** is a discrete location that is usually depicted on a GIS-generated map by a symbol or label. A point feature is analogous to a pin placed on a paper wall map. A GIS uses different symbols to depict the locations of data relevant to the analysis, such as crimes, motor vehicle crashes, traffic signs, buildings, police beat stations, and cell phone towers. Figure 6.1 shows circles on the map that could represent any of these types of locations. Table 6.1 illustrates how a database would display the attribute data associated with each point. In this example, the points represent robberies. Each point on the map in Figure 6.1

Figure 6.1   Point and Line Feature Map

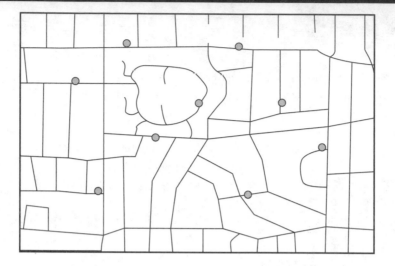

corresponds with a record (row) in Table 6.1. The variables in the database provide additional information about that location, such as the incident number, address, and type of location where the robbery occurred. This is just a simple example, as geographic attribute data can contain many more variables to describe each point.

A **line feature** is a real-world element that can be represented on a map by a line or set of lines. In Figure 6.1, the lines represent street segments. Other types of line features include rivers, streams, power lines, and bus routes. As with points, each segment of a street corresponds to a record in the attribute data shown in Table 6.2. The variables describe the attributes of that particular street segment and contain the addresses at the beginning and the end of the street segment. The variables *left from* and *left to* contain the addresses that start and end the range on one side of the street segment, and *right from* and *right to* contain the other side's range. The direction, street name, and type of street are also shown.

A **polygon feature** is a geographic area represented on a map by a multisided figure with a closed set of lines. Polygons can represent areas as large as continents or as small as buildings; in GIS-generated maps they may be used to depict county boundaries, city boundaries, parks, school campuses, or police districts. The polygons in Figure 6.2 show police districts. Each district corresponds to a record displayed in Table 6.3. With the polygon feature, the unit of analysis is the area, so the lines (borders) of the polygon do not have attribute data—only the area itself does. In Table 6.3, the variable called *feature* describes the type of feature these data are, and *district* is the name/label for that polygon.

Table 6.1 Point Feature Attribute Data

Incident No.	Address	Type of Location
2017-0025	15 Exchange Pl	Business
2017-0026	169 York St	Apartment
2017-0027	111 1st St	Business
2017-0028	685 Grand St	Street
2017-0029	344 Pacific Ave	Business
2017-0030	920 Bergen Ave	Park
2017-0031	438 Summit Ave	Apartment
2017-0032	921 Bergen Ave	Park
2017-0033	234 16th St	Street

Table 6.2 Line Feature Attribute Data

Left From	Left To	Right From	Right To	Prefix	Street Name	Type
2201	2249	2200	2248	E	Columbia	Pl
2301	2399	2300	2398	E	Columbia	Pl
2101	2199	2100	2198	E	Columbia	Pl
2251	2271	2250	2270	E	Columbia	Pl
2273	2299	2272	2298	E	Columbia	Pl
2167	2231	2166	2208	E	Dartmouth	Cir
2101	2165	2100	2164	E	Dartmouth	Cir
2233	2299	2210	2298	E	Dartmouth	Cir
2999	2901	3030	2900	S	Fillmore	Way
3099	3001	3098	3032	S	Fillmore	Way
3099	2901	3124	2900	S	Milwaukee	Cir
2899	2701	2998	2700	S	Dallas	Way
2999	2901	3098	3000	S	Dallas	Way
2701	2899	2700	2898	E	Linvale	Pl
3081	3139	3074	3098	E	Yale	Way

Crime analysts use many different types of vector data. Many of these are familiar to most people because they represent elements of the real world and are used for purposes other than crime analysis. Among the types of geographic

Figure 6.2   Polygon Feature Map

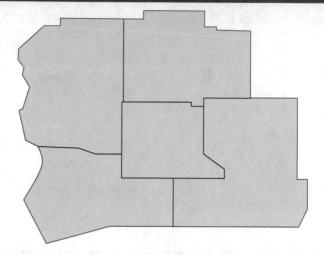

databases commonly used in crime analysis are those devoted to the following geographic features:

- Point features:

    Police stations

    Schools

    Hospitals

    Businesses

    Retail stores/restaurants

    Offices

    Places of worship

    Government buildings

    Mass-transit stops and stations (e.g., bus stops, train stations)

- Line features:

    Streets

    Highways

    Rivers

    Railroads

    Mass-transit routes (e.g., subways)

- Polygon features:

    Parcels

    Buildings

    Census block groups and tracts

    Parking lots

    School campuses

    Airports

    City, county, and state boundaries

    Police areas (grid, beat, precinct, district)

    Drug markets

    Gang territories

    Areas targeted for special policing efforts

Raster Data

In addition to vector data, crime analysts also use **raster data** to display features on the earth's surface. Raster data are an arrangement of grid cells or pixels that overlay the surface and are assigned attribute data (typically a numeric value). Raster files are typically used to store satellite images or remote-sensing pictures and are often displayed in color (Chainey & Ratcliffe, 2005; Hick, Bair, Fritz, & Helms, 2004). These images are often photographs taken from a satellite (see Figure 6.3) or an airplane and are placed within the appropriate coordinates. Satellite images are typically used in crime analysis along with vector data to show the details of streets, buildings, parking lots, and environmental features (landscaping). Other types of raster data files are used in crime analysis for density mapping, which is covered at the end of this chapter.

Table 6.3 Polygon Feature Attribute Data

Feature	District
Polygon	1
Polygon	2
Polygon	3
Polygon	4
Polygon	5

Figure 6.3 Satellite Photo Example

Source: Photo courtesy of the Chula Vista (California) Police Department.

Projections

When translating either vector or raster data into a GIS, it is necessary to make adjustments to the data files as they are incorporated into the software and used for analysis. These adjustments, called **projections**, are necessary because the earth is round, but a GIS depicts geographic data in a flat format. Unfortunately, the data from a round surface can never be perfectly displayed on a flat surface, so projections distort the surface in some way. Before conducting spatial analysis, the crime analyst selects the type of projection (e.g., cylindrical, planar, conic), depending on the size and location of the area of interest. (For more about projections, see Chainey & Ratcliffe, 2005, and Harries, 1999).

Coordinate Systems

Coordinate systems are at the heart of a GIS because these are the values that analysts use to locate data on a map. Latitude and longitude (also called *x-y coordinates*) are the universal reference system. They describe data in spherical terms that reflect the earth as being round and are expressed in degrees, minutes, and seconds. The State Plane Coordinate System is another system developed for greater user convenience. A grid is placed over the earth's surface, with coordinates expressed in meters, yards, or feet (Harries, 1999). The coordinate system that analysts use depends on the data and the purpose of the analysis. It is most important that when analysts use multiple data sources, the sources share the same coordinate system and projection (for more about coordinate systems, see Chainey and Ratcliffe, 2005, and Harries, 1999.)

Scale

Because maps are a miniature representation of the earth, a map's scale depicts how miniature a particular map actually is. **Scale** is expressed as a ratio of the map distance and the distance on the ground (for example 1:10,000 feet). Small-scale maps show large areas, and large-scale maps show small areas (Harries, 1999).

Getting Events on a Map

The most accurate and reliable way to locate events within a database on a map is the exact latitude and longitude coordinates of the event. Nearly all incidents that crime analysts need to map (i.e., crimes, calls for service, arrests, offender addresses, etc.) have a corresponding address. In current records management systems (RMS) and computer-aided dispatch (CAD) systems, the corresponding x and y coordinates are populated into the database when the address is entered using a GIS system. However, not all incidents happen at known addresses (e.g., parks or on vacant land), so in some cases, officers or detectives carry devices that can provide the coordinates on site. The use of the x and y coordinates allows the analyst to instantaneously put the events on the map.

However, there are instances when data may not have x and y coordinates associated with crime or calls-for-service incidents. When this happens, crime analysts must geocode the data by locating the events on the map based on the addresses. **Geocoding** is the process of linking an address with its map coordinates so that (a) the address can be displayed on a map, and (b) the GIS can recognize that address in the future. Most commonly, the address of a record (e.g., call for service, crime, or arrest) is geocoded to street segment data. Less often, data are geocoded by different levels of spatial precision, such as to the centroid (middle) of a zip code, beat, or grid. Fortunately, over the last decade or so, the need for crime analysts to geocode data has decreased as more and more CAD and RMS software automatically generates x and y coordinates. Although it is becoming less common, it is still important for the crime analyst to understand the geocoding process.

Geocoding is a five-step process in which the analyst prepares the geographic and tabular files, specifies the geocoding preferences, runs matches within the GIS, reviews the results, and respecifies parameters and begins the process again. Each of these steps is described briefly here:

> *Step 1: Preparing the geographic and police data files.* The analyst's task in this step includes making sure the addresses within the location variable of the database to be geocoded are accurate and consistent. To obtain accurate and complete geocoding results, the analyst must also ensure that geographic data (e.g., street segment file) are up-to-date and

accurate. This can be challenging in cities that are growing rapidly and undergoing changing street development.

Step 2: Specifying geocoding preferences. The analyst must determine and set the preferences for matching the reference data to the tabular data. Preferences include the spelling sensitivity of the matches (i.e., whether the police data street names and geographic street names are spelled exactly the same), address style (e.g., whether to match on "address only" or on "address and zip code"), and the acceptability of partial matches (i.e., whether to accept matches that are considered "close"). Geocoding produces a match score for each record that denotes how closely the address from the police data file matches the street segments in the geographic file, with a score of 100 signifying a perfect match.

Step 3: Matching within the GIS. Once the preferences are set, the analyst's next step is simply the push of a button. GIS software packages use a fairly simple method to accomplish the placement of an address along a street segment. Each street segment contains a range of addresses, and the GIS places the point along the segment relative to its value within the range. For example, an address of "200 E Main St" would be placed halfway along a street segment that ranges from 100 to 300 East Main Street (see Figure 6.4).

Step 4: Reviewing results. After the geocoding process is complete, GIS software programs generate statistics showing the numbers and percentages of addresses that were successfully matched, addresses that were partially matched (i.e., with scores lower than 100), and addresses that were not

Figure 6.4 Geocoding: Street Segment Matching

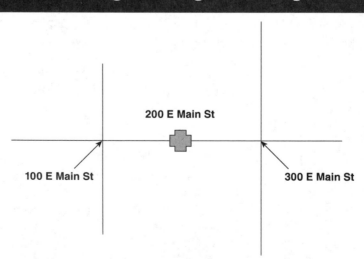

geocoded (matched) at all. The ideal **geocoding match rate** is 100%, which means that *all* records from the police data file were matched to the geographic file. Depending on the number of cases and the purpose of the analysis, a score of 95% may be acceptable, provided there is a legitimate reason why perfection was not reached (e.g., cases that were not matched occurred outside the jurisdiction) and the missing cases will not compromise the analysis results. Whenever geocoding match rates are lower than 100%, analysts should reexamine and correct the data and go through the geocoding process again.

Step 5: Respecifying parameters and geocoding again. Geocoding is a painstaking and often trying process, commonly requiring numerous adjustments and repetitions before a high enough match rate is achieved.

The geocoding method uses a mathematical model to locate each address within an address range (e.g., "100 E Main St" is located halfway between 0 and 200 East Main Street), but in reality, addresses do not occur proportionally along street segments. Some addresses take up entire blocks, whereas others share space on a block, with one address behind another. Thus, there is an accuracy issue with this method, which is why having coordinates is ideal and most police data systems are now producing them for each record.

INTERNATIONAL CRIME ANALYST PERSPECTIVE

Alyson Yaraskovitch

Crime Intelligence Analyst

Ottawa Police Service

Ottawa, ON, Canada

Certain types of crime often fall into geographic patterns; not only do multiple incidents sometimes reoccur over time within short distances of each other and at similar types of locations, but the offenders responsible for these crimes also tend to live within close proximity to their targeted area. At the Ottawa Police Service, it has been found, for example, that many theft from vehicle and residential break and enters are committed by offenders who live within a short distance of the incident. Also, many of these offenders are repeat offenders, who commit similar crimes even after being caught before. While this is of course not universally true, examining ongoing crime trends and attempting to identify known offenders who have committed similar crimes in the past and live near the trend's geographic location can often provide new investigative leads and persons of interest.

Ideally, this task would be completed by plotting the crime incident locations on a map and then adding another layer on top indicating the current home addresses

(Continued)

(Continued)

of known offenders for this offence type. Using different symbology to distinguish the crime from the known offenders, potential persons of interest are often almost immediately obvious.

Although this task may not seem particularly complex, the tools and record management system (RMS) available at the Ottawa Police Service made it impossible to directly extract offender addresses, though unloading incident x-y coordinates and other associated details was very simple. Using a work-around, a solution was discovered. RMS permitted the extraction of offender identities, addresses, and roles. By extracting the information for all entities associated with the relevant crime type (selecting only a single crime type at a time to avoid mixing different types of offenders together) within the past 3 years and removing the nonoffenders (witnesses, victims, guardians, etc.), the dataset could be imported into ArcGIS for geocoding. Because our RMS provides x-y information for crime incidents but not for the involved parties, the geolocator created by the city of Ottawa could be used instead to create a feature class using the address information unloaded as text from RMS. Using the Identify tool in ArcGIS, each offender address can be examined once plotted; the resulting pop-up window contains a variety of information, including the dates, details, and locations of that individual's past similar crimes. Therefore, the ability to link a potential person of interest to a crime trend goes beyond mere geographic proximity; the dataset attached to each point provides information that can further link offenders to crime trends based on MO. As our RMS system also updates offender addresses as they are changed, it is recommended that each offender database update is completed for the full date range, rather than just the new incidents committed since the time of the last update. Doing so ensures that offender addresses are as up-to-date as possible and also helps eliminate any offenders who are currently incarcerated and therefore could not be responsible for any ongoing trend.

Crime Mapping Techniques

Crime mapping is used in policing in many different ways. Chainey and Ratcliffe (2005, p. 4) outline some examples:

- Recording and mapping police activity
- Supporting the briefing of operational police officers by identifying crimes that have occurred recently
- Identifying crime problem areas or "hot spots" for implementing crime prevention responses
- Helping to effectively understand crime distribution along with other local data
- Monitoring the impact of crime prevention initiatives
- Communicating crime statistics to the public

Crime analysts take two distinct approaches to the spatial analysis of crime and disorder problems. In the first approach—called *descriptive mapping*—police data and statistics are displayed to show the results of analysis using geographic units of analysis. In the second approach—called *analytical mapping*—analysts use the exact locations of incidents to determine problem areas or clusters of activity. This chapter provides an overview of the various types of descriptive mapping and describes the methods in which statistics are used to classify data in descriptive maps. It ends by covering one type of analytical mapping—density mapping.

Types of Descriptive Crime Mapping

There are numerous types of descriptive crime mapping. Those covered here are used most frequently in crime analysis. They include single-symbol mapping, buffers, graduated mapping, chart mapping, and interactive Internet crime mapping.

Single-Symbol Mapping In **single-symbol maps**, individual, uniform symbols represent features such as the locations of stores, roads, or states. Figure 6.5 is an example of a single-symbol map showing homicide locations and streets.[1] An important thing to keep in mind about single-symbol maps is that a GIS places all points on such a map that share the same address directly on top of one another, making it impossible for the map to show how many points there really are. For example, in the map shown in Figure 6.5, if two homicides occur at the same location, the GIS will have placed two gray circles in the same spot, so there is no way someone looking at this map can see all the homicides. This drawback of single-symbol mapping is particularly relevant for the mapping of crime and other

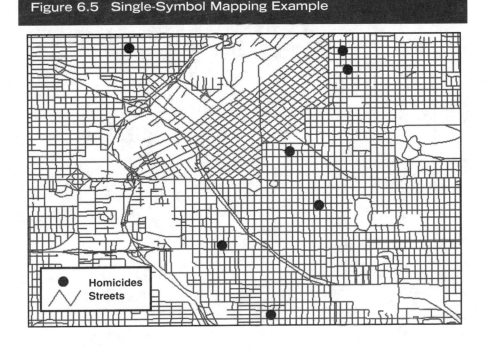

Figure 6.5 Single-Symbol Mapping Example

● Homicides
∧∕ Streets

police data because crime and other police-related incidents often occur repeatedly at particular locations. Thus, single-symbol maps also are not useful when analysts are dealing with large amounts of data. Imagine the map in Figure 6.5 with the locations of 100 different crimes marked. The points would overlap, and the map would be difficult to read.

Because of this, crime analysts use single-symbol mapping primarily to display small amounts of data as they are mapped for crime patterns and geographic information in which there is no overlap; they employ other types of maps to convey information about multiple incidents at particular locations.

Buffers A **buffer** is a specified area around a feature on a map. Buffers can be set at small distances, such as 50 feet, or larger distances, such as 500 miles, depending on the purpose and scale of the map. Buffers help in crime analysis by illustrating the relative distances between features on a map. The example map in Figure 6.6 shows an elementary school (polygon feature) with a 1,000-feet buffer and one subject stop within in the area. The map can be used to determine where and how many stops or other types of activity (e.g., arrests, calls, crimes) were made in and within 1,000 feet of the school.

Graduated Mapping Crime analysts often use **graduated maps**—that is, maps in which different sizes or colors of features represent particular values of variables. Figures 6.7 and 6.8 are general examples of graduated-size and graduated-color

Figure 6.6 Buffer Map Example

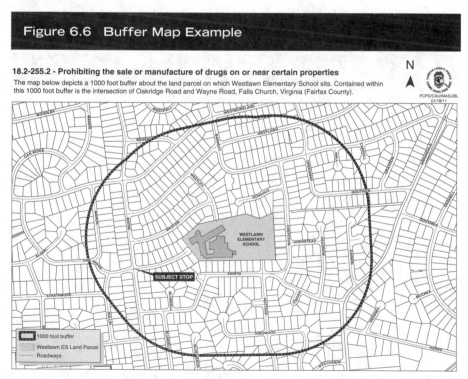

18.2-255.2 - Prohibiting the sale or manufacture of drugs on or near certain properties
The map below depicts a 1000 foot buffer about the land parcel on which Westlawn Elementary School sits. Contained within this 1000 foot buffer is the intersection of Oakridge Road and Wayne Road, Falls Church, Virginia (Fairfax County).

Source: Fairfax County (Virginia) Police Department, Jessica LaBlanc.

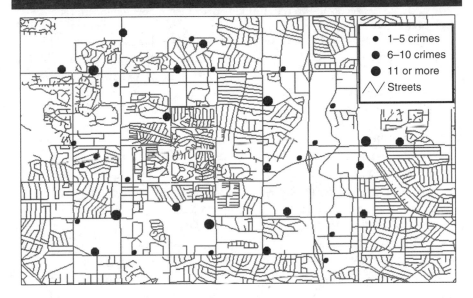

Figure 6.7 Graduated-Size Map Example

Legend:
- 1–5 crimes
- 6–10 crimes
- 11 or more
- Streets

maps, respectively. In a graduated-size map, the sizes of the symbols used for point and line features reflect their value (typically, how many incidents occurred at that address or on that street). As previously noted, single-symbol maps are not appropriate for displaying data about crimes that occur at the same locations repeatedly. Analysts use graduated-size maps for this purpose because these maps can account for multiple incidents at the same locations. However, like

Figure 6.8 Graduated-Color Map Example

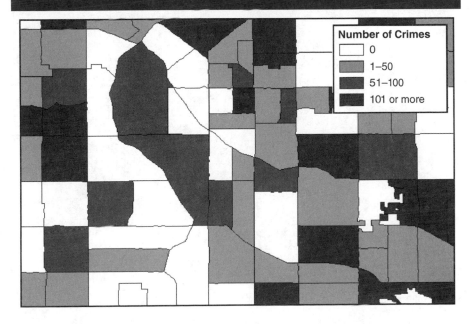

Number of Crimes
- 0
- 1–50
- 51–100
- 101 or more

single-symbol maps, graduated-size maps are subject to overlapping points if too many data points are analyzed at once. Figure 6.7 is a map in which points are graduated by size, according to the numbers of crimes at specific locations.

In a graduated-color map, the colors of the symbols reflect their values; this kind of mapping can be used with points (in a single-symbol map only),[2] lines, and polygons. Figure 6.8 is a map that uses colors to show the total numbers of crimes in particular areas—the lighter-shaded areas are those with fewer crimes, and the darker-shaded areas are those with more crimes.

Chart Mapping **Chart mapping** allows the crime analyst to display several values within a particular variable at the same time (e.g., variable = crime, values = robbery, assault, and rape). There are two types of chart mapping: pie and bar. In **pie chart mapping,** the relative percentages (represented by slices of a pie) of values within a variable are displayed. Figure 6.9 is an example of a pie chart map that depicts the Part I crime breakdown for each beat zone. The pies are placed in the middle of the zone to represent the data for that zone. The sizes of the pies are graduated to depict the total amount of crime, and the slices reflect the percentage of the type of crime. In **bar chart mapping,** the relative frequencies of values within a variable are displayed, but instead of percentages, the heights of the bars show the relative frequencies of incidents.

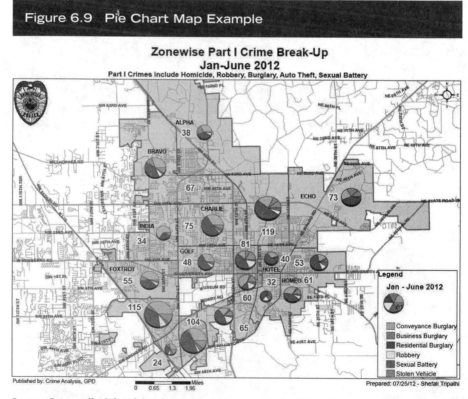

Figure 6.9 Pie Chart Map Example

Source: Gainesville (Florida) Police Department, Dr. Shefali Tripathi

Interactive Crime Mapping Rather than a type of mapping, the term **interactive crime mapping** refers to simplified geographic information systems made available to novice users over the Internet. Instead of simply posting analysis results, many police agencies are moving toward providing audiences with the ability to conduct analyses themselves through interactive crime mapping systems. Website visitors use these systems to search databases for the information that interests them and to map the results. This type of format gives audiences more flexibility in the information they can obtain and also reduces the amount of work for department personnel.

It has become more common in recent years for police departments to develop business partnerships with online companies to provide their citizens an interactive crime mapping service. Police agencies provide their crime data and pay a fee to these companies that have developed interactive crime mapping software and provide the service to the public. This relationship saves police agencies from having to develop and continually update the software themselves.

Currently, most interactive crime mapping websites are using single-symbol mapping for this purpose, but a few use graduated-color maps of areas and density mapping. Still other websites provide interactive features that give website visitors the same querying capabilities as mapping systems but provide the resulting information in the form of lists of cases or summary reports instead of maps. Doing a search on the Internet will reveal a large number of interactive crime mapping sites on both police and private websites. However, these applications typically are not flexible or sophisticated enough to be useful to crime analysts. There is another issue with these websites, which is the users' levels of knowledge of crime data and mapping. As this book makes clear, crime analysis and crime mapping are complex fields of study; thus, the possibility exists that novice users of Internet crime mapping systems might misuse or misinterpret the data they find and the maps they produce.

Methods for Descriptive Crime Mapping

One type of descriptive mapping is thematic (also called *choropleth*) mapping, which is a common technique for representing data summarized by statistical or administrative areas and is particularly useful for obtaining a general picture of the overall spatial distribution of crime (Eck, Chainey, Cameron, Leitner, & Wilson, 2005). This section describes the statistical techniques that crime analysts use to produce graduated-symbol and graduated-color maps, including categorical, statistical, and manual methods. There are many ways to display data geographically, and it is important that analysts select the methods that are most appropriate to the data and the purposes of their analyses.

By Category Data can be broken down by category and displayed on a map either as different types of symbols or as symbols in different colors or degrees of shading. Crime analysts use this method primarily for categorical variables because the values of such variables are nominal rather than numeric. Some examples of categorical variables are race, sex, method of entry, point of entry, weapon used, type of location, type of business, and land use. In this method, the values within each of the variables (e.g., male and female for the sex variable) are illustrated differently.

Shading by categorical value is used only with single-symbol maps and primarily with polygon and point features. Categorical mapping cannot be used with graduated-size maps because it requires that each point be shaded according to one categorical value. For example, if two robberies have occurred at one location, a graduated-size map would represent that location with a larger point than the points used for addresses with one robbery. One cannot then shade that point by weapon used during the robbery because different types of weapons may have been used in the two robberies represented by that single point (e.g., one robbery was committed with a knife and the other with a gun).

Figure 6.10 is a map that was created for an analysis of a robbery. The areas are shaded to indicate whether they contain any interstate highways because an interstate provides an offender with a quick way to flee the scene of a robbery. The categorical variable mapped here is: Is there an interstate in the area? The values that dictate the different colors are "yes" (an interstate

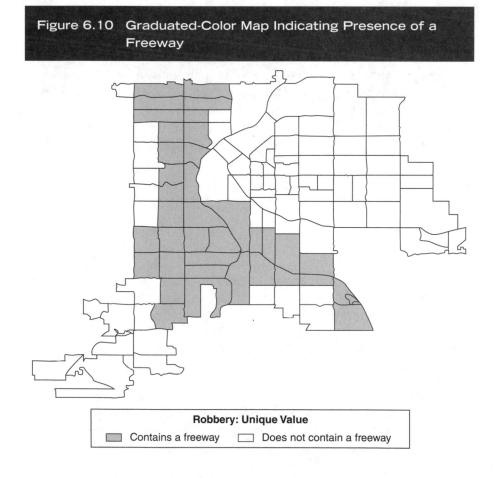

Figure 6.10   Graduated-Color Map Indicating Presence of a Freeway

Robbery: Unique Value

Contains a freeway   Does not contain a freeway

is present) and "no" (no interstate is present). An analyst might use this map with a graduated-symbol map of robberies to determine whether more robberies occurred in areas that contain an interstate. The example map in Figure 6.11 uses different symbols (instead of shading) for different types of businesses. An analyst could use this map in an analysis of robbery to help distinguish among locations regarding their susceptibility to robberies.

By Statistical Classification A statistical classification used in mapping is a formula that determines the break points of how the data will be shaded or sized (information about break points is displayed in a map's **legend**). The features on a map are distinguished from one another depending on the classifications into which their values fall. For example, the colors used to symbolize ranges may be broken down as follows:

- White: No crimes
- Light gray: 1 to 10 crimes
- Dark gray: 11 to 20 crimes
- Black: 21 to 30 crimes

In a map using these categories, an area feature, such as a police beat, with 15 crimes would be shaded dark gray. It is recommended to use no more than six classes or shadings in a thematic map (Harries, 1999). Four statistical classifications are typically used in crime mapping: natural breaks, equal

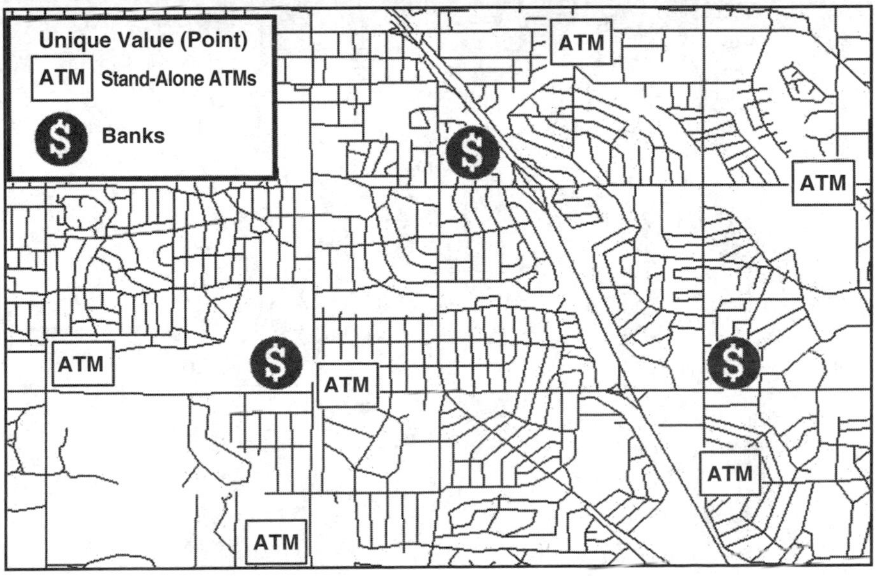

Figure 6.11   Unique-Symbol Map Indicating Banks or Stand-Alone ATMs

interval, quantile, and standard deviation. Analysts use these classifications for different purposes.

An analyst applying the **natural breaks classification** uses GIS software to identify the natural gaps in the distribution of the data; these gaps act as break points for the classifications in the legend. This type of classification is the default in many GIS programs and is one of the types used most frequently in crime analysis. It is most useful for exploratory or descriptive analysis of a snapshot of data (e.g., a general map of a problem) and is not applicable for making comparisons over time.

Figures 6.12, 6.13, and 6.14 are point, line, and polygon maps that illustrate the natural breaks classification. Note that the values of the categories in the map legends seem arbitrary, with intervals that are not equal. That is because the ranges have been decided by the GIS based on break points in the distributions of the data being mapped.

The graduated-size point map in Figure 6.12 depicts robberies at individual addresses using three categories. The natural breaks in the data set are between 1 and 4, 5 and 9, and 10 and 13 robberies at a single address. Table 6.4 displays several of the addresses and their counts of robberies to show the data that were used to create this map.

The graduated-size line map in Figure 6.13 depicts the number of robberies along the street segments in a specific area (listed in Table 6.4) in three

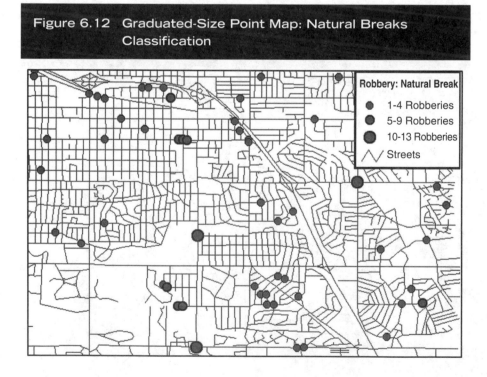

Figure 6.12   Graduated-Size Point Map: Natural Breaks Classification

Table 6.4 Number of Robberies by Address

Address	Number of Robberies
4980 E Main St	3
3920 S Clover Rd	10
930 S Bridge St	9
4500 N River Rd	4
3952 S Thompson St	0
230 S Bridge St	5
4560 N River Rd	1
465 S Bridge St	8
1520 S Bridge St	12

categories. The natural breaks in these data are between 1 and 7, 8 and 10, and 11 and 24 robberies per street segment. The graduated-color polygon map in Figure 6.14 shows the number of robberies per geographic area. These three map legends are different because the data have been summed differently (e.g., by address, by street segment, and by area), which causes the gaps in the data distributions to be different.

Figure 6.13 Graduated-Size Line Map: Natural-Breaks Classification

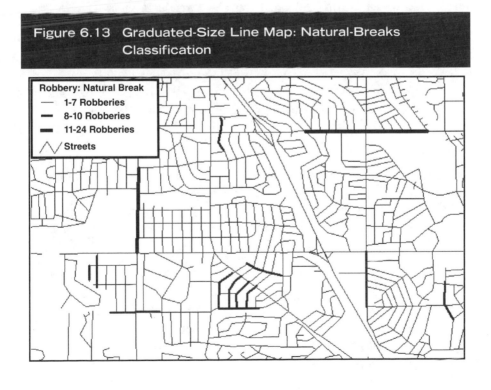

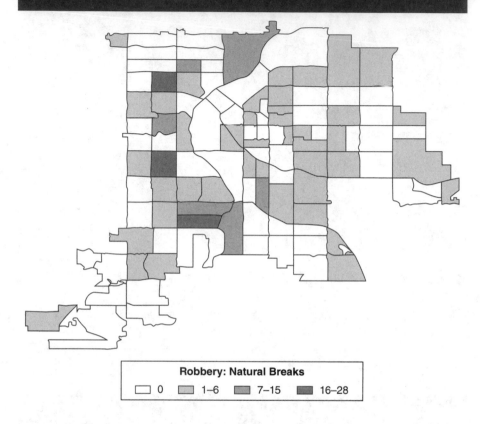

Figure 6.14 Graduated-Color Polygon Map: Natural-Breaks Classification

Robbery: Natural Breaks

☐ 0   ▢ 1–6   ▨ 7–15   ▩ 16–28

In the following discussions of the remaining types of classifications, only polygon maps are used to illustrate statistical formulas, but all of these classifications can be used to create graduated-size or graduated-color point and line maps as well. The following examples use the same data set as that used in the natural breaks example to show how the same data can be displayed differently, depending on the classifications employed by the analyst.

To arrive at an **equal interval classification,** the analyst uses a GIS to apply a statistical formula that divides the difference between the highest and lowest value into equal-sized ranges. In Figure 6.15, the lowest value of robberies per area is 0 and the highest is 28; four categories were selected, and each range is 7, which is 28 divided by 4 (e.g., 0–7, 8–14).

The equal interval classification yields different results depending on the values of the data (e.g., values ranging from 0 to 80 with four categories would be divided into 0–20, 21–40, and so on). This type of map is best suited for data in which there are similar numbers of incidents in all classes. Crime analysts typically use this classification in combination with other maps to get a sense of the nature of the problems they are examining. However, they do not usually

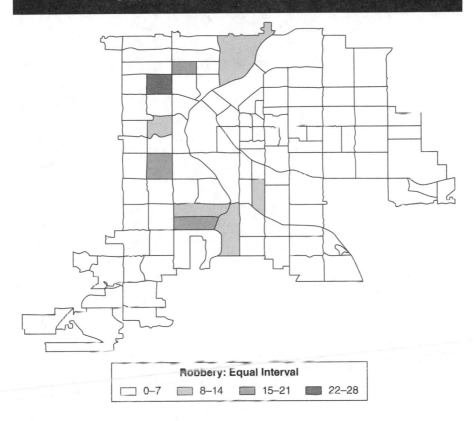

Figure 6.15 Graduated-Color Polygon Map: Equal-Interval Classification

Robbery: Equal Interval

□ 0–7   ▨ 8–14   ▨ 15–21   ▨ 22–28

disseminate such maps to police because most crime analysis data distributions are skewed (i.e., notice all the white areas in Figure 6.15), and this classification does not typically yield results that are useful for police purposes.

An analyst produces a quantile map by dividing the number of records in the database by the number of categories (selected by the user), which results in categories with equal numbers of records. Whereas other classifications are based on values in the selected variable to be mapped, **quantile classification** is first concerned with the number of records in the database and then with the values within the selected variable.

The following example illustrates the method that generates the quantile classification categories. Table 6.5 contains 20 records with areas (polygons) and number of robberies. In a quantile map with four categories created from these data, each range would include 5 cases because there are 20 cases total (20/4 = 5). To determine the break points, the GIS software sorts the data by number of robberies (ascending), with the first five cases representing the first range and so on. The sorted data are shown in Table 6.6. The break points for the four categories are 0, 1 to 2 robberies, 3 to 5 robberies, and 6 to 28

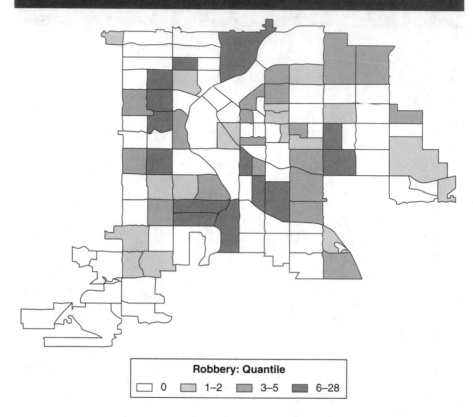

Figure 6.16   Graduated-Color Polygon Map: Quantile Classification

Robbery: Quantile

☐ 0   ▦ 1–2   ▦ 3–5   ■ 6–28

robberies (shown in Table 6.6 in gray). Geographic units in the four categories are shaded different colors, with each color representing 25% of the total number of records. Figure 6.16 is a quantile map with four categories. The break points come from the values of the first, second, third, and fourth 25% of the cases.

Crime analysts most often use quantile maps to make comparisons between data sets with very different values. For example, an analyst might use two quantile maps to compare robberies and burglaries in 1 year by area. Because there are significantly fewer robberies than burglaries, the values of the categories would be much different in the maps' legends. Using quantile maps enables the analyst to identify and compare areas within the highest 25% (using four ranges) for both types no matter the actual frequencies, and it allows the analyst to see whether the areas highest in burglaries were also the highest in robberies.

When using the **standard deviation classification**, an analyst uses mean (i.e., average) and standard deviation of the selected variable to determine the break points of the categories, which are shown in the legend not as whole numbers but as standard deviations (e.g., +1, −1 standard deviation from the

Table 6.5 Number of Robberies by Area (Polygon)		Table 6.6 Number of Robberies by Area, Sorted in Ascending Frequency to Determine Quantiles	
Area	Number of Robberies	Area	Number of Robberies
1	6	2	0
2	0	5	0
3	0	6	0
4	2	18	0
5	0	3	0
6	0	16	1
7	5	19	1
8	15	17	2
9	2	4	2
10	3	9	2
11	4	10	3
12	3	12	3
13	22	11	4
14	23	15	5
15	5	7	5
16	1	1	6
17	2	8	15
18	0	13	22
19	1	14	23
20	28	20	28

mean). For the map in Figure 6.17, the GIS determines the mean number of robberies in the polygons by adding the number of robberies in the polygons and dividing the total by the number of polygons. The GIS then computes the standard deviation of the distribution and adds and subtracts it from the mean to determine the break points of each category. This type of map is most useful for determining polygons, points, or lines that are outliers (+/− 3 standard deviations from the mean) and for comparing the outliers of one database to those of another (similar to quantile). That is, for each data set, the polygons that have values significantly higher or lower than the mean are shaded a particular color. Because the standard deviation is a standardized measurement and provides the same measures relative to the distribution of a specific variable, the analyst can compare unlike distributions across different maps. Note that in such maps usually no area is shaded the color of the mean value because

Figure 6.17   Graduated-Color Polygon Map: Standard-Deviation
Classification

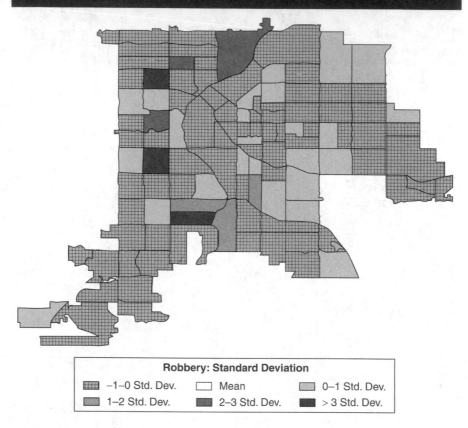

Robbery: Standard Deviation

▦ −1–0 Std. Dev.	☐ Mean	▨ 0–1 Std. Dev.
▨ 1–2 Std. Dev.	▨ 2–3 Std. Dev.	■ > 3 Std. Dev.

the mean is often not a value that exists in the data distribution, For example, a mean of 4.57 robberies does not exist in reality (i.e., there can be four or five robberies but not 4.57), so none of the areas would be shaded this color.

By Manual Method The last type of graduated map is a "custom" map; that is, in a map created using **manual method classification,** the ranges displayed in the legend are *not* determined by the values of a variable or a statistical formula but by the creator of the map. Crime analysts often use custom ranges to compare multiple maps with the same type of data over time, such as to analyze monthly robbery maps in which the same colors represent the same ranges. A comparison of actual values of the variable mapped cannot be done using any of the other classifications discussed so far because the colors represent different ranges each time the data changed in those classifications. Figures 6.18 and 6.19 are examples of two maps with the same custom legends that allow the analyst to compare differences in robbery by area in two time periods (i.e., January and February of the same year). Notice that in these maps the label for the fourth category does not have an upper value; instead, it reads *or more*. Analysts create such categories when

Figure 6.18 Graduated-Color Polygon Map: Custom Classification (January)

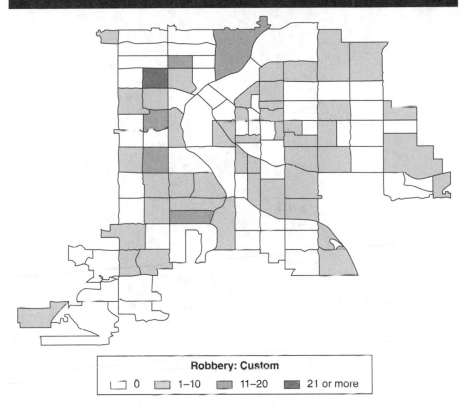

Robbery: Custom

☐ 0   ▨ 1–10   ▨ 11–20   ▨ 21 or more

they use the same legend for more than one map because the upper limit might be different for each data set. In most cases, the break points in custom legends fall on 5s, 10s, 25s, 50s, 100s, and so on.

Choosing the classification that will set the break points in the legend is an important element in creating a map, and crime analysts do not choose classifications haphazardly; rather, they base their decisions on their examination of the data and the planned purposes of the maps. In making these decisions, they often consider local laws, agency policies, and the context of the problem being studied. For example, an analyst who is creating a map to show the number of burglar alarms at specific locations in a city might select as the highest range "5 or more" if the city assesses fines to locations that have five or more alarms in a particular time period.

Classification Guidelines and Summary All of the maps presented thus far in this chapter have used frequency of robberies to illustrate the different classifications. However, analysts can map many statistics other than frequency—such as rates, means, and percentages (see Chapter 12)—and

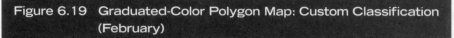
Figure 6.19 Graduated-Color Polygon Map: Custom Classification (February)

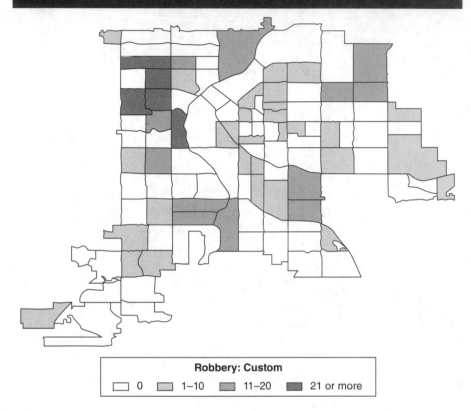

Robbery: Custom

☐ 0   ☐ 1–10   ▨ 11–20   ■ 21 or more

such maps may be more relevant to the issue at hand than frequency. Crime analysts should keep the following guidelines in mind when creating maps to describe data:

- In deciding which classification and how many categories to use, the analyst should first determine the purpose and audience of the map.

- Decisions regarding how a map should be made are part of the analysis process; the analyst should not rely on the default settings of a GIS program.

- With the exception of the custom or manual method classification, all of the classification methods are dependent on the data; that is, the ranges in the legend will differ from data set to data set, depending on the distributions and values within the data.

- When describing data using these classifications, the analyst should experiment with the classifications and the number of categories as well as with different statistics (e.g., rate vs. frequency). Often, comparisons among the different maps can provide insight into and promote understanding of a problem.

- The analyst should be aware that shading an entire area based on the aggregate number of events can give readers of the map the impression that the activity is occurring equally across the area, when in fact it may not be.

- When creating area maps, the analyst should not draw conclusions based on the area about individuals or particular locations within that area (i.e., ecological fallacy).

Table 6.7 provides a summary of mapping classification methods and some examples of their use.

Table 6.7 Summary of Mapping Classifications						
	Unique Value	Natural Breaks	Equal Interval	Quantile	Standard Deviation	Custom
Type of variable needed	Categorical	Numeric	Numeric	Numeric	Numeric	Any
Type of feature point (point, line, polygon)	All	All	All	All	All (typically polygon)	All
Ranges dictated by	Values of the variable	Data set	Data set	Data set	Data set	Crime analyist
How often used in strategic crime analysis	Often	Very often	Seldom	Seldom	Often	Very often
Practical example of use	Shading banks by whether they have drive-up ATMs	Mapping robberies for the past month using graduated symbols	Mapping the number of robberies per area to understand the skewed distribution	Comparing levels of bank robbery to levels of convenience store robbery	Determining areas with unusually high numbers of robberies	Comparing levels of robbery on a monthly basis

Analytical Mapping: Density Mapping

In analytical mapping, crime analysts use the exact coordinates of incidents to determine clusters of incidents and concentrations of crime and disorder. There are many ways of examining clusters and concentrations of crime, but the most common in crime analysis is density mapping. The technique is explained here, but its practical application is discussed in Chapter 14. Unlike the mapping techniques discussed thus far, density mapping does not limit the analyst to examination of predetermined areas (e.g., polygons), lines, or points; rather, the density results show how the incidents cluster and concentrate across space. Crime analysts use standard GIS packages as well as specialized software to create density maps. This section includes only a general discussion and examples of the technique of creating density maps; however, there are various statistics and techniques that are used. (For a more detailed discussion, see the GIS software manual or an analytical mapping textbook.)

The process of creating a simple density map includes the following components:

1. An arbitrary grid is placed over the study area. The analyst selects the size of the grid; however, in this type of map the size tends to be very small to approximate the immediate area of an incident location (i.e., the size used is typically between 50 and 100 feet).

2. A density "score" for each cell is derived as follows: The software searches a predetermined (by the map creator) radius around each cell (the **search radius**), counts the number of incidents within that radius, and divides that count by the size of the search area.

3. The cells are shaded according to their resulting scores. Thus, a cell's score does not represent the number of incidents in that cell but the number of incidents "near" that cell divided by the area "around" that cell, approximating the concentration of activity. In other words, a cell may not contain any incidents at all but have a high score because it is surrounded by areas in which incidents have occurred. This is also how continuous shading is produced.

4. The legend for the map is created. Most GIS software programs default to an equal interval classification. The legend does not illustrate "real" counts of events; rather, it provides a ratio of events in an area by the size of the area (e.g., the number of incidents per square mile).

With changes in cell size and the radius of the search distance, the same data can produce visually different density maps. For example, Figures 6.20 and 6.21 show the same data with a cell size of 50 feet but with search radii of 0.5 miles and 2 miles, respectively. This method is not limited by geographic areas and is suitable for examining large amounts of data. Analysts need to keep the following issues in mind when they use density mapping:

- Because density maps show crime locations as a continuous surface, they may give the impression that crimes have occurred in places where they actually have not occurred (Groff & La Vigne, 2002). In other words, the shading approximates areas that have high concentrations of crime, not the exact number and location of the crimes.

- Changes in cell sizes and search distances can result in very different maps. A general rule in crime analysis is to keep the grid cell size to about 50 to 100 feet (the approximate size of where a crime or call for service might occur) and adjust the search radius according to the scale of the study area.

- The legends can be confusing to those who are unfamiliar with density maps, and in practice, many crime analysts use legends with labels such as *low density*, *medium density*, and *high density* instead of ranges of numbers. However, such categories are not useful for comparison of different databases (e.g., the same type of data for different time periods or different types of data for the same time period). For example, if a map of 500 simple assaults is compared with a map of 50 aggravated assaults and the maps have categorical legends, both maps may appear to show the same level of crimes because the colors and the values are the same. In contrast, if the legends show actual values, it will be clear that simple assault occurs at a much higher rate per square mile. Thus, for purposes of comparing similar data, "custom" legends should be used. It is also recommended that if *low*, *medium*, and *high* density labels are used that the values also be included in the legend, so users can compare legends across maps.

- Density maps have an inherent border bias because cells that are close to the edges of the study area may not have the potential for incidents to occur.

Figure 6.20   Density Map: Search Radius 0.5 Miles

Source: Shawnee (Kansas) Police Department, Doug Hemsath.

Figure 6.21   Density Map: Search Radius 2 Miles

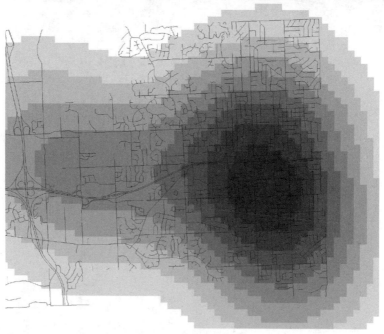

Source: Shawnee (Kansas) Police Department, Doug Hemsath.

SUMMARY POINTS

This chapter provides an overview of geographic data and descriptive crime mapping. The following are the key points addressed in this chapter:

- A GIS uses three types of features to represent objects and locations in the real world; these are vector data for which the basic units of spatial information are points, lines, and polygons.

- A point feature is a discrete location that is usually depicted on a GIS-generated map by a symbol or label.

- A line feature is a real-world element that can be represented on a map by a line or set of lines.

- A polygon feature is a geographic area represented on a map by a multisided figure with a closed set of lines.

- Raster data are an arrangement of grid cells or pixels that overlay the surface and are assigned attribute data (typically a numeric value). Raster files are typically used to store satellite images or remote sensing pictures and are often displayed in color.

- When translating either vector or raster data into the GIS, it is necessary to make adjustments to the data files as they are incorporated into the software and used for analysis. These adjustments are called projections and are necessary because the earth is round, but a GIS depicts geographic data in a flat format.

- Coordinate systems are at the heart of a GIS because these are the values used to locate data on a map. Latitude and longitude (also called x-y coordinates) are the universal reference system. The State Plane Coordinate System is another system developed for greater user convenience.

- Because maps are a miniature representation of the earth, the scale of a map depicts how miniature a particular map actually is. Scale is expressed as a ratio of the map distance and the distance on the ground.

- Geocoding is a five-step process that is used to bring tabular and geographic data together for mapping. The steps are as follows: (a) preparing the geographic and tabular files for geocoding, (b) specifying the geocoding preferences, (c) matching within the GIS, (d) reviewing results, and (e) respecifying parameters and geocoding again.

- Two other ways of locating tabular data on maps are matching records to parcel data and using latitude and longitude. These methods are both improvements over geocoding but are more difficult to conduct.

- In single-symbol maps, individual uniform symbols represent features.

- Buffers are areas that represent specified proximate zones around features on a map.

- In graduated maps, the sizes or colors of features represent the values of the variables.

- Chart maps, which can use either pie or bar charts, allow the illustration of several values within a particular variable.

- The term *interactive crime mapping* does not refer to a type of mapping; rather, it refers to simplified geographic information systems made available to novice users over the Internet.

- Crime analysts take two distinct approaches to the spatial analysis of crime and disorder problems: descriptive and analytical mapping.

- Crime analysts use categorical, statistical, and manual methods in displaying data and statistics in graduated-size and graduated-color maps.

- In the categorical method, different shading or different symbols are used to represent features (e.g., points, lines, and polygons) by unique values of a categorical variable.

- In the statistical method, points, lines, and polygons are shaded or graduated according to one of four formulas: natural breaks, equal interval, quantile, and standard deviation.

- In the natural breaks classification, a statistical formula is used to identify the natural break points inherent in the data. Crime analysts often use this classification in their initial examinations of problems.

- In the equal interval classification, a statistical formula is used to divide the difference between the highest and lowest value into equal-sized ranges. This method is best suited to a uniform distribution, where there are similar numbers of incidents in all classes.

- To produce a quantile map, the GIS divides the number of records in the database by the number of categories (selected by the user), which results in categories with equal numbers of records. Whereas other classifications are based on values in the selected variable to be mapped, quantile maps are first concerned with the number of records in the database and then with the values within the selected variable.

- In the standard deviation classification, mean and standard deviation of the selected variable are used to determine the break points of the categories, which are shown in the legend not as whole numbers but as standard deviations.

- In the manual method, the creator of the map (which is called a custom map) determines the legend. Crime analysts often use custom classifications to compare the same type of data over time, such as analyzing robbery by area each month.

- Crime analysts need to be aware of the following issues when using the descriptive methods described in this chapter: (a) For categorical and statistical classifications, break points are determined based on the uniqueness of the database and are not comparable; (b) in mapping, using different numbers of categories can yield different results; (c) analysis should include experimentation with a variety of classifications; (d) decisions about how maps are made should not rely on the default settings of GIS software; (e) a polygon map may give the impression that incidents are occurring equally across the area when in fact they might be clustered or located along a particular street; (f) one cannot draw conclusions about individual incidents based on analysis of incidents by area

- In density mapping, crime analysts use the exact coordinates of incidents to determine concentrations of incidents that are not limited to predetermined areas.

- The process of creating a density map includes the following: (a) placing an arbitrary grid over the study area; (b) computing a density "score" for each cell; (c) shading the cells according to their resulting scores; and (d) using colors to depict not the "real" counts of crime, but the ratio of incidents within an area (e.g., the number of incidents per square mile).

- Crime analysts need to be aware of the following issues when using density mapping: (a) They may give the impression that crimes have occurred in places where they actually have not occurred, (b) changes in cell sizes and search distances can result in very different maps, (c) the legends can be confusing, and (d) density maps have an inherent border bias because cells that are close to the edges of the study area may not have the potential for incidents to occur.

DISCUSSION EXERCISES*

Exercise 1

You are asked by the chief of police to create a map of residential burglary over the past year to indicate the areas with the highest risk for burglaries. First, what type of tabular data would you use to create the map? Second, what type of map, and if relevant, what classification would you create, and why that one? Third, is there a second type of map that could also be appropriate?

Exercise 2

As part of an evaluation of a program to reduce commercial burglary, you are asked to prepare two maps, comparing the data on commercial burglaries for a set period before the program's implementation with data for the same amount of time after the program's completion. What type(s) of maps and subsequent classification(s) would you use in your two maps to enhance the comparison of these time periods? Why?

Exercise 3

Identify two interactive web mapping sites that map crime, and compare and contrast how the data are presented and how easy they are to use. Point out three strengths and weaknesses of each site.

NOTES

1. The maps presented in this chapter are not "final" maps—that is, they are not complete maps that would be suitable for distribution to particular audiences. Rather, these maps are intended only to illustrate particular types of maps or techniques.

2. Graduated color and graduated size cannot both be displayed using the same points on a map. For example, if two robberies occurred at one location, the point for that location would be larger in size than the points where only single robberies occurred. One cannot then shade that point to show, for example, that two different types of weapons were used in the robberies (one a gun and the other a knife).

Crime Analysis Purpose and Audience

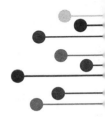

As discussed in Chapter 3, stratified policing creates a structure in which different types of crime analysis products are stratified by problem type and rank. This is vital because with the wealth of data and information that can be provided, crime analysis must be focused and prioritized so that police personnel aren't overwhelmed and are provided crime analysis results that are relevant to the problem at hand, their daily activities, and their job responsibilities. Therefore, before we cover the specific data, methodology, and techniques of the specific types of crime analysis (i.e., tactical, strategic, and administrative), this chapter discusses how the results of crime analysis processes differ by type of problem, purpose, and audience in order to provide an overview of the many different uses of crime analysis by police. A typology of crime analysis results is presented in this chapter, and at the end, practical examples are used to illustrate how these results are used in a variety of contexts. Subsequently, the rest of the book covers the specific data, methodology, and techniques that are used by crime analysts to produce the various results for tactical, strategic, and administrative crime analysis.

Crime Analysis Purpose

To review from Chapter 3, problems can be categorized by their temporal nature and complexity. That is, simpler problems, such as isolated incidents, are typically manifested over a very short period of time, whereas more complex problems, such as problem locations, develop over a longer period of time. In this book, they are broken down into these categories: (1) immediate problems, (2) short-term problems, and (3) long-term problems. Within each problem category, crime analysis results are created to be used for different purposes by different audiences. This first section presents a discussion of the two distinct purposes of results produced through crime analysis—to facilitate **situational awareness** and to guide crime reduction strategies. The section following discusses the different types of audiences.

Situational Awareness

In the policing context, **situational awareness** is the development of a perception of the environment in which an officer works, no matter the rank. To fulfill this purpose, crime analysts produce "information" for police personnel about crime and other activity to provide context about when and where these personnel work on a day-to-day basis. **Information** refers to knowledge that is communicated about a particular fact or circumstance, and **crime analysis information** results simply provide details about individual incidents (e.g., crime, calls for service, arrests, traffic crashes) or aggregate counts of incidents by different time periods (e.g., 1 week or month for short-term problems; 1 or 5 years for long-term problems). For example, crime analysis information results include a list of calls at an address over several days, a list or map of all offenders on parole living in a particular area, or the counts of crime by geographic areas over a year.

Importantly, crime analysis information results are created to simply report facts but *do not present conclusions* about what the facts mean, how they are related to other issues, or why they are occurring. Thus, information results do not guide or lead to specific police responses but are examined by personnel who must make conclusions for action themselves. For example, crime analysis information results depicted in a map and a list of current prisoner releases is provided to a robbery detective looking for suspects for a particular robbery he or she is investigating. The list contains all prisoner releases, so the detective must examine the information and identify a specific parolee who might have committed the robbery after looking at the parolee's crimes, location of residence, and physical description, among other things. Consequently, the list of prisoner releases simply relays facts about all the parolees that the detective then has to conduct analysis on while making conclusions to identify a potential lead from the list.

Crime Reduction

The second purpose of crime analysis results is to assist police with their crime reduction efforts, which means that crime analysis results are created with the intention of guiding police in implementing specific strategies for crime reduction. To create crime analysis results for this purpose, essential characteristics of factual information are examined (i.e., analyzed) by the crime analyst, and *conclusions are made* about the relationships that exist among the facts. In the police context, crime reduction analysis results distinguish and prioritize the elements of the information that have been examined and determine whether potential relationships exist with the purpose of directing police crime reduction strategies. Thus, these results are "action oriented" in that examination is not required by police personnel, but the results themselves lead police to a range of possible strategies that can be implemented. For example, six recent residential burglaries have been linked together by an analyst because entry in each case was made through the rear slider within a two-block area, during the day. These results are used to direct officers to patrol and make field contacts in the pattern area, to disperse crime prevention flyers to residents in the two-block area, and to dispatch undercover crime suppression units in that area during the time of the pattern.

Contrasting the Purposes of Crime Analysis Results

Although it may appear that situational awareness and crime reduction crime analysis results are similar because the data on which they are based are the same, the important differentiation is the process by which they are developed. That is, results for situational awareness typically require a simple search of a database, and the creation of a list or a map. The results for guiding crime reduction require the identification of relationships among the different facts by an analyst. Importantly, the systematic use of both types of results is important for police agencies to be effective in crime reduction. Officers, sergeants, managers, and commanders need information to help them understand the environment in which they work as well as analysis results to prioritize and direct specific crime reduction strategies. The following are several more examples of crime analysis results created for situational awareness and crime reduction to highlight their differences:

Situational Awareness Analysis Results

- List or map of all juveniles currently on probation in the jurisdiction
- List of all calls for service at a particular address over several months
- List of all burglaries occurring in a beat over 1 week
- Counts of all crime by crime type for the past 6 months
- Map of areas with the most Part I crime over 2 years

Crime Reduction Analysis Results

- A list or map of the 10 most serious violent juvenile offenders on probation
- A list of addresses with five or more false burglar alarm calls for service in the last 3 months
- Six convenience store robberies thought to be committed by the same suspect
- Ten apartment complexes that have the highest number of loud parties, fights, or public intoxication over 6 months
- A map showing areas in which a specific type of crime has increased or decreased before and after a particular police strategy was implemented

Importantly, results for these two purposes are typically created and published somewhat differently by crime analysts. Although this is not an exclusive difference, information produced for situational awareness is typically automated, and the results illustrate exhaustive lists of what is contained in the data (e.g., all prison releases, counts of all UCR Part I crime). This is oftentimes why information results can be and are produced by agencies without crime analysts or by personnel not designated by analysts. On the other hand, analysis produced for crime reduction is typically created by analysts who, through a systematic process, exclude extraneous information as well as unnecessary details, make conclusions, and create a product in a specific format, containing specific information. Albeit, some analysis results for crime reduction can be automated. In these cases, the important analytical decisions are made before automation so that the output is an analytical product (i.e., provides conclusions, not simply facts). The product ensures the results have been prioritized to guide police strategies.

INTERNATIONAL CRIME ANALYST PERSPECTIVE

Credit to:

Mattis Michaelsen

Law Enforcement Analyst

Oslo Police District

Oslo, Norway

As part of the knowledge base necessary for drawing new boundaries between station areas in the Oslo Police District, the CAU was tasked with analyzing the distribution of calls for service (CFS). We illustrated the concentration of over 27,000 calls for service in 2015 in the downtown area of Oslo, using kernel density mapping. These were calls that were assigned either of the three highest priority levels in the system. By coupling the distribution map with knowledge of call types, CFS became available to command as decision support by corroborating new city center boundaries based on the concentration of crime types (the solid line area in the center of the map). The dotted lines show the old boundaries; note that one of them cuts through the middle of the CFS hot spot.

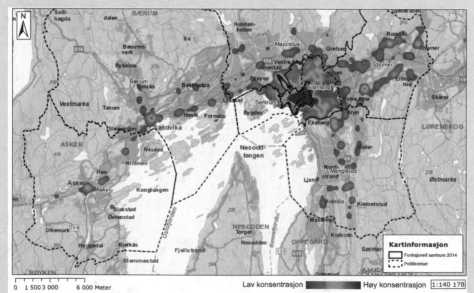

OPPDRAG I OSLO POLITIDISTRIKT: Pri ALARM, 1 og 2 (2015)

N = 27.481. Geokodingsprosent: 94,5. Operasjoner: "112 OPERASJONSSENTRALEN" og "A & B ASKER OG BÆRUM".
27 % av oppdragene fant sted i GDE 1, 42 % i GDE 2 og 31 % i GDE 3. Det første koordinatsettet i hvert oppdrag er benyttet.

Crime Analysis Audiences

When distinguishing the purpose of crime analysis results, another important consideration is differentiating the intended audience since different audiences require different types of analysis. This chapter focuses on crime analysis results that are relevant for internal police personnel using tactical and strategic crime analysis to implement and evaluate crime reduction strategies. Audiences within a police agency require different types of analysis for situational awareness and crime reduction. The easiest way to categorize what is useful is to think both about the job responsibilities of the people for whom the results are being created and the temporal nature of the activity (i.e., problem complexity) they are tasked with addressing.

Figure 7.1 illustrates the general relationship of responsibility to the temporal nature of activity; notice that it is similar to the stratified-policing figure in Chapter 3. Although there is overlap of responsibility among personnel in a police agency, lower-ranking personnel primarily deal with activity of smaller scale in the shorter term, and higher-ranking personnel (i.e., those with more responsibility) deal with activity on a larger scale in the longer term. That is, line-level officers and first-line supervisors require crime analysis results that address immediate and short-term concerns, such as responses to calls for service and recent crime patterns, while managers and commanders (i.e., lieutenants and above) require information addressing short-term and long-term activity.

For example, information results that facilitate situational awareness for line-level officers are likely to focus on individual incidents and may include lists of sex offenders, recently released prisoners, and lists of calls at individual addresses. In contrast, information results for police managers and commanders are likely to focus on aggregate information, such as the overall counts of crimes by type and patrol area (e.g., district or beat). Similarly, crime reduction results that facilitate responses from officers and sergeants are likely to address immediate activity and may include patterns of crime occurring in an area in the past few days or week, whereas managers' and commanders' crime reduction results are likely to address more long-term activity, such as whether crimes are increasing or decreasing over time or an examination of parks, bars, or hotels where a disproportionate amount of activity is happening, so that long-term solutions can be initiated.

In this chapter, three types of internal police audiences are categorized by their job responsibilities within the organization. Different-sized agencies assign responsibilities to ranks in different ways. Thus, the general terms and examples of what ranks are included in each are as follows:

1. **Operational personnel** refers to line-level officers (e.g., officers, corporals) and first-line supervisors (e.g., corporals, sergeants).

Figure 7.1 Relationship Between Responsibility and Problem Complexity

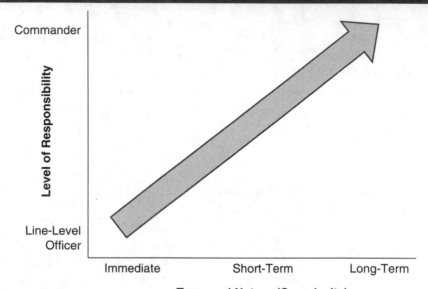

Source: Adapted from Taylor and Boba (2011).

2. **Management personnel** refers to midlevel police managers, such as lieutenants and in some cases captains.

3. **Command personnel** refers to those who serve as the leadership of the police organization, such as the chief or sheriff, deputy chiefs, majors, and in some cases captains.

Crime Analysis Typology

By breaking down potential crime analysis results by (1) category of problem, (2) purpose of crime analysis, and (3) types of internal police audience, a **crime analysis typology** emerges that allows us to classify crime analysis results and helps us apply crime analysis in a practical environment. Figure 7.2 is an illustration of the typology. Based on the typology, the following two sections provide simple, but realistic, examples for each of the classifications in the typology. Note that there are many different analyses that can be conducted that produce results in each classification within the typology as well as many different styles and formats that might be used by crime analysts. Although examples may overlap categories (e.g., the same results may be useful for different audiences), the intent here is to show at least one example in each category to provide the student further understanding of the how results are produced for different problems, purposes, and audiences.

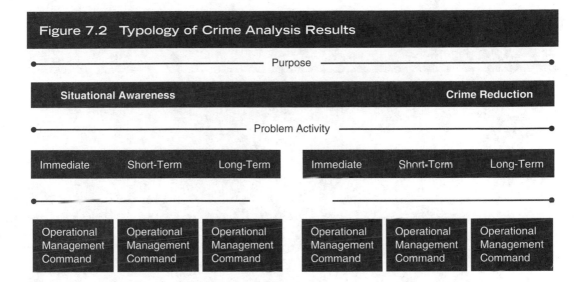

Figure 7.2 Typology of Crime Analysis Results

Purpose	
Situational Awareness	**Crime Reduction**

Problem Activity					
Immediate	Short-Term	Long-Term	Immediate	Short-Term	Long-Term

Operational Management Command	Operational Management Command	Operational Management Command	Operational Management Command	Operational Management Command	Operational Management Command

Situational Awareness Examples

This section illustrates situational awareness examples for immediate problems, short-term problems, and long-term problems for each of the internal police audience types—operational, management, and command. For each example, there is a description of the crime analysis results that are shown in each figure and a discussion of their potential use.

Immediate

To review from Chapter 3, problems considered "immediate" are isolated incidents that occur and are resolved within minutes, hours, or in some cases, days. They are responded to by patrol officers and detectives who use investigative skills learned in basic police training and more intensive investigative training.

Operational

Description: Table 7.1 is a list of calls for service produced on June 15, 2017, that occurred at one residential address in the previous 2 weeks (e.g., June 1, 2017, through June 14, 2017).

Potential Use: Patrol officers might review this information before they respond to a new call for service at this address to make them aware of the previous contact with the police the residents have had (e.g., previous crime reports, arrests, etc.).

Management

Description: Table 7.2 is a table that depicts an aggregate count of arrests that have occurred for each shift by district (e.g., days, evenings, midnights) in the previous 2 days.

Potential Use: Patrol or criminal investigations managers might review this information to get a sense of shift productivity.

Table 7.1	Calls for Service at 345 S Apple St				
Incident No.	**Call Date**	**Day**	**Time**	**Call Type**	**Disposition**
2017013294	6/1/2017	Wed	2102	Loud noise	No action taken
2017141524	6/5/2017	Sun	2012	Disturbance	Gone on arrival
2017142509	6/6/2017	Mon	1954	Domestic disturbance	Unable to locate
2017142640	6/6/2017	Mon	2325	Domestic disturbance	Arrest
2017142676	6/9/2017	Thu	1406	Barking dog	No action taken
2017142878	6/10/2017	Fri	2205	Criminal trespass	Report
2017143275	6/11/2017	Sat	0321	Domestic disturbance	Arrest
2017143496	6/13/2017	Mon	1604	Burglary	Report
2017144169	6/14/2017	Tue	1855	Parking violation	No action taken

Command

Description: Table 7.3 is a list of all commercial robberies that occurred over the last 24 hours (from May 2, 2017, 9:00 a.m. to May 3, 2017, 9:00 a.m.), with the suspect description and a brief summary of each case.

Potential Use: The chief and command staff might review this information to be aware of these serious gun crimes, as well as to be prepared for any questions about the cases that might come from the media or business associations.

Short-Term

To review from Chapter 3, short-term problems are repeat incidents and patterns. A repeat incident is a cluster of two or more incidents that are similar in nature and have happened at the same place (typically) or to the same

Table 7.2	Arrests by District Per Shift			
Shift	**District 1 Arrests**	**District 2 Arrests**	**District 3 Arrests**	**Total**
Day shift	2	6	7	**15**
Evening shift	0	10	7	**17**
Midnight shift	6	14	2	**22**
Total	**8**	**30**	**16**	**54**

Table 7.3 Commercial Robberies, Previous 24 Hours

Case #	Report Date	Time	Location	Business Name	Suspect Information	Short Description
20170132	5/2/2017	1800	470 Lake Rd	Cell Phones R Us	Black male, 22 years old, 200 pounds, 5'11"	Suspect entered business, pretended to be a customer, displayed a blue steel revolver, and demanded property.
20171425	5/2/2017	2200	2801 N Fithutt Ave	Harry's Food Store	Hispanic or Black male with shirt over his face, 20–30 years old, 180 pounds	Suspect entered business, displayed a handgun, and demanded property.
20171426	5/2/2017	2315	772 Farragut Ln	Subs and More	White male, 40 years old, 220 pounds, 6'	Suspect entered, exited, and returned. Suspect went to restroom, exited, attempted to get drink, waited in line, displayed black semiautomatic, and demanded property.
20171426	5/3/2017	0015	12516 E North Ave	Exgo Gas Station	White male, wearing a hoodie, 18 years old, 150 pounds, 5'5"	Suspect entered business, asked if clerk was alone, displayed handgun, and demanded property.
20171441	5/3/2017	0130	1959 N State St	Quick Mart	Asian male, beard, 18–25 years old, 160 pounds, 5'10"	Suspect entered business, made purchase, got second item, took to counter, produced handgun, and demanded property.

person and are (usually) common. Noncriminal or interpersonal criminal incidents may, but do not always, result in a crime report. Patterns are groups of two or more crimes reported to or discovered by police that are treated as one unit of analysis because they share one or more key commonalities that make them notable and distinct; there is no known relationship between victim and offender, and the criminal activity is typically of limited duration (IACA, 2011b).

Operational Description: Figure 7.3 is a map depicting density and single symbols for car prowls (theft from vehicle) over 4 weeks and single symbols for offenders living nearby in 2015.

Potential Use: Provides officers and sergeants information about where thefts from vehicles are occurring over 4 weeks in the southwest precinct as well as whether offenders live nearby. The density shading and the single symbols for the crimes represent the same crime data. The map is only descriptive as it does not provide conclusions that lead to specific crime reduction strategies; it only provides a general overview of where the thefts from vehicles are occurring. Additional analysis would be required to guide any specific crime reduction strategies.

Management

Description: Table 7.4 is a chart depicting counts of types of calls for service in the most recent month compared to the previous month for one district.

Potential Use: Managers can use this to compare number of calls by type in their district and to determine recent changes in calls for service for their own district. However, these results do not provide conclusions that lead to specific crime reduction strategies; they only provide an overview of general aggregated data.

Command

Description: Table 7.4 depicts counts of selected Part I crime types for two districts for the most recent month compared to the previous month and the percentage change.

Potential Use: Commanders can use this to determine changes from one month to the next and to compare districts. However, these results do not provide conclusions that lead to specific crime reduction strategies; they only provide an overview of general aggregated data.

Long-Term

To review from Chapter 3, a long-term problem is a set of related activity that occurs over several months, seasons, or years that stems from systematic opportunities created by everyday behavior and environment. Problems can consist of common disorder activity (e.g., loud parties or speeding in residential neighborhoods) as well as serious criminal activity (e.g., bank robbery or date rape).

Figure 7.3 Four Weeks of Car Prowls in Seattle, Washington—2015: Southwest Precinct

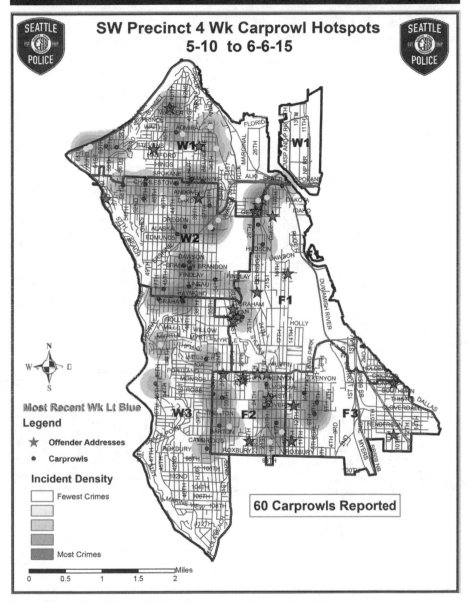

Source: Seattle (Washington) Police Department, Detective Dan Benz.

Operational

Description: Figure 7.5 is a map depicting the city of Gainesville, Florida, with equal grids, graduated by color to indicate 2010 crime counts for the entire city for the last year.

Potential Use: This alerts officers to the areas of the city that have the most crime over a long period of time. However, the map does not indicate the

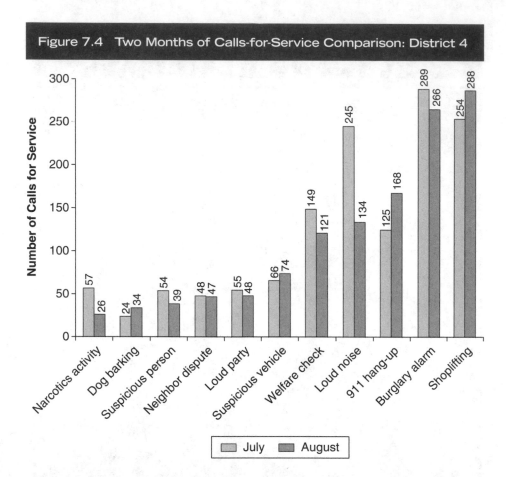

Figure 7.4 Two Months of Calls-for-Service Comparison: District 4

Table 7.4 Counts and Percentage of Change: Part I Crime Types

	Eastern District				Southern District			
	Jan.	Feb.	Difference	Percentage of Change	Jan.	Feb.	Difference	Percentage of Change
Homicide	0	0	0	NC*	1	0	−1	−100%
Rape	3	5	2	67%	7	3	−4	−57%
Robbery	26	35	9	35%	56	50	−6	−11%
Aggravated assault	75	66	−9	−12%	125	174	49	39%
Burglary	154	190	36	23%	201	175	−26	−13%
Larceny	254	288	34	13%	341	325	−16	−5%
Auto theft	167	188	21	13%	154	122	−32	−21%
Arson	0	2	2	NC*	0	0	0	NC*
Total	679	774	95	14%	885	849	−36	−4%

*NC = Not calculable

reason why these areas have the most crime or does it distinguish what types of Part I crimes are occurring where.

Management

Description: Figure 7.6 is a line chart of the aggregate counts of residential burglary crime for each month for the last year for one region in the city.

Potential Use: It provides managers information about increases or decreases in residential burglary in their region for 1 year.

Command

Description: Figure 7.7 is a map that compares counties in California by their rates of unsolved homicides over 20 years.

Potential Use: Command personnel, particularly those in county-level agencies, would review this map to compare their own levels of unsolved homicides to those of other counties in the state. Note that the map depicts the rate per unit of population, which helps to compare across counties of different populations.

Crime Reduction Examples

This section illustrates crime reduction examples. For each example, there is a description of the crime analysis results and a discussion of their potential use. Note that the rest of the book goes into detail about the analytical methodology and techniques needed to produce these results.

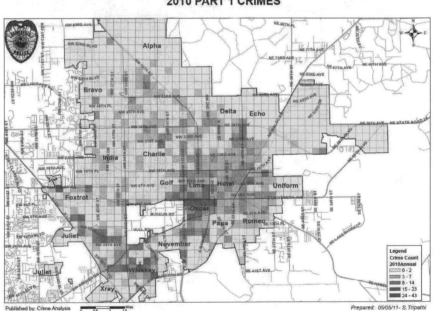

Figure 7.5   Part I Crime in Gainesville, Florida—2010

Source: Gainesville (Florida) Police Department, Dr. Shefali Tripathi.

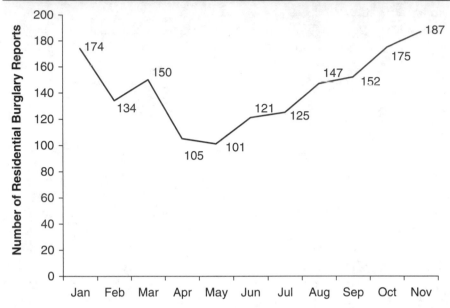

Figure 7.6   Western Region: Residential Burglary by Month

Immediate

Operational

Description: Table 7.5 is a list of only four burglary offenders who have recently been released from jail and live in a three-block area where there have been reports of several residential burglaries that appear to be related.

Potential Use: Officers and detectives might use this list to contact these burglars during their workday to determine if they might be responsible for the burglaries that have been occurring since they are known offenders who have been recently released and might be committing crime again. As discussed in Chapter 2, research shows that offenders commit crime near where they live, so it makes sense for detectives to start their search for suspects with these individuals.

Management

Description: Table 7.6 is a short report that is either disseminated or read to patrol officers during their daily roll call. It contains brief descriptions of analytical results from the previous day and week as well as direction for responses based on analysis that officers will conduct during their **uncommitted patrol time**, which is the time officers have for proactive activity between dispatched calls for service and writing reports.

Potential Use: This is a report that would be used by a variety of personnel. Managers help develop the report and use it to inform officers and sergeants about current short-term activity and long-term problems that are being

Figure 7.7 California Unsolved Homicides, 1987–2006

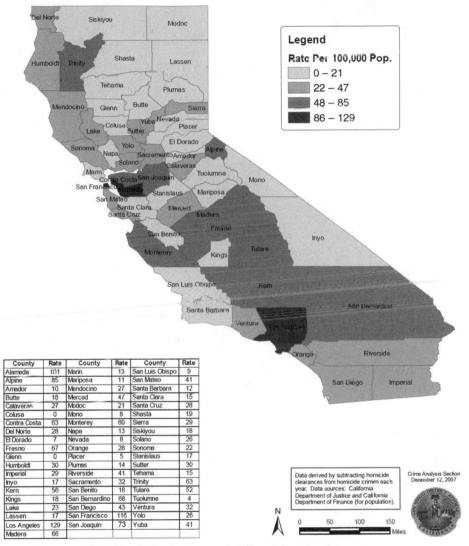

California Unsolved Homicides
From 1987 Through 2006
Total = 24,533

Legend

Rate Per 100,000 Pop.

- 0 – 21
- 22 – 47
- 48 – 85
- 86 – 129

County	Rate	County	Rate	County	Rate
Alameda	101	Marin	13	San Luis Obispo	9
Alpine	85	Mariposa	11	San Mateo	41
Amador	10	Mendocino	27	Santa Barbara	12
Butte	18	Merced	47	Santa Clara	15
Calaveras	27	Modoc	21	Santa Cruz	28
Colusa	0	Mono	8	Shasta	19
Contra Costa	63	Monterey	60	Sierra	29
Del Norte	28	Napa	13	Siskiyou	18
El Dorado	7	Nevada	8	Solano	26
Fresno	67	Orange	28	Sonoma	22
Glenn	0	Placer	5	Stanislaus	17
Humboldt	30	Plumas	14	Sutter	30
Imperial	29	Riverside	41	Tehama	15
Inyo	17	Sacramento	32	Trinity	63
Kern	56	San Benito	16	Tulare	52
Kings	18	San Bernardino	68	Tuolumne	4
Lake	23	San Diego	43	Ventura	32
Lassen	17	San Francisco	116	Yolo	26
Los Angeles	129	San Joaquin	73	Yuba	41
Madera	66				

Data derived by subtracting homicide clearances from homicide crimes each year. Data sources: California Department of Justice and California Department of Finance (for population).

Crime Analysis Section
December 12, 2007

N

0   50   100   150
Miles

Source: San Diego (California) District Attorney's Office, Julie Wartell.

addressed; it directs their proactive crime reduction responses. It can also be used by managers to hold their subordinates accountable (i.e., "Did you conduct the response outlined in the May 12th report, and if so, what did you do?").

Command

Description: Table 7.7 is an excerpt from a list of *selected* crimes that have occurred in a jurisdiction in the previous 1 to 3 days. This is an example of

Table 7.5 Released Burglary Offenders Living in a Pattern Area

Name	Date of Birth	Current Address	Race/Sex	Convictions
Jones, Mark	4/21/1986	156 E Main St	White/Male	Burglary, shoplifting, grand theft
Smith, John	7/17/1991	129 E Main St	Black/Male	Burglary, theft
Harold, Jason	8/1/1984	403 S Grand Ave	Hispanic/Male	Burglary, vandalism, robbery
Samuels, Denis	2/15/1988	470 S Grand Ave	White/Male	Burglary, auto theft, grand theft

a report in which the analytical decision comes *before* the product is created and could also be automated. The types of crimes included in the report are those that were selected by the chief and command staff when the report was initially developed because they are a priority for the agency. Instead of waiting to hear about the crimes through a police report, this report provides information on a daily basis so that the agency leaders can take action or ensure responses are being implemented immediately. Some examples of crime types that are typically selected for such a report include homicides, attempted homicides, home invasion robberies, shootings, serious, violent gang-related incidents, hate crimes, damage to city property, crimes involving city officials, and stranger-on-stranger gun crime such as armed robbery, violent sex crimes, abductions, and serious aggravated battery. The types selected are often different in different police departments since they have contrasting amounts and types of crime as well as distinct priorities for crime reduction.

Potential Use: The chief and command staff would discuss the list in each command briefing to ensure that crimes deemed a high priority are investigated thoroughly.

Short-Term

Operational

Description: Table 7.8 is a report that identifies addresses with more than a certain level of disorder type of activity within one police precinct. This report is generated by selecting those addresses with three or more types of disorder calls for service (e.g., disturbance, loud noise, loitering, etc.) that occurred within 3 weeks. This example only shows three addresses, but there are likely more addresses that had at least three disorder calls. This is a report that can be automated because the analytical decisions are made before the report is created. That is, the agency has decided it wants to respond to addresses that have short–term disorder problems. Because the agency has to prioritize its response based on resources, in this example it has decided to only respond to addresses that have had three or more calls in 4 weeks. Another agency with more resources might lower the threshold to two calls, or one with even fewer resources might increase it to five calls for service so that fewer addresses are on the report.

Table 7.6 Daily Roll Call Sheet

District 1: Saturday, May 12, 2017

Crime Patterns	Analysis	Response
Pattern #: 2017-089	Seven residential burglaries occurred in Beat 14 during the day over the last week; entry was made through the rear slider. Cash, jewelry, and small items were taken. No suspects.	Increase proactive patrols in Beat 14; conduct checks on suspicious subjects; continue to conduct thorough canvases on all burglary investigations and complete the security survey.
Pattern #: 2017-092B	Four street robberies have occurred in the Westwood area in the midmorning hours over the last several weeks. Two white males on foot approach victims from behind in a retail or apartment parking lot, threaten them with a weapon (or simulated weapon) and demand money and other possessions. Victims are primarily women.	Increase proactive patrols in Westwood area and in retail and apartment parking lots; make contact with business owners and apartment managers about pattern and crime prevention advice (see flyer developed by the Crime Prevention Unit for this pattern).
Problem Locations	**Analysis**	**Response**
Jay's Truck Stop: 1654 E Highway 176	Citizens have reported day laborers hanging around the truck stop causing disorder and traffic problems along Highway 176. Officers have also reported prostitution and drug activity.	Several weeks ago, Captain Smith (District 1) initiated contact with the truck stop's management to develop long-term solutions for this problem. However, because the activity has increased in recent weeks, officers are to patrol in the area, look for suspicious behavior, and give trespass citations (not warnings) to those individuals not on the property for business with the truck stop.

Table 7.7 Command Briefing Report

Monday, April 16, 2017			
Case #	Offense	Location	Synopsis
201714248	Murder, attempted	1204 S Stonegate Dr	On 4/15/2017 at 2100, Suspect (Larry Thompson, B/M, 12/14/1991) and Victim (Thomas Gonzolez, H/M, 01/19/1990) got into an argument at the PubNGrub bar. A shot was fired by the suspect, and the victim suffered a bullet graze to his head. He was transported to St. Mary's Hospital and will survive. K-9 and Air Unit conducted a search for suspect, who was found in bushes on the next block and was arrested.
201714166	Aggravated assault	2519 W Wake Rd	On 4/14/2017 at 2000–2200, Suspect (Christopher Allen, W/M, 7/1/1986) fired shots in the air at Club Y. Suspect was apprehended immediately by security and off-duty officers. Said to be an initiation for a local skinhead group.
201714288	Burglary, other	2301 N Janey St	Sometime between 4/13/2017 at 1900 and 4/15/2017 at 0900, the Holy Trinity Church was vandalized, with approximately $50,000 in physical damage. Also, racist, antireligious graffiti was painted throughout the church.

Potential Use: Operational personnel use these results to implement proactive problem-solving responses for these particular locations to prevent future calls for service and stop the problematic activity.

Management

Description: Table 7.9 is a brief summary of a crime pattern that includes information about the crimes an analyst has linked together by crime type (commercial burglary), the area of their occurrence (Beat 42), the method of the crimes (accessed through air conditioning ducts), and the time in which they occurred (overnight hours). These summaries are produced as crime patterns occur and are not a regularly produced report.

Potential Use: This is another example in which multiple personnel would use the report. Management personnel use these results to direct operational personnel from the patrol division as well as other support divisions to collaboratively implement short-term crime reduction strategies. The responses would include directed and undercover patrol, providing crime prevention advice to residents in the pattern area, contacting the known offenders living in the pattern area, and so on. Note that the daily roll call report directs patrol resources on a variety of problems for a particular day, whereas this

Table 7.8 Top Addresses for Disorder: Precinct 33

September 11, 2017–October 1, 2017

124 E Main St (Righty's Bar)

Date	Time	Day	Call Type	Disposition	Case #
9/30/2017	2200	Sat	Disturbance	Unable to locate	None
9/28/2017	1954	Thu	Loud noise	Citation issued	201709789
9/25/2017	2103	Mon	Loud noise	Warning Issued	None
9/17/2017	2356	Sun	Disturbance	Peace restored	None

3519 SE Cedar Ave (Hotspot Gas and Go)

Date	Time	Day	Call Type	Disposition	Case #
10/1/2017	0032	Sun	Loitering	Citation issued	2017121023
9/30/2017	2100	Sat	Disturbance	Trespass warning	None
9/15/2017	0120	Fri	Trespassing	Unable to locate	None

4428 N Grand Ave (Public Library)

Date	Time	Day	Call Type	Disposition	Case #
9/30/2017	945	Sat	Loitering	Peace restored	None
9/29/2017	1034	Fri	Loitering	Warning issued	None
9/29/2017	1345	Fri	Disturbance	Arrest made	201709945
9/22/2017	1622	Fri	Disturbance	Peace restored	None
9/14/2017	1007	Thu	Loud noise	Peace restored	None

report directs a collaborative response of patrol, criminal investigations, crime prevention, and actions from the public information officer until the pattern is resolved (for more detail see Part II Tactical Crime Analysis).

Command

Description: Figure 7.8 is a map depicting (with dots) the locations of all thefts from vehicles occurring over 3 months in District 2 as well as patterns of crimes (with large circles) that have been identified during the same time period. The labels for each pattern indicate the month in which the pattern was identified as well as its unique assigned number.

Potential Use: This map, produced each month for the previous 3 months, assists command personnel in determining 1) whether proactive responses to these crime patterns are working, or 2) whether individual crime as well as crime patterns are continually occurring in the same area and might be escalating into larger long-term problems that may require additional response.

Table 7.9 Crime Pattern Summary Information

Hot Spot of Commercial Burglaries in Beat 42	
# of Incidents:	Five crimes, two attempts
Date range:	September 15, 2017–September 21, 2017
Time range:	All incidents occurred overnight (between 2000 and 0700) during the week
Target:	Commercial businesses in plazas with roof-accessed air conditioning ducts
Property taken:	Computers, printers, cash, and in two cases a safe
General location:	Northwest area of Beat 42
Method (MO):	In five cases, entry was made into the business through the roof via an air conditioning duct. In two cases, entry was made from a neighboring business (that was entered through the roof the same night). In all cases, only the most expensive equipment was taken, even if it was large and heavy. Burglar alarms were activated in only the two attempts; officers found evidence of attempted entry through the roof, but after a canvas of the area, no suspects were found.

Figure 7.8 Theft From Vehicle Incidents and Patterns: April–May

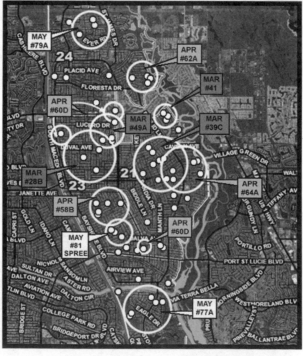

Source: Port St. Lucie (Florida) Police Department, Michelle Chitolie.

Long-Term

Operational

Description: Table 7.10 is a list of the five offenders with the most violent criminal offenses that live in a particular area of the city. This report uses 6 months of arrest data to identify these offenders, so it is considered a long-term analysis report. Note that using 12 or even 24 months of data could result in different individuals on the report.

Potential Use: Both patrol and criminal investigations personnel can use this information to implement responses to deter these offenders from future criminal activity.

Management

Description: Figure 7.9 illustrates a comparison analysis created for an apartment community that was identified as a problem location. This example is a part of a more comprehensive analysis product that would be used to guide long-term crime reduction responses. The report shows a chart of the number of calls for service per year at ABC apartments, with a line depicting the city goal of calls for service, indicating that this complex consistently has high

Rank	Name	Date of Birth	Current Address	Race/Sex	Convictions	Corrections Status
1	Marshall, James	5/23/1956	1456 E Harvard Ave	White/Male	Armed robbery, auto theft, aggravated assault, domestic assault, stalking, DUI	On parole until 5/2019
2	Holden, John	4/12/1967	1219 S Harrison St	Black/Male	Sexual assault, armed robbery, assault of a police officer	On parole until 1/2018
3	Venarila, Manuel	8/24/1979	980 S Appenton Rd	Hispanic/ Male	Domestic assault, sexual assault, DUI	On probation until 8/2021
4	Gregory, Josh	9/18/1983	1280 E Main St	Black/Male	Armed robbery, burglary, aggravated DUI, aggravated assault with a weapon	House arrest until 6/2019
5	Adams, Michael	1/12/1992	400 N Lexington St	White/Male	Sexual assault, stalking, domestic assault, armed robbery	Due to be released from prison 4/2018

Table 7.10   Top Violent* Offenders Residing in District 5: January–June 2017

*Convicted of any type of violent crime, sexual or nonsexual, domestic or nondomestic.

Figure 7.9 Problem Analysis Results: ABC Apartment

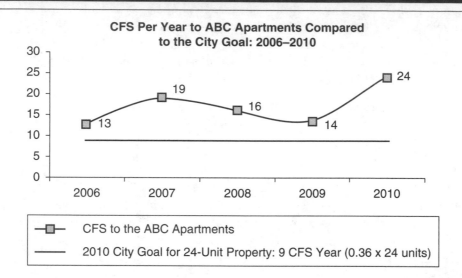

CFS Per Year to ABC Apartments Compared to the City Goal: 2006–2010

■ CFS to the ABC Apartments

— 2010 City Goal for 24-Unit Property: 9 CFS Year (0.36 x 24 units)

2010 Police CFS per unit, per year ratio for the ABC Apartments (24 CFS/24 units)

1.00

Median Police CFS per unit, per year ratio for city apartments with 8+ units

0.36

Compared to other city properties, the ABC Apartments' 2010 CFS per unit, per year ratio is

2.8 times higher

Total Number of CFS to Each Unit
From Most to Least

Address	Unit	2010 CFS
1234 ABC Street	Unit 5	9
1234 ABC Street	Unit 3	3
1234 ABC Street	Unit 22	3
1234 ABC Street	Unit 12	2
1234 ABC Street	Unit 7	1
1234 ABC Street	Unit 10	1
1234 ABC Street	Unit 11	1
1234 ABC Street	Unit 17	1
1234 ABC Street	No unit specified	3

Call Types to Your Complex From
Most Common to Least Common

CFS Type	2010 CFS
Domestic Violence	4
Psychological Evaluation	4
Vandalism	3
Disturbance - Family	2
Disturbance - Person	2
Check a Person's Well Being	1
Disturbance - Noise	1
Incident Evaluation	1
Other Incident	1
PR Contact	1
Stalking	1
Suspicious Circumstances	1
Suspicious Person	1
Vehicle Theft	1

Source: Chula Vista (California) Police Department, Karin Schmerler.

Note: A number of call types are not counted in this report, including traffic collisions, lost or found property, vehicle impounds, any calls canceled prior to dispatch, or any officer-initiated CFS without associated case reports.

numbers of calls for service. It also shows that this community has almost 3 times as many calls for service per apartment unit than other communities in the city and provides a frequency of calls by building and the most common types of calls at the location.

Potential Use: Police managers use these results to understand what specific problem this apartment community is experiencing as well as how it compares to others in the city. Along with other information not shown here but covered in depth in Part III: Strategic Crime Analysis, the analysis helps to determine appropriate responses and prioritize which responses should be implemented first. It also establishes a baseline for comparison once the responses have been implemented to determine if the crime reduction strategies were effective. These and other measures would be collected again to show how the community compared to others in the city and how the specific problem addressed had been impacted.

Command

Description: Figure 7.10 is an example of a chart that depicts monthly counts and the linear trend line of residential burglary before and after police response was implemented in November of 2017. For comparison, the chart includes the monthly counts and linear trend line for all other Part I property crime (commercial burglary, theft, and auto theft) for which specific proactive responses were not implemented. Including a comparison to other property crime occurring in the same jurisdiction assists in understanding whether

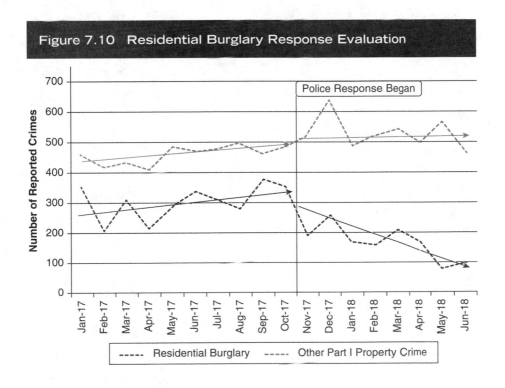

Figure 7.10 Residential Burglary Response Evaluation

property crime is going down generally or just for residential burglary, for which the agency has implemented specific crime reduction efforts. The chart provides linear trend lines for the crime occurring before and after the responses have been implemented, allowing the commanders to more easily see the differences.

Potential Use: Commanders would use these results to evaluate whether the agency's crime reduction efforts for residential burglary had been effective and whether the response could, if successful, be concluded or, if not, needed adjustment.

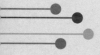

SUMMARY POINTS

This chapter describes a typology that classifies crime analysis results by type of activity, purpose, and audience. The following are the key points addressed in this chapter:

- The crime analysis typology is a classification system that provides a structure for crime analysis results based on the stratification of type of problem, purpose of crime analysis results, and type of audience.

- Three types of problems are broken down by the temporal nature of the activity and the complexity of the problem; they include immediate problems, short-term problems, and long-term problems. (For definitions, see Chapter 3.)

- There are two distinct purposes of crime analysis results—to facilitate situational awareness and to guide crime reduction strategies.

- Situational awareness is the development of a perception of the environment. Crime analysts produce "information" for police personnel about crime and other activity. This information is created simply to report facts and does not present conclusions about what the facts mean, how they are related to other issues, or why they are occurring.

- Crime reduction analysis results are created with the intention of guiding police in implementing specific strategies for crime reduction. Essential characteristics of factual information are examined, and conclusions are presented about the relationships that exist among the facts.

- Three types of internal police audiences are discussed in this chapter—operational, management, and command.

- The term *operational personnel* generally refers to line-level officers (e.g., officers, corporals) and first-line supervisors (e.g., corporals, sergeants).

- The term *management personnel* generally refers to midlevel police managers, such as lieutenants and, in some cases, captains.

- The term *command personnel* generally refers to those who serve as the leadership of the police organization, such as the chief or sheriff, deputy chiefs, majors, and, in some cases, captains.

DISCUSSION EXERCISES*

Exercise 1

Describe an example of crime analysis results for both situational awareness and crime reduction purposes (any problem or audience) for the following data:

- Traffic crash data

- Registered sex offender data

- 911 hang up calls-for-service data

Exercise 2

Contrast the types of information for situational awareness that the different audiences within a police agency require. What are the key differences? How does the information overlap? Describe how each type of audience might use Figure 7.3 and Figure 7.5.

Exercise 3

Contrast the types of analysis for crime reduction that the different audiences within a police agency require. What are the key differences? How do their requirements overlap? For example, describe how each type of audience might use Table 7.8 and Figure 7.9.

Tactical Crime Analysis

The focus of this book now shifts from description of the crime analysis discipline, theory, data, concepts, and examples to presentation of the methods and techniques used in the three types of crime analysis covered in depth in this book. Part III covers tactical crime analysis. To reiterate the definition provided in Chapter 4, *tactical crime analysis* is the analysis of police data directed toward the short-term development of patrol and investigative priorities and deployment of resources. Its subject areas include the analysis of space, time, offender, victim, and modus operandi for individual high-profile crimes, repeat incidents, and crime patterns, with a specific focus on crime series [sic].

The following four chapters introduce the data, analysis techniques, and products of tactical crime analysis and provide examples of effective crime patterns and the ways in which police can use the information for crime reduction. Chapter 8 includes a discussion of repeat incidents (i.e., the first type of short-term problem) as well as a description of tactical crime data. Chapter 9 covers the methodologies for identifying initial patterns (i.e., the second type of short-term problem), finalizing patterns, developing investigative leads, and clearing cases. Chapter 10 illustrates how to identify meaningful patterns and how they guide crime reduction efforts implemented by police. And Chapter 11 covers specific techniques that analysts can use to understand known crime patterns and provides an outline for the content and format of an ideal crime pattern bulletin.

CHAPTER

8

Repeat Incidents and Tactical Data Collection

The first chapter in Part III covers repeat incident data collection and analysis techniques and includes a discussion of the characteristics of the data used for tactical crime analysis. Because the analysis used to identify repeat incident locations is fairly simple and straightforward, repeat incident analysis is covered here as part of tactical crime analysis (short-term analysis) instead of in its own chapter.

Repeat Incidents

To review from Chapter 3, a repeat incident is a cluster of two or more incidents that are similar in nature and have happened at the same place (typically) or by the same person; these clusters occur less frequently than individual incidents. A repeat incident usually includes common noncriminal or interpersonal criminal incidents that may, but do not always, result in a crime report, such as loud noises, barking dogs, neighbor disputes, disruptive juveniles, domestic disturbances, bar fights, traffic crashes, and the like. The individual incidents that make up a repeat incident happen within hours, days, and, in some cases, weeks of one another. Identifying places where a repeat incident has occurred is one way to focus crime reduction on short-term disorder and interpersonal criminal activity.

Thus, guiding crime reduction efforts to address a repeat incident begins with identifying addresses that have received multiple calls for service in a short time period. Examination of calls-for-service data is used to initially scan for locations that may be having ongoing disorder and quality of life issues. Once identified, the analysis of the potential problem occurring at the repeat incident location requires police officers to conduct qualitative data collection (e.g., observation and interviews) before addressing the problem with a response. Importantly, when the calls for service are not related to one particular issue, the location does not require a response.

For example, a repeat calls-for-service report might show that 234 East Maple Avenue, a single-family residence, has had two calls for a disturbance, one for a fight, and another for a loud noise in the last 2 weeks. As we learned in Chapter 5, calls-for-service information from computer-aided dispatch (CAD) is limited, as it only includes the date, time, disposition, and a short narrative about the call. Since there is no other way to determine exactly what is happening at the location, an officer would talk to other police officers who initially responded to the calls as well as to the residents. Oftentimes, more than one officer answers multiple calls at a single address because of shift work and the timing of the calls for service. For example, consider that the officer discovers that the calls are related to disputes between a male resident and his brother who is temporarily living with him. Once this information has been gathered and the true nature of the problem has been determined, the officer develops a response that seeks to resolve the issue and stop future calls. Thus, the calls-for-service data were used for scanning and identifying the address initially, and the officers conducted the analysis to understand the nature of the activity at that location.

The role of crime analysis in addressing repeat incidents, then, is developing the report from which the repeat incident locations are identified. There are several considerations in the development of the repeat incident report that include the type of data used, the temporal length of the data, and the format of the report, which are covered here.

Repeat Incident Data

In the examination of short-term problems, repeat incident analysis products complement pattern analysis products in that they relay the results from analysis of different types of data. Calls-for-service data relating to disorder, quality of life, and interpersonal disputes are examined for repeat incident products. Crime data are not used for repeat incident products because they are used for pattern analysis products discussed later in this chapter. However, as noted in Chapter 5, there are many different types of calls for service. Because the purpose of a repeat incident location report is to identify locations with an ongoing short-term problem, specific types of calls for service are selected for one report, and crime analysts often create multiple reports that focus on different types of disorder and interpersonal crime problems in order to identify distinct types of repeat incident locations. The following are examples of several reports and the types of calls for service that might be included:

General disorder and family issues report the following incidents:

- Family fight/domestic trouble
- Neighbor trouble
- Juvenile trouble
- Loud noise/loud party
- Disturbance
- Welfare check

Suspicious activity and narcotics activity report the following incidents:

- Suspicious person
- Suspicious vehicle
- Loitering

- Unwelcome subject
- Narcotics activity
- Shots fired

Burglar alarms report (false alarm activity) the following incidents:

- Residential burglar alarm
- Business burglar alarm

These are only examples; each police agency would select the type of activity on which to focus and the type of calls for service that represent that activity based on its own calls-for-service codes, the nature of activity occurring in its jurisdiction, and what it considers important for crime reduction efforts.

Repeat Incident Location Report

The nature of the report and data used to develop a repeat incident location report are typically selected through a collaboration of a police agency's managers and crime analysts. Because the results will guide crime reduction efforts of the police department, it is important that police managers are involved in the process and that analysts do not make these decisions on their own (Boba & Santos, 2011; Santos & Taylor, 2014). There are several considerations for the development of the report that are related to the time period of the report, the number of calls that may constitute a repeat incident location, and the final content of the report (e.g., time of day, day of week, type of call, and disposition). All of these considerations again depend on the agency and the nature of activity in its jurisdiction.

Because repeat incident crime reduction has a short-term focus, the time period of the report should also be short term. The goal of crime reduction efforts for this type of problem is to identify and resolve the issue as soon as possible. Because of this, the time period of the report would most likely be between 2 and 4 weeks. The report would be considered a "rolling report" in that each week, the previous 4 weeks of activity would be part of the report—that is, as one new week is added, one drops off. This allows officers and sergeants not only to identify new repeat incident locations, but it also allows them to evaluate locations they responded to in the previous weeks.

The number of calls for service that constitutes a repeat incident location depends on the specific police department and its overall number of calls for service for the activity and the length of the time period under examination. That is, a police department may have 10,000 disturbance calls per year, and another one may have 2,000. The smaller number of call types selected for the report, the fewer the number of calls for service, and the shorter the time period, the lower the threshold. When the report is initially developed, the crime analyst will examine various combinations of time periods and call thresholds to determine what is realistic for crime reduction efforts and the police agency's resources. I have worked with many police agencies whose reports used 4 weeks of data as well as between three and five calls for service as the minimum number of calls necessary for an address to be considered a repeat incident location. With these considerations, typically agencies identified between five and 10 new repeat incident addresses each week.

Lastly, the content of the report is important because sworn personnel need to see the relevant information of the calls for service in order to begin to understand the nature of the activity. Typically, the following fields are included on a repeat incident location report:

- Date and day of call
- Time of call
- Type of call
- Disposition of call
- Report number (if generated)
- Officer who responded (to follow up with each officer about nature of that call)

Depending on the quality of the calls-for-service data, which can be different for each agency, the report also may include the narrative information from each call to allow the officer to read what the dispatcher wrote at the time of the call. Table 8.1 is a sample of what a repeat incident report may look like.

The information on the report is used, typically by first-line supervisors (Boba & Santos, 2011), to determine whether further analysis is necessary in order to understand the activity at that location. In some cases, it is fairly obvious that calls to a single address are not related (e.g., they may be several weeks apart at different times of the day), so having as much of the available call information on the report as possible is important.

Summary

The role of crime analysis in addressing repeat incident locations for crime reduction is fairly simple and straightforward, as the report produced is primarily used for scanning for and identifying repeat incident locations. Crime analysts would assist police personnel in determining the initial data, the format, and the timing of the report (i.e., produced every week). Analysts would produce the report (or in many cases it can be automated, as noted in Chapter 5) and might revisit the report every 6 to 12 months to be sure it is satisfying the needs of those using it (i.e., the feedback step in the crime analysis process discussed in Chapter 4). Police personnel would then use the repeat incident report to determine which locations require additional analysis and response as well as whether their ongoing responses have worked (i.e., the calls have stopped at a particular repeat incident location).

Table 8.1 Repeat Incident Location Report Example

General Disorder and Domestic Repeat Incident Report					
Date of Report: September 5, 2017–October 2, 2017					

Threshold: Four Calls for Service

District 4 Zone A

124 E Main St (single-family home)

Date	Time	Day	Call Type	Disposition	Case #
9/30/2017	2200	Sat	Disturbance	Unable to locate	None
9/28/2017	1954	Thu	Loud party	Citation issued	201799817
9/25/2017	2103	Mon	Domestic	No action taken	None
9/17/2017	2356	Sun	Disturbance	Peace restored	None

3519 SE Cedar Ave (duplex)

Date	Time	Day	Call Type	Disposition	Case #
10/01/2017	0032	Sun	Domestic	Report	201710252
9/30/2017	2100	Sat	Disturbance	Trespass warning	None
9/15/2017	0120	Fri	Juvenile trouble	Unfounded	None
9/15/2017	2230	Fri	Juvenile trouble	Unable to locate	None
9/05/2017	1654	Tue	Fight	Report	201798122

4428 N Grand Ave (single family home)

Date	Time	Day	Call Type	Disposition	Case #
9/30/2017	0145	Sat	Disturbance	Peace restored	None
9/27/2017	2210	Wed	Fight	Unfounded	None
9/27/2017	2101	Wed	Disturbance	Arrest made	201799974
9/20/2017	2200	Wed	Fight	Peace restored	None
9/14/2017	2036	Thu	Loud noise	Peace restored	None
9/08/2017	2103	Fri	Fight	Report	201798802

Collection and Collation of Tactical Crime Analysis Data

The other type of short-term problem addressed in crime reduction is patterns, which are the primary focus of tactical crime analysis. One of the most important aspects of tactical crime analysis, and the first step in the crime analysis process, is the collection of the necessary data. The remainder of this chapter describes the kinds of data used in tactical crime analysis. The data used for pattern identification include information about how, when, and where crimes have occurred and come from both quantitative and qualitative information within police reports. Quantitative data such as date, time, location, and type of crime typically come from specific variables collected in reports. Other quantitative variables are gleaned from the narratives of reports—that is, from qualitative information. Analysts create new quantitative variables by reviewing and categorizing qualitative information contained in reports, such as what the suspect said during the commission of the crime or the description of unique property stolen. Analysts also examine additional qualitative information gathered from the field, such as from patrol briefings, ride-alongs, and discussions with officers and detectives.

Before the systematic use of computers in pattern analysis, analysts recorded the data in paper matrices, such as the one depicted in Figure 8.1. Analysts coded limited numbers of variables manually and examined them in order to determine patterns. The matrices used today have a similar structure, as Figure 8.2 shows, but they are electronic, allowing analysts to include many more variables and to rearrange variables as needed for easier visualization. In addition, electronic matrices allow analysts to collect and review large numbers of cases quickly and easily—the only limitations lie in the creativity of the analyst. Analysts can create such matrices in any number of programs, including Excel, Access, SPSS, and programs created specifically for tactical crime analysis (see also Burrell & Bull, 2011).

Crime Report Data

Tactical crime analysis seeks to identify patterns of crimes that are not easily linked together and generally is not used to examine crimes in which the victim

Figure 8.1   Paper Matrix Example

Tactical Crime Analysis Matrix

Case #	Type of Crime	Dates	Times	Weekdays	Location	MO
78·9746	Res. Burg	5/1/78 - 5/2/78	0900- 0830	Mon - Tue	2483 E Apple St	·Unforced entry ·Took TV, cash, 8 track ·no suspect information
78·9750	Robbery	5/3/78	1020	Wed	562 S Main St	·Suspect approached ped. with gun, demanded purse ·see report for suspect info.
78·9761	Com. Burg.	5/8/78 5/9/78	1900- 0730	Mon - Tue	497 W Tech Rd.	·Suspect(s) entered thru air vent on roof ·took large computer eq. ·no suspect info avail.
78·9799	Auto Theft	5/21/78	2000- 2300	Sun	975 N Movie Dr.	·car stolen from east end of parking lot while victims at movie (Star Wars)
78·9841	Res. Burg.	5/30/78	0900- 1700	Tues	2597 E Apple St	·pry tool used to open front door ·tv, cash & record player taken, no suspect info

Figure 8.2 Electronic Matrix Example

Case Number	Crime	Location Type	First Date	Last Date	First Day	Last Day	First Time	Last Time
201700056	Criminal trespass	Single family	11/2/2017	11/2/2017	Thu	Thu	2349	2349
201700070	Burglary commercial	Commercial yard	11/2/2017	11/2/2017	Thu	Thu	1600	0830
201700081	Burglary residential	Apartment/Multi-housing	11/3/2017	11/3/2017	Fri	Fri	1200	1330
201700089	Burglary residential	Single family	11/10/2017	11/10/2017	Fri	Fri	1030	1350
201700093	Burglary residential	Apartment/Multi-housing	11/13/2017	11/14/2017	Mon	Tue	2043	2043
201700107	Burglary residential	Single family	11/14/2017	11/14/2017	Tue	Tue	0930	1145
201700112	Burglary residential	Single family	11/17/2017	11/17/2017	Fri	Fri	1800	1700
201700123	Burglary residential	Single family	11/20/2017	11/20/2017	Mon	Mon	0800	0800
201700131	Burglary commercial	Amusement	11/20/2017	11/22/2017	Mon	Wed	1500	1500
201700336	Burglary residential	Apartment/Multi-housing	11/26/2017	11/26/2017	Sun	Sun	1200	1000
201700371	Burglary commercial	Commercial yard	12/2/2017	12/3/2017	Sat	Sun	2100	0034
201700374	Burglary residential	Apartment/Multi-housing	12/7/2017	12/8/2017	Thu	Fri	1000	2330
201700697	Burglary residential	Single family	12/15/2017	12/18/2017	Fri	Mon	1200	1600
201700701	Burglary commercial	Construction site	12/17/2017	12/19/2017	Sun	Tue	1500	0630
201700869	Burglary residential	Apartment/Multi-housing	12/18/2017	12/18/2017	Mon	Mon	0030	1100
201700871	Burglary residential	Apartment/Multi-housing	12/22/2017	12/23/2017	Fri	Sat	2300	0800
201700877	Burglary commercial	Medical/Dental/Hospital	12/28/2017	12/28/2017	Thu	Thu	2127	2127
201700880	Criminal trespass	Single family	12/30/2017	12/30/2017	Sat	Sat	2220	2220
201700881	Burglary residential	Single family	12/30/2017	12/30/2017	Sat	Sat	0930	1600
201700883	Robbery	Street	12/31/2017	12/31/2017	Sun	Sun	2017	2017

and offender know each other (e.g., burglary by an ex-roommate, acquaintance rape, or robbery of one drug dealer by another), crimes in which the acts are consensual (e.g., prostitution, drug dealing/buying and gambling), or crimes involving conflicts (e.g., assault and domestic violence). The types of crimes most often examined include the following:

- Robbery
- Residential burglary
- Commercial burglary
- Theft from vehicle
- Auto theft
- Grand theft
- Vandalism
- Rape
- Indecent exposure
- Public sexual indecency

Because the legal description of a crime is not as important as the type of criminal behavior in the incident, other crime types might also be examined if the behavior they describe seems to be related to one of the crimes in the list. Examples might include a kidnapping that was an unsuccessful stranger rape or a criminal-damage incident that seems more like an unsuccessful burglary.

Currently, no national standards dictate what characteristics (variables) should be collected for tactical analysis purposes. However, both standard practice in tactical crime analysis and most records management systems (RMS) organize the characteristics of a crime into three categories: (a) *modus operandi;* (b) *persons* involved in the crime; and (c) *vehicles* involved in the crime. The number of characteristics known about the crime and the quality of the information varies by crime type, making some types more difficult to link together than others. For example, robbery and rape incidents are rich with data because a person (the victim) was present and able to describe when, how, and by whom the crime was perpetrated. Conversely, auto theft incidents lack many characteristics because not only is there usually no witness to the crime, but the target itself (the car) is gone. Pattern analysis is still conducted on crimes with fewer characteristics, but the patterns are harder to specify and link to a particular suspect. The following sections describe a wide range of characteristics that would be collected for incidents, depending on the information available.

Modus Operandi Modus operandi (MO), a Latin term meaning literally "method of procedure," refers to the method of the crime—that is, the key elements of the crime incident itself.

- *What*: The type of crime (e.g., commercial burglary, residential burglary, rape).

- *How*: How the crime was carried out (varies by type of crime). Characteristics include but are not limited to the following:

  Point of entry: Where the suspect(s) entered the property (e.g., front door, window, roof entry, unknown); important for property crimes

  Method of entry: How the suspect(s) entered the location (e.g., kick, pry tool, rock, drive in, unknown); important for property crimes

  Suspect's actions: What the suspect(s) did during the crime (e.g., beat the victim, tied the victim, acted compassionately toward the victim); especially important for persons crimes

  Action against property: What the suspect(s) did to the property (e.g., ransacked, set on fire); important for property crimes

  Object of attack: The type(s) of person or property attacked (e.g., cash register, safe, clerk, pedestrian, car)

  Method of departure: How the suspect(s) left the scene (e.g., in car, on foot); important for persons crimes

  Weapon type: The type(s) of weapon(s) used in the commission of the crime (e.g., gun, pipe, simulated weapon)

  Property taken: The items stolen during the commission of the crime (e.g., jewelry, cash, TV)

- *Where*: Where the crime was committed. Characteristics include but are not limited to the following:

  Address: The exact address where the crime occurred, including apartment, suite, or hotel room number if applicable

  Location name: The commercial name, if any, of where the crime occurred (e.g., ValueMart, Garden Apartments, Lucky's Convenience Store)

  Type of location: The category of location where the crime occurred (e.g., convenience store, apartment, storage shed, beauty salon)

  Area: The area in which the crime occurred (e.g., reporting district, beat, grid, section)

- *When:* When the crime was committed. Characteristics include the following:

  Exact time and date of the crime: Used when the exact time and date are known; typically for persons crimes

  First date and time: The first possible date and time the crime could have occurred (beginning of a time span); typically for property crimes that are not witnessed

  Last date and time: The last possible date and time the crime could have occurred (end of a time span). (Note that the date of report is not included here because the purpose is not to count crimes but to examine when they occurred.)

Qualitative information about crime incidents may also be included in a tactical crime analysis database. This would include information about incidents that does not fall within the characteristics listed here or that provides further explanation concerning the modus operandi or MO (e.g., the suspect in a bank robbery sent all the women in the bank to the bathroom, or a rape suspect left a flower with each one of his victims).

Persons Involved in the Crime The data about a person involved in a crime typically include a description of the type of contact, the name and address of the person, a physical description of the person, and a description of the physical condition of the person at the time of the crime. The individual's actions during the crime are not included here; as previously noted, these fall within the MO category because actions are part of "how" the crime occurred and often change from incident to incident.

- *Type of contact*: The classification of the individual within the crime incident (made by the reporting officer in most cases). Categories include the following:

  Investigative lead: A person who is a potential suspect for a crime

  Suspect: A person who was seen committing the crime or about whom there is enough evidence to "suspect" that person committed the crime (the person's name may not be known; only a physical description may be available)

  Known offender: A person who has been *convicted, not just arrested,* for any crime other than a sex offense; this information typically comes from databases external to a police agency, such as those housed in probation and parole or state criminal history databases

Sex offender: A person who has been convicted, not just arrested, for a sex offense

Victim: A person who is the victim of the crime (information about property as victims—i.e., targets—is normally included in the MO category as type of location or property type)

Witness: A person who is able to provide information about the crime

- *Name/address/date of birth*: The name, address, and birth date of the individual, when these are known, as well as any aliases

- *Physical description*: A description of the person's static physical characteristics (i.e., characteristics that do not change from one day to the next) as they are described by a witness or officer or are retrieved from official information such as a driver's license. Characteristics include the following:

  Age: Computed from a known date of birth or a range for a suspect whose birthday is not known (e.g., suspect appeared to be between 25 and 35 years old)

  Sex (male or female): Based on driver's license information of a known person or on witness description

  Height: Observed by an officer or a range based on witness description (e.g., suspect appeared to be between 5'6" and 5'8" tall)

  Weight: Observed by an officer or a range based on witness description (e.g., suspect appeared to be between 210 and 230 pounds)

  Eye color: Observed by an officer or based on witness description

  Race/ethnicity: Based on the person's self-classification or driver's license or on witness description (note that these two classifications can be very different)

  Build: The general body type of the individual (e.g., slight, medium, large, heavy, tall), based on an officer's observation or witness description

  Teeth condition: The nature of the individual's teeth (e.g., crooked, yellow, black, missing, gold), observed by an officer or based on witness description

Hand use: Whether the individual used one hand or another dominantly (e.g., held the gun in his right hand), based on witness description

Scars, tattoos, marks, or other distinguishing characteristics: Permanent unique visible characteristics (e.g., tattoos, scars, birthmarks, missing limbs), observed by an officer or based on witness description

- *Physical condition*: A description of characteristics of the person that are not static (i.e., that can be different or changed on purpose from one day to the next or from one crime to the next). Characteristics include the following:

Hair color: Observed by an officer or based on witness description

Hair length: Observed by an officer or based on witness description

Physical condition: The immediate physical condition of the person (e.g., intoxicated, belligerent, incoherent, nervous), observed by an officer or based on witness description

Facial hair: The type of facial hair (e.g., beard, mustache, goatee, clean shaven), observed by an officer or based on witness description

Appearance: The individual's general appearance (e.g., well-groomed, dirty, wearing a disguise, gang clothing), observed by an officer or based on witness description

Complexion: The texture and tone of an individual's skin (e.g., fair, tan, dark, pocked), observed by an officer or based on witness description

Speech: How the individual spoke during the crime (e.g., accent, slurred, quietly), based on witness description

Not all of the characteristics mentioned thus far are collected for each crime incident, but this list provides a framework for collecting potentially important information about persons that can be used to link them to crimes and crimes to one another. In addition to this information on a suspect, a photograph of the person is attached to the case record when available. Also, as in the case of MO data, an analyst can include qualitative information describing anything unique about the person that may not be covered by the previous characteristics or that provides further explanation (e.g., description of the exact clothing worn, including name brand items).

Vehicle Involved in the Crime The third general category of information collected for pattern analysis concerns vehicles. These data are important because vehicles often serve key roles in the commission of crimes. Offenders can use vehicles as transportation to and from the locations of their crimes, as weapons (e.g., running over a person), or as methods of entry (e.g., in a "smash and grab," the offender runs a vehicle through a storefront window and takes property inside). Stolen vehicles are often used in the commission of crimes.

Three types of information are collected about vehicles: official information, physical description, and the condition of the vehicle at the time of the incident. The official information on a vehicle consists of its vehicle identification number, or VIN, which is a unique identifier; the license plate number; and the state of issue. In some cases, only a partial license number is available, but that information can still be useful, as computer search capabilities enable police agencies to examine motor vehicle databases for possible matches using various combinations of plate numbers and letters.

The physical description of a vehicle is the permanent aspects of the vehicle and includes the make (e.g., Chevrolet, Ford, Honda), model (e.g., Corvette, Explorer, Accord), style (e.g., four-door, two-door, hatchback, coupe, truck) and color. Note that color of the vehicle can be changed, but in most cases is not. Information on the condition of the vehicle relates to temporary characteristics existing at the time of the incident, much like the physical condition of a person. It includes any after-market modifications (e.g., large tires and rims, spoilers) and damage (e.g., dent in the passenger door, broken window, primer on front end).

Field Information

Field information is another important type of data used in tactical crime analysis. In many police departments, patrol officers still fill out paper **FI cards** (i.e., *field information* or *field interview* cards) when they respond to a call and find that it is not necessary to take an official police report, but additional information about the incident, the person, or a vehicle is worth collecting (e.g., a person acting suspicious in an area with an increased number of burglaries). When on paper, FI cards are usually small so that officers can easily keep them in their pockets and access them in the field. Figure 8.3 is an example of a paper FI card. As technology has advanced, in most medium and large police departments, officers now put this information into an app on their smartphones, but interestingly, they are often still called "FI cards" or "FIs."

Not all types of incidents about which officers collect field information are useful for pattern analysis, but analysts sometimes find that such information helps them to identify potential leads (e.g., when someone is stopped in a residential neighborhood for being suspicious during the time frame associated with a burglary pattern) or individuals who are continually being contacted by the police for suspicious behavior (e.g., individuals sleeping behind commercial places and digging through garbage). The following four types of field information are most relevant in tactical crime analysis:

- *Suspicious persons*: For example, officers may record information on persons contacted while loitering in a commercial area after business hours or persons driving or sitting in a vehicle under suspicious circumstances.

- *Suspicious vehicles*: For example, a resident may provide an officer with the license plate number and description of a vehicle that has been driven through the neighborhood suspiciously on more than one occasion.

- *Persons warned for trespassing*: For example, officers may record information on such persons if they are engaged in disturbing or suspicious activity at specific locations.

- *Individuals with unique scars, marks, or tattoos*: Many police agencies compile databases on individuals with clearly identifiable, nonchanging characteristics such as visible scars, marks, or tattoos.

The data collected about an incident include general information about the characteristics of the incident, the person, and the vehicle involved. These variables are similar to those collected for crime incidents and allow analysts to examine field information and crime information together. Information about the incident includes the type of incident; the date and time of the incident; the address of the incident, including apartment, suite, or hotel room number, if applicable; the address name and type of location; and summary information about the purpose and nature of the incident (e.g., individual warned for trespassing at ValueMart and left the premises). Notice Figure 8.3 also contains check boxes for quick completion by the officers and categories that are particularly helpful for analysis (e.g., type of incident, behavior of the individuals, and environment where the incident occurred).

In most cases, officers collect field information from individuals through personal interaction and their drivers' licenses or identification cards, so information about many of the following characteristics of the person are available at the time of contact: name, date of birth, and home address; physical description (e.g., height, weight, race/ethnicity, sex); unique information (e.g., scars, marks, tattoos); and physical condition at the time the field information was collected (e.g., appearance, hair color). Finally, if a vehicle is involved, the information collected is the same as that collected in a crime incident (VIN, license plate information, make, model, style, color, etc.). Many police agencies also take photos of individuals in the field to document their current physical condition (e.g., individuals with scars, marks, and tattoos), which are then saved with the FI card information.

Figure 8.3 Sample FI Card

Field Information Card	
Date:	Time:
Location:	

Type of incident:

☐ Trespass warning	☐ Suspicious person/vehicle
☐ Information	☐ Other:_____

Type of behavior:

☐ Sitting/standing	☐ Driving
☐ Walking	☐ Sleeping
☐ Riding a bike	☐ In parked vehicle
☐ Other:_____	

Type of environment:

☐ Gas station/convenience store	
☐ Roadway/street	☐ Woods/vacant lot
☐ Park	☐ School
☐ Commercial/industrial	☐ Other:_____
Name:	DOB:
Height: Weight:	Hair: Eyes:

Scars/marks/tattoos:

Description:

_____

_____

_____

_____

_____

_____

SUMMARY POINTS

This chapter describes techniques for analyzing repeat incidents and collecting the data used in tactical crime analysis. The following are the key points addressed in this chapter:

- A repeat incident is a cluster of two or more incidents that are similar in nature and have happened at the same place (typically) or by the same person; these clusters occur less frequently than individual incidents. A repeat incident usually includes common noncriminal or interpersonal criminal incidents that may, but do not always, result in a crime report.

- Addressing of repeat incidents begins with identifying locations with multiple calls for service.

- The role of crime analysis in addressing a repeat incident is developing the report from which repeat incident locations are identified.

- Several considerations factored in the development of the repeat incident report include the types of calls for service, the time period examined, and the format of the report.

- Calls-for-service data are used to identify repeat incident locations—specifically, data relating to disorder, quality of life, and interpersonal disputes.

- Once the type of report and calls-for-service types have been selected, other considerations for the development of a repeat incident location report include the time period of the report, the number of calls that may constitute a repeat incident location (i.e., threshold), and the final content of the report.

- Tactical crime analysis seeks to identify patterns of crimes that are not easily linked together by focusing on crimes in which the offender and the victim do not know one another and on crimes that are predatory in nature.

- The types of crimes examined typically include robbery, residential and commercial burglary, theft from vehicle, auto theft, grand theft, vandalism, rape, indecent exposure, and public sexual indecency.

- Tactical crime analysts examine information about the crime incident, the persons involved in the crime, and vehicles involved in the crime.

- Modus operandi (MO), a Latin term meaning literally "method of procedure," refers to the method of the crime. The key elements of MO include the type of crime, how the crime was carried out, where the crime was committed, and when the crime was committed.

- The data about a person involved in a crime typically include a description of the type of contact, the name and address of the person, a physical description of the person, and a description of the physical condition of the person at the time of the crime.

- The types of contacts include investigative lead, suspect, known offender, sex offender, victim, and witness.

- The physical description is a description of the person's static physical characteristics (i.e., characteristics that do not change from one day to the next) and include age, sex, race, height, weight, eye color, build, teeth condition, hand use, scars, tattoos, marks, and other distinguishing characteristics.

- Physical condition is a description of characteristics of the person that are not static (i.e., that can be different or changed on purpose from one day to the next or from one crime to the next). They include hair color, hair length, immediate physical condition of the person, facial hair, appearance, complexion, and speech.

- The third general category of information collected for pattern analysis concerns vehicles. These data are important because vehicles often serve key roles in the commission of crimes.

- Offenders can use vehicles as transportation to and from the locations of their crimes, as weapons, or as methods of entry. Stolen vehicles are often used in the commission of crime.

- Three types of information are collected about vehicles: official information, physical description, and the condition of the vehicle at the time of the incident.

- The official information on a vehicle consists of its vehicle identification number, or VIN, which is a unique identifier, and the license plate number and state of issue.

- The physical description of a vehicle includes the make, model, style, color, the model year, and the general type of vehicle.

- Information on the condition of the vehicle at the time of the incident includes after-market modifications and damage.

- Field information is another important data source used in tactical crime analysis and is collected on paper cards by officers or through electronic data entry.

- Typically, field information is collected on suspicious persons, suspicious vehicles, persons warned for trespassing, and individuals with unique scars, marks, or tattoos.

DISCUSSION EXERCISES*

Exercise 1

You have been asked to develop a repeat incident location report that helps to identify domestic violence situations at residential addresses before they get too serious. These situations include disputes between parents, between parents and children, and between children. Decide the following in the development of the report: types of calls for service to be included (use Chapter 5 lists of call types), time frame of the report (e.g., 2 weeks vs. 6 weeks), number of calls to make a repeat incident location (because you are not working for an agency, decide based on how many calls in the time period you chose would constitute a potential domestic violence problem), format of the report, and timing of the report (e.g., how often it is provided to officers).

Exercise 2

For each of the following crimes, list (in order of importance) 10 characteristics described in this chapter from MO, suspect, or vehicle information that are important for pattern analysis of that crime. Remember that certain types of crime have more detailed information in their reports. There will be more than 10 characteristics that are important, but list only the top 10 and then rank them by importance.

- Robbery

- Theft from vehicle

- Residential burglary

- Stranger rape

CHAPTER 9

Pattern Identification Process

Once tactical data have been collected, crime analysts use them to identify patterns, to identify investigative leads, and to clear cases. This chapter outlines the processes for each of these goals of tactical crime analysis, separately

Pattern Identification Methodology

The first goal of tactical crime analysis is pattern identification, which consists of linking crimes by type, modus operandi (MO), person, and vehicle characteristics, among other things. Pattern identification makes up most of the work conducted for tactical crime analysis. This section describes the types of tactical crime analysis patterns that are identified, the approaches for pattern identification (e.g., deduction and induction), and the systematic methods for initial pattern identification and pattern finalization.

Types of Patterns

As discussed in Chapter 3, a crime pattern is a group of two or more crimes reported to or discovered by the police that is treated as one unit of analysis because (1) the crimes share one or more key commonalities that make them notable and distinct, (2) there is no known relationship between victim and offender, and (3) the criminal activity is typically of limited duration (IACA, 2011b). The International Association of Crime Analysts (2011b) categorizes crime patterns into seven main types, both to structure the identification of patterns and to provide a common language for communication about patterns within police departments and their communities. The following are definitions of the seven types according to the IACA (2011b, pp. 3–4):

- **Series** is a group of similar crimes thought to be committed by the same individual or group of individuals acting in concert. Examples: Four commercial arsons citywide in which a black male between the ages of 45 and 50 wearing yellow sweatpants, a black hooded sweatshirt, and a yellow "Yankees" cap was observed leaving the commercial structures immediately after the fire alarm was triggered; five home invasion–style robberies involving two to three white males in their 20s wearing stockings over their faces, displaying a silver, double-barreled shotgun, and driving a red 2000 to 2010 Honda Civic.

- **Spree** is a specific type of series characterized by high frequency of criminal activity within a remarkably short time frame, to the extent that the activity appears almost continuous. Examples: A rash of thefts from autos at a parking garage over the course of 1 hour; multiple apartments in a high-rise building burglarized during daytime hours on a single day.

- **Hot prey** refers to a group of crimes, committed by one or more individuals, involving victims who share similar physical characteristics and/or engage in similar behavior. Examples: five home invasion robberies of new immigrant Asian families occurring throughout the city over 6 weeks; seven fraudulent check scams targeting elderly victims over 1 week; 10 robberies, committed by different offenders, of intoxicated persons walking home alone from the bars on the weekend over 2 months.

- **Hot spot** refers to a group of similar crimes committed by one or more individuals at locations within close proximity to one another (IACA, 2011b); it is also called a **micro-time hot spot** (Santos & Santos, 2015d). It is important to more clearly differentiate micro-time hot spots from long-term or macro-time hot spots (i.e., problem areas) since the micro-time hot spot is the most common type of pattern identified by crime analysts. Thus, a micro-time hot spot is the emergence of several closely related crimes within a few minutes' travel distance from one another (i.e., micro-place) that occurs within a relatively short period of time (i.e., micro-time)—a crime "flare-up" (Santos & Santos, 2015c). Examples: four daytime burglaries over the past 2 weeks at a suburban residential subdivision, with no notable similarities in method of entry or known suspects; 10 commercial burglaries over the course of 3 weeks at businesses located within a 0.5-mile radius during overnight hours.

- **Hot setting** refers to a group of similar crimes committed by one or more individuals that are primarily related by type of place where the crimes occurred. Examples: seven late-night robberies of 24-hour convenience stores throughout the city by different offenders over 2 weeks; five burglaries of duplex homes adjacent to the same abandoned railway bed over a single weekend; 10 thefts from commercial vans/trucks parked at night in residential neighborhoods over 3 weeks.

- **Hot place** refers to a group of similar crimes committed by one or more individuals at the same location. Examples: a local movie theatre that has experienced 10 thefts from auto, three incidents of graffiti on the building, and two strong-arm robberies in the parking lot over the course of 1 month; an apartment community that has experienced two stranger-on-stranger sexual assaults, one drug-related shooting, and five residential burglaries within 3 weeks.

- **Hot product** refers to a group of crimes committed by one or more individuals in which a unique type of property is targeted for theft. Clarke (1999) coined this term, defining *hot products* as "those consumer items that are most attractive to thieves" (p. 23). Examples: four thefts of handguns taken out of vehicles at residential and commercial places in 2 weeks; 15 burglaries of vacant homes and construction sites in which only copper wiring and piping was taken over 6 weeks; 10 thefts of laptops and smartphones occurring across one college campus during the first month of school.

It is important to note that these pattern types are not mutually exclusive (i.e., a pattern can be more than one type). However, when deciding which to assign to a pattern of crimes, the type with the most specificity should be chosen. For example, if a pattern is identified in which the same suspect is robbing convenience stores, it is both a series and a hot setting. The analyst would title it as a *series* because that title provides more specific information about the pattern in that the same suspect is more specific than the same type of place.

Deduction and Induction

When a crime analyst sets out to identify a pattern, one of two general circumstances exists: (1) the analyst has a large number of cases from which to identify a pattern, or (2) the analyst has one crime to which others can be linked. In social science, these methods of inquiry are called **deduction** and **induction**, respectively (see also Burrell & Bull, 2011).

A researcher using the deductive method starts with general ideas about the phenomenon of interest and moves to specific facts that support these general ideas. In pattern analysis, analysts using this method examine all crimes at the same time and search for commonalities. Figure 9.1 illustrates how an analyst would deduce a pattern from a large number of incidents based on shared characteristics. The analyst begins by examining all burglaries and then focuses on commercial burglaries, then on commercial burglaries occurring in Beat 46, and then on commercial burglaries occurring at doctors' offices. Finally, the analyst focuses on commercial burglaries in Beat 46 at doctors' offices that occur overnight and on the weekends when the businesses are closed.

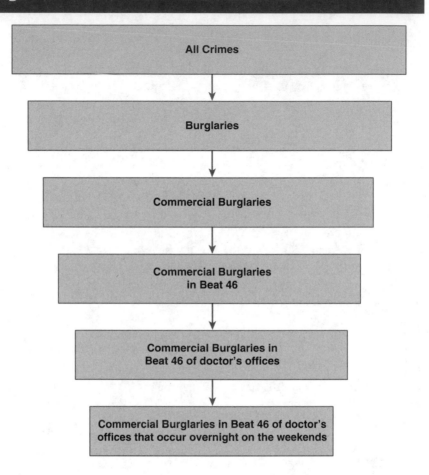

Figure 9.1   Pattern Identification: Deduction

All Crimes

Burglaries

Commercial Burglaries

Commercial Burglaries in Beat 46

Commercial Burglaries in Beat 46 of doctor's offices

Commercial Burglaries in Beat 46 of doctor's offices that occur overnight on the weekends

The decisions the analyst makes at each level are based on shared characteristics of the included incidents as well as on critical thinking. For example, if there was only one commercial burglary in Beat 46 at doctors' offices, the analysts would look for crimes in Beat 46 at a different location type.

The inductive method, in contrast, involves taking individual facts or specific ideas and relating them to general concepts. In pattern analysis, an analyst using induction focuses first on one crime and then looks at a group of other crimes for similarities. Figure 9.2 illustrates how an analyst would use the inductive method to find a robbery pattern. The first case is one in which a white man dressed as a woman robs a bank. Starting with this case, the analyst looks for other robberies with characteristics similar to those of the first.

Crime analysts can find the case for which they begin the inductive method of pattern identification in several different ways. One way involves searching the crime database for anomalies—that is, identifying rare or distinctive characteristics that are relatively unusual for that crime type and or that jurisdiction (e.g., a robbery by a man dressed as a woman; grand theft of valuable paintings; commercial burglaries in which the offender enters by cutting a hole in the wall of a neighboring business). Analysts also have cases brought to their attention by detectives who are investigating the crime and looking for related incidents or from other police personnel who take the report or make note of an unusual crime.

Initial Pattern Identification

To identify crime patterns, analysts must be skilled in critical thinking and be able to recognize commonalities among characteristics of crime incidents (Paulsen et al., 2009). This process is not mathematical nor can it be specifically laid out, but it requires knowledge of crime and analytical skills. However, a two-step process of identifying a pattern is presented in this chapter as a general guide for conducting pattern analysis. First, the analyst must link together all of the cases that might make up a pattern (initial pattern identification), and second, the analyst must look more closely at those cases to ensure that the pattern detected is sound (pattern finalization, discussed later in this chapter).Crime analysts use three methods to arrive at the initial identification of a pattern: 1) **ad hoc linking**, 2) **weights and thresholds**, and 3) **query method**. Using any of these methods, analysts can examine cases inductively or deductively.

The most informal pattern identification method, referred to as ad hoc linking, consists of persons linking cases by memory in the course of their everyday work. Even though this method is not systematic, analysts often identify many patterns this way. Most often, analysts follow up on ad hoc linking by applying one of the other two more formal methods of pattern identification: the query method and the weights and thresholds method. The query method involves the use of critical thinking and the application of deductive/inductive methods as the analyst searches a database and links cases that have similar characteristics.

The second method to identify initial patterns is through a mathematical method in which the analyst assigns weights to various characteristics of crimes and then uses a statistical or other type of program to sum up the weights for each crime. Once the weights are set, the analyst can either take one case and match its characteristics to the entire database (inductive method) or look for any cases that meet a particular threshold of similarity to one another (deductive method). The analyst can set different weights for a variety of crimes (e.g., residential burglary, commercial burglary, bank robbery, street robbery) and characteristics (e.g., point of entry, suspect description, time).

Of the three methods, the query method is most often used by crime analysts, so it is explained more fully here. In initial pattern identification, querying is an iterative process in which the analyst manipulates, searches, and sorts the characteristics of crimes in a database matrix to link crimes with similar characteristics. The analyst first uses induction or deduction to look for

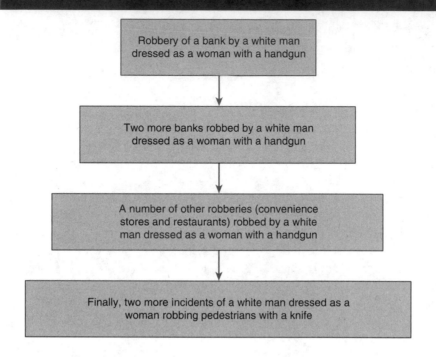

Figure 9.2 Pattern Identification: Induction

Robbery of a bank by a white man dressed as a woman with a handgun

Two more banks robbed by a white man dressed as a woman with a handgun

A number of other robberies (convenience stores and restaurants) robbed by a white man dressed as a woman with a handgun

Finally, two more incidents of a white man dressed as a woman robbing pedestrians with a knife

patterns. Figure 9.3 shows the results of an initial query (selection) that searched for 1) residential burglaries, 2) at single family homes, 3) from March 1, 2017, to March 30, 2017, 4) in Beat 24.

To view the results more easily and inspect them visually, the analyst typically sorts the crime report cases. Figure 9.4 shows the cases sorted by point of entry; the analyst can see that there are a number of cases in which entry was made through the master bedroom window, the side door, and another window. Even more interesting, the table shows that during the crimes in which the offender entered the master bedroom window, the closets were neatly searched. These cases might be the beginnings of an initial pattern. Another possible pattern may contain the cases in which the offender pried the sliding door to get into the home. The analyst would look at the dates and times of these incidents as well as read the narratives of the police reports to see if there are any more initial similarities.

The use of electronic data matrices through software such as Microsoft Excel or Access, IMB's SPSS, or specific crime analysis software is imperative in pattern analysis because analysts must be able to compare multiple cases and columns rapidly as well as scan fields quickly for pertinent information. For instance, to identify a robbery series, an analyst might organize the matrix so that those variables most salient to robberies—such as location type, weapon, suspect's actions against the victim, and suspect description—are contiguous and easily examined together. To identify a residential burglary pattern, an analyst might

Figure 9.3 Initial Results of Query

Case No.	From Date/Time	To Date/Time	DOW1	DOW2	Point of Entry	Method	GEO X	GEO Y
201704603	3/2/2017 18:09	3/2/2017 18:20	TH	TH	Window	Screen removed	86942600	108677050
201704742	3/4/2017 9:45	3/4/2017 11:25	SA	SA	Side door	Prying tool	85797519	108067775
201704950	3/6/2017 9:00	3/6/2017 17:09	MO	MO	No force	Biological evidence	86408875	106134150
201704974	3/7/2017 4:11	3/7/2017 4:11	TU	TU	Side door	Prying tool	84790906	106238888
201705064	3/8/2017 19:32	3/8/2017 19:32	WE	WE	Side door	Prying tool	88775531	107363038
201705580	3/14/2017 21:34	3/14/2017 21:34	TU	TU	Master bed window	Closets neatly searched	86746650	107221250
201708709	3/15/2017 12:00	4/19/2017 14:30	WE	SU	No force	No force	86809625	107871900
201705826	3/16/2017 2:00	3/16/2017 6:30	TH	TH	Master bed window	Closets neatly searched	86774288	107113975
201705818	3/18/2017 10:16	3/18/2017 10:16	SA	SA	Slider	Screen removed	86249719	107688113
201706050	3/19/2017 17:00	3/20/2017 2:18	SU	MO	Window	Screen removed	89172925	107383913
201706161	3/20/2017 18:00	3/22/2017 16:30	MO	WE	Master bed window	Closets neatly searched	86408900	108686700
201707103	3/26/2017 19:00	4/3/2017 21:56	SU	MO	No force	No force	86556944	108418363
201706608	3/27/2017 0:00	3/31/2017 6:00	MO	FR	Side door	Prying tool	84841794	107159788
201707084	3/29/2017 12:30	4/3/2017 17:01	WE	MO	Master bed window	Closets neatly searched	85772925	105159013

Figure 9.4 Initial Pattern Cases Sorted by Point of Entry

Case No.	From Date/Time	To Date/Time	DOW1	DOW2	Point of Entry	Method	GEO X	GEO Y
201705580	3/14/2017 21:34	3/14/2017 21:34	TU	TU	Master bed window	Closets neatly searched	86746650	107221250
201705826	3/16/2017 2:00	3/16/2017 6:30	TH	TH	Master bed window	Closets neatly searched	86774288	107113975
201706161	3/20/2017 18:00	3/22/2017 16:30	MO	WE	Master bed window	Closets neatly searched	86408900	108686700
201707084	3/29/2017 12:30	4/3/2017 17:01	WE	MO	Master bed window	Closets neatly searched	85772925	105159013
201704950	3/6/2017 9:00	3/6/2017 17:09	MO	MO	No force	Biological evidence	86408875	106134150
201708709	3/15/2017 12:00	4/19/2017 14:30	WE	SU	No force	No force	86809625	107871900
201707103	3/26/2017 19:00	4/3/2017 21:56	SU	MO	No force	No force	86556944	108418363
201704742	3/4/2017 9:45	3/4/2017 11:25	SA	SA	Side door	Prying tool	85797519	108067775
201704974	3/7/2017 4:11	3/7/2017 4:11	TU	TU	Side door	Prying tool	84790906	106238888
201705064	3/8/2017 19:32	3/8/2017 19:32	WE	WE	Side door	Prying tool	88775531	107363038
201706608	3/27/2017 0:00	3/31/2017 6:00	MO	FR	Side door	Prying tool	84841794	107159788
201705818	3/18/2017 10:16	3/18/2017 10:16	SA	SA	Slider	Screen removed	86249719	107688113
201704603	3/2/2017 18:09	3/2/2017 18:20	TH	TH	Window	Screen removed	86942600	108677050
201706050	3/19/2017 17:00	3/20/2017 2:18	SU	MO	Window	Screen removed	89172925	107383913

organize the matrix so that the information on point of entry, method of entry, property taken, and location is close together. If the variables in a matrix are in fixed positions (e.g., as they were originally stored in the database or as they are in a paper matrix), the analyst is likely to find it difficult to see the relevant variables by different crime types. The query method of analysis is simple yet powerful. It accommodates the analyst's need to examine information visually in order to recognize patterns. By manipulating the matrix and by grouping, sorting, and refining the results through data queries, the analyst can "see" patterns in the data.

Pattern Finalization

Pattern finalization is the process of refining the list of crimes identified initially and determining which crimes are strongly related and have key characteristics in common. For example, initial identification of a commercial burglary pattern might include all crimes occurring in the preceding month at businesses in a particular area. In the process of finalizing this pattern, the analyst might eliminate several crimes that occurred on weekday afternoons because the rest occurred at night or on weekends. The methodology for finalizing a pattern is inductive and involves three steps: identifying the principal case, identifying other key cases in the pattern, and identifying any additional related cases.

Identifying the Principal Case The analyst's first step is to select one crime from the initial list that best represents the pattern and contains the most detail. The analyst then uses this **principal case** to determine the other key cases in the pattern. The method that the analyst uses in determining the principal case is based on the key characteristics of that particular crime type (e.g., suspect actions for robberies, proximity and type of location for residential burglary; see Chapter 10 for a discussion of the key characteristics of different types of crimes typically examined in tactical crime analysis). Sometimes an analyst will identify two principal cases when two crimes share nearly all of the key characteristics. The following steps can be conducted for either one or two principal cases. If the analyst used the inductive method in the initial pattern identification, the case that began that identification would be the principal case in this process.

Identifying Other Key Cases in the Pattern To identify the cases that are strongly related to the principal case, the analyst must identify the characteristics most indicative of the pattern; these are usually the characteristics that were used to determine the principal case (e.g., suspect actions for robberies, proximity and type of location for residential burglary). Then, using an inductive method, the analyst compares the key characteristics of each crime in the initial list to the principal case. The analyst's final decisions regarding which crimes should be included in the pattern are based on critical thinking since it is rarely known if crimes are actually related.

Identifying Additional Related Cases At this point, the analyst has determined whether each of the crimes that were in the initial pattern should be included in or excluded from the final pattern. By querying the original database one more time using the key characteristics of the final pattern, the analyst can ensure that no other crimes have been missed. In addition, the analyst needs to examine other databases that could contain crimes related to the pattern, progressing from databases of current crimes (e.g., those in the most recent 4 months) to older, or archived, databases. Here again, the analyst uses the key characteristics of the principal case to query the archived data.

Thoroughness is the key to successful pattern analysis. Many police agencies maintain individual databases that may not be linked to the tactical data, and analysts query these also for potential links to current patterns. In addition, analysts solicit the help of neighboring police departments in finalizing patterns because criminals do not stay within police jurisdiction boundaries. Particularly in crimes that are committed across larger areas, such as commercial robberies and burglaries, analysts would communicate with other analysts to determine if they had similar crimes before publishing the pattern bulletin. Consequently, before finalizing and distributing information about a pattern, an analyst needs to check all internal and external sources that might provide relevant data.

Identifying Investigative Leads

The second goal of tactical crime analysis is to identify investigative leads for both individual crimes and patterns. Because many crimes do not have identified suspects (e.g., names and addresses of the individuals responsible for the crimes), tactical crime analysts will work with detectives and assist the investigative process by identifying potential suspects for individual crimes and for patterns. Just as in identifying the principal case, the analyst's first step in identifying an investigative lead for a pattern is to find the most relevant and reliable suspect description or other information to which a person can be linked (e.g., date, time, and location of a burglary can be linked to the date, time, and location of field information of a suspicious person).

Thoroughness and critical thinking are as important in suspect identification as they are in pattern identification; analysts must take care to consider all potential suspects. For example, if witnesses have described a suspect as a pale black man or a tan white man with an unidentifiable accent, it would derail the analysis to exclude either blacks or whites from a list of potential leads. In fact, given this rough description, the analyst would be wise to include Hispanics, Arabic, and Native Americans as well, given that these groups also include members who could fit the witnesses' description. In some instances, analysts can infer information about a suspect from the data available, such as strength (e.g., a door broken down during the crime), use of tools (e.g., pry marks on a window), and access to a location (e.g., the time span of the crime is 15 minutes vs. several hours).

Once a key suspect description is identified, the analyst examines the characteristics of that description against various databases of offenders and suspect information. As noted in Chapter 2, theory and research indicate that offenders commit crimes near where they live, so a search of the following databases would also focus on an offender's current residence and its proximity to the crimes in the pattern.

- *Arrest database*: This database is contained in the agency's RMS and includes information on individuals that have been arrested by the analyst's agency. A search of the arrest database by residential address, type of crime, MO, and suspect description can produce the names of individuals who have been arrested for committing the type of crime of the pattern and/or who live in the pattern area.

- **Probation and parole database**: This database is housed in the department of corrections and contains records of individuals who have been or are on parole or probation. A search of this database can produce names of individuals who were convicted of a particular type of crime and were recently released from prison or are currently on probation or parole.

- **NCIC database**: Discussed in Chapter 5, this database contains records of all individuals throughout the United States who have been arrested and/or convicted of crimes. This database is often too broad if a crime analyst does not know the name or address of an offender, but it can be used in conjunction with other databases to provide information on an individual.

- **Registered sex offender database**: This database contains information on individuals who have been arrested and convicted of sex crimes and have registered with the state as required by law. While the individuals will be in the other databases mentioned in this section, it provides a mechanism to search only sex offenders living in the jurisdiction, no matter where they committed their crimes (i.e., sex offenders are required to register based on where they live; they also must re-register when they move). Analysts can search the sex offender database by residential address, description, and type of crimes committed to identify potential suspects for related sex crimes (e.g., sex offenders convicted for abusing children living in the area of a current pattern of child abduction).

- **Field information database**: As discussed earlier in this chapter, this database contains information about individuals who have exhibited suspicious behavior and individuals who have unique features and have been contacted by police officers. Analysts may identify potential leads by searching this database for information that matches a current pattern by proximity to the pattern, time of day, day of week (e.g., suspicious vehicle in an area), unique features (e.g., a person with particular scars, marks, or tattoos), or other unique information (e.g., a person found behind a commercial place with a hammer or other tools that can be used for burglary).

- *Vehicle databases*: These are databases in which vehicles are represented as cases. They can be either a departmental database that lists vehicles that have been in crashes, stolen, recovered, found, or used in a crime within the analyst's jurisdiction or a database maintained by the state's motor vehicle division that has records of all registered vehicles. Both types of databases allow searches by various characteristics (e.g., VIN, plate number, and make/model) of vehicles, and analysts search them to identify the owners of vehicles used in the commission of crimes and identify potential suspects. Officers and citizens are more likely to identify vehicles than people, and vehicle ownership can be easily determined with tag information. They can also be identified or the possible vehicles narrowed down with less specific information through more complex searches. In more recent years, some agencies have implemented license plate reader technology equipment that captures license plates of vehicles that drive by (Koper, Lum, Willis, Woods, & Hibdon, 2015). The vehicle plate information is captured as well as the date, time, and location of when the plate was read. Analysts can search the database to identify cars that were in the vicinity of individual crimes or of patterns.

In addition to these databases, analysts examine information provided by other sources, including individuals contacted by neighboring county sheriff offices, state troopers, private security companies, federal agencies, and others who collect data on offenders. Analysts often share these data through formal meetings and networks as well as through more informal methods (e.g., e-mail messages).

Clearing Cases

Another goal of tactical crime analysis is to assist police in **clearing cases.** This is the process of linking unsolved cases to a recently solved case in order to close them and to enhance the prosecution of an individual suspect. It is important to note that crime analysts assist in this process, but it is up to detectives and prosecutors to make the legal determinations regarding whether or not cases can be linked. For example, a detective arrests a suspect for committing two residential burglaries in a particular area. An analyst searches data for the past 6 months and finds that four additional burglaries were committed in that area. The detective could use this information to interrogate the suspect (e.g., "Did you commit these as well?"), or the suspect could be matched to the other cases by fingerprints or DNA evidence. If the crimes are linked, six burglaries instead of two are cleared by the one arrest, the police department closes four additional burglary cases, and the prosecutor is able to charge the individual with more offenses.

Clearing cases is an inductive process. It follows the method of pattern finalization since one crime (the solved case) is identified and compared with others to determine whether meaningful relationships exist. Another aspect of clearing cases is the closing of entire patterns. In this process, analysts reexamine formerly published information on known patterns for arrested connection to recent arrests.

For instance, a crime pattern was published about a rash of robberies in which a suspect was armed with an AK-47. Four months later, there were additional robberies, but during a traffic stop, patrol officers arrested a man with an AK-47 in his car. A crime analyst would check this person's description against the suspect description in the robbery pattern and pass this along to the officers for additional comparisons of the gun and/or so they can use the pattern information in the suspect's interview in hopes of linking him to these crimes and clearing them.

Conclusion

Even though the processes of identifying patterns, identifying investigative leads, and clearing cases are systematic and involve specific techniques and methods, each analysis situation is uniquely shaped by the analyst's critical thinking, which is driven by the analyst's abilities, experience, and the task at hand. These processes are more intellectual than technical. Chapter 10 provides a discussion of identifying different patterns of crime and a myriad of examples that help illustrate these processes.

SUMMARY POINTS

This chapter describes the methods for identifying and finalizing patterns, identifying investigative leads, and clearing cases. The following are the key points addressed in this chapter:

- A crime pattern is a group of two or more crimes reported to or discovered by police that is treated as one unit of analysis because (1) the crimes share one or more key commonalities that make them notable and distinct, (2) there is no known relationship between victim and offender, and (3) the criminal activity is typically of limited duration.

- A series is a group of similar crimes thought to be committed by the same individual or group of individuals acting in concert.

- A spree is a specific type of series characterized by high frequency of criminal activity within a remarkably short time frame, to the extent that the activity appears almost continuous.

- Hot prey refers to a group of crimes committed by one or more individuals, involving victims who share similar physical characteristics and/or engage in similar behavior.

- Hot spot refers to a group of similar crimes committed by one or more individuals at locations within close proximity to one another.

- It is important to clearly differentiate pattern hot spots from long-term or macro-time hot spots (i.e., problem areas). Thus, the hot spot is also called a "micro-time hot spot" and is the most common type of pattern identified by crime analysts. The micro-time hot spot is the emergence of several closely related crimes within a few minutes' travel distance from one another (i.e., micro-place) that occurs within a relatively short period of time (i.e., micro-time)—a crime "flare-up."

- Hot setting refers to a group of similar crimes committed by one or more individuals that are primarily related by type of location(s).

- Hot place refers to a group of similar crimes committed by one or more individuals at the same location.

- Hot product refers to a group of crimes committed by one or more individuals in which a unique type of property is targeted for theft.

- Deduction is the process of finding a pattern from a large number of cases (i.e., general to specific).

- Induction is the process of finding a pattern from one case to which others can be linked (i.e., specific to general).

- Identifying a pattern is a two-step process: The analyst must link together all of the cases that may make up a pattern (initial pattern identification) and then look closely at the cases to determine whether they should be included in or excluded from a pattern (pattern finalization).

- The three general methods of initial pattern identification are the ad hoc, weights and thresholds, and query method.

- Ad hoc linking of patterns consists of persons linking cases by memory in the course of their everyday work.

- The second method of identifying initial patterns uses weights and thresholds within a computer system to identify patterns.

- The query method of identifying patterns involves the use of critical thinking and the application of deductive/inductive methods as the analyst searches a database and links cases with similar characteristics. It is the method primarily used to identify patterns.

- Pattern finalization is the process of refining a pattern by including only strongly related cases. The methodology for finalizing a pattern is inductive and consists of three steps: identifying the principal case, identifying other key cases in the pattern, and identifying any additional related cases.

- Identifying investigative leads is an inductive process that begins with identifying the most relevant suspect description or MO (modus operandi) characteristics to match offenders typically living in close proximity to the pattern.

- Tactical crime analysts use several kinds of databases to provide police with investigative leads; these include an arrest database, a probation and parole database, an NCIC database, a registered sex offender database, a field information database, and a vehicle database.

- Clearing cases is an inductive process in which an analyst links unsolved cases to a recently solved case in order to provide information to detectives who are ultimately responsible for closing cases and pressing multiple charges against an individual suspect.

DISCUSSION EXERCISES*

Exercise 1

For each of the following descriptions, determine which type of pattern it is. Justify your answer using the definitions in this chapter.

1. Five motor vehicle thefts from the Happy Days Apartments parking lot occurred over 1 week. All of the vehicles were found partially stripped at various locations around the city.

2. In December, there were seven thefts of motor vehicles left running at gas stations (when victims went inside to pay) around the city and in neighboring cities, with no common suspect information among the crimes.

3. Seven thefts from vehicles in the Valley Mall parking lot occurred in 3 hours during one afternoon.

4. Over 10 days, four commercial arsons occurred overnight in District 2 and District 4, a man with a similar description in each crime was observed leaving the retail stores with jewelry immediately after the fire alarm was triggered.

5. Four home invasion robberies of Haitian immigrant families occurred in the Water's Edge neighborhood by the same suspects.

6. There have been thefts of GPS units from rental cars in hotel parking lots as well as rental car parking lots in District 2.

7. There have been four daytime residential burglaries of single-family homes over the past 2 weeks in a 0.19-mile radius within the Shady Acres gated community; two crimes began with entry through the back slider, and two started with entry through the cabana door.

8. Six late-night robberies of pizza delivery drivers by different suspects across the city have occurred; one driver was victimized twice.

Exercise 2

Use the process of pattern finalization to determine the cases in the final pattern from the following table. Not all the information has been provided, but do the best you can with what is here. All of these crimes are robberies of pedestrians who were either on the street or in an alley in the same general area.

*Additional exercises using data and other resources can be found on **http://www.sagepub .com/bobasantos4e.**

Case No.	Date	Time	Day	Suspect's Actions Against Person	Weapon Type	Property Taken	Property Value	Suspect's Race	Suspect's Sex	Suspect's Facial Hair
1	3/1/2017	0200	Wed	Hit victim	Hands/ Feet	Cash/ Notes	$200.00	White	Male	
2	3/4/2017	1720	Sat	Deceptive practices	Handgun	Jewelry	$300.00	Unknown		
3	3/5/2017	1800	Tue	Deceptive practices	Handgun	None	NONE	Unknown		
4	3/19/2017	1930	Tue	Deceptive practices	Simulated	Purse/Wallet	$100.00	Hispanic	Male	Goatee
5	4/1/2017	1700	Sat	Followed victim	Simulated	None	NONE	Hispanic	Male	Goatee
6	4/4/2017	1900	Tue	Followed victim	Handgun	Purse/Wallet	$50.00	Hispanic	Male	
7	4/15/2017	1000	Sat	Hit victim	Hands/ Feet	Jewelry	$700.00	Unknown		
8	4/18/2017	2000	Tue	Deceptive practices	Handgun	Purse/Wallet	$100.00	Hispanic	Male	Goatee
9	4/19/2017	2100	Wed	Followed victim	Handgun	Jewelry	$100.00	Black	Male	
10	5/3/2017	0900	Wed	Followed victim	None	None	NONE	Unknown		
11	5/4/2017	1800	Thu	Hit victim	Simulated	Purse/Wallet	$80.00	Hispanic	Male	Goatee
12	5/5/2017	0100	Fri	Hit victim	Handgun	Purse/Wallet	$800.00	Unknown		

CHAPTER

10

Identifying Meaningful and Useful Patterns

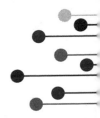

The purpose of this chapter is to illustrate how crime analysts identify meaningful patterns that are useful for police. In order to do this, it will first discuss the difference between how persons crime and property crime patterns are identified and second, how police can use the results of pattern analysis to implement problem-solving responses. The remainder of the chapter will discuss specific types of crime commonly examined in tactical crime analysis, key characteristics used to identify patterns for these crimes, and potential responses used by police for these patterns. The discussion is illustrated with examples of real crime patterns provided by working crime analysts.

To prepare for pattern identification, crime analysts should become familiar with the research related to the crimes they are examining. Although they do not focus specifically on short-term pattern analysis, the *Problem Guide* series at the Center for Problem-Oriented Policing (www.popcenter.org) provides analysts with a wealth of knowledge about types of offenders, victims, and places for the crime types discussed in this chapter.

Persons Crime and Property Crime

Pattern identification in tactical crime analysis is guided by the distinction between persons crime and property crime patterns. That is, persons and property crimes are normally examined separately because the characteristics that link persons crimes to one another are inherently different from those that link property crimes. **Persons crimes** are those crimes in which people are the targets of an offender. The crimes commonly examined for persons crime pattern analysis are robbery, stranger sexual assault, indecent exposure, and public sexual indecency. Other persons crimes may be examined in pattern analysis by some analysts (e.g., aggravated assaults and shootings between strangers), but the discussion here will focus on robbery, stranger sexual assault, indecent exposure, and public sexual indecency since they are the most common.

In most persons crimes, the victims are also witnesses, so these types of crimes provide analysts with abundant detail about the actions of the suspect, the suspect's description, and any vehicles involved. The types of patterns typically found for persons crimes are series or sprees because the wealth of information about each crime is used to link incidents by offender. Less often, analysts identify patterns involving hot spots, hot prey, or hot settings. These types of patterns do not have common suspects but share other characteristics such as proximity, type of victim, and type of place. The following are examples of some specific persons crime patterns:

- *Series, indecent exposure:* A suspect on a mountain bike approaches female pedestrians and exposes himself. Four incidents have occurred over a 1-month period, and the suspect's description, bicycle description, and actions are very similar in all four incidents.

- *Spree, carjacking:* Three carjackings have occurred within the city in a period of 3 hours. Two suspects use a car to cut the victim off in traffic and force the victim to stop; then one suspect approaches the victim's car and orders the victim out of the car at gunpoint. That suspect drives away in the victim's car, and the other drives away in the suspect car.

- *Hot place, mall parking lot:* Several incidents of robbery of pedestrians and indecent exposure have occurred in a mall parking lot near the movie theaters over a 1-month period. The crimes appear to have been committed by different people, based on various suspect descriptions by witnesses.

- *Hot prey, female pedestrians:* Several types of vehicles have been observed driving through a residential area during evening hours. On several occasions, the driver of each vehicle is alone and exposed himself to a female pedestrian. Because the incidents have all occurred at night, officers have not been able to obtain detailed suspect and vehicle descriptions, but the targeted victims have all been women walking on the street.

- *Hot setting, convenience stores:* Several incidents of strong-arm robbery have occurred in the past week at a particular chain of convenience stores throughout the city, yet different MOs and suspect descriptions indicate that multiple suspects are responsible for the crimes.

Property crimes are those crimes in which property is the target of an offender. The crimes commonly examined for property crime pattern analysis are theft from vehicle, auto theft, residential burglary, and commercial burglary. Incidents of theft from buildings, criminal trespass, grand theft, and criminal damage are also examined as they relate to these other crimes or as they indicate overt vandalism and theft of property (e.g., graffiti, mailbox destruction, theft of construction materials). Because witnesses are often not present during the commission of property crimes, crime analysts usually have little or no suspect information available to use for identifying patterns. Typically, analysts link property crimes together by examining information on types of crimes (e.g., residential vs. commercial burglary), types of settings (e.g., office buildings, apartments, single-family homes), and proximity of the incidents. Modus operandi (MO) and temporal characteristics are also used but to a somewhat lesser degree. The patterns most often identified in the analysis of property crimes are hot spots, hot settings, hot products, and sprees. Here are some examples:

- *Micro-time hot spot, residential burglaries:* Three residential burglaries have occurred in a specific neighborhood within a 0.15-mile radius of one another. In all of the burglaries, suspects gained entry to the homes by breaking or prying open a rear window. Various types of property have been taken, from small electronics to jewelry and cash. Suspect information is not available, as there have been no witnesses to any of the incidents.

- *Hot place, apartment community:* Ten incidents of theft from vehicle have occurred at the same 100-unit apartment community over 14 days. All incidents have occurred overnight, with several nights having multiple cars hit. Property taken varies from cash and electronics to parts of the vehicles (e.g., emblems, car covers). In some cases, no force was used, and in all cases, no suspect information is available.

- *Hot setting, new home construction sites:* Seven burglaries have occurred in the past 6 days at new home construction sites at a new 500-home development. Suspects break into or enter unlocked houses in their final stages of construction to steal appliances or on-site construction equipment. The incidents have all taken place at night, and no suspect information has been obtained. Different tire marks have been found at the scenes, indicating the use of several different types of vehicles.

- *Hot product, pool equipment:* Fifteen thefts from residential backyard pools have occurred over a 4-week period during the day and night. Portable pool equipment is the only property taken in each incident.

- *Spree, vandalism of vehicles:* Thirteen vehicles along the same street were damaged over 1 night. It seems as though the same suspect(s) committed the crimes because the cars were next to one another and damaged in the same way— taillights broken, mirrors damaged—with what seems to be a baseball bat.

Even though persons crime and property crime warrant the examination of different characteristics, crime analysts sometimes examine the two kinds of crimes together. Some examples of such patterns include the following:

- *Series, burglary and robbery:* Two "cat" burglaries (when the suspect enters the house at night while the residents are home) and two robberies of residents walking down the street have occurred in the same neighborhood. Suspect information is available and similar for all of these incidents.

- *Spree, burglary and carjacking:* A young man burglarizes a business suite late at night and leaves the scene by carjacking a vehicle. The man then crashes the vehicle into a different retail store's front window, enters the store, and steals additional property. All of these incidents take place within a 1-hour period.

- *Hot place, water park:* Over the past 2 weeks, a water park had 10 thefts from vehicle and four robberies of customers in its parking lot, as well as five public sexual indecency incidents inside the park itself. There are a range of suspect descriptions, and there have been no crimes at the park in the 2 months previous while it has been open.

- *Hot product, video games and consoles:* During the past 2 months, nine houses across the city have been burglarized, and video game consoles and games have been the only property taken. In addition, two robberies have occurred in which video games have been taken from individuals in a gaming store's parking lot, and there was one commercial burglary from a large box store in which 50 gaming consoles were taken.

Potential Responses to Patterns by Police

It is important for crime analysts to understand how police use the results of pattern analysis for crime reduction responses in order for them to identify meaningful and useful patterns. A pattern represents both the scanning and analysis steps of the problem-solving process, or SARA (scanning, analysis, response, assessment), so the response is tailored based on the specific pattern information provided in the analysis results. For example, if a pattern is daytime residential burglary in a particular neighborhood, successful resolution of that pattern would be stopping residential burglaries during the day in that area. If subsequent burglaries occur at night, in a different neighborhood, or to businesses within that area, this is not seen as a failure of the response since the response to the pattern would not address burglaries with these characteristics (e.g., at night, to businesses, or in a different area). Just as with repeat incidents, the idea is to identify specific activity and respond appropriately to these smaller-scale, short-term problems so they do not develop into larger-scale, long-term problems.

The types of responses that police employ for patterns are fairly straightforward and focus on arresting and deterring offenders, as well as on crime prevention (Boba & Santos, 2011; Bruce, 2008b). More specifically, the following explains the strategies typically used by police for patterns. Notably, the directed patrol, field contacts, surveillance, and sting operations are implemented during the times and in the places of the crimes within the pattern, which could be any day of the week and any hour of the day. In contrast, investigating the pattern and clearing cases, contacting potential victims directly, and providing pattern information to the public are conducted during normal business hours (i.e., weekdays from 8 a.m. to 5 p.m.) and/or normal waking hours any day of the week.

- *Directed patrol:* This strategy focuses on police patrol in the areas and at the times in which a pattern is occurring. Police patrol in cars, on bikes, or on foot. The objective of the directed patrol is for the police to arrest offenders committing a crime or to deter offenders by increasing guardianship and the offenders' perceived risk of being caught.

- *Field contacts:* While conducting directed patrol, police officers make contact with individuals in the pattern area and, in some cases, at the time when the pattern is occurring (i.e., daylight hours for residential burglary). They contact individuals who appear to be suspicious and/or who might have information about the crime pattern. This strategy can deter potential offenders from committing crime by talking to them specifically, as well as provide potential investigative leads or intelligence that can help solve the individual crimes or the entire pattern. (For more information on both directed patrol and field contacts, see the Center for Problem-Oriented Policing [POP Center] response guide *The Benefits and Consequences of Police Crackdowns* [Scott, 2004] at www.popcenter.org.)

- *Surveillance:* This response involves the police to watch and wait in a particular area at a particular time for a crime to happen in order to make an arrest. This is different than directed patrol in which officers drive around the entire area because surveillance is often static and focused on one street block or location. When officers conduct surveillance, this response is used only in the most specific patterns (e.g., robberies of one movie theater's employees when they leave work at the end of the night). This is because personnel costs are very high (e.g., officer overtime). However, with modern technology, static or movable surveillance cameras can be used to observe and record the activity around a particular location or street block. (For more information, see the POP Center response guide *Sting Operations* [Newman, 2007] and *Video Surveillance of Public Places* [Ratcliffe, 2006].

- *"Sting" or "bait" operations:* This response requires a situation in which people or property that have been targeted in a particular pattern are put out as "bait" for offenders. Police then directly observe the bait or have electronic monitoring that allows them to arrest the offender or record (on video) offenders committing the crimes when the bait is taken. Some examples include a "bait car" for theft from vehicle or vehicle theft, or an undercover police officer for a robbery (For more information, see the POP Center response guide *Sting Operations* [Newman, 2007].)

- *Investigating the pattern and clearing cases:* Because a pattern becomes a unit of response for the police department, in addition to being assigned individual crimes, detectives can be assigned a pattern to investigate. The detective would then investigate all the crimes in the pattern together, looking at how, for example, fingerprints and evidence might cross over cases, which allows them to piece together information about the suspect, victims, and related information from the group of related cases (instead of one case at a time). Notably, not all crime reports taken by patrol officers in the field are actually assigned to detectives to investigate. This might be because of lack of evidence or just because the police department prioritizes based on its resources. Thus, in any given pattern, there might be cases that are not otherwise being investigated, so doing this gives the detectives the opportunity to clear more cases. That is, if an arrest is made related to one or more crimes in that pattern, the pattern can be used to clear the other related cases.

- *Contacting potential victims directly:* Crime prevention education works best when it is targeted at specific victims, times, and areas. This response can include either volunteers or police officers contacting specific groups of citizens, residents, or businesses that are most relevant to a particular pattern. The contact can be made in person, over the phone (e.g., reverse 911), through a letter via postal mail, through flyers left at homes or businesses, or through the Internet, e-mail, or social media. The information would include details of the pattern, crime prevention advice, and contact information for the police. Crime prevention advice would include suggestions with immediate results (e.g., lock doors and windows) and those with more long-term results (e.g., installing video surveillance equipment or alarms). (For more information about crime prevention publicity campaigns, see the POP Center response guide *Crime Prevention Publicity Campaigns* [Barthe, 2006].)

- *Providing pattern information to the public:* By disseminating patterns to the general public, police encourage the public to provide additional information ("tips") on known crimes as well as to report crimes that have not yet been reported. Also, when offenders see that the police know about their activities, they might be deterred from continuing their offending. Information about patterns also would provide specific crime prevention advice and would encourage individuals to protect themselves. Media such as newspapers, radio, television, and the Internet are used to provide this information. (For more information about crime prevention publicity campaigns, see the POP Center response guide *Crime Prevention Publicity Campaigns* [Barthe, 2006].)

What follows is a brief discussion of how these responses can be employed by police for persons crimes and property crimes, separately.

Persons Crime

As discussed earlier, persons crime patterns are typically series or sprees, which means that the analyst thinks the crimes have all been committed by the same person or group of people. Because the pattern will contain suspect descriptions and specific MO information, police responses focus on enhancing the investigation and facilitating the arrest of the offender(s). Persons crime patterns can increase the likelihood of arrest of suspects because when multiple crimes are linked together, all of the information is combined to create a more complete picture of the suspect and his behavior. For example, the victim of a rape may provide a general description of the suspect with specific information about the suspect's actions. In a second rape incident that has been linked through the suspect's behavior, the victim may have provided a more detailed description of the suspect. By combining the information from both crimes, the investigators have more complete information that could increase the likelihood of arrest.

Police also respond to persons crime patterns with surveillance and directed patrol. Crime analysts can use crime pattern information to assist in this process by attempting to anticipate when and where the offender may hit again. Offenders often repeat their behavior when it is successful and may choose similar situations to commit their crimes based on their own routine activities and activity space. Linking similar crimes together is the only way to discern whether an offender is repeating his behavior. For example, if the offender has been robbing people at bank ATMs around malls on weekends during the evening, patrol officers can focus their uncommitted patrol time in these areas, stopping suspicious people, and detectives can conduct surveillance on locations where it seems likely that people might be robbed.

Police also respond to persons crime patterns with crime prevention education for specific place managers and potential victims. For example, police may provide pamphlets with crime prevention advice based on situational crime prevention (discussed in Chapter 2) to convenience store managers at a time when there is a series of convenience store robberies. They may also provide information to bar owners, managers, and patrons about crime prevention at a time when there is a series of stranger rapes at bars in which the suspect is slipping his victims a "date rape" drug.

Finally, police typically provide information to the public on persons crime patterns. The most common method of disseminating persons crime pattern information to the public is through the media (e.g., newspapers, TV, Internet, social media, radio). The public is typically informed of robbery series, stranger rape series, and the like. Although individual cases are often reported in the media, series of persons crime are much more serious and get more attention since the suspect is repeating his behavior. Once the public is provided this information, many different things can happen. Crimes that have already been committed but have not been reported to the police may be reported. Another result of media exposure is that witnesses of crimes already included in a pattern may come forward with more information when they realize the crimes are part of a larger series. Lastly, providing pattern information to the public allows them to protect themselves. In the case of the Washington, DC, sniper, when 10 people were seemingly shot at random in public places in 2002, the media's attention to this crime series encouraged people in the DC area to stay in their own homes and go outside only when necessary since the shooters were targeting people in public places.

Property Crime

Because the likelihood of arresting suspects for property crime is much lower than for persons crime, police responses to property crime patterns focus more on deterring offenders and encouraging victims to protect their property, and less on arresting offenders. Most importantly, police respond to property crime patterns by informing potential victims to protect themselves. As previously noted, people are much more likely to employ crime prevention methods if they feel an immediate threat. The police use property crime patterns to target specific people in pattern areas. Methods such as reverse 911 (i.e., leaving an automated phone message for a group of citizens living in a particular area), going door-to-door, and sending letters to citizens or businesses to inform them about the pattern and recommend relevant crime prevention techniques are all different ways police can inform potential victims. Other methods include, but are not limited to, posting patterns on the Internet or through social media and meeting with specific neighborhood or business groups. The goal is to provide information about the crime pattern as well as specific things that people can do to protect their property (e.g., lock their car doors), change their behavior that contributes to the crime (e.g., remove valuables from their cars), or increase awareness (e.g., look out for suspicious people in their neighborhoods).

Because property crime often is linked by proximity (i.e., hot spots), police use directed patrol to deter offenders and, less often, catch offenders in the act. As discussed in Chapter 3, hot spots policing does work for reducing crime, especially for short-term issues like patterns. Directed patrol can be conducted in police cars, on bikes, or on foot with the goal of increasing the visibility of police and increasing the offenders' perception of risk of being caught. Additionally, while doing this type of patrol, police can also make field contacts with suspicious people and vehicles. This can help to deter offenders from committing crime through increasing police contact and can also provide potential investigative leads for individual crimes and patterns.

Although property crime patterns do help with arresting suspects in some situations, they are likely to assist in clearing cases once a suspect is arrested for one crime. For example, when a detective arrests a suspect for breaking into cars in a particular area, the crime analyst can produce a pattern of vehicle burglaries that are in the same area during the same time period. The detective could then use that information to interview the suspect or review the evidence to see if he committed any of these crimes.

Finally, for very focused and specific patterns of property crime, police employ responses with the goal of arresting offenders in the act, such as surveillance and bait operations, but these patterns are less common. Some examples include a pattern of auto theft in which a specific type of vehicle (such as a Honda Civic) has been modified for racing; a pattern of theft from vehicle in which a specific type of property is taken from a vehicle, such as smartphones or high-end stereo speakers or expensive wheels; or a commercial burglary pattern in which the offenders drive a car through the glass window of a particular electronics store. For these patterns, police often use bait vehicles containing the targeted property, or they may use surveillance by either individuals (e.g., undercover detectives) or video surveillance equipment (either permanent or movable) to observe locations that are similar to those in the pattern in hopes of catching the offender in the act.

Identifying Meaningful Patterns

In most cases, tactical crime patterns are made up of multiple events of one type of crime. However, there are instances, as discussed earlier, in which similar types of crimes make up a single pattern. For example, unsuccessful burglaries can be classified as criminal damage and examined along with successful burglaries. Also, public sexual indecency, indecent exposure, and rape can make up a pattern if an offender is escalating in violence or performs different behaviors depending on the circumstances. An important point is that police officers classify similar crimes differently based on specific legal criteria; however, the crime acts with different legal codes may be similar in nature and can be part of the same crime pattern. A crime analyst needs to take both the classification and the nature of the activity into account in order to identify patterns.

Because modus operandi (MO) characteristics can be very specific (e.g., a robber who forces the victim to remove clothing), they can provide obvious links among cases that are months or even years apart. However, there is no way to establish a pattern entirely by MO. In other words, unless the suspect is arrested and confesses, there is no way to be sure that a particular suspect has committed all crimes with similar MO characteristics. In most cases, patterns are linked in other ways as well (e.g., suspect description, type of place). It is unlikely that an offender would deliberately or coincidentally copy another offender's vehicle or physical description, but it is easy to copy general MO characteristics; for example, a suspect enters a bank and demands money from a clerk using a gun and a note.

Another factor that can confuse the examination of MO characteristics is that situational circumstances may result in an offender's altering his or her MO. For example, depending on how a victim reacts, an offender may use less or more violence within the same crime pattern. Or depending on the environment, a burglar may not kick the door open—his usual MO—because the side window is open and much easier to enter. Also, characteristics that are based on witness descriptions are often problematic. Factors such as lighting, amount of time the victim and offender were together, and fear can influence the accuracy of information provided by witnesses. An important thing to remember is that linking crimes in a pattern for police response is not building a case for a prosecution of an offender in court. Thus, the patterns are really a "best guess" that the analyst has to direct police to particular responses. If and when a suspect is arrested, probable cause and the rules of evidence are paramount and the pattern is much less important.

Persons Crime Pattern Key Characteristics and Examples

When identifying any pattern, crime analysts must think of the potential police responses and make sure their patterns are focused, relevant, and helpful for implementing the appropriate responses. The main focus of persons crime pattern responses is arresting the suspect(s). Therefore, examination of persons crimes would focus on linking crimes through suspect actions and description to develop series and spree patterns. To assist in the pattern finalization process, the following sections are a discussion of the key characteristics and examples of robbery and sex crimes patterns, the two types of persons crimes most commonly examined.

Robbery Patterns Key characteristics of robbery patterns are the actions of the suspect(s) during the crime and the type of victim or place. Although the same robbery offender may commit crimes in different ways, those crimes are more difficult to link as patterns. Research shows that offenders who commit commercial robbery are different than those who commit street robbery (Wright & Decker, 1997), so using type of place to distinguish robbery patterns is logical. Suspect descriptions are important in persons pattern analysis, but because a witness can be unreliable, as discussed earlier, the suspect descriptions are considered secondary in importance to the suspect's behavior. For example, if a robbery is similar to another in terms of the suspect's actions (e.g., using a gun and striking the victims after robbing them) but the suspect of one crime is described as an Arabic man with wavy hair and the other is described as a Hispanic man with curly hair, the analyst may include both in the pattern because the victims may not have described the suspects accurately, but the behavior is very similar.

Although robberies at commercial locations are not as likely to be identified through proximity of the incidents because the businesses themselves are typically spread throughout a community (e.g., two Best Buy stores are not likely to be located right next to one another), proximity is relevant in street robbery patterns where offenders may be targeting people in areas familiar to them (i.e., crime pattern theory). So even within one type of crime, the key characteristics might be somewhat different. Finally, the use of a vehicle in a robbery makes proximity less important because of the offender's ability to travel and get away after committing the crime. This is why some robbery patterns overlap jurisdiction boundaries and the finalization of a robbery pattern should typically include soliciting information from a neighboring agency.

Example: Hot prey, street robberies, Seattle, Washington. This robbery pattern consisted of six strong-arm robberies (i.e., victims threatened with physical force) and one armed robbery (i.e., victim threatened with a handgun) of teenagers (juveniles under 18) walking on their way to or from high school over a 14-day period throughout the city. There were different descriptions of suspects in the crimes (e.g., black males and white males), so the pattern is not a series. It is a "hot prey" pattern because the victims were similar in that they were either male or female students walking alone to or from school. In each crime, the suspect asked to use the victim's phone, and when the phone was produced, the suspect threatened the victims and/or assaulted them and forcibly took the phone. In one of the crimes, the suspect approached the victim pointing a gun and demanded the cell phone. In all crimes, the suspect typically fled on foot. A backpack and money were taken in separate incidents. Figure 10.1 shows two maps for all six incidents in which the crimes are in blue and the high school locations are in red.

Based on the nature of the pattern, response by detectives could include investigating the similar crimes together (e.g., the armed robberies vs. the

Figure 10.1   Hot Prey Maps: Student Robbery Around High Schools

Source: Detective Dan Benz, Seattle (Washington) Police Department

strong-arm robberies) to identify potential suspects. The pattern could be released to the media to provide parents crime prevention information and to solicit additional information from citizens to assist with identifying and apprehending the offenders. Police could contact school officials directly so they could educate their students and their parents of the threat and provide ways to protect themselves. Lastly, police officers could conduct directed patrols within a walking distance from the high schools before and after the school day to deter offenders.

Example: Series, commercial robberies, Salisbury, Maryland. This commercial robbery pattern (see Figure 10.2) appears to be a series, as the suspect description is similar in each crime (i.e., white male around 6' tall). It is also both a hot setting and a hot product since it consists of robberies at one type of location (i.e., retail pharmacies) in which a specific product is targeted (i.e., oxycontin). Within the city of Salisbury, between November and February in the early afternoon, three separate and locally owned (i.e., nonfranchised) pharmacies were targeted by a white male wearing a mask and gloves who displayed a handgun to the pharmacy clerk and asked for "oxy." The suspect brought his own bag to carry out the stolen items. The suspect took over 20 bottles of pills with strengths of between 5 mg and 30 mg—thousands of dollars' worth—from each store. Cash was also taken in each robbery, but no video evidence was collected. Fingerprints were lifted in one of the cases.

Based on the nature of the pattern, responses by detectives could include investigating the three crimes together (e.g., examining video evidence and reinterviewing victims and witnesses with the other crimes in mind), working with detectives from neighboring agencies that had similar robberies,

Figure 10.2 Series, Commercial Robbery Map

Source: Salisbury (Maryland) Police Department, Kendahl Hearn.

contacting local pharmacies directly, and releasing the pattern to the media for citizens to provide additional tips to catch the offenders. Directed patrol is not likely an appropriate response for this pattern since the crimes are not proximate to one another in terms of geography or time. They are also not easily anticipated to direct patrol toward certain times, days, or specific pharmacy locations.

Example: Series and hot prey, cell phone robberies, Fairfax County, Virginia. This robbery pattern (see Figure 10.3) is a series of six robberies that occurred over 2 months. The victims were all individuals who sought to either buy or sell an iPhone through Craigslist or Facebook. Based on the similarity of the MO, this is a series, and based on the similarity of the victims and how they are victimized, this is also a hot prey pattern. In all the crimes, the suspect and victims connected through social media. Once they met in person, the suspect threatened the victim and took the cash or iPhone by force. In two incidents, the suspect used a firearm to threaten the victim, but no shots were fired. Also, in two cases, a brown or green older-model four-door vehicle was driven by the suspect. The incidents occurred throughout the county in public parking lots at various times of the day and evenings.

Based on the nature of the pattern, responses by detectives could include investigating all crimes together (e.g., examining evidence, reinterviewing victims, and looking at social media correspondence with all related crimes in mind). More importantly, the police could release the pattern to the media to warn citizens about selling and buying cell phones to strangers through the Internet and provide crime prevention advice for conducting that type of transaction. For example, some police departments suggest citizens make these transactions at the police department itself. The media release could also solicit information from citizens who might have been victims but did not report the crimes to the police, which would provide the police more information that could be coalesced to identify the offender(s) and stop the crimes. Directed patrol would not be an appropriate response for this pattern since the locations of the crimes depend on the discussion between the victim and offender and could be anywhere, but setting up a sting operation to identify and catch this offender would be appropriate.

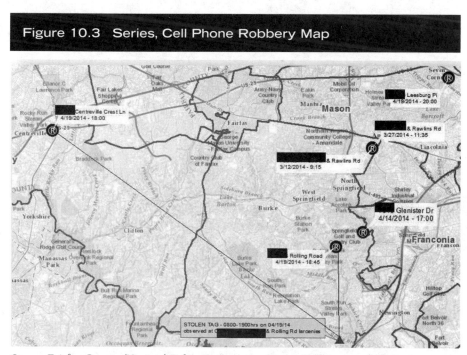

Figure 10.3 Series, Cell Phone Robbery Map

Source: Fairfax County (Virginia) Police Department, Jessica LeBlanc.

Example: Series and hot spot, home invasion robberies, Salisbury, Maryland.
This robbery pattern consists of two incidents in which two black males
wearing ski masks forced entry into two-story single family homes around
10:00 p.m. while the residents were at home. Once inside the homes, the
offenders threatened the victims with handguns and demanded money. The
crimes occurred within 5 days of one another and within a 0.13-mile radius.
Because the suspects appear to be the same in each crime, this is a series, but
because the crimes are close to one another in the same neighborhood, this
could also be a hot spot. In the first robbery, around $400 in cash was taken.
In the second robbery, the victim told the suspects his money was in his car
behind one of the speakers. The offenders went to the car and took the speaker
but no money. Note that these crimes are robberies not burglaries since the
offenders threatened the victims before taking property, which is why it is called
a "home invasion." Had the offenders entered the home and taken the property
without threatening the residents, the crimes would be considered burglaries,
even though the residents were at home when the crimes happened.

Based on the nature of the pattern, responses by detectives could include
investigating these two crimes together (e.g., examining evidence, reinterviewing
victims with both related crimes in mind). Because these crimes occurred in a close
proximity and in the same residential neighborhood, the police could conduct
directed patrol, stop suspicious individuals matching the suspect descriptions, and
contact residents in the area who might be potential victims. A media release could

Figure 10.4   Home Invasion Robberies Map

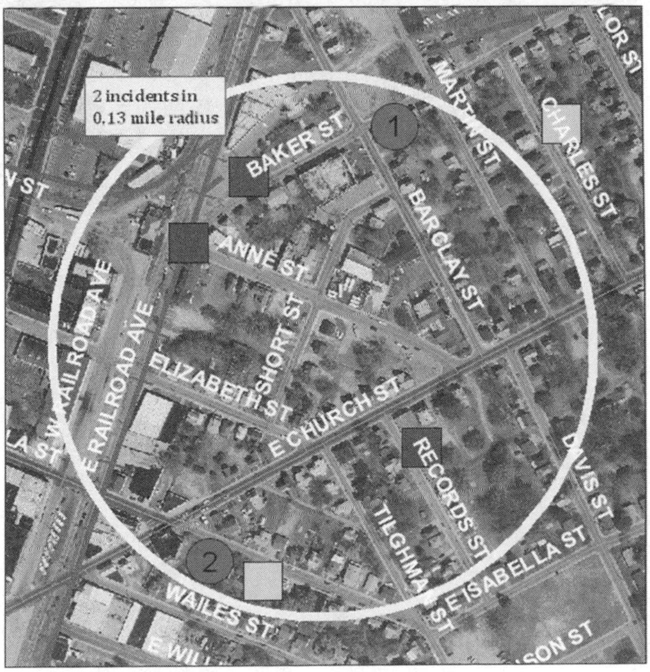

Source: Salisbury (Maryland) Police Department, Kendahl Hearn.

also be done to solicit information (i.e., intelligence) from citizens who might have seen something and/or who might have been victims of similar crimes but did not report them so that more information can be brought together to identify the offenders and stop the series. Note that in Figure 10.4, the circles with numbers in them (i.e., 1 and 2) represent the crimes, the dark gray boxes represent locations of field interview cards for suspicious persons in the area around the time of the pattern, and the light gray boxes are the home addresses of known gun offenders that detectives might contact as part of their response as well.

Sexual Crime–Related Patterns Sex crimes patterns are identified least often in tactical crime analysis because the crimes themselves are not as frequent as robbery and property crimes. Rapes are typically committed by acquaintances, so there are very few stranger rape patterns. Incidents of public sexual indecency and indecent exposure occur more often than stranger rapes but are still fairly rare. For all sex crimes, identifying patterns can be simpler than with other crimes because of their rarity and uniqueness of the offenders' MO.

Key characteristics of sex crime patterns are the actions of the suspect(s) during the crime (i.e., series) and/or the type of victim (i.e., hot prey). Similar to those in robbery patterns, suspect descriptions are important but are less reliable than actions of the suspect. In these cases in particular, the victims are surprised and shocked by the behavior and may not be able to identify the suspect easily (e.g., a flasher stepping out from behind a tree or a rapist attacking them from behind). However, unlike robbery, cases within a sex crime pattern may be more proximate to one another. A person who is exposing himself to people on the street may be doing this in an area he is familiar with and that has a significant number of pedestrians with minimal guardianship, such as a park. A rapist attacking college students would have to go to a college area to find his victims. Informing the public and specific groups of potential victims about sex crime patterns is particularly important because many of these crimes go unreported. If victims know others have been victimized and the offender is committing multiple offenses, they may be more likely to report the crime. These unreported incidents can provide additional information to a pattern that can assist in the investigation and apprehension of the offender.

Example: Series, indecent exposure, Gainesville, Florida. This pattern consisted of four separate incidents that occurred over several weeks in which a Hispanic male was seen masturbating in a silver compact-sized four-door vehicle. In the first incident, two Gainesville High School female students saw a Hispanic man, mid- to late 40s, masturbating in a silver vehicle near a Citgo station in the afternoon. Two weeks later in the morning before school, the same two female students saw a similar silver car at a gas pump at the same Citgo station. The male driver was wearing long, dark shorts and was masturbating while pumping gas. The suspect looked at the victims while masturbating, but when one victim attempted to photograph him for evidence, he got inside his car and drove away. Figure 10.5 is the picture she took of the vehicle. In a third incident, a different female high school student saw a man in

Figure 10.5   Picture of Suspect's Silver Vehicle at Citgo Station

Source: Gainesville, Florida Police Department and Ericka Jackson

a silver vehicle in the Gainesville High School parking lot after school. When she walked by the car, the subject was not wearing pants and was masturbating. Finally, a fourth incident was reported after these crimes, but it occurred a month previously; in the afternoon, a young woman saw a Hispanic man in khaki shorts masturbating while sitting in what looked to her like a gold four-door vehicle. The victim noted it was rainy that day so the description of the vehicle color might not be accurate.

Based on the nature of the pattern, detectives might investigate these crimes as a pattern, looking in particular at video evidence obtained from the businesses and school, if available. In addition, they might also conduct surveillance at specific locations in an attempt to apprehend the offender. That is, if the offender appears to be following a pattern of being at particular businesses around the high school and in the school parking lot at similar times, the police may conduct surveillance at those times and areas. Also, patrol officers could look out for the vehicle and suspect as described while conducting directed patrol around the high school before and after school since the offender likely wants to be where young women are walking around. The police could contact school officials so that students are warned about the pattern, and information of additional sightings of the man can be reported immediately to the police to further develop a pattern of behavior, as he is likely doing this much more than is being reported. Lastly, the police may choose not to publish this pattern in the media as it might alert the suspect to change or stop his behavior for a time to avoid being caught.

Example: Series, stranger rape. During my tenure as a crime analyst in the 1990s, we identified a pattern in which a white male suspect approached Asian students around a college campus and asked them for directions to a location, speaking in either Chinese or Japanese. If they answered and did not speak English, he would ask them to get in his car. If they complied, he would subsequently rape them. The crimes occurred in a variety of areas, but the women were initially contacted by the suspect in a small area near campus where foreign students resided. However, it was the specific actions of the suspect that linked the crimes together.

Based on the nature of the pattern, a response by officers included releasing the information to the public through the media, after which we received additional reports of women who were not Asian but had dark hair and eyes who had been approached but not raped. Even though these women had not been victimized, they provided additional information about the suspect's car and his physical description. Detectives were able to arrest the suspect after piecing together information about the suspect's vehicle (e.g., partial license plate and description) from the various victims and witnesses.

Property Crime Pattern Key Characteristics and Examples

Because the main focus of property crime pattern responses by police is having victims protect their property and deterring offenders, crime analysts focus on linking these crimes primarily through the type of crime, type of place, and proximity in location and time. The types of patterns typically found are sprees, hot spots, hot settings, and hot products. As noted earlier, the MO of a property crime often depends on the opportunities left by the managers or guardians of the property (e.g., unlocked doors, valuables in view, windows in a home with faulty locks). These factors, such as method of entry, point of entry, and type of property taken, are used for linking crimes only when they are very specific, which usually indicates a crime series or sprees (same suspect). For example, when working as an analyst, I identified a crime series of homes being burglarized by drilling a hole in the garage door, using a hanger to release the door lock cable, and entering the house through the unlocked internal garage door. An example of a spree is a group of vehicles in the same parking lot being burglarized in a 3-hour time period. The MOs may be different for each car, but the likelihood of multiple offenders committing these crimes in such a short time period and centralized place is unlikely, making the pattern a spree and a series, even though there is no suspect information.

Theft From Vehicle Patterns Theft from vehicle is the most frequently occurring type of crime examined in tactical crime analysis and is the topic of the highest number of patterns in police agencies. Often, there is little to no suspect information and minimal MO information since many of these thefts occur with no witnesses and when car doors have been left unlocked. Consequently, the key characteristics of theft from vehicle patterns are primarily based on type of place where the cars are located (e.g., businesses vs. residences), proximity of the thefts, and time of occurrence. Even though one offender may be committing these crimes across the entire city, the crime analyst typically does not have any suspect information and must distinguish patterns primarily by proximity (hot spots).

Importantly, micro-time hot spot patterns are helpful for police responses since the primary goal is not to arrest but to protect victims and deter offenders from committing the crimes in a particular area. Specific patterns may be identified by MO (e.g., use of a spark plug or window puncher to break a window) and type of property taken (e.g., hot product—cell phones, GPS equipment) or type of place (e.g., hot setting—day care centers, gyms). However, proximity is still an important factor in the final determination of most of these patterns.

Example: Micro-time hot spot, thefts from vehicles, Port St. Lucie, Florida.
Unknown suspects targeted six unlocked vehicles that were parked in the driveway or along the street in a residential neighborhood. The incidents occurred over 8 days in the late evening or early morning within a 0.41-mile radius of one another (see Figure 10.6). Property taken included loose change and other items left in the vehicles, but nothing of high value.

Figure 10.6   Theft From Vehicle Hot Spot Map

Source: Port St. Lucie (Florida) Police Department, Cheryl Davis.

Based on the nature of the pattern, responses by detectives could be to investigate these crimes together as well as contact known theft-from-vehicle offenders who live in the pattern area since this is occurring in a residential neighborhood. Responses by officers could include conducting directed patrol in the pattern area, making field contacts while on directed patrol, and contacting residents in the pattern area through flyers, door-to-door visits, social media, or reverse 911, warning them about the pattern and providing specific crime prevention advice.

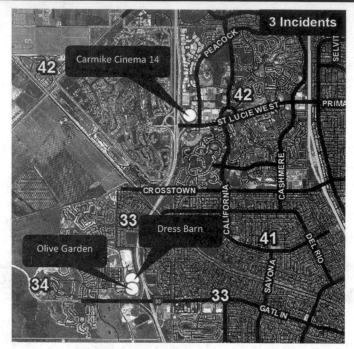

Figure 10.7 Theft From Vehicle Spree at Retail Parking Lots Map

Source: Port St. Lucie (Florida) Police Department, Michelle Chitolie.

Example: Spree and hot setting, thefts from vehicles at retail parking lots, Port St. Lucie, Florida. On a Sunday, between 4:00 p.m. and 10:00 p.m., three vehicles were burglarized at public parking lots (hot setting) at a retail store, restaurant, and movie theatre within several miles of one another (see Figure 10.7). In two of the incidents, the driver's door lock was "popped" (i.e., removed from the door with a drill or other tool). In the other incident, there was no sign of force to the vehicle. A cell phone was taken from one vehicle, a purse with a wallet and credit cards from another, and nothing from the third. The credit cards were used at a gas station and two restaurants within several hours of the initial theft and within 50 miles of when and where the crimes occurred.

Based on the nature of the pattern, detective responses could include investigating these crimes together, as they were likely committed by the same individual(s) based on the times, locations, and MO (popping the door lock). Responses also could include crime prevention officers contacting specific businesses in the pattern area to provide crime prevention advice for their employees and customers, as well as encouraging them to watch for suspicious people in the parking lots. Directed patrol and in-person surveillance by police would not be realistic here because the crimes happen so quickly, and it is not clear whether offenders will hit the location again. However, installing video surveillance might assist with identifying offenders after the fact to catch and prosecute them.

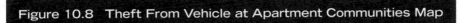

Figure 10.8   Theft From Vehicle at Apartment Communities Map

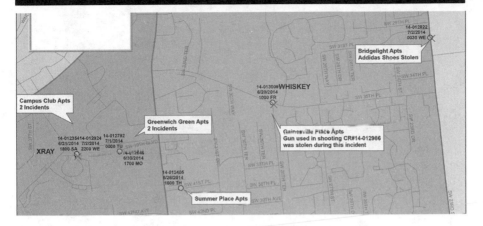

Source: Gainesville (Florida) Police Department, Ericka Jackson.

Example: Hot setting, thefts from vehicles, Gainesville, Florida. Over a
4-week period, unknown suspects targeted seven unlocked cars at apartment
communities (hot setting; see Figure 10.8) within about a 0.5-mile radius,
occurring throughout the week, primarily in the early afternoon and evening,
with one occurring at 10:00 a.m. Property taken included various items left in
the vehicle. In one incident, a gun was stolen that was later used in a shooting.
In another incident, nothing was taken.

Based on the nature of the pattern, detectives could investigate these crimes
as one pattern and contact known theft-from-vehicle offenders living in
these apartment communities or nearby. Police may also conduct directed
patrol and make field contacts in and around these communities, as well
as contact the managers and residents in each apartment community
about locking their vehicles and removing valuables. Lastly, two of the
communities were victimized twice, so police may also implement a bait
vehicle operation at either of these locations, as offenders seem to be
returning to commit more crimes.

Example: Hot place, thefts from vehicles at the YMCA, Gainesville, Florida.
From February to June, there were 10 thefts from vehicles that occurred on
three different days in the YMCA parking lot (see Figure 10.9). On
February 24, six vehicles were victimized between 5:45 p.m. and 7:30 p.m.
while parked in the first row of the parking lot. On March 6, two vehicles
were victimized between 5:00 p.m. and 8:00 p.m., and on June 10, two
vehicles were victimized between 9:50 a.m. and 11:00 a.m. Property taken
from the vehicles varied, and all of the vehicles were unlocked. Note that
vehicles in the parking lots that were not hit were those that were locked.
Based on the nature of this pattern and the repeat activity at this one

Figure 10.9 Theft From Vehicle Hot Place

Source: Gainesville (Florida) Police Department, Ericka Jackson.

location over many months, police could work with the managers of the YMCA to encourage their employees and members to lock their vehicles and remove valuables, as well as install video surveillance cameras and restrict access to the parking lot. Because the offenders hit several cars at a time, making employees and visitors aware of this and encouraging them to report anything suspicious right away could also be done.

Vehicle Theft Patterns Vehicle theft is similar to theft from vehicle except there is even less information to examine for pattern analysis because the entire vehicle is missing. Information about how and why vehicles are stolen can later be deduced from its condition when recovered (e.g., no items taken and the vehicle is out of gas might indicate joyriding), but vehicles are typically recovered days and weeks after the initial crime or sometimes not at all, which is not helpful for identifying immediate crime patterns. As a result, there is limited information to link these crimes, so the key characteristics for vehicle theft are simply proximity (hot spot), time, type of place (hot setting), and type of vehicle (hot product).

Example: Hot product, moped thefts, Roanoke, Virginia. Over a 19-day period, four newer-model (2009–2015) mopeds were stolen while in plain sight in front of a residence (see Figure 10.10) during daylight hours on various days of the week. None of the mopeds was secured to a structure, but each had the handle bars or front wheel locked. This meant that the offender could not push or drive the moped from the property. A white, male juvenile between 15 and 18 years old was seen in one of the incidents before the theft. Two known offenders matching the suspect's description live in the pattern area. One has a history of moped thefts and the other a history of vandalism and motor vehicle (e.g., car) theft. Based on the information provided by this pattern, responses by officers are likely to include disseminating the pattern in this neighborhood as well as publishing the pattern in the media to alert moped owners in the city. Detectives would contact the known offenders living in the area, and officers might conduct directed patrol in the neighborhood during the day.

Figure 10.10   Moped Theft Map

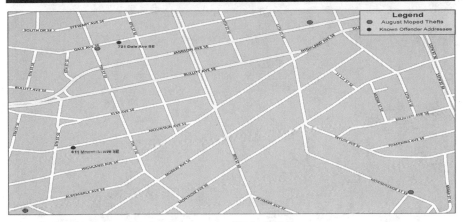

Source: Roanoke (Virginia) Police Department, Alisha Wilson.

Example: Hot product, auto theft of pickup trucks, Arlington, Texas.

Between August 1 and September 13 in Sector Z, there were 23 motor vehicle thefts and attempted thefts of full-sized pickup trucks. All of these thefts occurred in the overnight hours. Only seven vehicles were recovered, and five of those were recovered by a neighboring jurisdiction. Additionally, almost all vehicles were taken from the victims' driveways rather than from the street (see Figure 10.11). The most common method of entry was to pry or punch the door lock. The suspects then damaged the steering column or defeated the ignition in order to steal the vehicle. Only one vehicle had a broken window, and in that case, the suspects damaged the door locks as well.

Based on the information provided by this pattern, responses by officers are likely to include publishing the pattern in the media since it would be hard to identify specific potential victims (i.e., individuals who own these types of vehicles and park them in their driveway). A bait operation might be conducted in one of the areas where several of the most recent incidents occurred. However, implementing this latter response would depend on whether the police had access to a vehicle matching the descriptions of those that had been targeted.

Residential Burglary Patterns Burglaries occur at both businesses and residential environments, and although one offender may target both types of places over a period of several weeks, the lack of suspect information makes it difficult to link such crimes together. This, and the fact that there are different opportunities for burglary at commercial and residential locations, is why residential and commercial burglary crimes are normally examined separately.

Key characteristics for identifying residential burglary patterns are the type of residence and proximity. Again, the goal of responding to property

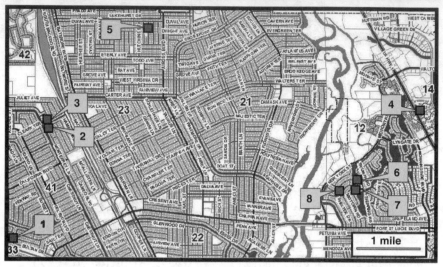

Figure 10.11   Vehicle Theft of Pickup Trucks Map

Source: Arlington (Texas) Police Department, Alex Schneider.

crime patterns is to educate potential victims and deter offenders. Because opportunities for burglary vary by types of residences, patterns are often distinguished by single-family, multifamily, mobile home communities, and the like. Proximity (hot spots) is important because often residences in close proximity to one another share characteristics, so crime prevention recommendations will be the same. In addition, directed patrol by police officers is done most effectively in a focused area. Commonalities in time of day and day of week can be important for residential burglary patterns when they are very specific; however, crimes occurring on different days and times would not necessarily be eliminated from a pattern when they occurred at the same type of residence in the same area. Lastly, MO is important in residential burglary patterns mostly when it is very specific. The fact that suspects entered one home through the sliding glass door and another in the same area through an open window would not prevent a crime analyst from linking these together.

Example: Micro-time hot spot, residential burglaries, Port St. Lucie, Florida.
Over a 4-day period, unknown suspects burglarized three homes within a 0.35-mile radius during the daytime and early evening hours. Property taken included household cleaning electronics, cash, and a video game console. In two incidents, no forced entry was used, as the screen door was unlocked in one incident and no evidence of force was found in the second. The third burglary was an attempt as no property was taken, but the front door lock was damaged from being kicked in.

Based on the nature of the pattern, responses by officers are likely to include directed patrol and field contacts in the pattern area (.35-mile radius) as

Figure 10.12   Residential Burglary Hot Spot Map

3 Incidents
.35 mile radius

Source: Port St. Lucie (Florida) Police Department, Michelle Chitolie.

well as direct contact with residents (potential victims) in the pattern area to provide crime prevention advice. The police could also contact the neighborhood association of that area to alert them to the pattern. Detectives may investigate the crimes together and contact known residential-burglary offenders who live in the pattern area as potential leads. Figure 10.12 shows the crimes in gray with known burglary/larceny/drug offenders' home addresses represented as white boxes.

Example: Hot setting, burglaries of sheds at apartment complexes, Frederick, Maryland. At four separate apartment communities (see Figure 10.13), multiple sheds within each apartment community were burglarized. Technically, these are not residential burglaries, but are burglaries at residential locations of "other buildings" because the sheds are not used as residences. The burglaries occurred over 4 weeks in the overnight hours. In most cases, the suspects either cut the padlocks off the sheds or removed the hinge locks. Property stolen included various tools, large kitchen/laundry appliances, lawn and snow equipment, compressors, and ladders. A possible suspect is described as a black male, approximately 50 years of age, driving a gray van.

Figure 10.13   Apartment Shed Burglary Map

Source: Frederick (Maryland) Police Department, Mark Bridge.

Based on the nature of the pattern, detectives could investigate these crimes together, focusing on the suspect description and possible video surveillance and fingerprint evidence as well as contacting known offenders living in or around the apartment complexes. Response by patrol officers could include direct contact with the apartment managers, who can then contact and warn their residents as well as help improve the security of the sheds on their properties. Police may also conduct directed patrols in the overnight hours and make field contacts of suspicious persons in and around the apartment communities as well as look out for the suspect.

Commercial Burglary Patterns Key characteristics for identifying commercial burglary patterns are similar to those for residential burglary patterns—proximity and type of business. Patterns will include crimes of different types of businesses being burglarized in the same area near one another—hot spots. However, oftentimes commercial burglaries are linked by type of business (e.g., electronics stores, medical offices) and/or by a specific MO (e.g., entering through air conditioning vent on roof or cutting through the wall of the next business in a plaza) across a larger area within a city or even across jurisdictional boundaries. Residential burglaries are rarely identified across neighborhoods or jurisdictional boundaries unless the MO is very specific and indicates a series. Crime analysts might examine burglar alarm calls for service to identify additional burglaries at neighboring businesses. Although there may be little to no information beyond the date, time, and location of the alarm, the call could indicate other places that offenders may have targeted unsuccessfully and would provide more information to develop responses and enhance the investigation of the pattern. This can also be done for residential burglar alarms in pattern areas.

Example: Series and hot setting, Radio Shack burglaries, Fairfax County, Virginia. From January to June, there were over 12 burglaries with a similar MO throughout Fairfax County and in the state of Maryland at Radio Shack locations. Based on the MO and surveillance photos (see Figure 10.14), these crimes are believed to be committed by the same suspect (i.e., series). Also, because they all occurred at Radio Shack stores, this pattern is also a "hot setting." Note it is not a hot place since multiple locations were victimized (i.e., a hot place is only one location). The suspect is a tall, thin black male wearing a light-colored hoodie who uses a rock or brick to smash the front door. The surveillance video shows that once inside, the suspect immediately goes to the stock area in the rear and targets the "cage" where high-dollar items are stored. The suspect brings a bag, screwdriver, a crow bar, and other tools to facilitate accessing the cage, as well as takes easily accessible items.

Based on the nature of the pattern, the crimes in the pattern would be investigated together to identify and apprehend the suspect. It is likely that the suspect is a current or former employee of Radio Shack, as this would give him the knowledge of the layout of Radio Shack stores and their practices (i.e., how and where they secure items). In addition, the police would work with Radio Shack store managers and particularly corporate executives on how to change the store design, security practices, and employee policies to prevent these crimes from happening in the long term. Directed patrol at Radio Shack stores would not be a realistic response since the crimes are widespread in both dates and geographic area. It would really be up to the Radio Shack stores and company executives to put in place preventative measures and protect their own property.

Figure 10.14 Radio Shack Surveillance Photos

Source: Fairfax County (Virginia) Police Department, Jessica LeBlanc.

Example: Hot spot and hot product, commercial burglaries, Fairfax County, Virginia. Over a 5-month period, there were six commercial burglaries along Richmond Highway (see Figure 10.15) in which cell phones and electronic tablets were taken. The businesses included a grocery store, a check-cashing store, and a "dollar" store. One location was hit three times, another two times, and the third only one time. In all incidents, the suspect(s) use a rock obtained nearby to smash the front glass door. The suspect(s), observed through surveillance cameras, seem to be either one or two black males who enter the store and take only cell phones and electronic tablets. The burglaries occurred on the weekdays only, between 1:00 a.m. and 3:00 a.m. Because the locations are close in proximity within the same commercial district, the pattern is a hot spot. However, this activity also represents a hot product since the same type of property was taken in each crime. In addition, this pattern might also be considered a series if the analyst decides from surveillance video that the same one or two offenders committed all the crimes.

Based on the nature of the pattern, detectives could investigate these crimes together. However, they would not necessarily contact known offenders living in the area because this is a commercial area, thus it is the "activity space" of a wide range of people who may or may not live nearby. Responses would also include working with the individual stores that were victimized to improve their security, especially since two locations were victimized more than once. Police may also contact other businesses in the commercial district highway that sell cell phones and tablets to alert them to the activity and provide them crime prevention and security information. Lastly, patrol officers may conduct directed patrol around these and other similar stores after midnight during the weekdays since the offenders are returning to the locations over several months—having been successful, they are likely to continue until they are arrested.

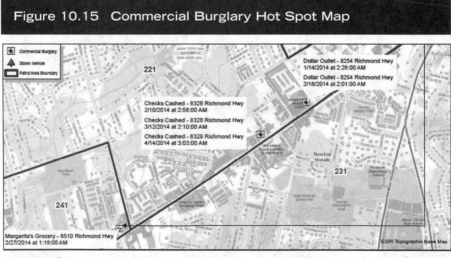

Figure 10.15   Commercial Burglary Hot Spot Map

Source: Fairfax County (Virginia) Police Department, Jessica LeBlanc.

Hot Product Patterns Some property crime patterns are not characterized by one type of crime, one suspect, or where they occur, but by a common type of property that is taken across different types of crimes and/or locations. A hot product is a type of property that is repeatedly targeted—or, as Clarke (1999) puts it, "those consumer items that are most attractive to thieves" (p. 23). In order for an item to be a hot product, it typically fits the following criteria: It must be "concealable, removable, available, valuable, enjoyable, and disposable" (p. 25). Examples include precious metal (e.g., gold, copper, platinum from catalytic converters), smartphones, tablets, laptop computers, and handguns. In tactical crime analysis, patterns focus on those items that are recently taken, but typically, these are also items that are taken over a longer term, such as jewelry and electronics. Identifying long-term trends of specific types of property being taken is important as well, but is considered strategic crime analysis and is covered in Chapter 13 and Chapter 14 as "problem property."

The key characteristics for identifying a hot product pattern are the characteristics of the product that is taken. Products can be taken in the same type of crime (e.g., theft) or in a variety of crimes (e.g., theft, robbery, and burglary). Importantly, to identify hot product pattern, the crime analyst looks for very specific characteristics. For example, cash is the "hottest" product, but a crime analyst would not identify a hot product pattern in which cash was taken in theft from vehicles, robberies, and burglaries since it is so common. However, a crime analyst might link cash for a hot product pattern if in each of the crimes (e.g., robbery, burglary, and theft from vehicle) the cash was thousands of dollars in $100 bills kept in a bank deposit zip bag. This would make the pattern and the property taken unique even if the offenders were not necessarily the same.

Example: Hot product and hot setting, burglaries of tractor trailer tires and wheels, Greensboro, North Carolina. Over a 3-month period from February to May, eight burglaries at truck and trailer dealerships (see Figure 10.16) occurred in which 10 to 50 tractor trailer wheels and/or tires were taken in each incident. In most of the incidents, suspects either cut the fence or locks to the gates to the storage yard and removed tires and wheels from existing trailers. That is, the tires and wheels were not stacked up but were actually installed on the trailers. In some cases, the suspects brought "blocks" with them to support the trailers so the tires could be removed. The crimes occurred in the overnight when the businesses were closed, and five occurred over the weekend. This pattern is likely also a series because of the specific nature, knowledge, and equipment necessary to remove the tires and transport them from the crime scene.

Based on the nature of the pattern, it is likely that the suspects are using large trucks or flatbed trailers to haul the property away from the crime scenes, so a response could be patrol officers conducting directed patrol

Figure 10.16   Map of Trailer Dealership Burglary Locations

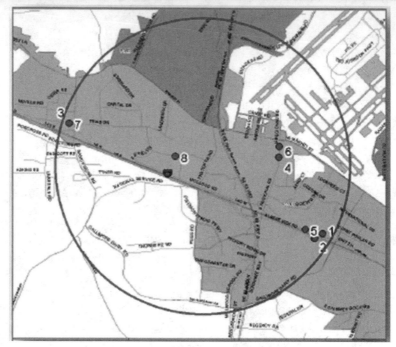

Source: Greensboro (North Carolina) Police Department, Brandon Inscore.

and conducting vehicle stops of large vehicles driving near the victimized and similar locations in the overnight hours and on the weekend. Detectives could investigate these crimes as one pattern to collate any evidence obtained. They would not contact offenders living in the area, but might look for individuals or at businesses in which trailer tires and wheels are sold either new or secondhand in other jurisdictions. Police may also contact all similar types of dealerships (i.e., potential victims) to provide information about the pattern and solicit information about possible suspects and intelligence about the nature of the trailer tire and wheel business.

Example: Hot product, packages left on residential doorsteps, Fullerton, California. In October and November, four thefts of packages occurred throughout the city (see Figure 10.17). In each case, a mail delivery truck left the package near the front door and in view of the street, and the package was stolen before the resident was able to retrieve it. The crimes occurred between the time of the drop-off, which typically occurred in the late morning and early afternoon, and the time when the victim arrived home and/or discovered the package was missing, which was sometimes a day or two later. There is no suspect information in any of the crimes, and the property taken varied from small electronics to clothing.

Figure 10.17 Hot Product Packages Map

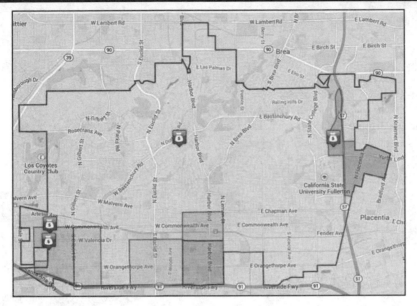

Source: Fullerton (California) Police Department, Tamara Otley.

Based on the nature of the pattern, there are a limited number of responses. For example, it is unlikely that the crimes are committed by the same person, as the time period and area in which the crimes occurred are widely spread. Because the timing of these crimes is the time before Christmas, the best response is likely a media release to remind citizens to have their packages delivered in more secure locations or request a "signature only" delivery. Police may also alert the delivery companies to the pattern, who can also tell their employees to leave packages in more secure settings.

Conclusion

The goal of this chapter is to show how to identify meaningful patterns that police can use to develop effective crime prevention and crime reduction responses. Crime analysts must understand what responses police employ for the various types of patterns in order to provide information helpful for their efforts. The goal for all tactical crime analysis is to create "actionable" products that prompt and require a police response. The examples here cover only a snapshot of all the possible patterns that can be identified during the crime analysis process. The most important point of this chapter is that analysts must think critically about the purpose of the information they are providing and use their knowledge of the crime type, the community, and their own department's responses to identify meaningful and actionable patterns.

SUMMARY POINTS

This chapter illustrates how crime analysts identify meaningful patterns that are useful for police. The following are the key points addressed in this chapter:

- Pattern identification in tactical crime analysis is guided by the distinction between persons crime and property crime patterns.

- Persons crimes are those crimes in which people are the targets of the offenders. The crimes commonly examined for persons crime pattern analysis are robbery, stranger sexual assault, indecent exposure, and public sexual indecency.

- Property crimes are those crimes in which property is the target of the offenders. The crimes commonly examined for property crime pattern analysis are theft from vehicle, auto theft, residential burglary, and commercial burglary. Incidents of theft from buildings, criminal trespass, grand theft, and criminal damage are also examined as they relate to these other crimes or as they indicate overt vandalism and theft of property.

- The types of responses police employ for patterns are fairly straightforward and focus on arresting and deterring offenders as well as on crime prevention. They include directed patrol, field contacts, surveillance, bait operations, clearing cases, contacting potential victims directly, reverse 911, and contacting the general public.

- Directed patrol is focusing police patrol in the areas and times in which a pattern is occurring.

- Field contacts are when officers make direct contact with people in the pattern area while conducting directed patrol.

- Surveillance requires police to watch and wait in a particular area at a particular time for a crime to happen in order to make an arrest.

- Bait operations use people or property that have been targeted in a particular pattern as "bait" for offenders. Police then directly observe the bait or have electronic monitoring that allows them to arrest the offender or record offenders committing the crimes when the bait is taken.

- Police contact potential victims directly and provide information about details of the pattern, crime prevention advice, and contact information for the police.

- Reverse 911 is technology that allows the police to call residents and businesses in a pattern area and leave a recorded message about the crime pattern and crime prevention advice.

- Police provide pattern information to the public to encourage the public to provide additional information ("tips") on known crimes, to report crimes that have not yet been reported, and to protect themselves. Offenders might also be deterred from committing further crimes after seeing this information.

- Police responses to persons crimes focus on enhancing the investigation and facilitating the arrest of the suspect(s) because the pattern will contain suspect descriptions and specific MO information.

- Police responses to property crime patterns are focused on deterring offenders and encouraging victims to protect their property because the likelihood of arresting suspects for property crime is much lower than for persons crime.

- Unless the offender is arrested and confesses, there is no way to be sure that a particular offender has committed all crimes with the same MO characteristics. The examination of MO characteristics and physical descriptions is not always clear. The analyst must be aware that situational circumstances may result in offenders altering their MO and that characteristics based on witness descriptions are often problematic.

- Examination of persons crimes focuses on linking crimes through suspect actions and descriptions to develop series and spree patterns.

- Key characteristics of robbery patterns are the actions of the suspect(s) during the crime and the type of victim or place.

- Key characteristics of sex crime patterns are the actions of the suspect(s) during the crime and the type of victim.

- Examination of property crimes focuses on linking crimes primarily through the types of crime, type of place, and proximity in location and time. The types of patterns typically found are sprees, hot spots, hot settings, and hot products.

- Key characteristics of theft from vehicle patterns are primarily based on the type of place where the cars are located (businesses vs. residence), proximity of the thefts, and time of occurrence.

- Key characteristics for vehicle theft are proximity (hot spot), time, and type of place (e.g., residences vs. commercial plaza).

- Key characteristics for identifying residential burglary patterns are the type of residence and proximity.

- Key characteristics for identifying commercial burglary patterns are similar to those for residential burglary patterns—type of business and proximity.

- Some property crime patterns are not characterized by one type of crime, one suspect, or where they occur, but by a common type of property that is taken. The key characteristic for identifying a hot product pattern is the type of product that is taken, whether it is taken as part of one type or several types of crimes.

DISCUSSION EXERCISES*

Exercise 1

Describe how you would go about identifying a convenience store robbery pattern both inductively and deductively. Be specific about which characteristics of the crime are most important and how you would search a database to identify cases within the pattern. Do the same for a commercial burglary pattern.

Exercise 2

First, classify each of the following patterns by pattern type (e.g., hot product, hot spot, series) and crime type (e.g., residential burglary, robbery, theft from vehicle). Second, discuss the combination of police responses you would employ for each pattern and why, focusing on only those discussed in this chapter.

- Four commercial arsons occurring throughout the city in which a man was observed leaving the stores with jewelry immediately after the fire alarm was triggered

- Seven thefts from vehicles in an apartment complex parking lot over the course of 3 hours

- Four home invasion robberies of Asian immigrant families in a particular neighborhood by the same suspects

- Theft of belongings from rental cars in hotel parking lots throughout the city

- Eight daytime burglaries over the past 4 weeks in a suburban residential subdivision with no notable similarities in method of entry or known suspects in the cases

- Fifteen thefts from vehicles, several incidents of graffiti, and two robberies of customers over 3 weeks in the parking lot of a retail area around a college campus

- Late-night robberies of 24-hour convenience stores by different suspects

CHAPTER
11

Describing and Disseminating Known Patterns

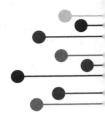

G iven that the purpose of crime analysis is to assist police, once an analyst has identified and finalized a pattern, an investigative lead, or other information, the analyst must disseminate that information to personnel who can use it. This chapter focuses on the techniques that crime analysts use to describe and disseminate known patterns. Analysts also can use many of these techniques to understand commonalities of characteristics among crimes and to identify patterns, such as by mapping burglaries according to the time of day and the day(s) of the week on which they occurred. Examples of how these techniques are used for analysis are included throughout, but this chapter focuses on developing information for the tactical crime analysis pattern bulletin versus other types of crime analysis products.

Describing Known Patterns

In general, information that is provided about a crime pattern focuses on how the crimes were committed (i.e., modus operandi [MO]), who committed them (i.e., suspect description), when they occurred (i.e., time series analysis), and where they occurred (i.e., spatial analysis). The goal in describing these aspects of a pattern is to summarize all the information from the crimes together as one unit of analysis, not to restate the details of each crime report. Importantly, this section covers how a pattern is described, and in doing so provides additional insight to identifying and finalizing patterns as well.

Modus Operandi Summary

The patterns identified by crime analysts are educated guesses about the relationships among incidents based on a variety of characteristics; therefore, when communicating the findings, analysts should be careful not to be too confident in their presentation of the information unless it is warranted. Only in a few patterns will the MO of each crime be almost exactly the same. It is more typical that they are all somewhat different. Describing the MO of a pattern should focus on the characteristics that are shared by all crimes and that distinguish the crimes in the pattern from other crimes occurring at the same time. For example, the following were the MOs for five crimes linked together for a street robbery series:

- Two black males approached the victim on the sidewalk in a residential area. They had their T-shirts pulled over their heads, flashed a handgun, demanded money, and took $46 from the victim.

- Two black males wore black ski masks, threatened the victim with a handgun, demanding money while on a residential sidewalk. The suspects took $50 in cash and fired one gunshot after the robbery but did not hit anything.

- One suspect wore a white Halloween mask; the other suspect wore nothing on his head. After threatening the victim with a handgun, the suspect(s) fired two or three gunshots toward the victim but did not take any money.

- Two black males approached victim outside of the victim's home, showed the victim a handgun, and demanded money. Suspect(s) took $10 and fired five gunshots into the air. No one was hurt.

- Three black males approached victim right outside victim's home, put gun to victim's head, and removed $30 from his wallet.

Each MO is slightly different and there are different numbers of offenders, but based on the information here and other information not shown (e.g., the location of the robberies, specific descriptions of the offenders), the crimes have been linked together. Thus, an MO summary for the pattern would be as follows:

> Between one and three unknown black males approach victims either walking along a residential street or outside the victim's home and demand money, using an unknown handgun. In one incident, the suspects put the gun to the victim's head. In three of the robberies, the suspects covered their faces with T-shirts, a Halloween mask, or ski masks. In three of the incidents, after the robbery the suspects fired between one and five rounds either toward the victims or in the air and did not hit anyone. The suspects took no money in one incident and between $10 and $50 in the other four incidents.

The purpose of the MO summary is to combine and synthesize the information from the incidents, not to restate what happened in each case individually. Also, in addition to synthesizing the information, it is also important to note something exceptional even if it is only one crime—for example, the suspects putting the gun to the head of one victim. This example is fairly complex because the crime involved a human victim and because there was a lot of interaction between the suspects and victims, even though the crimes themselves may have only taken a few minutes. Property crime MO summaries tend to be much simpler, especially when there is no forced entry into a vehicle or a building.

Suspect and Vehicle Descriptions

Suspect and vehicle descriptions are treated similarly when describing a pattern. In most patterns, there are a number of different suspect descriptions from the various cases that make up the pattern, and they range in specificity. The goal is to provide the most specific information about the overall suspect descriptions without excluding any of the case descriptions. As discussed in Chapter 9, more weight is placed on the physical description than on the physical condition of the person (e.g., height and weight vs. clothing). For example, the following is a list of suspect descriptions from a stranger rape pattern:

- White male, average height, medium build
- White male, 5'10" to 6' tall, 180 to 200 pounds, brown hair
- White male, 6'1" tall, 210 pounds, brown curly hair, tattoo of snake on right arm

The description for the entire pattern would be a white male, 5'10" to 6'1" tall, 180 to 210 pounds, brown curly hair, with tattoo of snake on right arm. The overall description is inclusive of all three descriptions in terms of height and weight but is more specific in terms of hair and the tattoo since that information was provided by only one witness and does not conflict with the other witnesses' descriptions. When there is conflicting information in the descriptions but the incidents are still considered related, the analyst has to be sure to note the differing descriptions. Inaccuracy often happens when describing the physical condition of the person or vehicle (e.g., drunken person or dirty vehicle), so just because the witness descriptions are different does not mean they are not related. Vehicle descriptions are handled the same way, in that information about the vehicle is summarized to the most specificity without excluding any of the cases, and the official description (e.g., tag, make, model, color) is given more weight than the vehicle's condition (e.g., dent on fender).

Time Series Analysis

An important characteristic of crime incidents, both for identifying patterns and for describing patterns, is the temporal nature of the crime, which is captured through the time of day, day(s) of week, and the order in which the incidents occurred. The method used to examine these characteristics is known as **time series analysis**—also called **temporal analysis** (Paulsen, Bair, & Helms, 2009). Crime analysts focus on describing small numbers of cases, typically fewer than 25, so statistics of central tendency, such as mean and standard deviation, are not appropriate. Rather, counts and percentages are used to describe the temporal nature of patterns.

Exact Time **Exact time series analysis** is the examination of incidents with an exact time of occurrence, such as robbery and sexual assault. It is common practice in crime analysis to use military time (so mathematical functions such as addition and subtraction can be applied to the time) and to round time variables to the nearest hour. Rounding makes the information slightly less accurate, but this is a necessary compromise to produce clear, understandable results. For example, the time of a crime occurring at 9:35 a.m. would be rounded to 0900 to 0959, and the time of a crime taking place at 10:15 p.m. would be rounded to 2200 to 2259. Table 11.1 displays a list of cases in a robbery pattern, showing the exact times at which they occurred and their rounded times.

Even though it may be interesting to know the exact time of each crime, the purpose of this analysis is to organize the information so that an overview of the entire pattern is presented. Table 11.2 shows the number of robberies by hour, which is a useful way of displaying information about the time events in a pattern. Although this information is an improvement over the list in Table 11.1, the results are even easier to understand when they are displayed in the form of a chart, as in Figure 11.1, which clearly shows that most of the robberies have occurred in the evening hours. This kind of format is useful for disseminating information about patterns to police.

Another way to display the time series analysis of this pattern is to convert each robbery into a percentage of the total number of robberies. That is, the value of each hour is no longer the count of incidents in that hour. Instead, it is the

Table 11.1 List of Cases: Robbery Pattern

Case	Time of Occurrence	Rounded
1	8:56 p.m.	2000 to 2059
2	10:45 p.m.	2200 to 2259
3	4:33 p.m.	1600 to 1659
4	5:45 p.m.	1700 to 1759
5	12:02 a.m.	0000 to 0059
6	7:48 p.m.	1900 to 1959
7	9:55 p.m.	2100 to 2159
8	7:16 p.m.	1900 to 1959
9	10:30 p.m.	2200 to 2259
10	5:46 p.m.	1700 to 1759
11	10:22 p.m.	2200 to 2259
12	8:16 p.m.	2000 to 2059
13	9:25 p.m.	2100 to 2159
14	7:56 p.m.	1900 to 1959
15	9:12 p.m.	2100 to 2159

Table 11.2 Number of Robberies by Hour			
Hour of Day	Count	Hour of Day	Count
0000 to 0059	1	1200 to 1259	0
0100 to 0159	0	1300 to 1359	0
0200 to 0259	0	1400 to 1459	0
0300 to 0359	0	1500 to 1559	0
0400 to 0459	0	1600 to 1659	1
0500 to 0559	0	1700 to 1759	2
0600 to 0659	0	1800 to 1859	0
0700 to 0759	0	1900 to 1959	3
0800 to 0859	0	2000 to 2059	2
0900 to 0959	0	2100 to 2159	3
1000 to 1059	0	2200 to 2259	3
1100 to 1159	0	2300 to 2359	0

count of incidents in that hour divided by the total number of incidents. In this example, because the total number of cases is 15, each incident is worth 6.7% (i.e., 1/15). Table 11.3 shows the counts of robberies by hour converted to percentages. The resulting chart in Figure 11.2 illustrates the percentage values. Although the charts in Figures 11.1 and 11.2 look similar, they serve different purposes. Analysts can use charts that depict percentages to analyze unlike distributions (e.g., a pattern with 10 cases and another with 25 cases) in relation to one another.

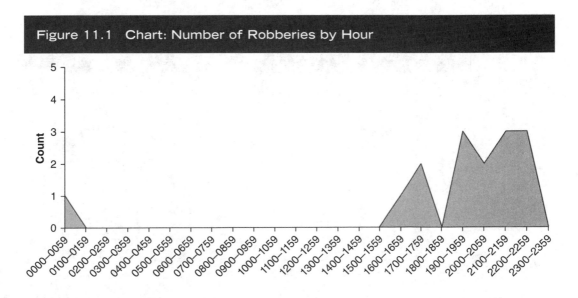

Figure 11.1 Chart: Number of Robberies by Hour

Figure 11.2 Chart: Percentage of Robberies by Hour

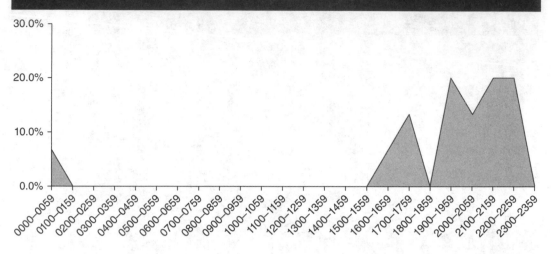

Exact Day of Week Using the same method for counting crimes by day of week, Table 11.4 illustrates the frequency of crimes and the percentage of the total by day. Figure 11.3 depicts the count and Figure 11.4 the percentage of the total of crimes by day of week. Crime analysts typically use bar charts to illustrate information about days of week.

Exact Time of Day and Day of Week The two techniques described in the previous sections illustrate information about time of day and day of week separately. However, it is important for analysts to know what combination of day *and* time is most common among incidents in the pattern. Table 11.5 is the list of cases showing time of day and day of week. Table 11.6 presents a **cross-tabulation** of these two variables, showing the count of crime by both time of day and day of week.

Figure 11.3 Chart: Number of Robberies by Day of Week

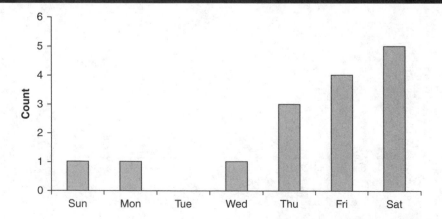

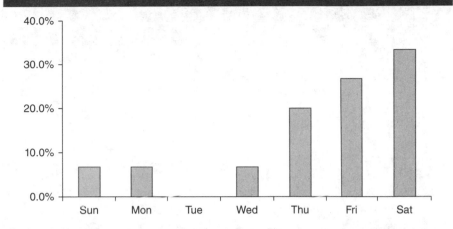

Figure 11.4 Chart: Percentage of Robberies by Day of Week

Table 11.3 Number and Percentage of Robberies by Hour

Hour of Day	Count	Percentage of Total
0000 to 0059	1	6.70%
0100 to 0159	0	0.00%
0200 to 0259	0	0.00%
0300 to 0359	0	0.00%
0400 to 0459	0	0.00%
0500 to 0559	0	0.00%
0600 to 0659	0	0.00%
0700 to 0759	0	0.00%
0800 to 0859	0	0.00%
0900 to 0959	0	0.00%
1000 to 1059	0	0.00%
1100 to 1159	0	0.00%
1200 to 1259	0	0.00%
1300 to 1359	0	0.00%
1400 to 1459	0	0.00%
1500 to 1559	0	0.00%
1600 to 1659	1	6.70%
1700 to 1759	2	13.30%
1800 to 1859	0	0.00%
1900 to 1959	3	20.00%
2000 to 2059	2	13.30%
2100 to 2159	3	20.00%
2200 to 2259	3	20.00%
2300 to 2359	0	0.00%

Table 11.4   Number and Percentage of Robberies by Day of Week

Day of Week	Count	Percentage of Total
Sun	1	6.70%
Mon	1	6.70%
Tue	0	0.00%
Wed	1	6.70%
Thu	3	20.00%
Fri	4	26.70%
Sat	5	33.30%

Table 11.5   List of Cases: Time of Day and Day of Week

Case	Time of Occurrence	Day of Occurrence
1	12:02 p.m.	Sunday
2	4:33 p.m.	Saturday
3	5:45 p.m.	Saturday
4	5:46 p.m.	Friday
5	7:16 p.m.	Saturday
6	7:48 p.m.	Thursday
7	7:56 p.m.	Thursday
8	8:16 p.m.	Friday
9	8:56 p.m.	Monday
10	9:12 p.m.	Saturday
11	9:25 p.m.	Saturday
12	9:55 p.m.	Friday
13	10:22 p.m.	Wednesday
14	10:30 p.m.	Thursday
15	10:45 p.m.	Friday

Like the results in the previous examples, these counts can be used to create a chart for visualization and dissemination of results, as in Figure 11.5. In this figure, the areas with the darker shading represent times and days when more crimes have occurred (note the legend); in this pattern, more robberies have occurred on Thursday, Friday, and Saturday evenings. It is important to keep

Figure 11.5   Chart: Time of Day and Day of Week

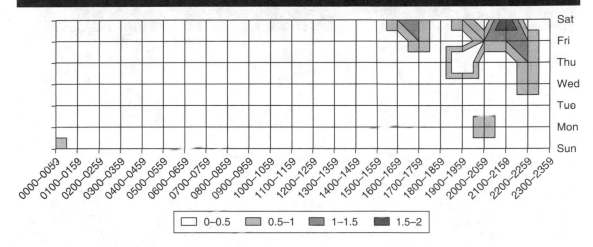

in mind that such a chart is more useful if it displays more cases (e.g., note the numerous empty cells in Table 11.6) and is put to good use in strategic crime analysis, where larger numbers of cases are examined at once.

Exact Date: Intervals Between Events Finally, an analyst may gain insight into the nature of a pattern by analyzing the number of days between crimes in the pattern. For example, a person committing robberies to support a drug habit may commit crimes closer together in time if his take in any given robbery is small. However, analysts must be careful not to assume too much about patterns or offenders when conducting this type of analysis, as many different factors can influence the time between incidents (e.g., weather, work, sickness, opportunity). Table 11.7 lists the dates of the crimes in the example pattern of robberies and the number of days between the events.

Figure 11.6 illustrates the information in Table 11.7 graphically. It shows the date range of the pattern along the x-axis (e.g., 12/01/2016 through 1/15/2017), lines that represent when the crimes occurred within that range, and diamonds along the lines that indicate the number of days between each incident and the next (y-axis). This chart is called a *tempogram* (Helms, 2004); note how it shows that the crime frequency is accelerating, or crimes are becoming more frequent. Analysts also can include information on intervals between events when mapping patterns, a technique discussed later in this chapter (in the section on spatial analysis). This type of analysis can clarify whether there is a particular tempo to a pattern—that is, whether the pattern is accelerating, stable, or decelerating. In a pattern with an accelerating tempo, intervals between events decrease as the pattern progresses. In a pattern with a decelerating tempo, intervals between events increase as the pattern progresses. When the intervals between cases remain fairly consistent, the tempo is stable. By examining the intervals between cases in a pattern, a crime analyst can help to anticipate future incidents in the pattern.

Table 11.6 Cross-Tabulation of Time of Day and Day of Week							
Hour of the Day	Sun	Mon	Tue	Wed	Thu	Fri	Sat
0000 to 0059	1						
0100 to 0159							
0200 to 0259							
0300 to 0359							
0400 to 0459							
0500 to 0559							
0600 to 0659							
0700 to 0759							
0800 to 0859							
0900 to 0959							
1000 to 1059							
1100 to 1159							
1200 to 1259							
1300 to 1359							
1400 to 1459							
1500 to 1559							
1600 to 1659							1
1700 to 1759						1	1
1800 to 1859							
1900 to 1959					2		1
2000 to 2059		1				1	
2100 to 2159						1	2
2200 to 2259				1	1	1	
2300 to 2359							

Weighted Time Span Analysis Exact time of day and day of week time series methods are not appropriate for the types of crimes (typically property crimes) for which only time span information is available (i.e., the crime occurred between 7:00 a.m. and 5:00 p.m.). Although time span information is not as accurate as exact time information, it can still help an analyst link cases together and more fully understand an established crime pattern. Two aspects of a crime-related time span are important: when

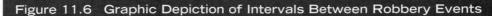

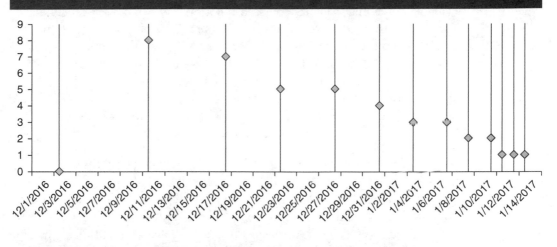

Figure 11.6   Graphic Depiction of Intervals Between Robbery Events

Table 11.7   Intervals Between Robbery Events

Case	Date of Occurrence	Days Between Events
1	12/3/2016	0
2	12/11/2016	8
3	12/18/2016	7
4	12/23/2016	5
5	12/28/2016	5
6	1/1/2017	4
7	1/4/2017	3
8	1/7/2017	3
9	1/9/2017	2
10	1/11/2017	2
11	1/12/2017	1
12	1/13/2017	1
13	1/14/2017	1

the time span begins and ends, and the length of the time span. For example, a time span beginning at 4:00 p.m. and ending at 12:00 a.m. is very different from one beginning at 4:00 a.m. and ending at 12:00 p.m., even though both are 8 hours in length. Additionally, a time span of 1 hour is a much more accurate estimate of when a crime occurred than a time span of 5 hours. It is important that analysts examine both aspects of time spans in time series analysis.[1]

In the **weighted time span analysis** method, each time span is assigned a value of 1, and each hour within the time span is a proportion of the time span.[2] For example, for a time span of 5 hours, each hour is one fifth of the overall time span and is assigned a value of .20 (i.e., 1 hour is 20% of a 5-hour time span). Similarly, in a time span of 8 hours, each hour is one eighth, and it is assigned a value of .125 (12.5%). Table 11.8 is a list of cases that shows, for each crime, the first possible time the crime occurred, that time rounded, the last possible time the crime occurred, that time rounded, the length of the time span, and the assigned value (weight) of 1 hour of the time span (e.g., in Case 1, with a time span of 6 hours, each hour in the time span is worth 1/6, or 17).

After assigning a value to an hour within the time span of each case, the analyst places these values in their appropriate hours of the day and examines these together. In Table 11.9, the rows represent the hours of the day, and the columns are the values of the time spans for each crime in the pattern (e.g., in Case 1, hours 1000 to 1059 through 1500 to 1559 are weighted .17 each). The important columns are on the right: *Total* represents the sum of the values by hour of the day, and *Percentage of Total* is "total" for that hour of the day divided by the total of all the hours of the day (e.g., the "total" for 1000 to 1059 is 1.12, which is 9.4% of 11.96, the total for all the hours of the day).

As with the methods previously described, a chart is useful for visualizing these results. Figure 11.7 illustrates the final column in Table 11.9, *Percentage of Total*.

Table 11.8 List of Cases: Time Span Data

Case	First Possible Time	Rounded	Last Possible Time	Rounded	Length of Time Span	Weight of Hour
1	10:00 a.m.	1000 to 1059	3:15 p.m.	1500 to 1559	6	0.17
2	11:15 a.m.	1100 to 1159	2:30 p.m.	1400 to 1459	4	0.25
3	9:15 a.m.	0900 to 0959	7:15 p.m.	1900 to 1959	11	0.09
4	8:00 a.m.	0800 to 0859	5:00 p.m.	1700 to 1759	10	0.10
5	7:30 a.m.	0700 to 0759	5:30 p.m.	1700 to 1759	11	0.09
6	8:15 a.m.	0800 to 0859	4:30 p.m.	1600 to 1659	9	0.11
7	10:30 a.m.	1000 to 1059	1:30 p.m.	1300 to 1359	4	0.25
8	12:30 p.m.	1200 to 1259	6:30 p.m.	1800 to 1859	7	0.14
9	12:15 p.m.	1200 to 1259	4:30 p.m.	1600 to 1659	5	0.20
10	9:45 a.m.	0900 to 0959	6:15 p.m.	1800 to 1859	10	0.10
11	8:45 a.m.	0800 to 0859	5:15 p.m.	1700 to 1759	10	0.10
12	8:30 a.m.	0800 to 0859	4:30 p.m.	1600 to 1659	9	0.11

Table 11.9 Hour and Percentage Totals for Time Spans

Hour of Day	Case												Total	Percentage of Total
	1	2	3	4	5	6	7	8	9	10	11	12		
0000 to 0059													0.00	0.00%
0100 to 0159													0.00	0.00%
0200 to 0259													0.00	0.00%
0300 to 0359													0.00	0.00%
0400 to 0459													0.00	0.00%
0500 to 0559													0.00	0.00%
0600 to 0659													0.00	0.00%
0700 to 0759					0.09								0.09	0.80%
0800 to 0859				0.10	0.09	0.11					0.10	0.11	0.51	4.30%
0900 to 0959			0.09	0.10	0.09	0.11				0.10	0.10	0.11	0.70	5.90%
1000 to 1059	0.17		0.09	0.10	0.09	0.11	0.25			0.10	0.10	0.11	1.12	9.40%
1100 to 1159	0.17	0.25	0.09	0.10	0.09	0.11	0.25			0.10	0.10	0.11	1.37	11.50%
1200 to 1259	0.17	0.25	0.09	0.10	0.09	0.11	0.25	0.14	0.20	0.10	0.10	0.11	1.71	14.30%

(Continued)

Table 11.9 (Continued)

Hour of Day	Case												Total	Percentage of Total
	1	2	3	4	5	6	7	8	9	10	11	12		
1300 to 1359	0.17	0.25	0.09	0.10	0.09	0.11	0.25	0.14	0.20	0.10	0.10	0.11	1.71	14.30%
1400 to 1459	0.17	0.25	0.09	0.10	0.09	0.11		0.14	0.20	0.10	0.10	0.11	1.46	12.20%
1500 to 1559	0.17		0.09	0.10	0.09	0.11		0.14	0.20	0.10	0.10	0.11	1.21	10.10%
1600 to 1659			0.09	0.10	0.09	0.11		0.14	0.20	0.10	0.10	0.11	1.04	8.70%
1700 to 1759			0.09	0.10	0.09			0.14		0.10	0.10		0.62	5.20%
1800 to 1859			0.09					0.14		0.10			0.33	2.80%
1900 to 1959			0.09										0.09	0.80%
2000 to 2059													0.00	0.00%
2100 to 2159													0.00	0.00%
2200 to 2259													0.00	0.00%
2300 to 2359													0.00	0.00%
Total													11.96	

Figure 11.7   Chart: Weighted Time Spans

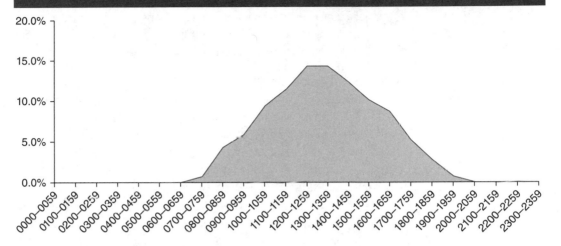

The chart shows that the crimes in this pattern have time spans that generally cluster from 7:00 a.m. to 7:00 p.m. and that the time spans cluster between the hours of 11:00 a.m. and 2:59 p.m. (just over 52% of the weighted hours of all the time spans in the pattern, the exact number obtained from Table 11.9). Analysts also can use this method for weekday spans in which each day is weighted by the number of days in the time span (e.g., for a crime that spans over Monday, Tuesday, and Wednesday, each day would be weighted .33 and would be assigned to the appropriate weekday).

INTERNATIONAL CRIME ANALYST PERSPECTIVE

Rachel Carson

Director

Inspired Acts, Ltd

United Kingdom

Data concerning recorded crimes or calls for service shown over time are often visualised as a control chart in the United Kingdom, meaning that patterns, shifts, and exceptions can be easily identified and tackled. Plotting average (expected) values with upper and lower confidence limits at different levels of certainty and looking for patterns in individual data points allows analysts to be alerted to points of note. Data can be viewed daily, weekly, monthly, and so on, but as an example, three monthly robbery data points consistently above average may be an early indication of a shift in crime levels, which requires investigation; three consecutive increasing data points may indicate a gradual increase to monitor and/or research; a data point above the upper-control limit indicates a significant factor is affecting the data series, which requires identification. This is a useful tool for identifying emerging issues quickly and tackling them effectively before they become a bigger problem.

Spatial Analysis of Patterns

Another key characteristic of crime patterns is their geographic nature. Crime analysts use spatial analysis in several ways to identify and understand crime patterns. Scholars and practitioners are currently doing advanced work in tactical spatial analysis, but the following discussion is confined to basic techniques.

As noted earlier, the micro-time hot spot is the most common type of pattern identified by crime analysts. They are typically identified by examining 1 to 2 weeks of data. The activity of a micro-time hot spot is the emergence of several closely related crimes within a few minutes' travel distance from one another (i.e., micro-place) that occurs within a relatively short period of time (i.e., micro-time)—a crime "flare-up" (Santos & Santos, 2015c). However, micro-time hot spots are not stable over time but flare up in one area and may not return to that same area for many months, years, or not at all. Micro-time hot spots are clusters of repeat incidents (discussed in Chapter 2) that occur within stable, long-term problem areas as well as in other areas that are not accustomed to high levels of crime or have an ongoing crime problem. This is why they are important to identify and distinguish from problem areas.

To identify and describe a micro-time hot spot, it is important for a crime analyst to understand how a micro-time hot spot evolves. As part of the crime analyst's pattern analysis process, a set of criteria that determines what makes a micro-time hot spot should be developed so that micro-time hot spot patterns are consistently identified and enable actionable responses by police. Each crime analyst would determine the criteria based on the size of the jurisdiction, the zoning, and the type of crime being examined (e.g., residential burglary patterns tend to occur more closely than commercial burglary patterns).

The following is an illustration of the evolution of a property crime micro-time hot spot based on the following criteria developed for residential crime in a suburban jurisdiction with average amounts of property crime: (1) two or more incidents of residential burglary and/or residential theft from vehicle; (2) occurring from 1 to 14 days of another; (3) within a 0.25-mile radius. Figure 11.8 illustrates an example of how a micro-time hot spot flares up and cools off.

The left panel contains a map that shows a micro-time hot spot at initial identification, with two crimes occurring inside a 0.10-mile radius within 4 days (i.e., February 1–5). In the middle panel, the map shows additional Crimes 3 and 4 occur and are part of the micro-time hot spot because they are located within a 0.25-mile radius of the mean center of the two original crimes, and they occur 2 and 3 days later, respectively. The right panel map shows how the micro-time hot spot continues to flare up, since Crime 6 falls inside the 0.25-mile radius and occurs only 7 days after Crime 4. Crime 5 is not included in the micro-time hot spot because it does not fall within the maximum-allowed 0.25-mile radius.

The micro-time hot spot is considered cooled off after Crime 6, since Crime 7 occurred 25 days (i.e., more than 14 days) after Crime 6. Therefore, in this

Figure 11.8   Evolution of a Micro-Time Hot Spot

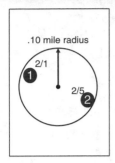
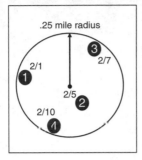
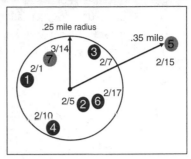

illustration the micro-time hot spot began with two crimes in a 0.10-mile radius over 4 days. It continued to "flare up," with three more crimes within a 0.25-mile radius, and lasted 12 more days before "cooling off." Importantly, it is possible that a new micro-time hot spot could develop around Crime 5 in terms of space and Crime 7 in terms of time, but they would each have to meet the criteria of a new micro-time hot spot (i.e., two crimes within 0.50 miles and 14 days). In other words, once a crime is part of a micro-time hot spot it cannot be part of a new one, and even though a micro-time hot spot may be close to another, it does not overlap in either time or space.

As noted previously, geographic proximity of incidents is a particularly important characteristic in the analysis of property crimes, such as residential burglary, residential theft from vehicle, and auto theft or persons crimes such as street robbery. However, analysts need to consider more than just geographic locations of incidents when conducting pattern identification. In addition to following a set criteria, the crime analyst would examine characteristics such as type of place, time, day, and MO to finalize the pattern.

Pattern Bulletins

To disseminate crime pattern and other tactical information to officers, detectives, and (in some cases) citizens, crime analysts use a format known as a *pattern bulletin*. Such a bulletin typically includes the following elements:

- *Publish date:* This is the date the bulletin was initially published (disseminated to the police department) by the crime analyst.

- *Bulletin number:* This is the sequential number of the bulletin. Normally, crime analysts use the year and a range of numbers (e.g., 2017–001, 2017–002). Also, when a bulletin is updated with new information, such as additional crimes or an arrest, the date is changed with an updated date, and a letter is added to the bulletin number (2017–001A).

Multiple updates use letters in order (e.g., A, B, C, D, etc.). This is done so that the subsequent versions of the same pattern bulletin can be easily referenced. An additional consideration is that crime pattern bulletins should be numbered separately from other tactical bulletins, such as arrest bulletins and BOLOs (i.e., be on the lookout).

- *Amended date:* Oftentimes, in an effort to get information to sworn personnel quickly, the crime analyst publishes a pattern before all the information is available (i.e., officers are still finalizing a crime report), and there may be mistakes or missing information in the first version of the bulletin. Thus, when more or corrected information about the original pattern comes about, a crime analyst will "fix" (i.e., amend) it, publish the bulletin again, and add an amended date so that individuals know the difference between the original and amended bulletin. The amended date does not replace the original publish date and both should be included; however, when a bulletin has been amended multiple times, only the most recent updated date is included.

- *Updated date:* A bulletin is updated when there is additional activity linked to the pattern after the bulletin has been published. Where amending the bulletin is correcting, changing, or adding information of the original bulletin, updating a bulletin is adding new information about activity that *occurred* after the original publication (i.e., additional crimes 2 days after initial publication; FI cards taken in the pattern area after publication; an arrest). When an update to a bulletin is published, as noted earlier, the bulletin number is changed to include a letter (e.g., A, B, C) at the end, so the updated date corresponds with this change. When multiple updates to a bulletin are created, the bulletin letter reflects how many times there has been an update, and the updated date reflects how long the pattern has been active (i.e., crimes are continuing) for response. (Note: Amending a bulletin has nothing to do with how long it has been active). For example, bulletin 2017-045, with a publish date of March 1, 2017, has been updated several times and is now 2017-045C, with a date of April 3, 2017. These two components indicate that the pattern has been updated three times and has been active for 34 days. The update date does not replace the original publish date on the bulletin (i.e., both should be listed); however, when a bulletin has been updated multiple times, only the most recent updated date is included.

- *Title:* The title contains the type of pattern (e.g., series, hot spot), the type of crime (e.g., robbery, burglary), and the location of the pattern (e.g., address, neighborhood, police beat, entire city). The title also may include other information, depending on the type of pattern (e.g., type of place for a hot setting, type of property for hot product).

- *Number of incidents:* This is the total number of incidents in the pattern. The bulletin also may describe other incidents that are discussed as possibly related (e.g., five burglaries and two burglar alarm calls).

- *Date range:* The date of the first and last crimes in the pattern.

- *Days and times:* A summary of the days of week and times of day when the overall pattern is occurring.

- *Summary of MO:* A short, straightforward narrative in bullet form describing the suspects' actions in the incidents in the pattern.

- *Property taken (if relevant):* A summary of the types of property or unique property taken.

- *Suspect information:* The most specific description(s) of the suspect(s) possible that covers all crimes.

- *Vehicle information:* The most specific description of the vehicle possible that covers all crimes.

- *Weapons (if relevant):* The most specific description of the weapons used that covers all possible descriptions.

- *Known offenders (if relevant):* Because we know individuals commit crimes near where they live (particularly burglaries, thefts, and robberies in residential areas), crime analysts include offenders who have been arrested or convicted of the pattern crime type and who report their residences in the pattern. Each person's information is included on the bulletin (e.g., picture, name, date of birth, and crimes committed). Note that offenders should be individuals who are most likely to have committed the crime and thus should be prioritized and the number kept low (e.g., between three and five offenders on a bulletin).

- *Field interviews and other information:* Information about field interviews, suspicious persons, or vehicles in the area that might be related to the pattern or information from other crimes that might be related but not enough to be considered a crime within the pattern.

- *List of cases:* A list of the incidents in the pattern with detailed information about each case. This would include a map reference number, case number, date/time span of crime's occurrence (not of the report), time/time span of crime's occurrence, and address of the crime. Other information in the list would depend on the type of crime and pattern and would include other characteristics, such as location name, suspect's actions, individual suspect descriptions, victim type, point of entry, method of entry, property taken, and whether fingerprints and evidence were collected. Importantly, the cases are listed by chronology; most analysts place the most recent crimes at the bottom of the list.

- *Map of the incidents in the pattern:* Single-symbol map with numbers next to the symbols corresponding to the list of cases so that the numbers indicate the sequence of the crimes; higher numbers are more recent crimes. The addresses of known-offender residences, field interview locations, or other relevant locations (e.g., all Radio Shacks in a pattern in which three of twelve stores were victimized) would also be mapped using different symbols than the crimes. The map should also include a circle drawn so its edges touch the outermost crimes in the pattern with a notation about the length of the circle's radius. Instead of providing a scale on the map, the circle and its radius tell the officers the relative distance of all crimes in the pattern and the area in which to implement the responses, if appropriate.

Across the United States, pattern bulletin formats and content vary by police agency and often by analyst. Over the last 22 years, I have examined and evaluated hundreds of bulletins, made recommendations, and trained crime analysts in pattern bulletin creation, as well as worked with police departments to effectively implement responses to patterns. Thus, based on my work, Figure 11.9 illustrates the recommended format for pattern bulletins, which has been produced using a bulletin making software.

Police agencies also produce other types of tactical crime analysis bulletins, such as arrest bulletins (i.e., information about an offender arrests for one or more crimes in a pattern), BOLOs (i.e., "be on the lookout" for a particular suspect, vehicle, etc.), and officer safety bulletins. Historically, tactical crime analysis bulletins have been distributed to police personnel on paper during briefings or in internal mailboxes. In recent years, however, many police agencies have begun to distribute bulletins through e-mail or by posting them to intranet sites (i.e., agency management systems discussed in Chapter 5). These methods are preferable because they are less expensive (e.g., paper and printing/copying costs) and officers receive higher quality products (e.g., color maps vs. black-and-white copies).

In agencies where officers have access to a police department intranet site through laptops in their vehicles, crime pattern responses can be documented within the system. For example, in the Port St. Lucie (Florida) Police

Figure 11.9 Crime Pattern Bulletin Example

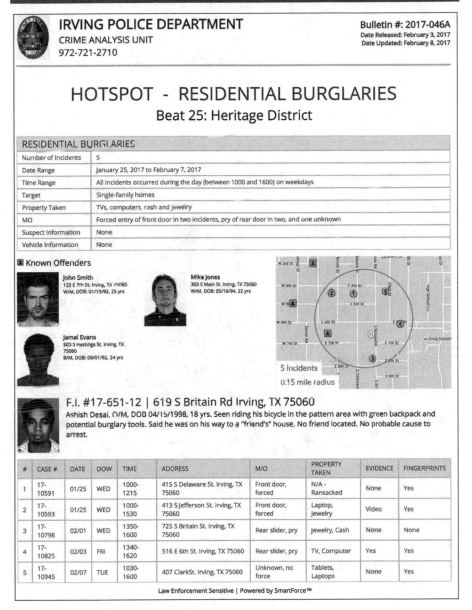

IRVING POLICE DEPARTMENT
CRIME ANALYSIS UNIT
972-721-2710

Bulletin #: 2017-046A
Date Released: February 3, 2017
Date Updated: February 8, 2017

HOTSPOT - RESIDENTIAL BURGLARIES
Beat 25: Heritage District

RESIDENTIAL BURGLARIES

Number of Incidents	5
Date Range	January 25, 2017 to February 7, 2017
Time Range	All incidents occurred during the day (between 1000 and 1600) on weekdays
Target	Single-family homes
Property Taken	TVs, computers, cash and jewelry
MO	Forced entry of front door in two incidents, pry of rear door in two, and one unknown
Suspect Information	None
Vehicle Information	None

Known Offenders

John Smith
133 E 7th St. Irving, TX 75060
W/M, DOB: 01/15/92, 25 yrs

Mike Jones
303 S Main St. Irving, TX 75060
W/M, DOB: 05/16/94, 22 yrs

Jamal Evans
503 S Hastings St. Irving, TX 75060
B/M, DOB: 09/01/92, 24 yrs

5 Incidents
0.15 mile radius

F.I. #17-651-12 | 619 S Britain Rd Irving, TX 75060
Ashish Desai, O/M, DOB 04/15/1998, 18 yrs. Seen riding his bicycle in the pattern area with green backpack and potential burglary tools. Said he was on his way to a "friend's" house. No friend located. No probable cause to arrest.

#	CASE #	DATE	DOW	TIME	ADDRESS	M/O	PROPERTY TAKEN	EVIDENCE	FINGERPRINTS
1	17-10591	01/25	WED	1000-1215	415 S Delaware St. Irving, TX 75060	Front door, forced	N/A - Ransacked	None	Yes
2	17-10593	01/25	WED	1000-1530	413 S Jefferson St. Irving, TX 75060	Front door, forced	Laptop, Jewelry	Video	Yes
3	17-10798	02/01	WED	1350-1600	725 S Britain St. Irving, TX 75060	Rear slider, pry	Jewelry, Cash	None	None
4	17-10825	02/03	FRI	1340-1620	516 E 6th St. Irving, TX 75060	Rear slider, pry	TV, Computer	Yes	Yes
5	17-10945	02/07	TUE	1030-1600	407 ClarkSt. Irving, TX 75060	Unknown, no force	Tablets, Laptops	None	Yes

Law Enforcement Sensitive | Powered by SmartForce™

Source: Adventos™; Brian McGrew.

Department when a pattern is identified by the crime analysts, the pattern bulletins are immediately posted to the department's agency management system (i.e., SmartForce®) for review by other sworn officers working in the same area and their supervisors. A pattern discussion board (i.e., "thread") provides officers the capability to post information about their responses as well as their knowledge of the pattern area, known offenders, or of field interviews

Figure 11.10 Pattern Bulletin Distributed to the Public

PORT ST. LUCIE POLICE DEPARTMENT

Would you like to help us?
Below are ways you can help deter crime in your neighborhood!

CRIME PREVENTION TIPS

Prevent a Vehicle Burglary
- Secure all vehicle doors.
- Ensure all windows are rolled up entirely and secured.
- Remove all items from plain view of any passer by.
- Activate vehicle alarm system.
- Promote good natural surveillance by always parking in a well lit location and never parking smaller vehicles between two larger vehicles.
- Use our online interactive public mapping for any additional activity occurring in this area at www.CrimeReports.com *(access the website via www.pslpd.us).*
- Report all suspicious activity to police immediately.

If you want to remain anonymous, please contact:

TREASURE COAST CRIME STOPPERS
www.tcwatch.org or call (800)273-8477

PORT ST. LUCIE POLICE DEPT.
121 SW Port St. Lucie Blvd Bldg. C
Port St. Lucie, FL 34884
(772)871-5000
EMERGENCY CALLS—DIAL 911

NEIGHBORHOOD CRIME NOTIFICATION

WE WANT YOU TO KNOW:
The below map depicts burglary incidents that have occurred within an approximate .45 mile radius in the area of SE West Snow Road from April 28th—May 5th, 2011.

Auto Burglaries (9 Incidents)
- 8 of the 9 vehicle burglary entries were made without force .
- Primarily targeting unlocked vehicles
- Occurring primarily in the late night/overnight hours
- Stolen Items: Cash (coins), GPS units, cellphone chargers, DVD player, garage opener, food items, and a car battery.

Our reports indicate the person or people responsible for committing these crimes might match the following descriptions:
- Two white males
- Clothing Descriptions of Suspects
    - **Suspect #1—** *wearing black gloves, white shorts and a black shirt*
    - **Suspect #2—** *wearing all black clothing*

Source: Port St. Lucie (Florida) Police Department, Cheryl Davis.

that have been conducted. In this type of system, the crime analyst can easily post an amendment or an update of the bulletin to the thread for all officers to see immediately as they are responding. Another example is software used by the Greensboro (North Carolina) Police Department (i.e., CrimeView). The software allows police managers to draw a geographic area and assign officers a "mission" or response. Officers can then click on the mission and enter the responses they have implemented.

Lastly, when citizens are provided with information about patterns, they receive "watered-down" or sanitized versions of the bulletins created for police agencies. Bulletins intended for citizens will not include information that might breach confidentiality or that is likely to jeopardize an investigation. For example, if a burglary pattern contains privately owned locations (e.g., single-family residences), the bulletin for citizens would include only information about the MO, times, dates, and general locations; the specific addresses of the homes burglarized would not be provided as that information is not necessary for homeowners in the area to protect themselves. Exact address information would be provided for publicly frequented locations contained in the pattern; for example, if cars are repeatedly being burglarized in the parking lot of a particular nightclub, that location would be specified because it would be important for citizens to have that information in order to protect their belongings at that place. Figure 11.10 is an example of a pattern bulletin that has been reformatted for distribution to citizens.

SUMMARY POINTS

This chapter covers specific techniques that analysts can use to understand known crime patterns and provides examples of tactical crime analysis products. The following are the key points addressed in this chapter:

- Information provided about a crime pattern focuses on how the crimes were committed, who committed them, when they occurred, and where they occurred.

- Because MO characteristics can be very specific, they can provide obvious links among cases that are months or even years apart; however, there is no way to establish a pattern definitely by MO alone.

- Some of the most important characteristics of crime incidents, both for identifying patterns and for describing patterns, are the times of day and the days of the week when they occur, and the order in which they occur. These characteristics are examined in various types of time series analysis, including exact time analysis, weighted time span analysis, and analysis of days between incidents.

- In spatial analysis, single-symbol maps enable analysts to examine the geographic nature of crimes and begin to identify patterns.

- A micro-time hot spot as the emergence of several closely related crimes within a few minutes' travel distance from one another (i.e., micro-place) that occurs within a relatively short period of time (i.e., micro-time) is called a crime "flare-up."

- Crime analysts should develop criteria for identifying patterns. Particular to pattern hot spots, the criteria should designate 1) type of crime, 2) number of crimes, 3) number of days for crime span, and 4) radius in which the crimes occur.

- Crime pattern bulletins typically include the following elements: publish, amended, and updated dates; bulletin number; title; number of incidents; date range; days and times; summary of MO; property taken; suspect and vehicle information; weapons; known offenders; field interview and other information; a list of cases; and a map of the incidents.

- There are several types of tactical crime analysis bulletins, including (but not limited to) pattern bulletins, repeat-offender and repeat-victim bulletins, BOLOs, and officer safety bulletins.

- Police produce "sanitized" bulletins to disseminate and raise citizen awareness, to try to catch offenders, to investigate crimes further, to clear old cases, and to prevent future crimes.

DISCUSSION EXERCISES*

Exercise 1

Synthesize the following MO information from five burglaries of businesses to be included in a pattern bulletin:

- Unknown suspects smashed a window in the rear of the building to gain entry into a vacant business. Once inside, they broke into the candy machine to take change and pried open a filing cabinet.

- Unknown suspects pried open a rear door of a business to gain entry. Once inside, they broke into the candy machines and took change.

- Unknown suspects broke glass in front door of the business and took two donation containers. They attempted to break into the candy machines but were unsuccessful.

- Unknown suspects entered by prying open the rear door to the business, cut phone/alarm wires, searched file cabinets, and took cash from a plastic bin.

- Unknown suspects pried open the rear bay door using a dolly. They took tin cash box and kicked a small candy machine to get the change inside.

Exercise 2

Synthesize the following suspect information for three robberies to be included on a pattern bulletin:

- Two suspects: black male, 19 to 23 years old, 5'9" to 6'1" tall, 170 to 190 pounds; and a white male with a goatee, 19 to 23 years old, 5'8" tall, 150 pounds

- Three suspects: two black males, 20 to 25 years old; and one Hispanic male, 20 years old, 150 pounds, beard

- Two suspects: one light-skinned black male with a goatee, 20 years old, 5'8" to 5'10" tall; and a black male, 5'10" tall, 170 pounds

NOTES

1. Some time series methods include examining "split time," or the middle of a time span, to determine when the pattern occurred. This method is not recommended, however, because it does not consider the beginning and end or the length of the time span, so the results provide the crime analyst with little relevant information.

2. Weighted time span analysis is also sometimes called *aoristic analysis* (see Paulsen et al., 2009; Ratcliffe, 2002).

3. In the spatial analysis process, numerous maps may be created, but only a few may yield interesting results.

Strategic Crime Analysis

As discussed in Chapter 4, strategic crime analysis is the "analysis of data directed towards development and evaluation of long-term strategies, policies, and prevention techniques. Its subjects include long-term statistical trends, hot spots [problem areas], and problems" (IACA, 2014b, p. 4). Similar to tactical crime analysis, the data used for strategic crime analysis comes from police databases; however, strategic crime analysis often includes the collection of data from a variety of other sources, such as the census data, geographic zoning data, and city data, and can include primary data collected through both quantitative and qualitative methods. Strategic crime analysis requires the same crime data but in aggregate form and over a longer period of time. The goal of strategic crime analysis is to identify long-term problems and understand why they are occurring to direct police resources to develop long-term crime prevention solutions.

Specifically, Chapter 12 is an overview of the problem-solving process and how it is used for strategic problems instead of for repeat incidents or patterns as discussed in Part III. It also covers the basic statistics used in strategic crime analysis as a foundation for Chapter 13 and Chapter 14, which illustrate the strategic analysis of problems by answering key analysis questions. Chapter 15 describes the types of crime analysis products that result from the strategic analysis described here. Just as a carpenter uses a variety of tools for building different things, crime analysts apply different techniques in different situations. The chapters in Part IV present a toolbox full of different analysis techniques that are used within the strategic problem analysis process, as well as examples of the techniques and case studies of problem analysis.

CHAPTER 12

Analyzing Problems
Process and Statistics

The purpose of this chapter is to provide an overview of the process and statistics that are used in strategic crime analysis to analyze various types of problems. This chapter provides the foundation for Chapter 13 and Chapter 14, which illustrate the application of these methods and techniques.

Methodology: SARA Process

Strategic crime analysis involves the study of long-term problems. To review from Chapter 3, a long-term problem is a set of related activity that occurs over several months, seasons, or years that stems from systematic opportunities created by everyday behavior and environment. They include problem locations (i.e., risky places), problem areas (i.e., hot spots), problem offenders (i.e., repeat or chronic offenders), problem victims (i.e., repeat victims), problem property, and compound problems. These types of problems are different than those discussed so far—repeat incidents and patterns—in that they are broader in scope and occur over a longer period of time. Because of this, the level of analysis and the responses required are more in depth and often require collaboration with non-police agencies and the community.

The problem-solving process is a way in which police and crime analysts approach a problem in order to implement crime prevention or crime reduction strategies. Thus, problem solving is applied to all types of problems, including immediate, short-term, and long-term problems. For immediate problems, problem solving is the process by which patrol officers respond to calls for service appropriately on a daily basis and detectives go about investigating a crime. For short-term problems, the problem-solving process is fairly straightforward as crime analysts assist in identification of repeat incidents and patterns that allow sworn personnel to respond tactically. Finally, long-term problems require a long-term approach to both analysis and response because the problems addressed are more complex. This chapter, then, discusses the problem-solving process in more detail, but specifically in the context of long-term problems to support strategic crime analysis.

As discussed in Chapter 3, John Eck and William Spelman (1987) developed the acronym *SARA* to help guide police in carrying out the problem-solving process for crime reduction. The following section describes the steps of SARA in more detail: (S)canning and defining specific problems, (A)nalyzing data to understand the opportunities that create the problem, (R)esponding to the problem using both police and nonpolice methods, and (A)ssessing whether the response has worked.

Scanning and Identifying a Problem

According to the Center for Problem-Oriented Policing (2016), also referred to as the POP Center, scanning includes identifying recurring problems of concern to both the public and the police, prioritizing those problems, and selecting problems for closer examination. Long-term problems are most likely selected by police personnel instead of crime analysts, though crime analysts may recommend a particular problem for problem solving. Analysts assist in this first step by providing general statistics of crime, disorder, and arrests that allow police to identify and prioritize current problems in their jurisdictions. Not all incidents of crime and disorder are brought to the attention of the police through analysis. Because of this, the ability of police to develop information about some problems may be difficult. This is why police–community relations are important, and the input of various community groups through interviews, surveys, and other forms of community outreach can be important sources of information for both identifying and prioritizing problems.

Once a problem is selected, the **scanning step** includes confirming that the problem exists, determining how frequently the problem occurs and how long it has been taking place, and identifying the consequences of the problem (Center for Problem-Oriented Policing, 2016). In this process, the analyst typically examines the relevant data that are immediately available within the police agency (e.g., crime reports, calls for service, and arrests). This initial examination of the problem merely describes what is occurring but does not yet seek to understand *why* the problem is occurring, which is done in the second step (i.e., analysis) of the SARA process.

Oftentimes, when conducting an initial descriptive analysis of a problem, it becomes apparent that the problem is too broad. For example, auto theft is identified as a problem in a city, and descriptive analysis shows that various types of auto theft are occurring—joyriding, theft for parts, insurance fraud— and in different types of places—apartment communities, shopping malls, residential neighborhoods. In order to make sure that a problem is identified correctly and distinguished accurately from other problems so that situational crime prevention responses can be implemented effectively, it is helpful to classify each problem using two major characteristics of the problem: the environment in which it occurs and the type of behavior associated with it. Clarke and Eck (2005, Step 15) have developed the following classifications for the environment and behavior of a problem:

Environments regulate the targets available, the activities people can engage in, and who controls the location. Specifying an environment allows comparisons of environments with and without the problem. Environments have owners who can be important for solving the problem. There are 12 distinct environments for most common police problems (the "technological" environment was added to Clarke & Eck's list here):

- *Residential*: Locations where people dwell. Houses, apartments, and hotel rooms are examples. Though most are in fixed locations, a few are mobile, such as recreational vehicles.

- *Recreational*: Places where people go to have a good time. Bars, nightclubs, restaurants, movie theaters, playgrounds, marinas, and parks are examples.

- *Offices*: Locations of white-collar work where there is little face-to-face interaction between the workers and the general public. Government and business facilities are often of this type. Access to these locations is often restricted.

- *Retail*: Places for walk-in or drive-up customer traffic involving monetary transactions. Stores and banks are examples.

- *Industrial*: Locations for processing of goods. Cash transactions are not important activities in these environments, and the public is seldom invited. Factories, warehouses, and package-sorting facilities are examples.

- *Agricultural*: Locations for growing crops and raising animals.

- *Education*: Places of learning or study, including day care centers, schools, universities, libraries, and places of worship.

- *Human services*: Places where people go when something is wrong. Courts, jails, prisons, police stations, hospitals, and drug treatment centers are examples.

- *Public ways*: Routes that connect all other environments. Roads and highways, footpaths and bike trails, and drives and parking facilities are examples.

- *Transport*: Locations for the mass movement of people. These include buses, bus stations and bus stops, airplanes and airports, trains and train stations, ferries and ferry terminals, and ocean liners and piers.

- *Open/transitional*: Areas without consistent or regular designated uses. These differ from parks in that they have not been designated for recreation, although people may use them for this. Transitional areas include abandoned properties and construction sites.

- *Technological*: Typically, an "electronic" place where problems can happen. Examples include the Internet, intranets, social media sites, cell phones, computer networks, and the like.

Behavior is the second dimension for classifying a problem. Specifying behaviors helps pinpoint important aspects of harm, intent, and offender–target relationships. There are six types of behavior:

- *Predatory*: Offender is clearly distinct from the victim, and the victim objects to the offender's actions. Most common crimes are of this type. Examples include robbery, child abuse, burglary, and theft.

- *Consensual*: Parties involved knowingly and willingly interact. This typically involves some form of transaction. Examples include drug sales, prostitution, and stolen goods sales. Note, however, that assaults on prostitutes are predatory behaviors.

- *Conflicts*: Violent interactions involve roughly coequal people who have some preexisting relationship. Some forms of domestic violence among adults involve this type of behavior, although domestic violence against children and the elderly is classified as predatory because the parties involved are not coequal.

- *Incivilities*: Offenders are distinguishable from victims, but the victims are spread over a number of individuals and the harms are not serious. Many concerns that are annoying, unsightly, noisy, or disturbing but do not involve serious property damage or injury fall into this category. Loud parties are an example. Whether vandalism fits in this category depends on the details. Some forms of vandalism are predatory. Some incivilities are troublesome regardless of the environment, while others are troublesome only in specific environments.

- *Endangerment*: Offender and the victim are the same person, or the offender had no intent to harm the victim. Suicide attempts, drug overdoses, and vehicle crashes are examples.

- *Misuse of police*: A category reserved for unwarranted demands on the police service. False reporting of crimes and repeated calling about issues that citizens can handle themselves are examples. This is a category of last resort: for use when the sole harm stemming from the behavior is the expenditure of police resources, and when none of the other categories fit.

Table 12.1 displays a list of problems and their characteristics of environment and behavior to help illustrate these concepts. Once the environment and behavior of a problem are specified, the descriptive analysis should be repeated with these constraints to inform the rest of the problem-solving process.

Table 12.1   Problems, Environment, and Behavior

Problem	Environment	Behavior
Assaults in bars	Recreational	Conflict
Construction site burglaries of homes	Transitional	Predatory
Traffic crashes at intersections	Public ways	Endangerment
Thefts from vehicles at a mall	Public ways	Predatory
False burglar alarms at factories	Industrial	Misuse of police
Street prostitution in a residential neighborhood	Public ways	Consensual
Intimate violence at work	Office	Conflict
Loud music at an assisted living facility	Residential	Incivilities
Robbery of bus drivers	Transport	Predatory

INTERNATIONAL CRIME ANALYST PERSPECTIVE

Prof. Dr. João Apolinário da Silva

Pós-Doutor em Administração –UFBA

Doutor em Desenvolvimento Regional e urbano –UNIFACS

Presidente da Agência Brasileira de Análise Criminal

Strategic crime analysis is one of the most used types of analysis in public security management in Brazil. Especially in the state of Bahia, its use is important for planning public policies and allocating resources to meet the needs of policing application and criminality reduction in cities. This analysis tool allows monitoring the operation of governmental actions and has aided the governing of the public security sector, including the application of performance assessment and prize-giving for achieved results on account of reaching crime reduction rates in the territories.

One important aspect of the use of strategic crime analysis is the maximizing of results in the face of the supervision of criminality development and policing performance. Since it is a type of analysis that requires the application of theoretical and technological knowledge for studying the phenomena involving crime and its control, the criminal analyst has to have academic preparation to understand the dynamics of cities and their territories. In Brazil, there has been used the Central Cities Theory to understand the relations between criminality, the urban area, and the connections of organized structured criminality in big cities and its influence in small, midsized, and big towns. For this purpose, there is used simple and multiple time regression analysis; correlation analysis to examine how much one variable interferes in the other, factorial analysis; cluster analysis to determine the group of cities with the same criminality profile; and spatial area analysis to designate the cities that need greater attention in policing reinforcement and application of public policies. Such tools combine with other knowledge to help understand criminality and determine possible solutions towards the problems of criminality in the territories.

Analysis

The **analysis step** of the problem-solving process begins with researching what is known about the specific problem type and potential responses, understanding the local context of the problem, and determining how the problem is currently being addressed in that particular jurisdiction (Center for Problem-Oriented Policing, 2016). This is followed by the analysis of data in which hypotheses are developed that speculate why the problem is occurring; then data are collected to test these hypotheses; and finally statistical analysis is conducted, from which conclusions are made about the immediate causes of the problem.

Research Related to the Problem The POP Center (2016) has developed a series of monographs—the *Problem-Oriented Guides for Police*—which contains three types of guidebooks that summarize knowledge about the nature of and responses to specific crime and disorder problems (i.e., *Problem-Specific Guides*), about responses that are used across a wide range of problems (i.e., *Response Guides*), and about how various analytical techniques are applied to understand crime and disorder problems (i.e., *Problem-Solving Tool Guides*). Some of the response guides were noted in Chapter 10, but all of these guides are mandatory reading in the analysis step because they provide all the known information about a given problem, potential responses, and useful analytical techniques, most of which are discussed in this book as well.

Even if the specific crime or disorder problem that the crime analyst is examining is not the subject of a particular guide, there may be a related guide that the analyst can use (e.g., the guide on assaults in and around bars can be used to help understand sexual assaults in and around bars). Importantly, an analyst should start with the guide titled *Researching a Problem* (Clarke & Schultze, 2005) in the *Problem-Solving Tool Guide* series (http://www.popcenter .org/tools/) since it provides step-by-step instructions on how to find additional research materials about a problem when a guide is not available.

Crime analysts can also gather information about problems from other practitioners who have dealt with similar problems. Sometimes neighboring jurisdictions that share a community's problem provide data, analysis results, and findings about successful or unsuccessful responses. Obtaining information about a problem from regional and national perspectives allows the analyst to make comparisons (e.g., national arrest rates for burglary are 15%, but local rates are only 3%). The findings of academic and practical research about problems provide analysts with insights into the causes of these problems, suggestions for data collection, descriptions of analytic techniques to use to study problems, and information on the success or failure of attempts to solve the problems.

Local Context of the Problem: Agency and Community As environmental criminology stresses, patterns of opportunities that create crime and other problems are specific to time, space, and environmental circumstances. In order to analyze a problem, a crime analyst must understand the nature of the community in which the problem exists and the police agency that will address the problem. Some needed information is general and easy to obtain, such as population of the community served, the number of officers in the agency, and the types of agency (e.g., local police, sheriff, state police) and community (e.g., rural, urban, suburban, large or small) that are involved. The analyst can use all of this information to make comparisons with other communities.

The other types of information that are necessary for problem analysis differ from problem to problem and may not be as easily obtained. Generally, the analyst needs to understand the political nature of the problem in the community (e.g., racial tensions between groups), who the audience for the analysis results will be (e.g., chief of police, community groups, city council), whether any recent significant changes have taken place in the community (e.g., increase in immigration, significant population growth), and if the city has any unique characteristics (e.g., contains a university, has seasonal visitors).

Furthermore, to determine the scope and intensity of the analysis, it is important for the analyst to know why the particular problem is a concern and has been chosen for study. A police agency may select a problem for analysis because addressing the problem is a strategic goal of the agency or because the problem has been an issue for years in the community. If problem analysis is being conducted for these reasons, the analyst can expect to spend significant time and energy on the project.

Developing and Testing Hypotheses A hypothesis is a statement about a problem that can be true or false. It is normally an answer to a question posed about the problem that is based on theory and experience. Crime analysts typically have a limited amount of time to devote to a particular problem analysis. By developing hypotheses relevant to a local problem, analysts can streamline their work and not waste time producing analysis results that are not relevant. Hypotheses suggest the type of data to collect, direct the analysis of data, and help interpret the results (Clarke & Eck, 2005).

Hypotheses are typically developed after the scanning process in which some initial descriptive analysis has been conducted. For example, an initial analysis might show that there are a large number of auto thefts occurring in the jurisdiction compared to other neighboring jurisdictions. A question asked about the problem might be: Why are cars being stolen in our jurisdiction? One hypothesis that could be developed is: Most of the cars are being stripped and the parts sold. An analysis of the number of cars found (i.e., recovery rate) after they are stolen might provide some insight. If the analysis shows that 85% of the cars are found in near original condition, the hypothesis would be proven false since the statistics show the majority of cars are not being stripped for parts since they are being recovered.

In many cases, the questions that generate hypotheses begin with *why*. For example, "Why is this bar more of a problem than others in the area?" "Why are burglars taking smart TVs?" For any question, numerous hypotheses can be formulated. However, theory and experience, as well as practicality (e.g., availability of data, whether the results would lead to an outcome the police could implement) dictate which hypotheses should be examined.

The process of collecting data and testing hypotheses is a highly specific process since the goal of problem solving is to narrow the scope of the problem as much as possible to develop situational crime prevention responses. Much of the data that are examined for problem analysis are primary data since the questions being answered focus on *why* the problem is occurring. Yet even though the data collection process may be somewhat difficult, the statistics used to analyze the data are fairly simple and are described later in this chapter.

Response: Role of Analysis

The **response step** of the problem-solving process includes identifying realistic responses from the POP guides, from situational crime prevention techniques, from what other communities have done successfully, and by brainstorming for new responses (Center for Problem-Oriented Policing, 2016). The results of the analysis step are then used to select one or a variety of responses. Once a response plan is developed, identifying responsible parties as well as specific objectives, the activities are then primarily carried out or initiated by police personnel (Center for Problem-Oriented Policing, 2016).

The role of crime analysis is somewhat smaller in the response step than in any of the other steps in the problem-solving process; however, crime analysts do assist in this step by conducting further analysis that helps to direct and prioritize the responses. For example, in a project addressing construction site crime, the Port St. Lucie (Florida) Police Department decided that one of its responses was to work specifically with the most victimized home builders. The 10 most victimized builders were identified in the analysis process, but once the response was selected, further analysis was necessary to determine the specific issues that each builder was having (e.g., theft of appliances, theft of building materials, burglary of secured construction sites) in order to tailor the situational crime prevention techniques to each one (Boba & Santos, 2007).

Assessment

Finally, the goal of the **assessment step** of SARA is to determine whether the response to the problem worked. There are two important factors to consider when evaluating whether a response worked. The first is to determine whether and how the response plan was implemented and whether it was implemented correctly. It is rare in organizations that a plan is carried out exactly as intended and, in some cases, responses are not carried out at all. So it is important to determine which goals were achieved and which activities were conducted and which were not. This is called a **process evaluation**.

If the process evaluation shows that the response has been implemented correctly, even if not completely, the **impact evaluation** is also conducted to determine whether the response reduced or eliminated the problem. This part of the assessment step includes examining data from before the responses were implemented, typically collected and examined during the scanning and analysis steps, and comparing them with the same measurements after the response was implemented for a period of time (i.e., pre- and postanalysis). Oftentimes, there is not a clear end to a response (e.g., when a partnership is developed between the police and another entity), so the impact evaluation is conducted not after the response has been completed but after a time in which the police department determines is an appropriate time to determine the impact.

Importantly, if the process evaluation finds that the responses were implemented incorrectly or not at all, it is not necessary to conduct an impact evaluation because its results would be irrelevant since any change in the problem could not be attributed to the responses. This becomes an ethical consideration for a crime analyst who might be asked to conduct an impact evaluation without any results from a process evaluation or when it is known that the response was not truly implemented. In these situations, an analyst should stress that it is inappropriate to conduct an impact evaluation.

Once the results of these evaluations are complete, the assessment step also includes readjusting or reimplementing responses if necessary and/or conducting ongoing assessment to ensure continued effectiveness (Center for Problem-Oriented Policing, 2016). For more information about assessment of problems, see the POP guide titled *Assessing Responses to Problems* (Eck, 2002). As noted in the beginning of this chapter, specific procedures for the evaluation of problem responses and organizational procedures are not included in this introductory book. However, in Chapter 13 and Chapter 14, some examples are provided for techniques that are used for assessment in addition to understanding problems.

Basic Statistics Used in Crime Analysis

This section is a brief review of the most relevant statistics used for strategic crime analysis—frequency or count, cross-tabulation, percentage, rate, mean, and standard deviation. This and the previous section provide a foundation for Chapter 13 and Chapter 14, which discuss examples of how these various statistics can be used to examine primary and secondary data for problem analysis, as well as for Chapter 15, which discusses crime analysis for accountability.

Frequency

The **frequency** or count is the number of cases within each category (or value) of a variable. It is the most basic statistic and is used the most often in crime analysis. For example, to see how many crimes occurred in each police **beat** (i.e., a geographic area designated by the police department for patrol officer deployment), a crime analyst would conduct a count of the "beat" variable in a crime dataset. Table 12.2 shows the results. The value (i.e., beat number) with

Table 12.2 Frequency of Crimes by Beat	
Beat	Frequency of Part I Crime
Beat 1	1,523
Beat 2	543
Beat 3	1,987
Beat 4	310
Beat 5	1,640
Beat 6	420
Beat 7	1,301
Total	7,724

Table 12.3 Frequency of Type of Crime	
Type of Part I Crime	Frequency
Murder	2
Rape	35
Robbery	150
Aggravated assault	361
Burglary	1,204
Theft	5,421
Auto theft	542
Arson	9
Total	7,724

the highest frequency is known as the **mode**, and in Table 12.2, the mode is Beat 3. Mode is not often used by crime analysts, but they create and disseminate frequencies through tables or charts for a majority of their products. Frequency can be used with any type of variable, whether it is numeric (e.g., age) or categorical (e.g., method of entry). Another example is shown in Table 12.3, which illustrates the frequency of all Part I crime types in the city.

Cross-Tabulation

A **cross-tabulation** (also called a *cross-tab*) is a way to examine the frequency of cases for two variables at once. The frequencies are computed for one variable separated by the categories (or values) of the other, and vice versa. Most often, cross-tabulation is used with categorical variables with a limited number of values, otherwise the tables are too large to be useful.

Using the data from the previous examples of crime by beat and type of crime, Table 12.4 shows the frequency of each type of Part I crime for each beat. Crime analysts use cross-tabs often to examine variables together, such as sex and race of arrestees, location type and crime type, and calls-for-service time of day and day of week.

Percentage

A **percentage** is the count of cases in one category of a variable divided by the total number of cases and multiplied by 100. For example, Table 12.5 shows there were 150 robberies, which is 1.94% of the robbery total, 7,724 (i.e., 150 divided by 7,714, and the result multiplied by 100). Table 12.5 includes the frequencies of Part I crime types along with the percentage for each category.

Table 12.4 Cross-Tabulation: Type of Part I Crime by Beat

Types of Part I Crime	Beat 1	Beat 2	Beat 3	Beat 4	Beat 5	Beat 6	Beat 7	Total
Murder	1	0	0	0	1	0	0	2
Rape	10	2	7	0	4	3	9	35
Robbery	25	12	12	9	49	16	27	150
Aggravated assault	59	23	174	46	22	16	21	361
Burglary	150	320	250	64	290	30	100	1,204
Theft	1,131	155	1,304	159	1,199	334	1,139	5,421
Auto theft	146	29	240	32	70	20	5	542
Arson	1	2	0	0	5	1	0	9
Total	**1,523**	**543**	**1,987**	**310**	**1,640**	**420**	**1,301**	**7,724**

Percentage is used to express how large one category of a variable is relative to another category. For example, in Table 12.5 the frequencies of burglary and auto theft, respectively, are 1,204 and 542, and even though we can determine from these counts that there are just over twice as many burglaries than auto thefts, we cannot determine whether these are high or low numbers in terms of all crimes. When we use the percentage of these categories, 15.59% and 7.02%, not only do we know that there are over twice as many burglaries as auto thefts, but we also know that they represent only 15% and 7%, respectively, of the total amount of Part I crime.

Table 12.5 Frequency and Percentage of Part I Crime by Type

Type of Part I Crime	Frequency	Percentage
Murder	2	0.03%
Rape	35	0.45%
Robbery	150	1.94%
Aggravated assault	361	4.67%
Burglary	1,204	15.59%
Theft	5,421	70.18%
Auto theft	542	7.02%
Arson	9	0.12%
Total	**7,724**	**100.00%**

Cross-Tabulation Percentage

Percentage also allows us to compare the same categories across variables, which is illustrated as cross-tabulation percentage. For every cross-tabulation table of frequencies, the corresponding percentages also can be computed, allowing the analyst to compare categories of the variables with a common measurement (i.e., 100%). Table 12.6 contains two rows of the cross-tab table used previously, as well as the row of percentages. It shows that even though Beat 6 has the same number of robberies and aggravated assaults (16), they represent different percentages (10.67% and 4.43%, respectively) when they are compared to the other beat's percentage for those two types.

The cross-tabulation percentages can also be computed by column, which allows comparison of the same frequency within the categories in a different way. Table 12.7 contains the first two columns from the original cross-tab table with column percentages that compare all Part I crime types by two beats. A

Table 12.6 Cross-Tabulation of Frequency and Percentage of Crime Type by Beat: Row

Type of Crime	Beat 1	Beat 2	Beat 3	Beat 4	Beat 5	Beat 6	Beat 7	Total
Robbery	25	12	12	9	49	16	27	**150**
Percentage	16.67%	8.00%	8.00%	60.0%	32.67%	10.67%	18.0%	100.0%
Aggravated assault	59	23	174	46	22	16	21	**361**
Percentage	16.34%	6.37%	48.20%	12.74%	6.09%	4.43%	5.82%	100.0%

Table 12.7 Cross-Tabulation of Frequency and Percentage of Type of Crime by Beat: Column

Type of Crime	Beat 1	Percentage	Beat 2	Percentage
Murder	1	0.07%	0	0.00%
Rape	10	0.66%	2	0.37%
Robbery	25	1.64%	12	2.21%
Aggravated assault	59	3.87%	23	4.24%
Burglary	150	9.85%	320	58.93%
Theft	1,131	74.26%	155	28.55%
Auto theft	146	9.59%	29	5.34%
Arson	1	0.07%	2	0.37%
Total	**1,523**	100.00%	**543**	100.00%

comparison of aggravated assault in Beats 1 and 2 shows that even though Beat 1 (59) has over twice as many aggravated assaults as Beat 2 (23), Beat 2 aggravated assaults make up a higher percentage of its total Part I crime than in Beat 1, 4.24% and 3.87%, respectively. This is because the totals for the two beats are much different (1,523 vs. 543). Lastly, cross-tabulation percentages can be computed a third way, which is by the total number of cases. An example is not shown, but each cross-tab value within the table would be divided by the total number of cases, which in this example is 7,724, and then multiplied by 100.

Percentile

Percentages also are used to determine **percentile**, or a value above and below which a certain percentage of cases lie. For example, when a student's score on a test is within the 95th percentile, it means the student has scored higher than 95% of other students taking that test. Percentile is computed from the cumulative percentage of ordered data (e.g., test scores, months, age, income) through addition of the percentages in the ordered sequence. Table 12.8 illustrates the frequency of robberies per month (ordered values) as well as the percentage and the cumulative percentage for each month. For example, the cumulative percentage for April is 33.33%, which is the sum of January (15.33%), February (6.67%), March (10.00%), and April (1.33%).

Percentiles are determined from cumulative percentages. For example, in Table 12.8, 45.33% of the cases occurred before the end of June. This is interesting, given that one might expect half of the robberies to occur before the end of

Table 12.8 Frequency, Percentage, and Cumulative Percentage of Robbery by Month

Month	Frequency of Robberies	Percentage	Cumulative Percentage
January	23	15.33%	15.33%
February	10	6.67%	22.00%
March	15	10.00%	32.00%
April	2	1.33%	33.33%
May	2	1.33%	34.67%
June	16	10.67%	45.33%
July	5	3.33%	48.67%
August	16	10.67%	59.33%
September	10	6.67%	66.00%
October	9	6.00%	72.00%
November	24	16.00%	88.00%
December	18	12.00%	100.00%
Total	**150**	100.00%	

June, as that marks the end of half of the year. Percentiles are often presented in terms of particular values called *quartiles*—that is, the 25th, 50th, and 75th percentiles—or the 95th percentile, as in the test score example. In the example displayed in Table 12.8, the 95th percentile occurs sometime in December, so this type of information is not useful. In crime analysis, the exact cumulative percentage from a table such as Table 12.8 is most often used to indicate the percentile. For instance, in Table 12.8 it is more realistic to say that just over 88% of the robberies occurred before December 1 than it is to say that 95% of the robberies had occurred by "sometime in December."

The 50th percentile is also the **median**—that is, the value or potential value (in that it does not necessarily occur in the distribution) above and below which one half of all the values lie. Percentiles are also used in the analysis of repeat victimization and repeat offending when determining whether the 80/20 rule applies to a particular type of crime (illustrated in Chapter 14).

Rate

A **rate** is another statistic that is derived from frequency. In calculating rate, one variable (the denominator) is used to determine the relative difference between values of another variable (the numerator). In geographic information systems software, this is often referred to as **normalizing**. The rate used in crime analysis that is most recognizable to the layperson is crime rate, which is the number of crimes (numerator) in an area divided by the population (denominator) of that area.

Table 12.9 contains the frequency of Part I crime and the rate per person (computed by dividing the number of crimes by the number of people) for each beat and the overall city. Notice that the number of Part I crimes per person (fourth column) is a very small number and thus hard to understand (i.e., How can there be .038 crimes?). This is why crime rates are typically reported per 1,000, 10,000, or 100,000 persons. To arrive at these rates, analysts multiply the

Beat	Frequency of Part I Crime	Population	Part I Crimes per Person	Part I Crime per 1,000 Persons
Beat 1	1,523	40,000	0.03808	38.08
Beat 2	543	87,000	0.00624	6.24
Beat 3	1,987	67,000	0.02966	29.66
Beat 4	310	6,400	0.04844	48.44
Beat 5	1,640	59,400	0.02761	27.61
Beat 6	420	25,000	0.01680	16.80
Beat 7	1,301	39,000	0.03336	33.36
Total	7,724	323,800	0.02385	23.85

Table 12.9 Frequency and Rates of Crime per Population by Beat

initial rate by the chosen number of persons and then report it that way (e.g., Part I crimes per 1,000 persons, per 10,000 persons, per 100,000 persons). In this table, notice that even though Beat 4 has the lowest amount of Part I crime, the Part I crime rate in Beat 4 (48.44 per 1,000 persons) is the highest since it has the lowest population. On the other hand, Beat 3 has 6 times more crime than Beat 4 (1,987), but its rate is much lower (29.66 per 1,000 persons) because its population is higher (67,000).

Mean and Standard Deviation

The **mean**, also known as the average, is the sum of the values of a variable divided by the number of values. It is used with ratio or interval variables. It is important to compute the **standard deviation** along with the mean because it provides, in simple terms, a standardized, average variation of the values from the mean and helps indicate the shape of a data distribution. Table 12.10 shows the frequency of calls for service at 20 apartment complexes, the number of apartment units in each (obtained from city records), and the rate of calls per apartment unit (sorted by rate). When the rates for the apartment complexes (fourth column) are averaged, the mean is 1.16 calls per unit. The standard deviation for these data is 0.73, indicating that the distribution is skewed because in a normal distribution the standard deviation would be about one third of the mean. In this case, it is more than half of the mean, which indicates there are some very high values in the distribution.

To illustrate the distribution of the rate variable, Figure 12.1 is a depiction of all 20 apartment complex rates, sorted lowest (.24) to highest (2.71),

Table 12.10	Frequency of Calls, Number of Units, and Rate of Calls per Unit for Apartment Complexes		
Apartment Complex Name	Frequency of Calls	Apartment Units	Rate (Calls per Unit)
Apartment Complex 1	59	250	0.24
Apartment Complex 2	199	500	0.40
Apartment Complex 3	230	500	0.46
Apartment Complex 4	234	500	0.47
Apartment Complex 5	249	500	0.50
Apartment Complex 6	260	500	0.52
Apartment Complex 7	160	250	0.64
Apartment Complex 8	79	100	0.79
Apartment Complex 9	88	100	0.88
Apartment Complex 10	49	50	0.98

(Continued)

Table 12.10   (Continued)

Apartment Complex Name	Frequency of Calls	Apartment Units	Rate (Calls per Unit)
Apartment Complex 11	102	100	1.02
Apartment Complex 12	154	150	1.03
Apartment Complex 13	164	150	1.09
Apartment Complex 14	297	200	1.49
Apartment Complex 15	310	200	1.55
Apartment Complex 16	97	50	1.94
Apartment Complex 17	310	150	2.07
Apartment Complex 18	321	150	2.14
Apartment Complex 19	466	200	2.33
Apartment Complex 20	542	200	2.71
Total	4,370		

along with lines representing the mean value of all the rates (solid line) and the standard deviations (SD; dotted lines). By charting these values, we can see how the data are skewed, that most (13) of the apartment complexes are below the mean, and that one particular apartment complex is over 2 standard deviations above the mean.

Normally, numbers that are more than 2 standard deviations from the mean are considered outliers. In this example, the mean plus 2 standard deviations is 2.62

Figure 12.1   Call per Unit Rate (Lowest to Highest), Mean and Standard Deviation Lines

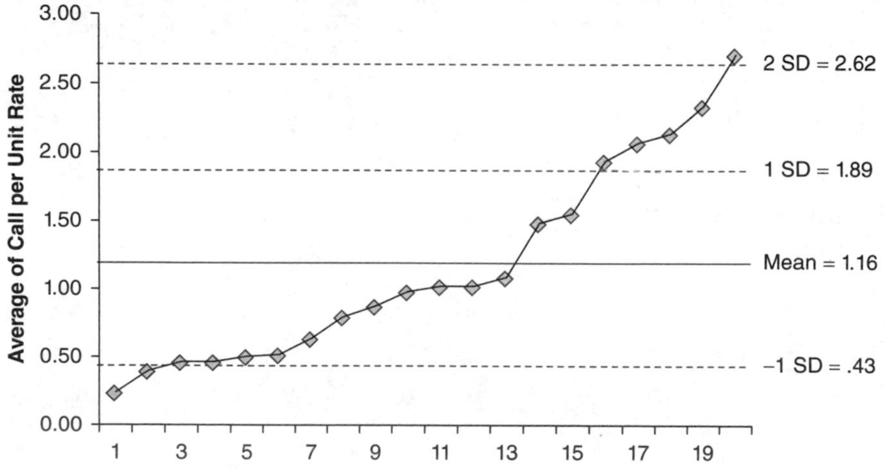

(1.16 +.73 +.73 = 2.62), which indicates that any apartment complexes with more than 2.62 calls per unit are outliers (e.g., Apartment Complex 20). In many situations in crime analysis, the mean does not accurately represent the distribution, especially because there are outliers in most data examined by crime analysts as shown in this example. Thus, the mean and standard deviation are typically used for purposes other than simple description (described in Chapter 13).

Conclusion

This chapter provides a more detailed explanation of the problem-solving process because strategic problems are complex and require the most complex analysis and response. The chapter also reviews statistics that are most likely to be used in strategic crime analysis. The goal here is to provide a foundation for the next two chapters, which apply these concepts.

SUMMARY POINTS

This chapter is an overview of the problem-solving process and how it is used for strategic problems. It also covers the basic statistics used in strategic crime analysis as a foundation for Chapter 13 and Chapter 14. The following are the key points addressed in this chapter:

- The problem-solving process can be applied to all types of problems. For immediate problems, problem solving is the process by which patrol officers respond to calls for service appropriately on a daily basis and detectives go about investigating a crime. For short-term problems, the problem-solving process is fairly straightforward as crime analysts assist in identification of repeat incidents and patterns that allow sworn personnel to respond tactically. Finally, long-term problems require a long-term approach to both analysis and response because the problems addressed are more complex.

- SARA stands for (S)canning and defining specific problems, (A)nalyzing data to understand the opportunities that create the problem, (R)esponding to the problem using both police and nonpolice methods, and (A)ssessing whether the response has worked.

- The scanning step includes identifying recurring problems of concern to both the public and the police, prioritizing those problems, and selecting problems for closer examination. Once a problem is selected, the scanning step includes confirming that the problem exists, determining how frequently the problem occurs and how long it has been taking place, and identifying the consequences of the problem.

- Environments regulate the targets available, the activities in which people can engage, and who controls the location. The types of environments include residential, recreational, offices, retail, industrial, agricultural, educational, human service, public ways, transport, open/transitional, and technological.

- By specifying the behaviors associated with a problem, the crime analyst can help to pinpoint important aspects of harm, intent, and offender–target relationships. The types of behavior include predatory, consensual, conflicts, incivilities, endangerment, and misuse of police.

- The analysis step of the problem-solving process begins with researching what is known about the specific problem type and potential responses, understanding the local context of the problem, and determining how the problem is currently being addressed in that particular jurisdiction. This is followed by the analysis of data in which hypotheses are developed that speculate why the problem is occurring; then data are collected to test these hypotheses; and finally, statistical analysis is conducted, from which conclusions are made about the immediate causes of the problem.

- The response step of the problem-solving process includes identifying realistic responses from the POP guides, from situational crime prevention techniques, from what other communities have done successfully, and by brainstorming for new responses. The role of crime analysis is somewhat smaller in the response step than in any of the other steps in the problem-solving process; however, crime analysts do assist in this step by conducting further analysis that helps to direct and prioritize the responses.

- The assessment step determines whether the response(s) to the problem worked by examining both how the response was carried out (process) and whether it made an impact on the problem.

- The frequency or count is the number of cases within each category (or value) of a variable. It is the most basic statistic and is used the most often in crime analysis. The mode is the value with the highest frequency in a distribution, but it is not often used in crime analysis.

- A cross-tabulation (also called a cross-tab) is a way to examine the frequency of cases for two variables at once. The frequencies are computed for one variable separated by the categories (or values) of the other, and vice versa.

- A percentage is the count of cases in one category of a variable divided by the total number of cases multiplied by 100.

- Percentiles are computed from cumulative percentages. Percentiles are often presented in terms of particular values called quartiles—that is, the 25th, 50th, and 75th percentiles—or the 95th percentile. Crime analysts typically use actual cumulative percentages computed for a particular dataset when presenting percentiles.

- The 50th percentile is also the median—that is, the value or potential value (in that it does not necessarily occur in the distribution) above and below which one half of all the values lie.

- A rate is another statistic that is derived from frequency. In calculating rate, one variable (the denominator) is used to determine the relative difference between values of another variable (the numerator).

- The mean, also known as the average, is the sum of the values of a variable divided by the number of values. It is used with ratio or interval variables. The standard deviation is the standardized, average variation of the values from the mean and helps indicate the shape of a data distribution and determine outliers.

DISCUSSION EXERCISES*

Exercise 1

Using Clarke and Eck's (2005) classifications of the environments of problems and the behaviors involved in problems, develop a matrix and place the following problems in the appropriate categories:

- Assaults in and around bars

- Acquaintance rape of college students

- Bullying in schools

- Loud car stereos

- Burglary of retail establishments

- Burglary of single-family houses

- Rave parties

- Robbery at automated teller machines

- Disorderly youth in public places

- Drug dealing in privately owned apartment complexes

- Speeding in residential areas

- Street prostitution

- Thefts of and from cars in parking facilities

- Disorder in budget motels

- Identity theft on the Internet

- Student party disturbances on college campuses

- Bomb threats against schools

- Sexual activity in public places

- School break-ins

- Open-air drug dealing

- Bank robbery

- Street racing

Exercise 2

Determine which statistics discussed in this chapter would be *most* appropriate to answer the following questions:

- Which bar has a significantly higher number of assaults per occupancy than the average for all the bars in the city?

- Which beat in the city has the highest number of commercial burglaries per commercial location?

- Comparing Beats 1 and 2, which one has the highest proportion of residential burglaries?

- Which beat has a disproportionate number of burglaries according to population?

- Which beat has seen the most increase in the number of auto thefts from 2016 to 2017?

- Which beat has seen the most decrease in relative proportion of auto thefts from 2016 to 2017?

- Which beat has more Part I crime than expected (i.e., if all beats were the same)?

- Which beat has the most crime?

- Considering all 20 beats in the city, what is the number of assaults that indicates that 10 beats have a fewer number assaults and 10 beats have a higher number of assaults?

CHAPTER 13

Analyzing Problems

Application of Techniques, Part I

Importantly, there are no step-by-step instructions for examining problems because the analysis depends on a variety of factors, including the nature of the problem, the data available for analysis, and the results of the initial analysis (i.e., scanning step). Problem analysis will always require critical thinking because just as with pattern analysis, there are no right or wrong answers but rather systematic techniques that are used when appropriate to help understand the immediate causes of a particular problem.

The application of strategic crime analysis techniques is discussed in this and the next chapter. The amount of information covered warrants two chapters, so Chapter 14 is simply a continuation of Chapter 13. These two chapters are framed around questions that analysts answer when scanning and analyzing problems, as well as when they provide general information for other strategic purposes, such as examining general crime trends, considering sociodemographic factors, or developing general problem area (i.e., long-term hot spot) analyses within the jurisdiction. These questions include the following:

Chapter 13

- What is the nature of the problem?
- How frequently is the problem occurring?
- Has the problem increased or decreased?
- When is the problem happening?

Chapter 14

- Where is the problem occurring?
- Who are the victims, and does repeat victimization exist?
- Who are the offenders, and does repeat offending exist?
- Why is the problem occurring?

The type of data considered and how in depth these questions are answered lies in the purpose of the analysis. As discussed in Chapter 12, the scanning step includes a more superficial descriptive analysis of available secondary data, whereas the analysis step digs deeper into the problem by developing hypotheses and collecting primary data on which in-depth analyses are based. The goal of the next two chapters is to provide a myriad of techniques that can be used together or separately in examining problems for both the scanning and analysis steps of the SARA process.

What Is the Nature of the Problem?

Not all analysis requires statistical analysis. To answer this first question, the analyst must begin to understand the problem in two different ways. The first is to look at the sequence and actions of those involved in the events that make up the problem (Clarke & Eck, 2005, Step 36), and the second is to look at the broader environment in which these events are occurring.

Once a problem has been narrowed in scope to a specific behavior and environment as discussed in Chapter 12, the events that make up the problem should be similar enough that a common process can be identified to accomplish the activity. More specifically, problem events might contain several steps from initiation of the activity to its completion (Clarke & Eck, 2005, Step 36). The analyst examines the problem events together in three stages:

1. The "prelude," which contains the processes that lead directly up to and into the problem behavior, such as getting drunk, driving through a neighborhood, or waiting until no one is looking;

2. The "incident," which is the immediate event or problematic behavior, such as punching someone, breaking a window of a home, or stealing a purse out of a vehicle; and

3. The "aftermath," which is what happens after or as a result of the incident, such as the offender fleeing the scene, the fencing of stolen goods, or use of a stolen credit card. (Felson, 2006, p. 42)

It is important to note that other crimes and problematic behavior can be committed in the aftermath, such as fencing stolen goods after a burglary or stealing a car to escape a crime scene quickly. All of these parts of the activity are important to examine in order to understand a problem.

The initial information about the nature of the problem will be primarily qualitative and can be gathered through reading police report narratives and talking to police officers, place managers, offenders, and victims. Notably, there may be multiple ways the problem activity occurs, so all need to be considered. For example, residential burglary could entail offenders watching the neighborhood (prelude), entering the home by force and taking property (incident), and fencing the stolen goods (aftermath); and it could entail offenders driving or walking through a neighborhood as part of their everyday activities (prelude), taking property exposed or not secured in a garage (incident), and using the property themselves (aftermath). The goal here is to identify all likely ways in which the activity for a particular problem occurs and determine through analysis which is occurring most often so that the problem-solving responses can be tailored to address the most prevalent and/or more serious activity.

In addition to understanding the process of the problematic behavior itself, it is also important to begin to understand what mechanisms and opportunities allow or encourage the problematic activity. At this stage of the analysis process, the analyst has only partial information, so the goal here is to speculate, or hypothesize, how the environment is creating opportunities for this activity. These hypotheses can then be used to guide additional data collection and analysis, as noted in Chapter 12.

It is here that the theory discussed in Chapter 2 becomes very important and is coupled with knowledge provided by the POP guide series (Center for Problem-Oriented Policing, 2016). The analyst uses the problem analysis triangle to hypothesize about the offenders, places, and targets/victims, as well as how the lack of control by handlers, managers, and guardians helps to facilitate the problem. The analyst uses the POP guides to develop relevant hypotheses based on findings from research and other problem-solving efforts.

Case Study, Port St. Lucie, Florida: In examining the problem of construction site crime at single-family houses, the Port St. Lucie Police Department interviewed police, builders (victims), and city building personnel about the nature of theft from construction sites. From the information obtained in these interviews, the problem-solving committee hypothesized that the prelude to the incident included offenders either living near the site, working on the site, or driving by the construction site and seeing vulnerable property. The incident was hypothesized to be primarily the taking of property unattached to and outside the building under construction, outside and attached to the building, inside the building unsecured, or secured. The aftermath was hypothesized to include personal use of the property, use of the property in other construction, or sale of property in secondhand markets. They also hypothesized that either people with inside knowledge of the construction business or people just looking for easy property to steal were the primary offenders in their community and that the builders, who were both the victims and the managers, were not protecting their construction sites adequately and were creating opportunities for this crime. (Boba & Santos, 2007)

Once hypotheses are developed, the analyst collects and examines relevant primary and secondary data to determine if the hypotheses are supported. This is one of the most important steps in the strategic problem-solving process. Police departments have been more likely to conduct the initial scanning, speculate what the causes of the problem are, and then jump directly to responses. The goal of the problem-solving process is to tailor crime prevention responses based on what is happening, not on what people hypothesize is happening.

There are a vast number of hypotheses that can be developed for every problem. It is important, however, to focus on those that are most realistic for analysis and police-initiated response. This means focusing on immediate causes and not on the underlying social issues. For example, one hypothesis about why teens are hanging out and causing disturbances in a retail plaza is that their parents have not taught them to be respectful and do not know where their children are (i.e., poor parenting). Although this may be a relevant hypothesis, this is a deeper cause of the problem (social issue), and a response to improving parenting is out of the span of police control. Once hypotheses are developed, they guide the analysis process. The rest of this chapter and the next chapter are spent describing how to answer a series of typical questions used to develop hypotheses in problem analysis.

How Frequently Is the Problem Occurring?

Although this seems like a simple question, the frequency of problem activity is very important in the entire problem-solving process, but is not always a simple question to answer. For example, it can be used to indicate whether activity should be considered a problem at all (scanning), how the problem compares to others (analysis), the amount of resources allocated for crime prevention measures (response), and whether the response was effective (assessment). What follows are a number of ways to determine and illustrate the prevalence of a problem. These techniques are used to count and compare any number of characteristics dictated by the nature of a problem, such as property taken, types of places victimized, addresses where the problem occurred, and so on.

Case Study, Raleigh, North Carolina: In trying to understand the magnitude of the street prostitution problem in Raleigh, researchers estimated the number of sexual transactions through a combination of methods. They used the information in the POP Guide on prostitution that suggested that prostitutes carried out three to five sexual transactions per day and worked 5 days per week. They confirmed this in interviews with their local prostitutes. Having identified approximately 60 chronic prostitutes in the key prostitution area of concern in their analysis, they estimated these women made 15 sexual transactions per week for 50 weeks per year, which would result in approximately 45,000 sexual transactions. Thus, over an 18-month period (the duration of the project), they estimated that 67,500 sexual transactions occurred (Weisel, 2004).

Frequency and Percentage

The most basic form of determining frequency is using count and percentage. However, in variables that have numerous categories (e.g., addresses and types of calls for service), analysts sort the categories in descending frequency by highest count, as this makes them easier to examine. Table 13.1 shows the count and percentage of robberies by beat, sorted in descending counts. Rather than list the beats in order, this table allows a quick assessment of which beats have the most street robberies.

In situations with a large number of values (in the Table 13.1 beats), it may not be necessary to provide the entire list but only the top five, 10, or 25 (e.g., addresses or call types). The rest would still be included in the table to show the incident total in aggregate form. Table 13.2 illustrates a list of the top

Table 13.1	Frequency and Percentage of Robberies by Beat in Descending Order	
Beat	**Frequency of Robberies**	**Percentage**
Beat 4	84	31.00%
Beat 3	49	18.08%
Beat 1	46	16.97%
Beat 7	38	14.02%
Beat 2	23	8.49%
Beat 6	19	7.01%
Beat 5	12	4.43%
Total	**271**	100.00%

Table 13.2	Frequency and Percentage of Top Five Call Types in Descending Order		
	Type of Call	**Frequency**	**Percentage**
1	Burglar alarm calls	1,254	8.29%
2	Suspicious behavior calls	983	6.50%
3	Domestic calls	950	6.28%
4	Traffic calls	810	5.35%
5	Check welfare calls	569	3.76%
	All other calls	10,567	69.83%
	Total	**15,133**	100.00%

five calls-for-service types for an entire city in descending order, with the rest of the call types aggregated.

Analysts often place frequency data in bar or line charts because this allows them to make visual comparisons among the categories. Figure 13.1 is a bar chart (also called a *histogram*) of the frequency of robberies per beat. Bar charts are typically used for categorical variables (e.g., beats and types of robberies). Because the bar chart is a visualization and the "frequency" category is obvious, it is not always necessary to arrange the categories in descending order, but in order of the categorical variable (e.g., Beat 1, Beat 2, Beat 3). Line charts are used for ordinal and ratio variables (e.g., months and age) and are illustrated in the next section.

Strategic crime analysts use frequency often, but they do not use this statistic alone to understand the prevalence of a problem for the following reasons:

- Just because an address or area has the "most" incidents of a problem does not mean it is the "worst" area. Many times analysis is based on "reported" crimes and calls for service, so levels of reporting influence the statistics. Both "good" and "bad" neighborhoods can have low frequencies—the former because there is little or no activity to report, and the latter because people are afraid to report the activity that occurs.

- In comparisons of units that are dissimilar, frequency may distort a problem (e.g., comparing an area of 200 square miles and a population of 300,000 to one of 20 square miles and a population of 10,000).

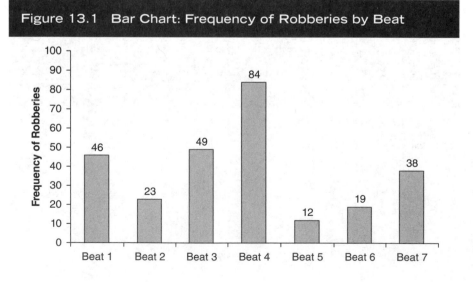

Figure 13.1   Bar Chart: Frequency of Robberies by Beat

- Variables with large numbers of categories may be difficult to illustrate using simple frequency (e.g., frequency of crime at individual addresses, frequency of offenders by age). These long lists are often aggregated into larger categories, such as individual addresses aggregated by street segment or neighborhood and offenders' ages aggregated into multiple years (e.g., 17 or younger, 18 to 24, 25 to 34, etc.).

- Frequency of a variable with small values can be meaningless. For example, counts of homicide for 4 years in a small community may be 0, 1, 3, 0. Clearly, these very small numbers do not tell us much about whether there is a homicide problem.

- It is important to note that before narrowing the scope of a problem, frequency can be misleading because different types of activity are represented in the more general category. An important example of this is aggravated assaults. There is a very important difference between aggravated assaults between intimates (i.e., domestic violence) and assaults between strangers or even acquaintances (i.e., fights at bars, drive-by shootings). A frequency of all aggravated assaults will hide the counts of these two distinct types of activity and may lead to erroneous conclusions about potential responses.

Including percentages in frequency tables and charts allows a comparison of categories and helps to indicate the prevalence of a problem. This is particularly relevant when comparing across different datasets. For example, Table 13.3 is a comparison of datasets for 2 years and shows 210 street robberies in Year 1 and 200 in Year 2. These counts appear similar when considering them alone. However, if we look at what percentage street robberies are of the total for the year, Year 1 has 85%, and Year 2 has 50%. These percentages are much different, even though the frequencies for Years 1 and 2 are similar. This is because the number of overall robberies increased from 247 in Year 1 to 400 in Year 2, making street robberies a much smaller portion of all robberies in Year 2. Percentage values could provide meaningful information for an assessment of a response to street robberies in this example. That is, even though the actual number of street robberies only decreased by 10, the percentage of the total robberies decreased by 35, showing that street robberies are much less frequent in Year 2 than in Year 1 relative to the total.

Like frequencies, percentages can also be depicted in charts. The type of chart most commonly used for this purpose is a pie chart. When creating pie charts, crime analysts typically include no more than five to seven categories so that the slices of the pie do not become too small to see and label. Just as

Table 13.3	Frequency and Percentage of Street Robbery Comparison		
	Street Robbery	Other Robbery	Street Robbery Percentage of Total
Year 1	210	37	85.00%
Year 2	200	200	50.00%

with tables, charts can be used to compare across distributions. Figure 13.2 and Figure 13.3 illustrate the relative percentage of street robbery in both years and allow for an easy visual comparison of the differences shown in Table 13.3. Note that the figure caption of each chart includes the total number of robberies (i.e., *N* means number of cases); this is important because it provides context for the percentage values illustrated in the chart.

Rate

In addition to using percentage, computing a rate is also an improvement over frequency to understand the prevalence of a problem. Rates allow the analyst to compare frequency of incidents for dissimilar areas and locations. The example given for rates in the previous chapter used population as the denominator. However, when an analyst is examining a problem, using population to compute a rate may not always provide relevant information for comparison. For instance, it would not be appropriate to use population to compare frequency of commercial burglaries over several areas because people do not live at commercial businesses. A commercial burglary rate using population would show high rates in commercially zoned areas because the population counts would be low. In contrast, a rate of commercial burglaries by number of commercial businesses would show the relative number of burglaries in different areas according to the

Figure 13.2   Pie Chart: Percentage of Street Robbery (*N* = 247), Year 1

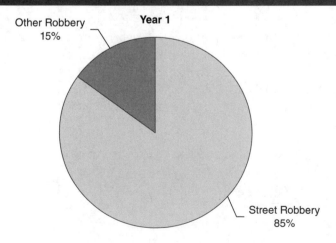

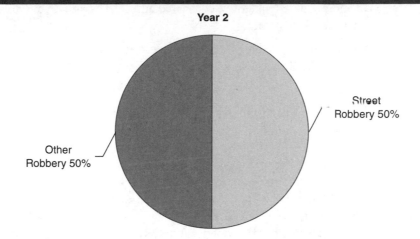

Figure 13.3 Pie Chart: Percentage of Street Robbery (*N* = 400), Year 2

number of relevant targets. Table 13.4 depicts commercial burglaries by 100 targets (commercial places) per beat.

Analysts compute rates for problems by using the appropriate denominator, depending on the comparisons they want to make. Here are some examples:

- Per dwelling or apartment unit (e.g., to compare the number of residential burglaries because the target is the residential unit, not the number of people living in it)

- Per room (e.g., to compare hotels and motels of different sizes)

- Per building (e.g., to compare commercial districts by their relative size)

- Per square foot (e.g., to compare commercial buildings contain multiple floors of commercial space)

Table 13.4 Frequency and Rate of Burglaries per Target

Beat	Frequency of Burglaries	Number of Targets	Burglaries per 100 Targets
Beat 1	164	131	125.01
Beat 2	82	75	109.17
Beat 3	174	130	134.18
Beat 4	299	348	85.93
Beat 5	43	84	50.86
Beat 6	68	286	23.65
Beat 7	135	212	63.81
Total	**965**	**1,266**	**76.21**

- Per occupancy rate (e.g., to compare bars, nightclubs, or other service establishments, given that the actual number of patrons is difficult to measure; note that occupancy rate and square footage are correlated and thus essentially measure the same thing)

- Per parking space (e.g., to compare parking lots, given that the number of spaces in a lot determines how many cars it can hold)

- Per acre (e.g., to compare parks or other land masses)

- Per building permit (e.g., to compare number of burglaries at construction sites by how many houses are under construction)

However, using such alternatives to determine rates does not always solve the comparison problem. For example, using parking spaces to determine the relative size of a parking lot does not account for how many spaces in the parking lot are actually used or how much time each car spends in the lot. Other information, such as the length of time per day the parking lot is open and the amount of time that cars typically spend in the parking lot, also would be useful for comparison purposes. However, some kinds of information can be difficult to obtain and update regularly, so analysts may have to rely on the most relevant and accessible information for the problem at hand. When communicating their results, they should be clear about what is being used for comparison.

Case Study, Chula Vista, California: In a study of theft from vehicle in Chula Vista, researchers and analysts found the following: "Our Risk Rate Subcommittee made some interesting findings. The target lots with the highest volume of thefts were not necessarily those with the highest risk rate. One of our target lots, the Swap Meet, open only 2 days a week, experienced 42 auto thefts in 2001 and two auto burglaries. We suspected that the Swap Meet would have the highest lot risk rate. This turned out to be untrue, as some of the smaller lots, open 7 days a week, even with lower volumes of theft were much riskier. When the Subcommittee took into account the volume of cars entering and exiting these lots, the number of parking spaces in these lots, the average length of time parked for these lots, and the number of days these lots were open to parking, they found that Chula Vista's trolley commuter lots had risk rates of up to ten times higher than the average of the other lots combined. Perhaps we should not have been so surprised as the trolley lots (amongst all the target lots) had the most favorable conditions for auto theft (a wide range of older vehicles, no regular security patrols, unfettered access, multiple exits, vehicle owners parked for very long periods of time, and proximity to the freeway—two minutes or less by car)." (Sampson, 2004, p. 13)

In the scanning and analysis steps, crime analysts use three rates regularly to compare local crime problems with national crime problems, as well as to describe particular general problems: **crime rate**, **clearance rate**, and **recovery rate**. A *crime rate* is typically the number of reported crimes in an area divided by the number of people living in the area. National and state crime rates are typically reported as the number of Part I crimes per 100,000 persons (number of crimes divided by population and the result multiplied by 100,000). At the local level, however, reporting crime rate by 100,000 persons may not be appropriate, especially in communities with populations smaller than 100,000 (i.e., reporting crime rate per 100,000 would give the impression that more crimes are occurring than actually are). If a town of 50,000 residents has 3,000 Part I crimes, this computes to a Part I crime rate of 6,000 crimes per 100,000 persons. Although it is important that analysts use "per 100,000" rates when comparing crime levels in their jurisdictions with national or state levels, those working in smaller jurisdictions can examine rates per 10,000 or 1,000 persons, depending on which is more relevant for comparing crime rates of smaller areas within a particular jurisdiction (e.g., census tracts, beats, precincts).

Another issue that crime analysts need to consider when using crime rates at the local level is the distinction between property crime and persons crime. Most people think that violent crime is more common than property crime, even though the reverse is true. For example, in 2014 law enforcement agencies across the United States reported a total of 1,165,383 violent crimes to the FBI; in the same year, they reported 8,277,829 property crimes (FBI, 2016), about a 1:7 ratio. Crime analysts need to be careful to separate the two types of crime into two different rates to avoid misinterpretation.

Another rate often used in problem analysis is the *clearance rate*. The Uniform Crime Report program acknowledges two ways in which crimes are cleared: (a) by arrest and (b) by exceptional means. A crime is cleared by arrest if at least one person is arrested for the crime, charged with the commission of the crime, and turned over to the court for prosecution. The UCR counts the number of crimes cleared, not the number of individuals arrested; the arrest of one individual may clear several crimes, and the arrest of many individuals may clear only one crime. A crime is cleared by exceptional means if circumstances beyond police control prevent the clearing of the crime by arrest. For the UCR program to count a crime as cleared by exceptional means, the police agency must have the following: knowledge of the offender's identity; enough evidence to support arresting, charging, and turning over the offender to the court for prosecution; and knowledge of the offender's exact location so that law enforcement can make an arrest (FBI, 2016). Examples of exceptional clearance include death of the offender, victim's refusal to prosecute, and denial of extradition.

Clearance rates are typically reported as percentages. For example, if 200 robberies were reported in the past year and 90 of them were cleared, the clearance rate would be 45 per 100 robberies, or 45% (instead of .45). As with national crime rates, national clearance rates are based on Part I crimes only. When analyzing problems, crime analysts use clearance rates to determine the numbers of crimes for which arrests have been made and to compare local to national rates (e.g., to see if the local clearance rate is lower than the national rate).

Finally, the third rate typically used in problem analysis is *recovery rate,* which is the percentage of vehicles that have been stolen in a jurisdiction and subsequently recovered (i.e., found) anywhere. It is also reported as a percentage. Analysts use this rate to help understand the nature of an auto theft problem. For instance, if the recovery rate in a city is 90% (i.e., 9 out of 10 stolen cars are later found), it is clear that the city's auto theft problem does not primarily involve offenders who dismantle cars for resale of parts or export them out of the country.

Mean and Standard Deviation

Lastly, as noted in Chapter 12, mean and standard deviation are not helpful to describe distributions of data because crime analysis data tend to have significant outliers. However, these statistics are very helpful in providing yet another way to compare areas, locations, and other aspects of a problem to determine how widespread or focused a problem might be. Because mean and standard deviation help estimate the central tendency of the values, they can be used to determine whether a particular count or rate is normal or unusual. For example, if a crime analyst is examining a problem of thefts from vehicles at retail establishments, the analyst might compute the rate for the number of thefts per parking space for each retail location in the city. When these locations are sorted in descending order, the location with the highest rate is at the top. However, is the rate of crime at this location problematic or that much different from the others? Mean and standard deviation help to determine this.

Table 13.5 shows a list of 10 such locations looking at data for 12 months. The Retail Plaza 1 has the highest rate of theft, but if the mean and standard deviation for the entire city (not all locations are shown for simplicity) are 2.67 and 0.86, respectively, we see that Retail Plaza 1 is within 1 standard deviation of the mean (2.67 +.86 = 3.53), which indicates the top location is not that much different than the other locations.

Table 13.5 Rate of Theft From Vehicle per 10 Parking Spaces for Retail Plazas	
Location	**Rate of Theft per 10Parking Spaces**
Retail Plaza 1	3.52
Retail Plaza 2	3.49
Retail Plaza 3	3.42
Retail Plaza 4	3.30
Retail Plaza 5	3.21
Retail Plaza 6	3.20
Retail Plaza 7	3.20
Retail Plaza 8	3.09
Retail Plaza 9	3.07
Retail Plaza 10	3.01

Table 13.6 shows a different example comparing assaults per 100 persons (i.e., occupancy of the bar) at the top five bars over 12 months. If the mean of all 100 bars in the city is 9.23 and the standard deviation is 4.01, 3 standard deviations (4.01 × 3 = 12.03) from the mean is a value of 21.26 assaults per person (12.03 + 9.23). With values of 25.30, 25.23, and 24.02, respectively, the top three bars have considerably more assaults than are typical in all the bars in the city and indicate that the assault problem and the tailored response might be focused on these three locations.

Table 13.6 Rate of Assaults per 100 Persons Occupancy for Bars	
Location	Rate of Assaults per 100 Persons
Bar 1	25.30
Bar 2	25.23
Bar 3	24.02
Bar 4	15.25
Bar 5	13.11

Like frequency and percentage, it can be helpful for the analyst to illustrate the results of mean and standard deviation in a chart. Figure 13.4 shows the rates of assault for the five bars from Table 13.5 along with lines that represent the mean and first, second, and third standard deviations above the mean. Those below the mean are not shown since our purpose is to identify bars with the highest rates. The chart illustrates the results and makes it easy to determine which bars are significantly higher than the overall mean. Note that this is just a simple example, and more locations can be included on such a chart.

Figure 13.4   Rates of Assaults per 100 Persons at Bars, Mean and Standard Deviations

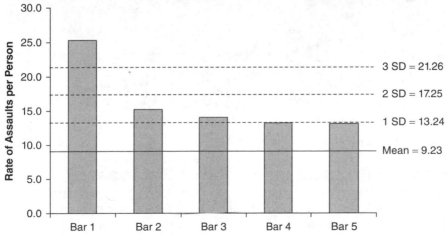

It is important to note that mean and standard deviation are less reliable and not always necessary when working with data sets with fewer than 10 cases because one or two unusual cases can significantly influence the statistics. However, this is not a hard and fast rule, and the results of these analyses should be closely scrutinized when working with small numbers of cases.

Case Study, Chula Vista, California: Median can also be used to determine the difference of one location from the others because it indicates that 50% of the locations are above and below a particular value. Figure 13.5 is from a problem analysis of budget motels in Chula Vista in which the hotels are shown by their calls for service per room (rate) in comparison to the median for all the hotels. The report states, "The problem analysis conducted up to this point in the project was very helpful in identifying basic problems that needed attention at the motels (such as room security) and factors associated with high CFS (renting to local and long-term guests), but these analytical findings did not fully explain the extreme variation in CFS per room ratios found at Chula Vista motels (from a high of 2.77 CFS per room to a low of 0.11 CFS per room. . . . While many motels that catered to a local clientele had high CFS per room ratios, some did not." (Chula Vista (California) Police Department, 2009, Appendix I)

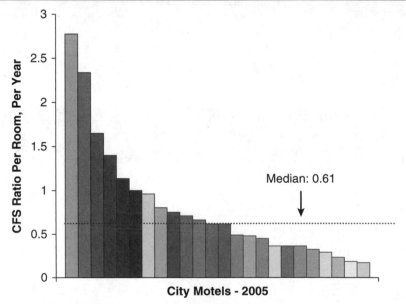

Figure 13.5 Calls for Service per Room per Year

Source: Chula Vista (California) Police Department (2009).

Has the Problem Increased or Decreased?

In addition to understanding how frequent a problem is, it is important to understand the long-term trends of the problem both before and after a response is implemented. That is, has the problem increased, decreased, or stayed the same over time? During the scanning step, analysts look for increasing trends to help prioritize and select problems for further examination. During the assessment step, analysts look for decreasing trends that help to indicate that responses have worked. Frequencies, percentages, rates, and averages can be computed and displayed according to temporal variables such as year, month, and week in order to determine whether the problem has changed over time. Analysis of temporal variables is normally displayed in line charts because this is a clear way to show continuity and chronological order. The percentage of change is also used to determine whether a problem has increased or decreased.

By Year

A year is the largest time unit used in strategic crime analysis to understand increases and decreases of a problem. Most crime statistics collected on a national level and by local police agencies are tabulated by year, allowing analysts to make comparisons to previous years and across jurisdictions. Figure 13.6 is an illustration of a line chart showing the frequency of robbery for 5 years.

Another comparison by year might include robbery rates per population that allow comparison across different levels (e.g., city vs. neighboring city, city vs. state, city vs. country). Table 13.7 provides the information necessary to make a chart comparing a city's robbery rate per 100,000 persons to the state's rate. The table shows that the city's robbery rate is much higher than the state's, even though the actual numbers of robberies are much lower. Although this table provides sufficient information about robbery rates, displaying the data in the form of a line graph, as in Figure 13.7, allows a reader to make comparisons more easily.

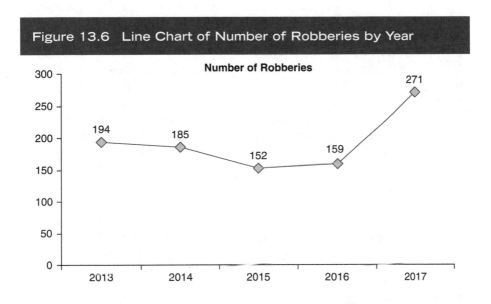

Figure 13.6   Line Chart of Number of Robberies by Year

Year	Robbery Frequency	City Population	City Rate per 100,000 Persons	Robbery Frequency	State Population	State Rate per 100,000 Persons
2013	254	120,000	211.67	19,291	12,852,000	150.10
2014	220	122,000	180.33	16,753	12,867,000	130.20
2015	219	125,000	175.20	19,136	12,886,000	148.50
2016	299	126,000	237.30	18,808	12,891,000	145.90
2017	271	136,000	199.26	19,400	12,916,000	150.20

Table 13.7 Number of Robberies, Population, City Rate, and State Rate

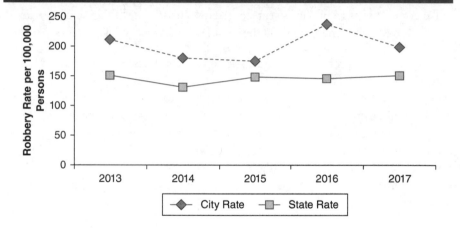

Figure 13.7 Chart Comparing City and State Robbery Rates

By Month or Quarter

Crime analysts report statistics as well as study problems by month primarily, as do most businesses and other organizations. A month is a small enough unit of time to allow the analysis of variation over a year, and at the same time, it is large enough to produce a sufficient amount of data to examine. Crime analysts also study statistics by quarter (i.e., a period of 3 months) when the values by month are too small to make meaningful conclusions. Analysts use the techniques described here when examining data for both month and quarter.

Figure 13.8 illustrates the number of loud party calls for service at apartment complexes in a city by month for the past 3 years. Notice that this figure contains many more data points than the previous year charts, which results in peaks and valleys within each year. This type of analysis allows the analyst to see incremental (monthly) changes in the data. The straight line on the chart represents the linear trend line and helps the analyst determine the overall linear trend of the frequency.

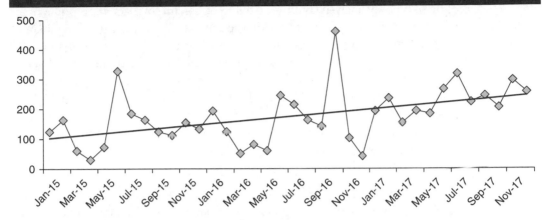

Figure 13.8   Chart of Loud Party Calls at Apartment Complexes, 3 Years

Trend lines are used to help determine the direction of a problem when the incremental increases and decreases in the data are not clear. The **linear trend line** is created by a statistical equation (linear regression), which produces a line that best estimates the direction of the month-to-month figures and is most often used in crime analysis. Other types of trend lines also can be produced since not all distributions are linear, such as exponential or moving average. However, the analyst should be sure to understand the statistics behind these trend lines before using them. Importantly, the direction of the trends indicated by the lines can be different for the same problem, based on the type of statistic used in the analysis (e.g., frequency, rate, mean).

One problem with using months to identify variations in problem activity is that months are not equal units—they vary in length from 28 to 31 days. A 3-day period can make a big difference in monthly counts of crime and other activity. One way in which crime analysts correct this problem is by computing the mean number of occurrences of the activity of interest per day for each month. So for example, instead of January and February having loud party frequencies of 123 and 164, respectively, they have averages of 3.97 and 5.86 (i.e., 123 divided by 31 and 164 divided by 28) per day.

By Week

Another problem with using month as the time unit for analysis is that months vary in the numbers of individual weekdays they contain; that is, one month may contain five Fridays, and the next month may have only four. These variations can affect the counts of certain types of activity that are particularly heavy on weekends as opposed to weekdays—loud parties at apartment complexes, for example. Analysts address this problem by comparing time periods using intervals of set numbers of weeks (e.g., 4-week, 2-week, or 1-week intervals). Within such intervals, each unit of time has the same number of days and the same types of days (e.g., four Fridays, four Saturdays). In conducting temporal analysis, crime analysts can use line charts to depict all of these types of analysis, but they need to be careful to select appropriate time units—that is, units that will provide enough data in each unit to allow them to draw substantive conclusions. However, one warning is that weekly counts of crime and disorder are not always helpful to determine the trends or evaluate a problem. Seven days is a very short time frame and counts fluctuate greatly from week to week, especially when the counts are low. Something as simple as a heavy rainstorm can influence the amount of activity in a city during one week, so it is recommended to use longer time periods and/or caution when examining weekly counts.

Percentage of Change

To answer this question, the **percentage of change** can also be used to examine the amount of relative increase or decrease in a problem between two time periods. This can be particularly helpful in the assessment step when examining the level of a problem before and after a response. The percentage of change expresses the amount of change as a proportion of the value at the first time period (Time 1), or the difference between a measurement at Time 1 and a measurement at Time 2, divided by the measurement at Time 1, and then multiplied by 100 (to arrive at a percentage). The formula for arriving at the percentage of change is as follows:

$$\frac{\text{Time 2} - \text{Time 1}}{\text{Time 1}} \times 100 = \% \text{ of Change}$$

For example, from July to December 2016 (before the response), 320 commercial burglaries were committed in a particular business district in Smalltown, and from July to December 2017 (after the response that took place from January to June 2016), 256 burglaries were committed. The percentage of change of burglaries in this area is computed as follows:

$$\frac{256(\text{Time 2}) - 320(\text{Time 1})}{320(\text{Time 1})} \times 100,$$

or

$$\frac{-64}{320} \times 100 = 20\% \text{ of Change}$$

The business district experienced a 20% decrease in burglaries in the 6 months after the response was implemented. The percentage of change can also be used more generally in the scanning process for yearly, quarterly, or monthly comparisons. Table 13.8 contains data on the change in frequency and the percentage of change of stranger rapes by beat for 2016 and 2017. It shows that

Table 13.8 Actual and Percentage of Change in Stranger Rape by Beat From 2016 to 2017

Beat	2016	2017	Change	Percentage of Change
Beat 1	20	46	26	130.00%
Beat 2	36	23	–13	–36.00%
Beat 3	15	49	34	227.00%
Beat 4	56	84	28	50.00%
Beat 5	0	12	12	NC*
Beat 6	3	19	16	533.00%
Beat 7	29	38	9	31.00%
Total	**159**	**271**	**112**	**70.00%**

*NC = Not Calculable

even though the overall number of rapes has increased by 70%, the numbers within individual beats have fluctuated differently and that Beat 6 has had the most significant increase.

There are some considerations to remember when computing percentage of change. Note that Table 13.8 shows no stranger rapes in Beat 5 in 2016, 12 in 2017, and NC (for "not calculable") in the last column instead of a percentage of change value. This is because it is a mathematical rule that a number cannot be divided by zero; thus, it is not possible to compute any percentage of change for Beat 5. In such a case, the crime analyst must revert to using the actual change in the count, reporting, for example, that "the number of stranger rapes in Beat 5 increased by 12 crimes, up from 0." Also, even though Beat 6 experienced a 533% increase in stranger rapes, the actual increase (16) is not nearly as high as in some other beats (e.g., 26, 34, 28). The percentage of change in Beat 6 is high because the value at Time 1 is relatively low, and when numbers are low, even slight increases can result in large percentage of change values.

Note that there are a variety of ways to signify that a percentage of change cannot be calculated. In Table 13.8, NC is used, and other analysts use *not calculable*, NA, or put a dash in the cell (e.g., "—"). Some readers may not understand why this calculation cannot be made, so it is usually necessary to include a footnote stating why the percentage of change value is not there. Lastly, crime analysts often created these tables in Microsoft Excel, which puts "#DIV/0!" in the cell. This should not be used in the final product since it indicates a mathematical error and will not make sense to most people outside of the software, even with a footnote.

Case Study, Arlington, Texas: Figure 13.9 is a chart produced by crime analysts at the Arlington Police Department every month for the command staff. The chart contains many of the statistics discussed in the chapter. First, it depicts the frequencies of theft by 4-week periods (e.g., reporting period 14 [RP14] had 1,027 thefts). Second, along the bottom, it depicts the percentage of change from each RP to the next (e.g., the change from RP08 to RP07 is −15%). Third, it depicts the average number of thefts for the entire time period considered on the chart (middle solid line), and 1 standard deviation above and below the average (two lines above and below the average). Finally, it depicts the overall linear trendline (dotted line) and the overall percentage of change of −17% (in the chart title).

Figure 13.9 Theft by Reporting Period, Arlington, Texas

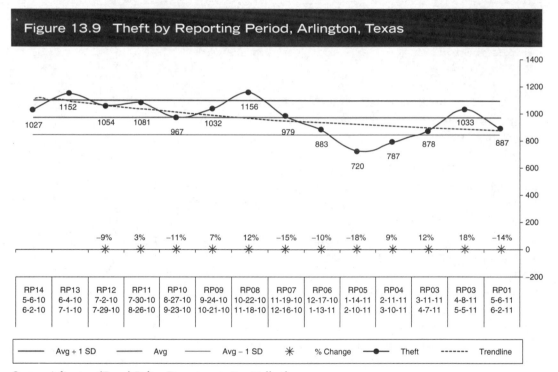

Source: Arlington (Texas) Police Department, Jim Mallard.

Anticipatory Benefit

During the assessment step when crime analysts examine whether there has been a decrease in the problem, they also must be aware of what is called the **anticipatory benefit.** As Smith, Clarke, and Pease (2002) argue, crime reduction may occur before a strategy is implemented because the work being done before implementation may actually change offenders' perceptions of risk and victims' awareness. Although other responses also may create this benefit, Johnson and Bowers (2003) found that crime prevention publicity does have a preliminary anticipatory benefit on the problem. For example, in Port St. Lucie's construction site theft project, the team had been analyzing, talking to builders, and observing sites nearly 6 months before the response period began. Although it was difficult to confirm, it appeared as though this may have caused the thefts to decrease before the responses were fully implemented (Boba & Santos, 2007).

INTERNATIONAL CRIME ANALYST PERSPECTIVE

Rachel Carson

Director

Inspired Acts, Ltd

United Kingdom

In the United Kingdom, strategic crime analysis is increasingly using alternative sources of information from partner agencies, such as ambulance/hospital records and fire services data, to build a richer intelligence picture. This helps to build a greater understanding of any problems identified and also enables a partnership response, working together to improve public safety. This is particularly useful for problems associated with the nighttime economy and has enabled local authorities to be creative when putting interventions in place to manage late night antisocial behaviour and violence and to ensure people return home safely, such as the use of street wardens, managed taxi ranks, staggered closing times of licensed premises, encouraged use of plastic glasses, and so on. Similarly, partner data is used within hotspot analysis as additional layers to help identify common problem areas between partner agencies.

In addition, strategic analysts in the United Kingdom are encouraged to identify common and emerging themes by looking holistically at the people, places, and crime factors prevalent across each of their priority crime categories. This is most effectively achieved through the use of a matrix. The left-hand side of the matrix lists the categories of people, places, and crime factors, and the top of the matrix lists the crime categories. Completing the matrix helps the analyst to identify common and emerging themes. For example, young adults may be increasingly susceptible to mobile phone theft, but also increasingly likely to commit forms of antisocial behaviour associated with the nighttime economy and speeding-related offences. The underlying reasons behind these increases may be the same, and hence a combined response may be more effective than just tackling one issue (e.g., mobile phone theft) in isolation.

When Is the Problem Happening?

According to environmental criminology, most problems are not distributed equally across time. In other words, because opportunities are based on everyday behavior, they cluster at certain times of year (seasonal), days of week, and times of day. For example, road rage is most likely to happen when people are frustrated with traffic. Traffic is frustrating when streets are overloaded and busy. Streets are overloaded and busy during rush hour,

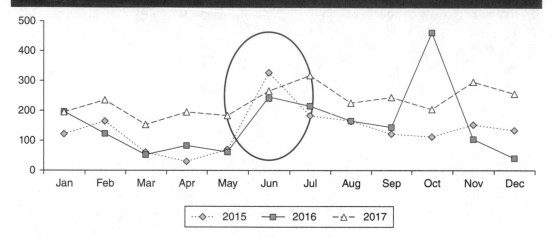

Figure 13.10 Loud Party Calls at Apartment Complexes: Seasonal Comparison

which in most cities is from 7:00 a.m. to 9:00 a.m. and 4:00 p.m. to 6:00 p.m. It is logical that road rage is most likely to happen during these times and even more specifically at the end of the day when people are tired and want to get home. However, this is only a hypothesis based on theory and may not be true in every community, so analysis of the local problem would have to confirm this.

In general, tactical crime analysts look for temporal patterns in small numbers of cases and in relatively short time periods (using a method known as *time series analysis*), such as hours and days. Strategic crime analysts use a larger number of cases to look for temporal patterns over short time periods (e.g., time of day and day of week), as well as over longer periods, such as months, seasons, and years.

Seasonality

To examine **seasonality,** the crime analyst examines several years of data on a problem to determine if there seems to be a similar pattern across years. Figure 13.10 depicts loud party data at apartment complexes from a previous example but places the same months from multiple years alongside one another so that monthly patterns are visible. This ellipse indicates that each year loud party calls increase in June.

Time of Day and Day of Week

Both tactical crime analysts and strategic crime analysts examine data by time of day and day of week. This technique is appropriate in tactical crime analysis in certain situations (as discussed in Chapter 11), but it is even more useful in strategic crime analysis when more cases are *analyzed*. Table 13.9 contains

Figure 13.11   Seasonal Chart of Crashes

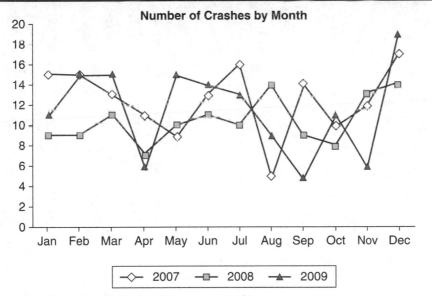

Number of Crashes by Month

Legend: 2007, 2008, 2009

Source: Fort Pierce (Florida) Police Department, April Lee.

data on the frequency of robberies at convenience stores over the past year by time of day and day of week, and the chart in Figure 13.12 illustrates these data. Analysis of Figure 13.12 indicates that over the past year robberies have occurred throughout the week between 8:00 p.m. and 11:00 p.m. and have been more frequent on Fridays and Saturdays during those times.

The weighted time span method, as described in Chapter 11, also is useful for determining when problems with time span data occur. This is frequently the case for property crimes such as burglary, auto theft, and vandalism, which often are

Table 13.9 Cross-Tabulation of Convenience Store Robberies by Time of Day and Day of Week

	Sun	Mon	Tue	Wed	Thu	Fri	Sat	Total
Midnight	24	5	1	0	9	3	30	72
1:00 a.m.	30	6	9	12	3	6	18	84
2:00 a.m.	6	0	3	0	3	0	12	24
3:00 a.m.	0	0	0	0	0	2	7	9
4:00 a.m.	5	0	0	0	7	0	0	12
5:00 a.m.	0	3	0	2	6	0	0	11
6:00 a.m.	1	0	1	3	0	8	3	16
7:00 a.m.	6	3	0	0	2	0	3	14
8:00 a.m.	3	0	9	0	0	0	0	12
9:00 a.m.	0	3	0	6	0	3	0	12
10:00 a.m.	1	0	3	9	3	0	12	28
11:00 a.m.	2	0	6	0	9	1	9	27
Noon	0	3	2	0	1	1	0	7
1:00 p.m.	15	0	0	0	9	12	9	45
2:00 p.m.	3	0	6	0	0	6	0	15
3:00 p.m.	0	12	0	6	0	1	3	22
4:00 p.m.	6	1	4	0	3	2	0	16
5:00 p.m.	0	0	0	2	0	0	6	8
6:00 p.m.	0	1	0	0	2	6	0	9
7:00 p.m.	6	9	15	3	0	0	6	39
8:00 p.m.	12	0	6	6	1	12	15	52
9:00 p.m.	3	15	6	9	15	33	45	126
10:00 p.m.	12	6	18	12	27	27	36	138
11:00 p.m.	9	12	6	3	21	24	18	93
Total	**144**	**79**	**95**	**73**	**121**	**147**	**232**	**891**

not discovered until some time after the crimes have taken place. Figures 13.13 and 13.14 show the time spans for commercial and residential burglaries over a 1-year period, with a total of 250 and 175 burglaries, respectively. It is easy to

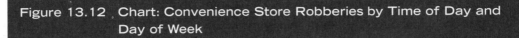

Figure 13.12 Chart: Convenience Store Robberies by Time of Day and Day of Week

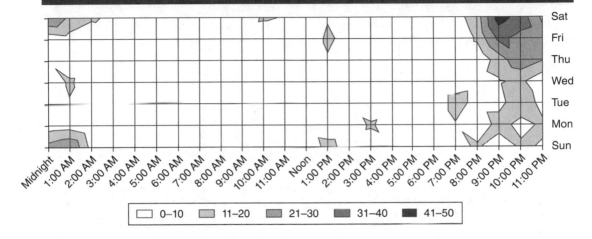

Figure 13.13 Weighted Time Span Chart: Commercial Burglaries

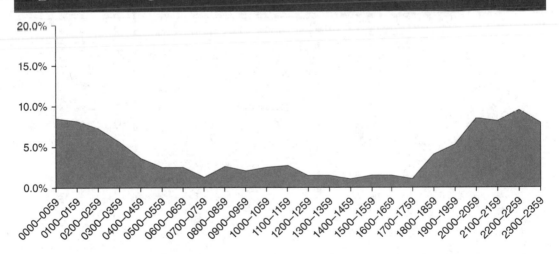

discern general patterns from these charts and to make comparisons between the two types of burglaries (e.g., commercial burglaries are occurring at night and residential burglaries are occurring primarily during the day).

Weighted time span also can be conducted on day of week for a problem but is not always as helpful because the time periods in which crimes occur can span over days and even weeks. Also, a combination of this type of analysis for time of day and day of week together is often not conducted because of the vagueness of the results (i.e., time spans and day of week spans).

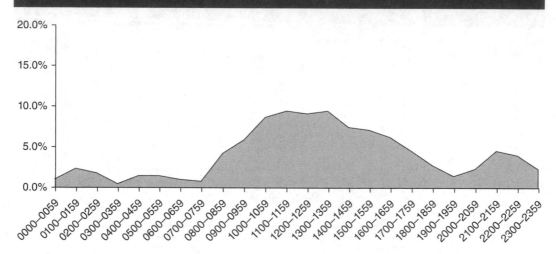

Figure 13.14 Weighted Time Span Chart: Residential Burglaries

SUMMARY POINTS

This chapter illustrates the strategic analysis of problems by answering key analysis questions. The following are the key points addressed in this chapter:

- What is the nature of the problem? To answer this first question, the analyst examines the sequence and actions of those involved in the events that make up the problem and looks at the broader environment in which these events are occurring.

- How frequently is the problem occurring? To answer this question, analysts use frequency, percentage rate, and mean and standard deviation. They may also use a combination of these and other more indirect methods for understanding the frequency of a particular problem.

- Crime analysts use three rates regularly to compare local crime problems with national crime problems as well as to describe particular general problems: crime rate, clearance rate, and recovery rate.

- Has the problem increased or decreased? To answer this question, analysts examine data according to temporal units (e.g., year, month, quarter, week) to determine if there have been increases or decreases in the problem over time. Percentage of change also can be used to examine the amount of relative increase or decrease in a problem between two time periods.

- When is the problem happening? To answer this question, analysts use a large numbers of cases to look for temporal patterns over short time periods (e.g., time of day and day of week) as well as over longer periods, such as months, seasons, and years.

DISCUSSION EXERCISES*

Exercise 1

Fill in the missing numbers for the following table. Also, compute the mean rate of assaults per 100 persons.

Location	Frequency of Assaults	Percentage	Occupancy	Rate of Assaults per Person	Rate per 100 Persons
Bar 1	25	2.50%	250		
Bar 2	50		1,000	0.05	
Bar 3	100	10.00%	500		
Bar 4	75	7.50%	1,000	0.08	
Bar 5	250		500	0.50	
Bar 6	125	12.50%	250		
Bar 7	50	5.00%	250	0.20	
Bar 8	200		1,000	0.20	
Bar 9	50	5.00%	500		
Bar 10	75		250	0.30	
Total	1,000	100.00%	5,500		

Exercise 2

What is the purpose of the following chart? If you were the chief of police, where would you first implement your responses for this problem and why?

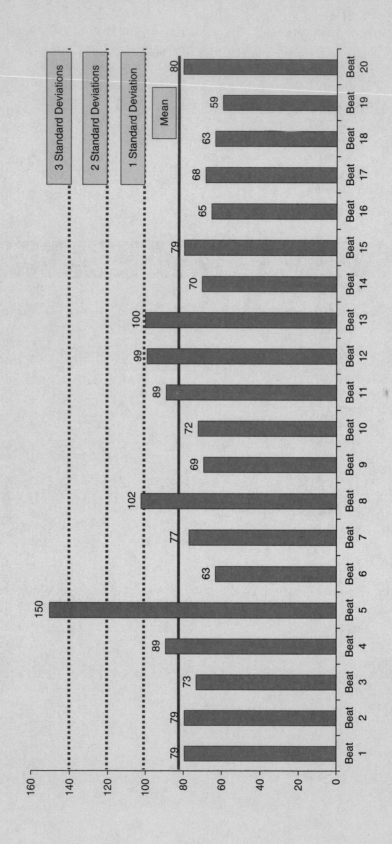

Exercise 3

How does the proportion of property crime compare to the proportion of persons crime in Beat 4; how do they compare to the proportions of property and persons crime for the rest of the city?

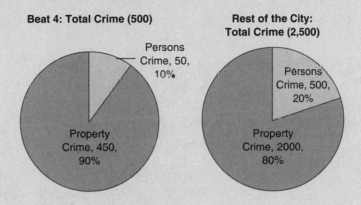

Beat 4: Total Crime (500)

Persons Crime, 50, 10%

Property Crime, 450, 90%

Rest of the City: Total Crime (2,500)

Persons Crime, 500, 20%

Property Crime, 2000, 80%

CHAPTER 14

Analyzing Problems
Application of Techniques, Part II

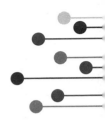

Where Is the Problem Occurring?

Just as problems are not distributed equally across time, most problems are not distributed equally across space (Felson & Boba, 2010; Tompson & Townsley, 2010). The terms used to refer to the spatial clustering of crime and disorder events in the long term (i.e., strategic) are the problem location and the problem area. In practice and research, the term *hot spot* is used oftentimes in practice and research to refer to both of these problem types as well as short-term hot spots. In this book, three terms are used to represent the different phenomenon to clarify both the analysis required and responses police implement. The *micro-time of pattern hot spot* is a short-term cluster of crime as described in Chapter 11. As defined in Chapter 3, the *problem location* or "risky place" can be an individual address (e.g., one convenience store) or a type of place (e.g., all convenience stores) at which there is a concentration of crime or problematic activity, and the *problem area* (i.e., long-term hot spot) can be one block face or entire square block areas, one street segment or clusters of street segments, or designated police geographic areas such as zones, beats, districts, or precincts. In both problem areas and locations, various victims and offenders are involved in the activity occurring at the location or in the area. Problem analysis focuses on identifying the types of problematic activity and understanding how opportunities are being created and acted upon that make up the problematic behavior.

Long-term geographic analysis is used as part of the assessment step within problem solving to determine whether there has been spatial displacement or diffusion of benefits after the response (see Chapter 2). Although there are more sophisticated spatial analysis methods, the primary way to use crime mapping for assessment is to compare similarly constructed maps before and after the response. This is because the maps are only one part of the assessment analysis product and do not stand on their own to determine if the response was effective.

The level at which a geographic unit of analysis is examined depends on the purpose of the analysis. However, the unit of analysis selected for long-term problem analysis—location, street segment, or area—will significantly influence the analysis results. The analyst should start at the lowest level (points) and work upward (areas) to avoid overlooking low-level clusters of a particular problem (Eck, Chainey, Cameron, Leitner, & Wilson, 2005). The methods used to answer the question "Where is the problem occurring?" seek both to identify and categorize problem locations and areas in order to understand and communicate the spatial relationships of the problem events.

INTERNATIONAL CRIME
ANALYST PERSPECTIVE

Carola Jersonsky

Crime Analyst/Data Quality Control

Metropolitan Police of Buenos Aires

Buenos Aires, Argentina

The Metropolitan Police in Buenos Aires was created just 6 years ago. As a new police, new departments are being developed with a different and innovative vision of a police that can do better things than as they were in the past. The Crime Analysis and Information Department is growing up in the same proportion of the Metropolitan Police, with an orientation to do strategic crime analysis. It is not easy for us to be sure about the analysis because the operative system is staying small (watching the growth in the number of officers and crime), and we do not have the other Forces data (with whom we share the capital city security). We work in hot spot analysis, trying to understand the movements of the different places (generally slums) where the crime is concentrated. Metropolitan Police have barely developed three police stations around the capital city (there will be 15), where we most work with the analysis (because is where we have more data). But we are still dealing with a problem: We now see more crime or the people now report more of them (because they feel comfortable with the new police station).

Identifying and Analyzing Problem Locations

Crime analysts use the 80/20 principle to identify problem locations where the problem has concentrated in order to guide police in prioritizing where their responses should be implemented. As discussed in Chapter 2, this concept comes from the observation that 80% (number of repeat offenses) of some kinds of outcomes are the results of only 20% (number of repeat victims or targets) of the related causes. The numbers 80 and 20 in the name of this "rule" are meant only to represent "large" and "small" amounts; the actual proportions change, depending on the type of activity and nature of the community in which it occurs. This analysis can also be used to identify repeat victims, but more often, crime analysts are asked to identify the problem locations that are experiencing the most problematic activity in the jurisdiction.

There are two key types of data used for an 80/20 analysis to identify problem locations. The first is the number and percentage of offenses that occurred by address, and the second is the number of addresses that have suffered multiple offenses. Because a problem location is a long-term problem, the analyst would use at least 1 year of data. In order to determine the repeat victim and offense percentages more easily, crime analysts take the following steps:

- Identify the type of places that are important for a particular problem and that the rule might apply to. This is an important step and is where the analyst focuses on a particular type of location and activity to analyze.

Some examples include assaults at bars, loud parties at apartment complexes, burglaries at storage facilities, and shoplifting at retail establishments.

- Get a list of the type of place to be analyzed with a count of the number of events associated with location.

- Rank order the locations according to the number of events associated with each—most to least.

- Calculate the percentages of the events each location contributes.

- Cumulate the percentages, starting with the most involved location.

- Calculate the proportion of the total number of locations analyzed that each single location represents.

- Compare the cumulative percentage of locations to the cumulative percentage of outcomes. (Clarke & Eck, 2005, Step 18)

Table 14.1 presents an example of this kind of calculation for robberies by addresses for 1 year. The following list describes each column of the table and how the method was conducted:

- *Column 1:* A rank of the addresses with the most robberies. The rankings reflect descending frequency.

- *Column 2:* The list of addresses, sorted by descending frequency of robberies. Note that after the first 10 addresses, the frequency for each addresses is not listed. This is because there are too many addresses to list in the table ($N = 106$, as noted in column 6). Instead, in this table, addresses with four or fewer robberies are aggregated into categories. For example, the row that says *Addresses With 4* ($N = 5$) means that there were five addresses with four robberies each. Column 3 shows there were a total of 20 robberies for this category, which was computed by multiplying 5 (addresses) by 4 (robberies). In the next column, 45 robberies occurred at 15 addresses since each address had three robberies ($15 \times 3 = 45$), and so on. The aggregate categories will depend on the each dataset examined and how many individual cases are listed. Some analysts will list five, 10, 15, or even 20 individual addresses, depending on the type of activity and the purpose of the analysis.

- *Column 3:* The descending frequency of robberies by address (the number of offenses that each location accounts for) and by category with multiple addresses.

- *Column 4:* The percentage of total robberies for each address or category.

- *Column 5:* The cumulative percentage of robberies for each address and category (this number represents the percentage of repeat offenses).

- *Column 6:* The percentage for each address is of the total number of addresses examined. In this example, to determine the total number, the individual number of addresses (10) is added to the number in each category

Table 14.1 80/20 Calculation for Robberies by Address

1	2	3	4	5	6	7
Rank	Address	Frequency of Robberies	Percentage of Robberies	Cumulative Percentage of Robberies	Percentage of Addresses (N = 106)	Cumulative Percentage of Addresses
1	134 E Main St	25	9.23%	9.23%	0.94%	0.94%
2	254 S Clover Ave	17	6.27%	15.50%	0.94%	1.89%
3	8012 N Grand Blvd	15	5.54%	21.03%	0.94%	2.83%
4	8210 N Grand Blvd	10	3.69%	24.72%	0.94%	3.77%
5	1430 E Main St	9	3.32%	28.04%	0.94%	4.72%
6	365 W Haverty Rd	9	3.32%	31.37%	0.94%	5.66%
7	3401 N Staple Dr	8	2.95%	34.32%	0.94%	6.60%
8	210 S Daisy Rd	7	2.58%	36.90%	0.94%	7.55%
9	4598 N Roan Rd	5	1.85%	38.75%	0.94%	8.49%
10	132 E Main St	5	1.85%	40.59%	0.94%	9.43%
	Addresses with 4 (N = 5)	20	7.38%	47.97%	4.72%	14.15%
	Addresses with 3 (N = 15)	45	16.61%	64.58%	14.15%	28.30%
	Addresses with 2 (N = 20)	40	14.76%	79.34%	18.87%	47.17%
	Addresses with 1 (N = 56)	56	20.66%	100.00%	52.83%	100.00%
	Total	271	100.00%		100.00%	

(5 + 15 + 20 + 56) to get the total (106). Thus, each individual address is 1/106 or 0.94% of the total. The percentage for each category depends on the number of addresses in that category. For example, addresses with four robberies make up 5/106 or 4.72% of the total.

- *Column 7:* The cumulative percentage of addresses (this number represents the percentage of repeat addresses).

- *Row shaded gray:* Look to Columns 5 and 7 to determine the 80/20 relationship for these data. That is, 40.59% of the repeat robberies are occurring at 9.43% of the repeat addresses. Any row can be used to show how the 80/20 rule exists for a particular problem. Crime analysts chose a particular row, depending on the numbers and the purpose of the analysis (e.g., 47.97% of the repeat robberies occur at 14.15% of the repeat addresses, or 64.58% of the repeat robberies occur at 28.30% of the repeat addresses).

The 80/20 analysis of addresses could be done for an entire jurisdiction, separately by each geographic area, or by location type and crime type.

Table 14.2 80/20 Calculation of General Disturbance and Fight Calls in Problem Bars by Address

Rank	Location	Disturbance and Fight Calls	Percentage of Calls ($N = 576$)	Cumulative Percentage	Percentage of Addresses ($N = 65$)	Cumulative Percentage
1	800 S Darwood Blvd	45	7.81%	7.81%	1.54%	1.54%
2	1449 E Morrow St	44	7.64%	15.45%	1.54%	3.08%
3	1055 S Main St	42	7.29%	22.74%	1.54%	4.62%
4	1675 N West Av	40	6.94%	29.69%	1.54%	6.15%
5	1850 S Gatland Rd	39	6.77%	36.46%	1.54%	7.69%
6	1655 E Walton Rd	32	5.56%	42.01%	1.54%	9.23%
7	166 W Peacock Blvd	25	4.34%	46.35%	1.54%	10.77%
8	973 S Deloir Rd	21	3.65%	50.00%	1.54%	12.31%
9	269 S Foster Av	20	3.47%	53.47%	1.54%	13.85%
10	220 N Irving St	19	3.30%	**56.77%**	1.54%	**15.38%**
	Other addresses (55)	249	43.23%	100.00%	84.62%	100.00%
	Total	**576**	100.00%		100.00%	

Table 14.2 is an example of an 80/20 analysis of problem bars (i.e., problem locations) for general disturbance and fight calls. It lists the top 10 bars in descending order, with all other addresses aggregated. The table shows that these 10 addresses (15.38% of the addresses) account for almost 60% (56.77%) of the calls.

Using this as a scanning tool, some or all of the top locations might be selected by sworn personnel for crime reduction and would be further examined before responses are initiated. Once the locations are selected for response, the crime analyst conducts analysis on each location individually to provide detailed information about all of the activity that is happening at the place. While all these locations might be selected for the same reason (e.g., they are bars with disturbances and fights), the reason behind the activity will likely be different for each one. The crime analyst will provide additional information to help sworn personnel create and implement tailored crime prevention and reduction strategies. Because the problem location analysis product can be somewhat long, instead of showing examples of each aspect of the product, the following are guidelines for creating the problem location product in terms of the content and format of the specific aspect of the product. Many of these are discussed already, but this provides a checklist for the final product that would be produced for an individual problem location.

1. *Read the relevant POP Center* Problem–Specific Guide *(e.g., theft from vehicle in residential neighborhoods, assaults at bars)*. As noted in Chapter 12, each guide summarizes knowledge, research, and practice about the problem activity and how police can reduce the harm caused by specific crime and disorder problems. This information would be used to provide introductory information about the reader as well as support and/or a citation for evidence-based responses recommended in the report.

2. *Citizen-generated calls-for-service analysis.* Using at least 12 months (up to 36 months) of citizen-generated calls-for-service data occurring at this location and, if relevant, addresses in close proximity, include the following:

   - Frequency and percentage of types of calls at the location—table
   - Frequency of calls by month (or by 4-week period)—line chart
   - Time of day/day of week analysis for all calls—surface chart
   - Time of day/day of week for selected calls (those that are concerning and/or most frequent)—surface chart
   - Frequency and percentage of disposition of the calls—table or pie chart

3. *Officer-generated calls-for-service analysis.* Using at least 12 months (up to 36 months) of officer-generated calls for service occurring at this location and, if relevant, addresses in close proximity, include the following:

- Frequency and percentage of types of calls at the location—table
- Frequency of calls by month (or by 4-week period)—line chart
- Time of day/day of week analysis for all calls—surface chart
- Frequency and percentage of disposition of the calls—table or pie chart

4. *Crime and arrest analysis.* Using at least 12 months (up to 36 months) of crime report and arrest data at the location and, if relevant, addresses at close proximity, include the following:

- Frequency and percentage of crime types—table
- Frequency of crime as well as most relevant crimes by month (or by 4-week period)—line chart
- Frequency of arrests occurring the location by month—line chart
- Frequency and percentage of types of arrests occurring at the location—table
- Frequency of arrests occurring at the location by each individual's age, sex, and race, if necessary—table or pie charts
- 80/20 analysis of arrests and individuals arrested—table
- Any crime patterns, including this location (provide a summary of each pattern in the report and attach the relevant bulletin at the end of the report)

5. *Qualitative analysis.* As relevant, include the following:

- History of the location's relationship with city, county, state, and federal government (i.e., licenses, code enforcement violations, taxes, etc.)
- Specific information about key individuals, such as owners, managers, renters
- Characteristics of other individuals who frequent or are familiar with the location, such as customers, neighbors, business community, neighborhood association

- Observation of the location (i.e., visit and take pictures to assess condition, conduct a crime prevention through environmental design [CPTED] study of the location and the surrounding environment)

- Interviews with officers about the recent activity and history of the location with the police and others

- Interviews and surveys of owner, manager, residents, customers, neighbors, and others (surveys taken before and after a response will contribute to the impact evaluation)

6. *Conclusions.* For each section of analysis, it is not enough to simply provide the statistics, tables, and charts, but the crime analyst should make conclusions based on the analysis and on the POP guides to assist in the development of responses (e.g., calls for service are occurring during the day; they are predominantly loud music calls; crimes and arrests are predominantly assaults).

Identifying Problem Areas

Similar to individual problem location analysis, an 80/20 analysis can be used to identify top areas in a jurisdiction without using a crime mapping program. Also, once a problem area is selected for a response, the crime analyst would use

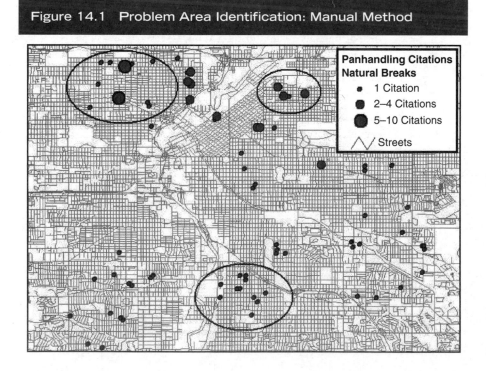

Figure 14.1 Problem Area Identification: Manual Method

a similar checklist to conduct a comprehensive problem analysis report. While it would not be exactly the same, it is similar enough (i.e., provide analysis of calls, crime, arrests, etc.) that another checklist is not provided. However, spatial analysis techniques are distinct in their use for identifying problem areas versus problem locations, so the next sections describe a variety of spatial analysis techniques that are most often used to identify problem areas.

Manual Method The most straightforward way of determining problem areas is the manual or "eyeball" method using point data; this is also the most often used method in crime analysis and policing. In Figure 14.1, which depicts panhandling citations as graduated symbols, an analyst identifies the areas where the concentration of citations appears to be the greatest (indicated by the circles).

It is important that analysts use graduated points when identifying problem areas manually because, as noted in Chapter 6, single-symbol maps place incidents that have occurred at the same location on top of one another so that a large number of incidents at the same location appear as one. Analysts

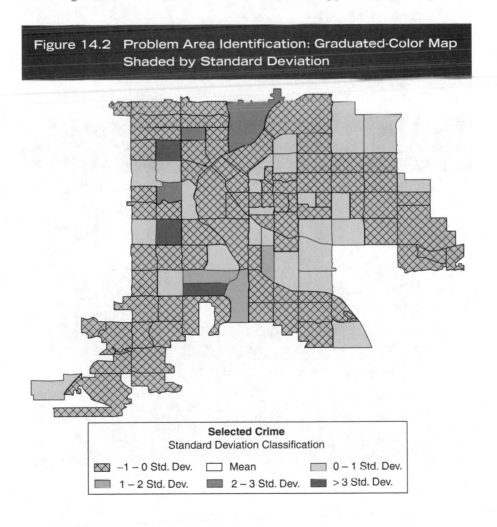

Figure 14.2 Problem Area Identification: Graduated-Color Map Shaded by Standard Deviation

Selected Crime
Standard Deviation Classification

- −1 – 0 Std. Dev.
- Mean
- 0 – 1 Std. Dev.
- 1 – 2 Std. Dev.
- 2 – 3 Std. Dev.
- > 3 Std. Dev.

also can aggregate incidents by street segment and area to determine manual problem areas but need to be aware that the areas appearing to be problem areas will vary depending on the unit of analysis, scale of the map, and the amount of data mapped.

Graduated-Color Mapping For data distributions with large numbers of incidents, using points, even graduated ones, to determine problem areas can be difficult. Graduated-color maps of areas (polygons) allow analysts to examine more incidents by aggregating them by area. Graduated-color area maps also allow analysts to map census information, such as population and income, along with crime analysis data, as census variables are available only by area (e.g., census blocks, census block groups, census tracts). The standard deviation classification is particularly helpful for determining problem areas because it highlights those areas that are considerably different from the mean—that is, areas with frequencies or rates that are 1, 2, or 3 standard deviations above the mean. In Figure 14.2, the darkest areas would be identified as problem areas, as their values are more than 3 standard deviations above the mean for all the areas.

When using graduated-color polygon maps, analysts need to be aware that the areas are not of equal size, which makes comparing frequency of incidents among unlike units problematic. Analysts can address this issue by using a normalizing variable, such as population, number of targets, or area of the

Figure 14.3 Comparisons of Actual Crime Locations and Shaded Polygons

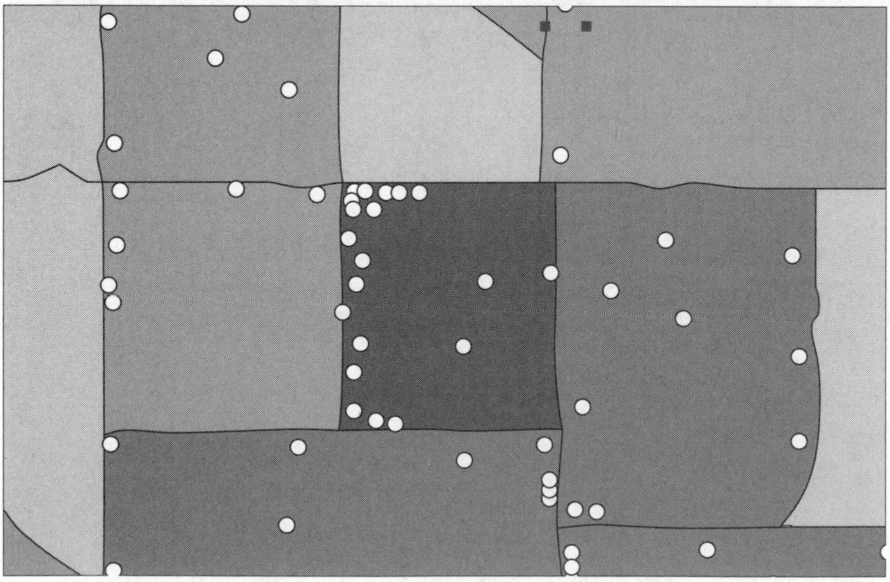

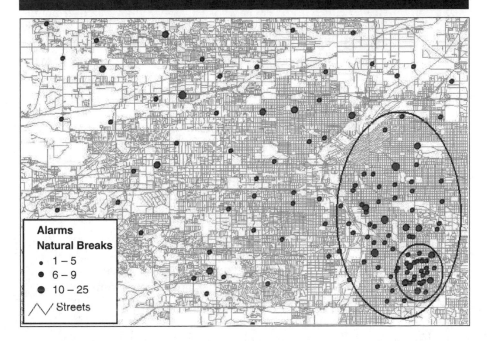

Figure 14.4 Problem Area Identification: Ellipses

Alarms
Natural Breaks
- 1 – 5
- 6 – 9
- 10 – 25
⋀⋁ Streets

polygon. Analysts using this or any graduated color polygon map to determine problem areas also need to be aware that incidents within an area could have occurred only along the border of that area, but because the entire area is shaded, no matter what classification is used, actual data and the resulting hot spot are distorted. Figure 14.3 shows the actual incidents along an area border (a major road) and how the shading distorts this concentration of incidents; however, without the clarification of the incident symbols, it appears that all of the area is equally dense with crime. Sometimes (e.g., when an analyst is faced with a large number of cases and limited software capabilities) analysts have no option but to use this method, but they should do so with caution.

Ellipses Crime analysts use ellipses to determine problem areas or geographic concentrations of activity in data distributions (i.e., points that are closer to one another than to any other point).[1] An **ellipse** is a closed curve that is formed from two foci or points in which the sum of the distances from any point on the curve to the two foci is a constant. Unlike a circle, which has an exact center, an ellipse has two foci, allowing it to accommodate the area of a hot spot both horizontally and vertically.

Software designed for spatial analysis, such as STAC (Spatial and Temporal Analysis of Crime), developed by the Illinois Criminal Justice Information Authority (ICJIA), uses a statistical method and user selections (e.g., study area) to determine both first-order and second-order clusters.[2] Figure 14.4 presents a rudimentary example of an ellipse that highlights first-order (larger ellipse) and second-order (smaller ellipse) problem areas of activity within a data distribution.

Density Mapping In the **density mapping** method of determining problem areas, analysts identify problem areas by examining graduated-color maps that depict concentrations of activity using the exact locations of the incidents. Unlike the graduated-area and grid mapping methods, density mapping does not limit the analyst to examination of predetermined areas; rather, in density maps "the flow of hotspots mimics the underlying crime patterns and often follows urban geographic features that are known to police officers and other users" (Ratcliffe, 2004b, p. 8). Figure 14.5 is an example of a density map that would be used to identify problem areas. However, once the problem areas are selected for further analysis and response, clearer boundaries for each area should be determined so that responses can be implemented and activity in the problem area can be consistently measured. That is, the density map creates areas that have vague boundaries because of the shading, which makes determining which incidents are occurring inside the problem area difficult over time. Also, density mapping does not consider natural or constructed characteristics of the area, such as rivers, roads, large buildings, and the like. It would be important to draw boundaries of the problem area considering these characteristics, so those responsible for problem solving would give the crime analyst the exact boundaries of the problem area. The analyst would draw a customized polygon in the GIS and save it as a layer so that any activity occurring in the problem area could be clearly distinguished and counted.

Summary of Problem Area Identification Methods

As with many of the other analysis techniques discussed throughout this book, each of the problem area identification methods described earlier has its own strengths and weaknesses. Table 14.3 provides a summary of problem area identification methods and the issues associated with their use.

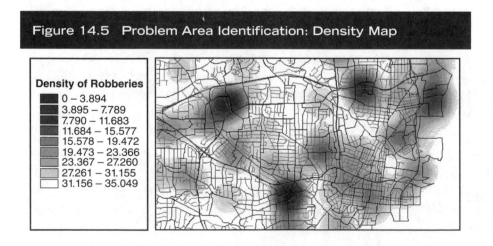

Figure 14.5 Problem Area Identification: Density Map

Density of Robberies
- 0 – 3.894
- 3.895 – 7.789
- 7.790 – 11.683
- 11.684 – 15.577
- 15.578 – 19.472
- 19.473 – 23.366
- 23.367 – 27.260
- 27.261 – 31.155
- 31.156 – 35.049

> Case Study, Gainesville, Florida: Figure 14.6 depicts a density analysis of gang-related crime in 2012 in the City of Gainesville, Florida. The map informs officers and police commanders of the Gainesville Police Department as well as city officials and community members where the highest concentration of crimes are being committed by gang members.

Figure 14.6 Gainesville, Florida, Gang-Related Crimes

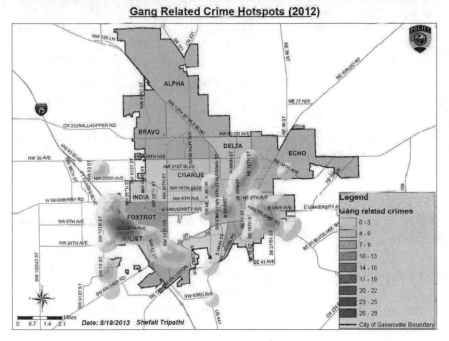

Gang Related Crime Hotspots (2012)

Source: Gainesville (Florida) Police Department, Dr. Shefali Tripathi.

Who Are the Victims, and Does Repeat Victimization Exist?

To understand the underlying causes of crime or disorder problems, analysts need to understand who and what the victims (people) and targets (property) of those problems are. Research suggests that "lightning does strike twice"—that is, individuals and targets that are victimized once are likely to be victimized again (Farrell & Pease, 1993; Grove, Farrell, Farrington, & Johnson, 2012; Weisel, 2005). There are two distinct questions to ask when examining victimization in a problem. The first is to determine who the victims are, and the second is to determine whether repeat victimization exists.

Table 14.3 Summary of Problem Area Identification Methods

	Manual Method	Graduated-Color Polygon Maps	Ellipses Maps	Density Maps
Type of feature (point, line, polygon)	Graduated points	Polygons	Points	Points
Software requirements	Basic GIS	Basic GIS	Advanced functions or specialized software	Advanced functions or specialized software
Issues	No standardized methodology, dependent on scale	Assumes equal distribution across area	Depends on user selections; erroneously used to predict future crime occurrences	Depends highly on user selections of search radius and cell size; problems with borders; comparison difficult
How often used in strategic crime analysis	Very often	Very often	Seldom	Very often

For most problems, people are victims in some way, and victims can often be identified through their sociodemographic characteristics (e.g., sex, race, and age, among others). However, more importantly, victims' systematic behavior is what contributes opportunities for the problematic activity, as noted in the discussion of the problem analysis triangle in Chapter 2. The simplest way that analysts search for repeat victimization by victim characteristics is by conducting cross-tabulations of particular data. For instance, Table 14.4 displays a cross-tab of frequency and category percentages of domestic violence victims in a particular city. The table shows that women make up 68.2% of the victims, and both men and women ages 36 to 55 make up the largest percentage (38.5%). In addition, women ages 36 to 55 are victims in 25% of the cases (45 divided by 179 multiplied by 100).

To determine common victim behavior that may contribute to a problem, the analyst must dig deeper by using qualitative data collection, such as interviews, focus groups, and observation (as discussed in Chapter 5) to understand the particular circumstances of a problem. Some examples include the following:

- Individuals who leave their vehicles unlocked and property in their vehicles in front of their homes
- Parents who leave their cars running when dropping off children at day care

Table 14.4   Cross-Tabulation of Intimate Violence Victims by Sex and Age

Age	Sex			
	Male	Female	Total	Percentage
Under 18	2	5	7	3.91%
18 to 35	15	38	53	29.61%
36 to 55	24	45	69	38.55%
Over 55	16	34	50	27.93%
Total	57	122	179	100.00%
Percentage	31.84%	68.16%	100.00%	

- Migrant workers who cash their paychecks instead of depositing them in banks
- Men in their 20s who get extremely intoxicated at bars and become belligerent
- College students who do not protect their laptops, phones, and the like in their dorms or in the library
- People who leave windows open and doors unlocked at their homes
- Elderly people who give their credit card and personal information to telemarketers on the phone

Victims can also be organizations, especially with commercial crime. For example, builders or subcontractors are victims of theft of tools and building materials from construction sites, and electronics stores are victims of overnight burglary. Whether the victims are people or organizations, it is important to determine any common behavior among them for a particular problem. An example of common behavior in commercial crime could be the installation of concrete barriers and alarms in stores that sell electronics, so offenders cannot use their vehicles to smash in the front doors to gain access to the store. Lastly, to examine repeat victimization of individuals, the same 80/20 analysis shown for problem locations is used. In the analysis, the addresses would be replaced with individual victims.

Who Are the Offenders, and Does Repeat Offending Exist?

When doing problem analysis, there are two ways a crime analyst analyzes offender information. The first way is understanding who the offenders are of the particular problem, such as assaults at problem bars or burglaries in residential neighborhoods. The second is to identify a prioritized list of "problem offenders" by frequency or seriousness of their arrests. As discussed in Chapter 3, a problem offender is an individual who commits a disproportionate amount of crime or groups of offenders who share similar characteristics. For the problem offenders, the key component is that one person or a group of people moves through different settings and takes advantage of different victims.

The crime analysis techniques (previously described) that help determine the characteristics of victims, behaviors that contribute to victimization, and the 80/20 analysis can also be used to determine both who are the offenders and whether repeat offending exists within a problem. Cross-tabulations can be computed using police arrest data on the age, race, and sex of the offenders, and an 80/20 analysis can also be done on the individual offenders (using a combination of name, date of birth, and/or social security number). However, answering questions about offenders for some types of problems can be difficult because the offenders for that crime are not often caught, so police do not have offender data to analyze.

Even using qualitative methods such as interviews and observations may be difficult since offenders may not be identified, or when they are identified, they may not be forthcoming with information about their criminal behavior. For example, arrest rates for property crime such as burglary and auto theft are both under 15%, so police do not know who the offenders are or have arrest data in over 85% of the cases. An analysis of arrests for these types of crimes would provide information about only a minority of the cases and arguably about people who may not be as smart or experienced (since they were actually caught) as those who were not caught.

To try to understand who the offenders might be for problems where there is little arrest data, crime analysts can look for indications of criminal behavioral patterns in the MOs (modus operandi) of the crimes and deduce who the offenders are and what their motivations might be. For example, an examination of auto theft recoveries may find that a large proportion of the vehicles are found with no damage and an empty gas tank, whereas a smaller number are found with radios and car parts stripped from the vehicles. Analysts could deduce that the first type of offenders may be individuals looking to have fun by "joyriding," where the other offenders are taking property to sell or use themselves. The analyst must think critically about how to determine patterns of offending in these cases in which there is no official information about the offenders. Other examples include the following:

- Residential burglaries of homes from which burglar alarms are defeated easily and only expensive jewelry is taken might indicate professional burglars.

- Construction site burglaries from which tools and equipment are taken might indicate employee theft.

- Graffiti depicting gang signs might indicate gang members or potential gang members.

- Drug paraphernalia and condoms in a park might indicate prostitution.

- Theft from vehicle incidents in which entry is made through unlocked doors and primarily change and small items are taken might indicate juveniles living in the area.

No matter how the individual problem offenders are identified, just as with problem locations and areas, a more in-depth analysis of them would be conducted, as long as their names are known to the police. The offender product created by the crime analysts is often called a "criminal résumé," which is a long-term analysis report of the offender's criminal history, personal characteristics, financial information, and so on. You'll remember that this analysis product was discussed as part of crime intelligence analysis in Chapter 4. This is an instance in which the types of crime analysis overlap. In both short-term and long-term analysis, the criminal résumé contains long-term information and is provided to sworn personnel who are responsible for developing either short-term or long-term solutions to reduce that offender's criminal activity.

The criminal résumé is a comprehensive document that takes a crime analyst a significant amount of time to put together. Thus, this product is not created for all offenders, but only for those that have been prioritized for long-term response. The product would contain a complete criminal history from the national crime database, corrections history and current probation status, and any other contacts made with the police department, including as a victim, a witness, calls for service, and traffic citations. Associates (presented with a link chart analysis), residence history, credit history, history with city services (e.g., utilities, code enforcement), and social media activity (e.g., Facebook, Twitter, Instagram) are also included. The content and length of the criminal résumé depends on the offender's criminal activity and personal background.

Much of the information in the criminal résumé comes from outside the crime analyst's agency data. The following are examples of the range of data sources that are typically used to create the résumé:

- Internal police data, such as crime, arrests, calls for service, field interviews, victim, witness, gang information; family members, associates, and other information collected through intelligence and surveillance

- National Crime Information Center (NCIC; same for each state database as well); gun permit search; requests of police reports, affidavits and field interviews from other agencies based on the criminal history

- Department of motor vehicle data to obtain vehicle, picture, address history, date of birth, social security numbers, ticket history, birth records and other historical documents

- External criminal justice data from department of corrections (incarcerations, gang affiliations, probation/parole information and contacts), department of juvenile justice, court records

- Financial records, such as wage/hour report, credit reports, utilities account requests, property appraiser information, marriage and divorce records, litigations

- Open-source data, Google/Yahoo and Internet searches, social media sources (e.g., Facebook, Twitter, YouTube)

- Other sources such as pawn data, schools, phone company, and the like

The crime analyst constructs a lengthy document that summarizes the information, provides details, and presents the information in a standard and easy to understand format. Figure 14.7 is a template for the front page of such a product.

Why Is the Problem Occurring?

This question represents the overall purpose of the analysis step of the problem-solving process. Selecting from the variety of the techniques described in this and the previous chapter, the analyst tests hypotheses and makes conclusions based on the evidence about why the problem is occurring. Unfortunately, there is never a way to know the absolute truth about why a problem is occurring, and there is no specific methodology that analysts can follow to determine the causes. The various results of the analyses have to be considered together along with local factors, results from research, and the theories of environmental criminology to develop a final understanding of the problem before responses can be developed.

To develop conclusions about why the problem is occurring, the analyst must consider evidence about each of the components of the problem analysis triangle: victims, offenders, place, time, guardians, handlers, and managers. In addition, the analyst considers factors that may be facilitating the problem and may consequently block crime prevention responses from working. Clarke and Eck (2005, Step 34) describe three types of facilitators:

Figure 14.7   Template for Front Page of a Criminal Résumé

Port St. Lucie Police Department	Intelligence Bulletin #: 2014I-0042
Crime Analysis Unit	*Released: November 25, 2014*
(772)344-4046, (772)873-6522	*Page 1 of 2*

Type of Program
Offender Resume

Name: Full Legal Name of Offender
AKA: Any alias or street names used by Offender
Priority Status: Priority Status of Offender

Probation: Adult/Juvenile, any curfew or restrictions, name of Probation Officer & contact info
Warnings: Any violent activity noted to alert officers such as gun violations, gang affiliations, etc
Last Agency Contact: Date of last contact – Agency – Type/reason for contact

Physical Description				Most Recent Image of Offender located here
Race		**Sex**		
DOB		**Age**		
Height		**Weight**		
Hair		**Eyes**		
Tattoos/Other	Type of identifier such as Tattoo or scar, location on offender/Description			

Identifiers				
DL		**DL info**	Valid/Suspended/ETC	
SSN		**Birthplace**		
SID #		**FBI #**		
DJJID:		**DNA on file**		
DOC #		**Alien #**		Where photo retrieved : Date of photo

Address	Dates Reported	Source(s)
Current Address	Date – Present	Source Information
Former Address	Date – Date	Source Information
Normally document at least 2 years		

Year	Color	Make/Model	Tag	Registered / Lien Status
		No Vehicles		

Charges and Violations					
Offense Date	Description	Disposition Date	Adjudicated?	Disposition	Notes

Employer/Business /School	Document employer/business/School, address & phone number
Phone Numbers	555-555-5555 – Source of phone number
Family/Associates	Full Name of Individual R/S DOB: 1/1/1911 Association/Family type IE: Mother Street Address, City, State, Zip • Information regarding associations (Include dates & case numbers when possible • C/H of individual summarized • Normally only include information of contacts within last year
Pawn History	Negative or Date: Item description, location of pawn
Social Media	Twitter: Negative Facebook: https://linkiscopiedhere (Last activity: Date) Also any other youtube, instragram, etc.
Miscellaneous	

FOR LAW ENFORCEMENT USE ONLY
Information provided from: Sources USED

Source: Port St. Lucie (Florida) Police Department, Michelle Wentz.

1. **Physical facilitators** are things that augment offenders' capabilities or help to overcome prevention measures. Trucks extend offenders' capacity to move stolen goods, telephones allow people to make obscene phone calls, and firearms help overcome resistance to robberies.

Some physical facilitators are tools, but others are part of the physical environment. Felson and colleagues (1996) describe how the old layout of the Port Authority Bus Terminal in New York facilitated a variety of crimes. Types of crimes had specific ecological niches created by the variety of design features in the old station.

2. **Social facilitators** stimulate crime or disorder by enhancing rewards from crime, legitimating excuses to offend, or by encouraging offending. Groups of young men, for example, can provide the social atmosphere that encourages rowdy behavior at sporting events. Gangs and organized criminal networks facilitate criminal activity by their members.

3. **Chemical facilitators** increase offenders' abilities to ignore risks or moral prohibitions. Some offenders, for example, drink heavily or use drugs before a crime in order to decrease their nervousness.

In the end, crime analysts answer this question with a series of "best guesses" that are based on evidence, not on intuition or limited experience. They will draw a number of conclusions about a problem, and during the response phase, police will prioritize these conclusions and decide the best plan to implement the responses based on the analysis and resources of the agency, as well as other local and political factors.

Going back to the example of construction site burglary of single-family homes, the Port St. Lucie Police Department concluded that a majority of the problem was caused by particular builders who had lax crime prevention practices. This was based on analysis that determined that only 20% of the builders accounted for nearly 70% of the crime, the majority of the property taken was building materials, and the property taken was easily accessible. A series of crime prevention responses were implemented that focused on improving the practices of a specific group of builders. In addition, one response was suggested in which the city's building department would implement an ordinance requiring builders to implement certain crime prevention responses. In the end, the agency decided not to pursue this because the number of thefts was much lower than originally thought and the amount of time, energy, and political capital that it would take to enact such an ordinance was not worth it at that particular point in time. (Boba & Santos, 2007)

SUMMARY POINTS

This chapter illustrates the strategic analysis of problems by answering key analysis questions. The following are the key points addressed in this chapter:

- Where is the problem occurring? To answer this question, analysts use methods to identify and analyze problem locations and problem areas.

- Crime analysts use the 80/20 principle to identify problem locations (as well as problem areas, problem victims, and problem offenders) in order to guide police in their responses. This concept comes from the observation that 80% (number of repeat offenses) of some kinds of outcomes are the results of only 20% (number of repeat victims or targets) of the related causes.

- Once the problem locations are selected for response, the crime analyst conducts a detailed analysis on each location individually to provide information about all of the activity that is happening at the place.

- The method of identifying problem areas that is used most often in crime analysis is the manual or "eyeball" method, in which the analyst studies a graduated-size point map and visually locates areas of high activity.

- By using a standard deviation classification in a graduated-color map of areas to identify problem areas, an analyst can examine more incidents together as well as examine additional information.

- To determine ellipses, crime analysts use statistical formulas that identify geographic concentrations of activity based on distances of the incidents from one another.

- In the density method, analysts identify problem areas by searching for dense concentrations of activity using the exact locations of the incidents. Unlike graduated-symbol and grid mapping, density mapping is not limited to predetermined areas and follows the course of the data.

- Who are the victims, and does repeat victimization exist? There are two distinct questions to ask when examining victimization in a problem. The first is determining the characteristics and behavior of the victims, and the second is determining whether repeat victimization exists.

- The simplest way in which analysts search for victimization patterns is by conducting cross-tabulations of the data. Qualitative data are used to understand victim behavior that might be contributing to the problem.

- Who are the offenders, and does repeat offending exist? The crime analysis techniques used to determine patterns of victimization and repeat victimization also can be used to determine patterns of offending and presence of repeat offending.

- Answering questions about offenders for certain types of problems can be difficult because most offenders are not caught, so police do not have offender data to analyze, and when they are caught, offenders may not be forthcoming. To try to understand who the offenders might be for problems where there is little arrest data, crime analysts can look for indications of behavioral patterns in the problem activity and deduce who the offenders might be and what their motivations are.

- Once an individual problem offender is selected for response, just as with problem locations and areas, a more in-depth analysis of each would be conducted.

- The criminal résumé is a comprehensive document that takes a crime analyst a significant amount of time to put together. Thus, this product is not created for all offenders, but only those that have been prioritized for long-term response. The product would contain a complete criminal history from the national crime database, corrections history, and current probation status, as well as any other contacts made with the police department, including as a victim, a witness, calls for service, and traffic citations. Associates, residence history, credit history, history with city services, and social media activity are also included. The content and length of the criminal résumé depends on the offender's criminal and personal background.

- Why is the problem occurring? This question represents the overall purpose of the analysis step of the problem-solving process. To develop conclusions about why the problem is occurring, the analyst must consider evidence about each of the components of the problem analysis triangle: victims, offenders, place, time, guardians, handlers, and managers.

- The analyst also considers factors that may be facilitating the problem and may consequently block crime prevention responses from working. Three types of facilitators include physical facilitators, social facilitators, and chemical facilitators.

DISCUSSION EXERCISES*

Exercise 1

You are asked to create a hot spot map of aggravated assaults in your city to see whether any particular areas have significantly higher rates of aggravated assault than the city average. What type of hot spot map would you create that would help you complete your task? Why?

Exercise 2

Fill in the missing values of the table; then interpret the table according to the 80/20 rule.

*Additional exercises using data and other resources can be found on http://www .sagepub.com/bobasantos4e.

Location	Frequency of Calls	Percentage	Cumulative Percentage	Percentage of Locations	Cumulative Percentage
Address 1	32	16.00%	16.00%	5.00%	5.00%
Address 2	30		31.00%	5.00%	10.00%
Address 3	26	13.00%		5.00%	15.00%
Address 4	24	12.00%	56.00%	5.00%	20.00%
Address 5	17	8.50%	64.50%	5.00%	25.00%
Address 6	15	7.50%	72.00%	5.00%	30.00%
Address 7	13			5.00%	35.00%
Address 8	9	4.50%	83.00%	5.00%	40.00%
Address 9	7	3.50%		5.00%	45.00%
Address 10	6		89.50%	5.00%	50.00%
Address 11	4	2.00%	91.50%	5.00%	55.00%
Address 12	4	2.00%	93.50%	5.00%	60.00%
Address 13	3			5.00%	65.00%
Address 14	2	1.00%	96.00%	5.00%	70.00%
Address 15	2	1.00%	97.00%	5.00%	75.00%
Address 16	2	1.00%	98.00%	5.00%	80.00%
Address 17	1	0.50%	98.50%	5.00%	85.00%
Address 18	1	0.50%	99.00%	5.00%	90.00%
Address 19	1	0.50%	99.50%	5.00%	95.00%
Address 20	1	0.50%	100.00%	5.00%	100.00%
Total	**200**	100.00%			

NOTES

1. Analysts also use ellipses to describe the amounts of data in particular areas (e.g., "95% of the cases fall within the ellipse"). Unfortunately, crime analysts sometimes use standard deviation ellipses with small numbers of cases to predict the location of the next case in a series; this is not an appropriate use of ellipses.

2. More information about STAC is available on the ICJIA website at www.icjia.state.il.us. For discussion of the categorization of spatial and temporal hot spots together, see Ratcliffe (2004b).

Strategic Crime Analysis Results and Dissemination

The three preceding chapters have outlined many different techniques that crime analysts use alone and in combination with one another to understand long-term problems. This chapter focuses on how analysts disseminate the results of their strategic crime analyses to police personnel. The first section addresses how analysts decide on what problem analysis information they should disseminate; the chapter then describes specific types of strategic crime analysis products and provides format guidelines for tables, graphs, and maps.

Choosing Analysis Information to Disseminate

The chapters in Part IV of this book are not intended to be a "recipe book" for crime analysis, with a step-by-step methodology for analyzing problems because much of the crime analysis process relies on the analyst's critical thinking skills and the kind of judgment that comes with experience. Crime analysts use different techniques in various combinations to evaluate information about problems, determine the gaps in that information, and collect additional information to fill those gaps. A problem analysis may result in 50 pages of information, but an efficiently prepared product resulting from that analysis may be comparatively brief. One weakness in current crime analysis practice is that many analysts create and disseminate to police personnel volumes of products and information without sifting through their findings to present only the information that is important and useful for police purposes.

There are two stages of reporting for the scanning and analysis steps of the problem-solving process. The first is reporting the initial descriptive analysis from the scanning process; the second is reporting the analysis findings, conclusions, and recommendations for responses. In both cases, crime analysts are beginning more and more to provide their products in a presentation software format (e.g., Microsoft PowerPoint) since the recipients of the products are often making presentations of the information for different audiences. While the crime analysts do not prepare each presentation, they provide the maps, charts, graphs, and analysis conclusions in a presentation format so the recipients can easily make adjustments within the presentation software for their own use. Fewer and fewer crime analysts are providing information on paper or in long PDF files.

Initial Analysis Results

To review from Chapter 12, the scanning step includes confirming that the problem exists, determining how frequently the problem occurs as well as how long it has been taking place, and identifying the consequences of the problem (Center for Problem-Oriented Policing, 2016). In this process, the analyst typically examines the relevant data that are immediately available within the police agency (e.g., crime reports, calls for service, arrests). This initial analysis merely describes who, what, when, where, and how the problem is occurring but does not seek to understand why the problem is occurring.

Oftentimes, the initial analysis of a problem indicates that the problem is too broad and must be narrowed in scope. For example, the initial analysis results of the construction site burglary problem in Port St. Lucie, Florida, revealed that one third of the crimes were actually vandalism—property was destroyed and nothing was taken (Boba & Santos, 2007). The department chose to eliminate these crimes from the final problem-solving project since vandalism had different offender motivations and warranted different crime prevention responses. Because the initial analysis was based on both theft and vandalism, it was necessary to redo the initial analysis on only construction site theft incidents before conducting the analysis to understand why the problem of theft from construction sites was occurring. Therefore, along with initial results, in the scanning step the analyst also makes recommendations about how a problem should be more focused.

The initial analysis may also begin to reveal that the available data are inadequate to study the problem in depth (i.e., part of the data modification subcycle discussed in Chapter 5). If this is the case, additional data collection measures would be developed and implemented before the full analysis step would take place. For example, in the construction site burglary project in Port St. Lucie, Florida, it was discovered that police reports did not contain important information that would be helpful for understanding the problem. A supplemental form was added to the construction site burglary report to collect additional information, such as the stage of building the home was in when the burglary occurred, who delivered the items that were stolen, who were the subcontractors working on the site, and where exactly was the property when it was stolen (Boba & Santos, 2007). Once these data were collected, the analysis step could begin. Overall, the initial analysis provides the results from police data readily available and helps to narrow the scope of the problem and identify additional data that must be collected.

Problem Analysis Results

The results of the analysis step of the problem-solving process contain three main areas of information. First, crime analysts provide the specific analysis results about the problem both from national research and the local findings (e.g., rate comparisons, maps of the problem, repeat victim analysis, temporal analysis). Second, crime analysts summarize the specific analysis results and make conclusions about the hypotheses derived as part of this process. Finally, recommendations are made by analysts, along with other police personnel working on the problem, for responses based on the research and analysis conclusions.

More specifically, the crime analyst would cover the following points in a full problem analysis product whether it is a written report or in a presentation format:

- The context of the city in which the analysis has taken place in relation to the problem

- Research findings from other (national or local) studies about the problem

- The data used in the analysis to understand the current nature of the problem and any limitations of those data

- The nature of the problem in that particular community

- Changes in the problem over time

- Temporal patterns of the problem (e.g., the problem has increased significantly in the past 2 years; it appears to have increased in the spring; it occurs primarily in the evening)

- The types of offenders, victims, property, and targets victimized and the rates of repeat victimization

- Spatial patterns of the problem

- Results from primary data collection (e.g., interviews of victims, officers, place managers, etc.)

- Conclusions of all the specific analysis results that include a discussion of how the various findings support or refute the hypotheses that were developed at the beginning of the analysis

- Recommendations for responses based on recommendations by the POP guides (e.g., increased lighting, focus on crime prevention campaign) and the analysis results (e.g., focus in a particular part of the city and on particular victims at a particular time)

Obviously, a problem analysis product that covers every one of these areas would be quite comprehensive. Often in crime analysis, however, the focus is on one aspect of a problem (with one or two hypotheses), and the resulting analysis statements and products are also narrowly focused. No rules exist to help crime analysts determine which of their findings are most important and interesting; to make such decisions, they need to consider both the purposes of their analyses (hypotheses) and the audiences for the resulting information. They often do not do this by themselves but have assistance from key police personnel working with them on the problem. In determining which of the analysis findings should be communicated to others, crime analysts should keep the following guidelines in mind:

- The methods and analysis are only as good as the data used. Analysts need to acknowledge any weaknesses of the data (whether in quality or quantity) in order to provide information about what the results do and do not reveal about the problems analyzed, as well as to make recommendations for improving data quality.

- In strategic crime analysis particularly, the amounts of data analyzed must be adequate in terms of both the total number of cases and amount of time (no less than 12 months' worth of data to analyze long-term problems) and the counts of individual categories (e.g., it is difficult to conduct a substantive analysis of homicide with counts of between zero and 10 per year). If they have conducted their analyses with only small amounts of data, analysts should acknowledge this and interpret their results with caution.

- There are many different ways to show information that can serve different purposes. Adjusting how findings are presented is part of the analysis process; however, analysts should be careful never to make up data or use their data to misrepresent the fact or "lie" for any reason.

- Analysts should keep the audiences for their findings in mind when choosing their analysis methods and deciding on the level of complexity to offer in their products. The analyst's best choice for communicating the findings effectively may not be to present large tables and statistical formulas but to present charts, graphs, and maps that illustrate findings quickly and easily.

- When the issues under examination are simple or subjective, analysts need not use complex methods or statistics. For addressing such issues, critical thinking and simple analysis of thoughtfully collected data can be much more effective than more complicated statistical methods.

The products that result from strategic crime analysts' work vary widely in length and style because the purposes of the analyses and the audiences for their findings also vary. Products can range from a three-slide presentation file containing the overview of a problem apartment community location to a 50-slide in-depth presentation on a compound problem of auto theft in an entire city. Dr. Jerry Ratcliffe has developed 10 tips for creating PowerPoint presentations to assist crime analysts with presenting their information effectively (Ratcliffe, 2011). The following is a summary of Ratcliffe's 10 tips:

1. Use a dark background and light text, not the reverse.

2. Use simple titles and bullet points, not long phrases and sentences.

3. Use fairly large and simple fonts.

4. Limit the number of bullets on a slide to about five.

5. Do not include distracting animation.

6. "Don't rely on the spel chequer."

7. Do not include unnecessary or extremely technical detail.

8. Maps, charts, and graphs should be simple and never have more than about five pieces or components.

9. Formatting and level of description should be consistent across slides.

10. The last slide should be the title slide or a black screen.

Strategic Crime Analysis Products

The results of strategic crime analysis can be presented in a wide array of formats, given the range of analysis techniques available and the many levels on which problems are examined. Although overall formats vary, a number of basic guidelines apply to the general content of analysis products as well as to the appearance and content of the tables, charts, and maps included in these products. This section discusses the general types and elements of strategic crime analysis products.

Types of Products

The types of products that result from strategic crime analysis include the following:

- *Memos:* The results of simpler queries or analyses are often sent in the form of memos that include text describing the analyses along with attached tables, charts, and maps as appropriate.

- *Monthly/quarterly products:* These products contain charts, tables, and maps as appropriate and are produced regularly. They can be distributed on paper through intradepartmental channels or electronically through e-mail or postings on intranet sites. Typically, they provide descriptive statistics on crime, calls, and traffic crashes for particular areas of the city, in addition to explaining notable findings within the results.

- *Annual products:* These yearly products present analysts' conclusions based on descriptive statistics for the entire jurisdiction for the preceding year and comparison of the data with previous years. Most annual products focus on crime, arrests, and clearances, but some also include information about calls for service, domestic violence incidents, traffic crashes, hate crimes, and so on, as well as results of citizen surveys. In some cases, rather than standing alone, annual products are included in general police agency annual reports, which present overall information about agencies.

- *Special products:* These products typically present the findings of analyses that were initiated in response to requests for information from particular levels or divisions of a police agency. A special product usually focuses on a specific location or problem activity. Examples include an analysis of the calls for service and crime at a local retail location over the past year, an examination of theft from vehicles in Beat 12 over the past 2 years, and an analysis of false burglar alarm calls for service.

- *Research, evaluation, and problem products:* These products tend to be fairly lengthy and complex and written with a word processor for electronic or paper publication. They generally include reviews of the literature on the problems or topics analyzed (e.g., assaults at bars, evaluation of photo radar, staffing analysis), discussion of the analyses of secondary and primary data, presentation of findings, and recommendations based on the findings. Evaluation products also include descriptions of the programs evaluated and conclusions concerning the programs' effectiveness.

Using E-Mail for Dissemination

Many crime analysts disseminate their products through e-mails to the entire agency. Because crime analysts disseminate their own products, information on behalf of other internal police personnel, and products from other police agencies, fusion centers, and federal agencies, police personnel often receive a lot of e-mails from crime analysts. This can be a problem for the analysts' "customers" who may not have the time or inclination to sort through and determine what is important, which can result in an "overload" of crime analysis information.

Importantly, not all the information that is distributed by crime analysts is useful or necessary for everyone who may receive it, so after a while, individuals may start deleting e-mails sent by the crime analysts instead of reading each one to determine which is relevant for them. To resolve this problem, some analysts set up different e-mail distribution lists for different products and information, but this can be cumbersome when personnel are moved to different job assignments, get promoted, or there is a shift change in patrol (i.e., patrol officers move to different shifts en masse).

A key problem with e-mailing information is that once the e-mail is deleted from the person's inbox, he or she may not easily find it and may have to ask the analyst to send it again. Some people do not organize their e-mails very well or download information to their computers because of the increasing use of the smartphone to check e-mail. In addition, information pasted directly into an e-mail and attachments with full color products with images cannot be seen well on smartphones or can be too large to e-mail at all. Sharing videos is even more difficult through e-mail, and using public media through a web link (e.g., YouTube) for dissemination is not preferable for police agencies because of its lack of security.

To solve this problem, analysts have begun using an intranet software communication system (i.e., agency management systems discussed in Chapter 5) to post important information products for individuals to access themselves. Such a system allows for archiving old products as well as searching them. Oftentimes, crime analysts organize their products by districts, divisions (patrol vs. investigations), crime type, and/or by level of activity (short-term or long-term) so that individuals can go directly to the information they need.

Yet e-mail can be an effective communication medium in many cases, but crime analysts must be strategic in their use of e-mail to ensure their customers are not "overloaded." If there are fewer e-mails sent by crime analysts that contain information that individuals need or should read, then the crime analyst's e-mail communication will be much more effective. The following are some guidelines that analysts use to decide whether to use e-mail or to use an agency management system to disseminate crime analysis products and information:

Crime analysts should use e-mail

- For anything that is the equivalent to an official departmental memo.

- For requesting information from a group of people that can be provided to the crime analyst by simply replying to the e-mail.

- To notify a large group of people where they can find information on an agency management system. However, a notification should not be necessary every time a regular product is published. For example, if the same product comes out every Monday at 10:00 a.m., once people are made aware of this, an e-mail is not necessary to remind them every week. E-mails such as these should be sent out sparingly and primarily when the product is introduced and new.

- For sending information to one person or a small group of people fulfilling a one-time specific request.

Crime analysts should use an agency management system

- For any regularly produced crime analysis product, whether it is produced daily, weekly, monthly, or even yearly for a few or many people.

- For crime analysis request policies, procedures, and explanations of crime analysis services and the purpose and components of crime analysis products (i.e., an explanation for the time of day/day of week chart might be posted separate from the actual products because some individuals struggle to understand it the first time they see it). These are types of things crime analysts disseminate to "market" what the unit can do.

- For providing products to a large number of people, even if only one time. Send an e-mail to let them know where it is. If they need it, they will go and get it.

- To organize products into categories for easy access and querying.

- To archive products for future access and querying.

Consequently, crime analysts should look at the files on their own computers as a "personal library" and the agency management system as the "public library." Not all that is in the personal library needs to be in the public library, but anything that is useful or provided to others should be public.

Guidelines for Product Contents

The many different formats that police agencies and individual analysts use in producing various kinds of products are often dictated by the experience and personal preferences of the people who create the products. All strategic crime analysis products, no matter the format, include the following elements:

- *Title:* The product title (or in the case of a memo, the "Re:" line) should include information about (a) the nature of the data, (b) the unit of geography on which the product focuses, and (c) the date range analyzed. For example, "Citizen-Generated Calls for Service in District 3: January

1, 2017, Through December 31, 2017" or "Commercial Burglary in the Downtown Beat: 2015–2017."

- *Tables, graphs, and maps:* The tables, charts, and maps that appear in a product reflect the specific analysis techniques used. As noted previously, the final product need not include every map and table produced during analysis; rather, only those should appear that illustrate important and interesting findings or that are useful for helping audiences understand the analysis.

- *Analysis findings:* The findings can be written in paragraph form or as bullets in a presentation. They should provide a synthesis and interpretation of the analysis and highlight important and interesting findings. In some cases, it may include information about tables and statistics that are not shown in the product but are only written up (e.g., 45% of the addresses account for 95% of the robberies). It is important for a product to provide more than just lists of data and tables of frequencies. At the same time, the findings should not be long and drawn out, but should be short, to the point, and meaningful to the audience.

- *Disclaimers:* The product should include clear statements detailing any limitations of the data and analysis techniques. For example: "Conclusions drawn from any product containing crime information are based only on data about crimes known to the police, not all crime"; "Crime per population figures may not account for all the differences among areas in the city"; "Juvenile arrest statistics do not indicate all the crimes committed by juveniles, only those crimes for which juveniles are arrested."

- *Recommendations:* The product should offer suggestions for improvement of data quality, areas for future analysis, or actions based on the analysis results. For example, "It is recommended that additional information on auto theft recovery be included in the recovery report to enable determination of why the auto theft occurred"; "It is recommended that the department provide crime prevention information to beauty salons and daycare centers, given that such locations have been victimized repeatedly over the past year."

- *Credits/date:* The name or division of the individual(s) who created the product and the date it was created should appear on the product so that anyone with questions can direct them to the appropriate person(s). An author credit also encourages recognition for the creator of the product. Examples of credit and date information: "Prepared by Crime Analysis Unit, December 2016"; "Prepared by Jane Doe, 01/06/17."

Guidelines for Table and Chart Contents

The tables and charts that appear in crime analysis product should be formatted consistently to enable comparisons among them. Also, because information from products is copied and pasted into other documents and/or presented in pieces, each table and chart in a product needs to be descriptive enough to stand alone. For example, what does Figure 15.1 show? It is a frequency of UCR crime for 2016 and 2017, but what types of crime, what type of statistic, and where? Although this chart may have been described in depth in the product it originally appeared in, by itself it is unclear.

Each table and chart in a crime analysis product should include the following elements:

- *Title:* As in the title of a product, the title of a table or chart should include information about the nature of the data, the unit of geography, and the date range of the analysis. This is important because tables and charts often show only parts of the analysis.

- *Labels:* All rows and columns of a table should be labeled, as should the *x*- and *y*-axes of a chart. Different colors, formatting, or additional text may be used to highlight interesting results or key features, but labels should be used in moderation and only where appropriate and readable within the table or chart.

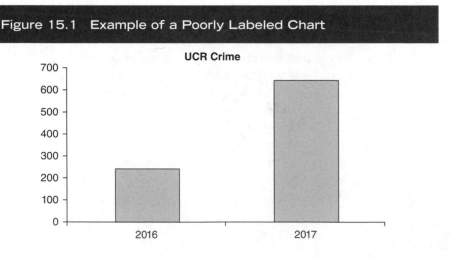

Figure 15.1   Example of a Poorly Labeled Chart

- *Credits/date:* The name or division of the individual(s) who produced the table or graph should appear on the table or graph itself, along with the date the item was created.

Table 15.1 is an example of a properly formatted and labeled table; it shows the frequency and percentage change of Part I crime in District 4. Notice that it provides (in a note at the bottom) additional information that may indicate a reason for the significant drop in crime in Beat 40. Figure 15.2, an example of correct formatting and labeling, depicts the data from Table 15.1 but provides additional information on the types of crime that are considered Part I crime and indicates the largest decrease in crime.

In creating tables and charts, analysts must make decisions about what information to include and highlight based on the audiences for their products. For example, if the audience for a product is police officers and other crime analysts, it would not be necessary to include a definition of Part I crime, whereas such a definition would be useful to an audience of laypersons. Another issue in the formatting of charts is the amount of space available. In the example in Figure 15.2, additional information is contained within the boundaries of the chart; however, if there is room in the product to devote an entire page to this chart, the analyst might include this type of information on the page but outside the boundaries of the chart, making the chart itself less cluttered.

Guidelines for Map Contents

Because maps differ substantively from other strategic crime analysis products, and strategic maps differ from tactical maps, analysts need to follow a different set of guidelines concerning their contents. To be understandable on their own, maps created for strategic crime analysis should include the following elements:

Table 15.1   Example of a Correctly Formatted and Labeled Table

Frequency and Comparison of Part I Crime in District 4, 2016–2017

	2016	2017	Actual Difference	Percentage of Change
Beat 40	253	164	–89	–35.18%*
Beat 41	261	275	14	5.36%
Beat 42	278	210	–68	–24.46%
Beat 43	285	301	16	5.61%
Beat 44	322	354	32	9.94%

* Hilldale Mall opened in 2016. Created by Jane Doe, Crime Analysis Unit, February 25, 2018.

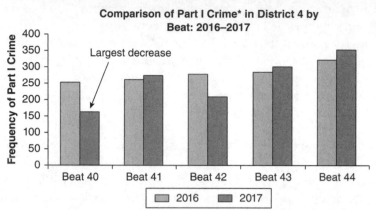

Comparison of Part I Crime* in District 4 by
Beat: 2016–2017

* Part I crime includes homicide, rape, robbery, aggravated assault,
burglary, larceny, auto theft, and arson.

Source: Created by Jane Doe, Crime Analysis Unit, February 25, 2018.

- *Title:* Like the title of a full product or a table, the title of a map should include information on the nature of the data, the unit of geography, and the date range of the analysis. This is important because maps within products often illustrate only subsets of the full data.

- *Legend:* The legend should list the tabular and geographic data sources displayed in the map in addition to indicating the symbols that are used to represent each data source. In a map that includes graduation by color or size, the legend should also state the classification used so that the audience knows what technique was used to create the map, which is the heart of that type of analysis. For example, "Classification = Custom" or "Natural Breaks Classification."

- *Geocoding or address match percentage:* As with statistics and tables that are presented in social sciences, the amount of data that have not been geocoded or matched to addresses on the map (e.g., missing data) should be noted. This is displayed as a percentage, such as "Geocoded Addresses = 99%" or "5% of Addresses Not Matched." Even if the incidents are located on the map with *x* and *y* coordinates, the analyst should indicate if some of the cases are not included for some reason.

- *Labels:* Text can be used to label key features of a map, such as streets and landmarks, as well as to highlight interesting findings on the map itself (see Figure 15.3 for an example). However, labels should be used in moderation and only where appropriate and readable within the map.

- *Scale bar:* This element illustrates the distance units used in the map. Note that the circle and radius that are recommended for crime pattern bulletin maps are not recommended for strategic maps.

- **North directional:** This element indicates the geographic orientation of the map. Normally, north is at the top of the page, but that is not always the case.

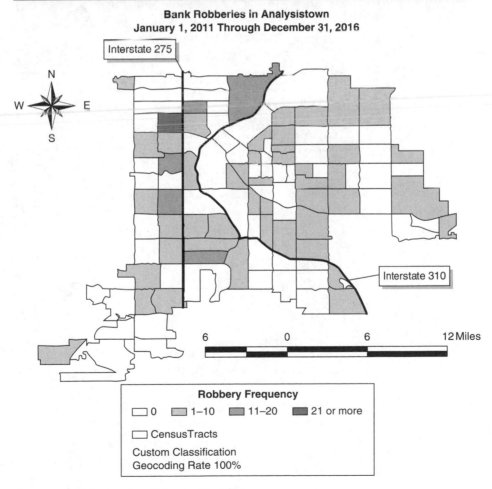

Figure 15.3 Example of a Correctly Formatted and Labeled Map

Bank Robberies in Analysistown
January 1, 2011 Through December 31, 2016

Interstate 275

Interstate 310

6   0   6   12 Miles

Robbery Frequency

☐ 0   ■ 1–10   ■ 11–20   ■ 21 or more

☐ CensusTracts

Custom Classification
Geocoding Rate 100%

Source: Created by Jane Doe February 11, 2017

- *Credits/date:* The name or division of the individual(s) who produced the map should appear on the map itself, along with the date the map was created. This is important because in some cases the maps in a product are created by someone other than the author(s) of the rest of the product.

Practical Examples

For this edition of the book, current practical examples of a variety of information and analysis products are provided on **http://www.sagepub.com/ bobasantos4e**. They cover all types of information and analysis products and have been created by a wide range of working crime analysts from the United States. However, not all products represent the best or the worst formatting and content, so students should look at each one critically to determine their strengths and weaknesses based on the content discussed in this chapter.

SUMMARY POINTS

This chapter discusses the various types of products strategic crime analysts produce, as well as how they select their most important and interesting analysis findings for dissemination. The chapter also presents guidelines concerning the elements that should be included in products as a whole and in individual tables, charts, and maps. The following are the key points addressed in this chapter:

- Crime analysts must apply critical thinking and judgment in determining which of their findings are important and interesting enough for dissemination.

- There are two stages of reporting for the scanning and analysis steps of the problem-solving process. The first is reporting the initial descriptive analysis from the scanning process; the second is reporting the analysis findings, conclusions, and recommendations for responses.

- The initial analysis merely describes who, what, when, where, and how the problem is occurring but does not seek to understand why the problem is occurring.

- The results of the analysis step of the problem-solving process contain three main areas of information: (1) the specific analysis results about the problem both from national research and the local findings, (2) conclusions about the hypotheses, and (3) recommendations for responses based on the research and analysis conclusions.

- As a general rule, a product on the findings of a problem analysis includes information on the following topics: the context of the city and jurisdiction, the data used, other research findings about the problem, the nature of the local problem, changes in the problem over time, temporal and spatial patterns, the types of offenders/victims/targets victimized and the rates of repeat victimization, results from primary data collection, conclusions of all the specific analysis results, and recommendations for responses.

- When determining which analysis findings are important enough for dissemination, analysts should consider the following: (a) The methods and analysis are only as good as the data, (b) analysis should be conducted with an adequate amount of data, (c) analysts must never make up data or use the data to "lie" for any reason, (d) analysts should select analysis methods and the formats they use to report findings with the audience for the findings in mind, and (e) analysis of simple or subjective issues does not always require the use of complex methods or statistics.

- Crime analysts should use e-mail for anything that is the equivalent to an official departmental memo; for requesting information from a group of people; to notify a large group of people where they can find information on an agency management system; and for sending information to one person or a small group of people, fulfilling a one-time specific request.

- Crime analysts should use an agency management system for any regularly produced crime analysis product; to market the services and capabilities of the crime analysis unit; to provide products to a large number of people; and organize and archive products.

- Crime analysts should look at the files on their own computers as a "personal library" and the agency management system as the "public library."

- Strategic crime analysis products include memos; monthly/quarterly products and maps; annual products; special products; and research, evaluation, and problem products.

- Every strategic crime analysis product should include the following basic elements: title; tables, graphics, or maps; analysis findings; disclaimers; recommendations; credits; and date of creation.

- Every table and chart that appears in a strategic crime analysis product should include the following basic elements: title, labels, credits, and date of creation.

- Every map that appears in an strategic crime analysis product should include the following basic elements: title, legend, geocoding or address match percentage, labels, scale bar, north directional, credits, and date of creation.

DISCUSSION EXERCISES* ——————————————

Exercise 1

Examine the following chart and table, checking for the components recommended in this chapter. List what the charts contain and what, if anything, is missing.

Exercise 15.1a

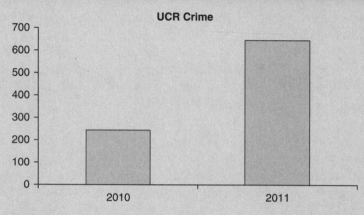

Source: Fort Pierce (Florida) Police Department, April Lee.

Exercise 15.1b

Citizen Generated: Animal Control 2017 Final Call Disposition by Type	
Ending Disposition	Freq
Stray animal picked up/Impounded	570
Case followed up by animal control	470
Stray animal gone on arrival	464
Trap set	421
Wildlife picked up	376
Animal dropped off at shelter	260
Animal DOA—called proper authority	239
Trap picked up	189
Animal control handled by phone	178
Not a law enforcement problem	163
Returned animal to owner	160
Information given	119

Citizen Generated: Animal Control 2017 Final Call Disposition by Type	
Ending Disposition	Freq
Picked up injured or sick animal	117
Stray animal loose/Couldn't catch	108
Incident verified/Gone on arrival	103
Unable to locate, complete, or verify	98
Animal control left door hanger	92
Unfounded	75
Trap checked	74
No disposition recorded	61
Report will be written	52
Animal control gave verbal warning	52
Animal control gave written warning	50
All other dispositions	294
02/09/2011 Command Meeting: 2010 Calls-for-Service Analysis	

Source: Fort Pierce (Florida) Police Department, April Lee.

Exercise 2

Examine the following two maps, checking for the map components recommended in this chapter. List what the maps contain and what, if anything, is missing.

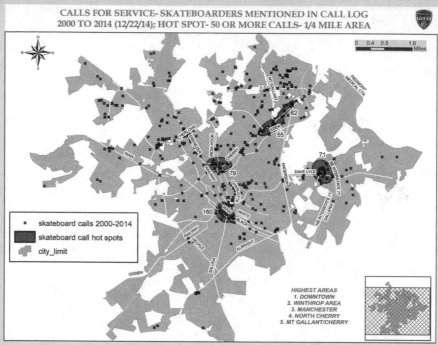

Source: Rockhill (South Carolina) Police Department, Damien Williams.

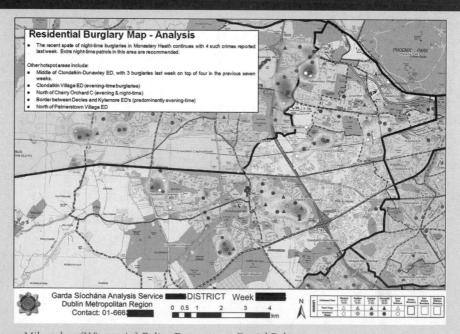

Source: Milwaukee (Wisconsin) Police Department, Daniel Polans.

Administrative Crime Analysis

Part V contains only one chapter, as the previous editions' discussion of the future of crime analysis has been moved to Chapter 1. To review from Chapter 4, the IACA (2014) defines administrative crime analysis as "analysis directed towards the administrative needs of the police agency, its government, and its community" (p. 7). Where tactical and strategic crime analysis are concerned with supporting crime prevention, crime reduction, and problem-solving activities of the agency, administrative crime analysis supports the internal operations of the organization as well as a police department's interactions with the community and other government entities.

Administrative crime analysis covers a wide range of techniques and processes that could be the subject of an entire textbook. As discussed in Chapter 4, these include accountability analysis, districting and redistricting analysis, patrol staffing analysis, community-focused analysis, and cost-benefit analysis, as well as support for grants and media requests. Because the majority of the techniques and processes discussed for tactical and strategic crime analysis focus on assisting police in their crime reduction work, the final chapter of the book will zero in on the aspect of administrative analysis that supports crime reduction as well—crime analysis for accountability.

Administrative Crime Analysis

Crime Analysis for Accountability

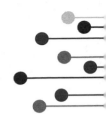

T his chapter covers crime analysis products that assist police agencies in their crime reduction accountability processes and meetings (i.e., Compstat and Compstat-like programs). As discussed in Chapter 3, crime analysis plays a significant role in crime reduction accountability processes. More specifically, crime analysts assist with the development and measurement of crime reduction goals, provide regular products to monitor the success of short- and long-term crime reduction activities, assess whether the crime reduction efforts are effective, and determine whether the crime reduction goals are being met.

The content in this chapter has been adapted from Boba and Santos (2011) and covers the following topics: 1) a brief discussion of crime reduction accountability to provide context of the role of crime analysis, 2) crime reduction goal development, 3) crime analysis for weekly action-oriented meetings, 4) crime analysis for monthly evaluation-oriented meetings, and 5) crime analysis for assessment of crime reduction goals.

There are many different crime analysis techniques, statistics, and final products that can be created for accountability that range from very simple to very complex. In administrative crime analysis, just as in tactical and strategic crime analysis, it is important to balance using difficult and complex analysis techniques with providing products that are relevant and helpful to police personnel and decision-makers. Based on my work since 1994 with police agencies in implementing effective accountability practices, I have carefully selected specific accountability products and techniques from the wealth of potential products to present in this chapter. Hundreds of analysts and police agencies have used these products and techniques successfully, so a crime analyst who starts with these accountability products will serve the police department well.

INTERNATIONAL CRIME ANALYST PERSPECTIVE

Tyr Steffensen

Law Enforcement Analyst

Oslo Police District

Oslo, Norway

Station command tasked the CAU with the following: "If we were to change the boundaries inside our district at the station level based on the current distribution of crime types, what

(Continued)

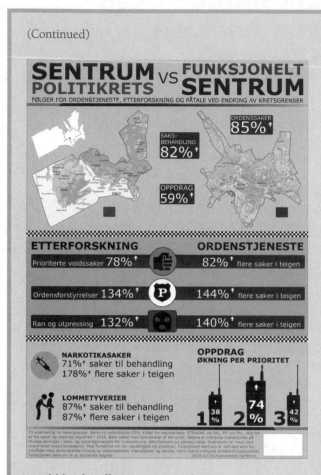

our RMS for two sets of data, both comprised of assaults, robberies, disturbances of the peace, pickpocketing, and narcotics cases. One query returned the set of cases the stations had investigated; the other, the set of cases that had taken place inside the current boundaries, regardless of where those cases had been investigated. We then contrasted these data sets with suggested boundaries based on city geography and the current concentration of crime types in the downtown area of Oslo. We also counted calls for service originating inside the different areas, sorted by three levels of severity, and illustrated the potential increase. We chose to present our data in an infographic-style poster. The product served as a reality check and provided a unified situational awareness for command going forward in the redistricting process.

would be the effect on our case load for investigation, as well as the number of incidents the uniformed division would have to handle?" We queried

Crime Reduction Accountability

In this book, **accountability** refers to the process by which police personnel are held responsible for implementing strategies to reduce crime and disorder in the community. The underlying theme of accountability for crime reduction is that individuals, units, and divisions within a police agency must take responsibility for implementing crime reduction strategies beyond answering calls for service and investigating crimes. As discussed in Chapter 3, the trend for police departments to have a formalized structure of accountability for facilitating crime reduction began in 1994 with the New York Police Department's (NYPD) Compstat program. What started as a program in one department has become a standard practice within many police departments around the world; however, most do not follow NYPD's model but have adapted it to their own needs. In the last decade, stratified policing (Santos & Santos, 2015b) has expanded and specified the framework of Compstat to stratify accountability by the different types of problems and ranks within the police organization. Consequently, the discussion of accountability in this chapter will also be stratified to address crime analysis products for different purposes.

Crime reduction accountability processes in a police organization center on creating realistic expectations, documenting the crime reduction activities, systematically reviewing the progress of crime reduction activities, and evaluating the success of crime reduction efforts at each level. An accountability process ensures that the entire organization implements and maintains crime reduction efforts consistently and effectively. The role of crime analysis in the accountability structure is significant. Crime analysts create routine products that are used to identify problems and direct resources, hold managers accountable for their effectiveness in reducing crime, and determine the effectiveness of the organization as a whole in reducing crime and disorder.

In both Compstat and stratified policing, regularly scheduled meetings make up the formal structure police departments create to facilitate their accountability process. Each type of meeting includes a standard list of attendees, a consistent agenda, and standardized crime analysis products. For Compstat, meetings might be once or twice a week, once every 2 weeks, or once a month. For stratified policing, there is a defined structure of three types of meetings—daily, once a week, and once a month—all of which are implemented in concert with one another.

Importantly, not only does accountability occur during these meetings, but it is also when crime reduction activities are evaluated. Crime analysts play a central role in preparing the products and presentations that are used to monitor and assess crime reduction efforts. While the previous chapters discussed specific products used to *direct* crime prevention and crime reduction efforts of police, this chapter covers the specific products that are created to *ensure* people are implementing strategies correctly and to *assess* whether their efforts are working.

Each type of accountability meeting is different in its purpose, in the types of crime reduction activities that are discussed, and in the rank and type of personnel who attend. Daily and weekly meetings are action oriented because they are used to ensure that police personnel are responding (i.e., the "action") immediately, collaboratively, and appropriately. Monthly meetings are evaluation oriented because they are used to assess the overall effectiveness of short-term crime reduction as well as the progress and effectiveness of long-term crime reduction efforts. The following is a brief description of each type of meeting:

- *Daily accountability meetings* facilitate action-oriented accountability for strategies implemented for immediate and short-term activity. The primary type of daily meeting is the "shift briefing" in which supervisors give patrol officers their crime reduction "mission" for that day based on crime analysis.

- *Weekly accountability meetings* facilitate action-oriented accountability within and/or among divisions (e.g., patrol, investigations, crime prevention, and media relations) so that police employees can come together to develop, coordinate, and assess strategies implemented for short-term activity. The main focus of weekly meetings is on patterns, as they require a coordinated response. These meetings are used for district commanders to "report out" what they are doing and for their bosses to ensure they are implementing the right number and type of responses, as well as decide whether the responses are working.

- *Monthly accountability meetings* facilitate evaluation-oriented accountability within patrol districts and investigations, as well as across the entire police department. Patrol and criminal investigations commanders are held accountable for their specific geographic area or division by the police chief. The meetings are used to discuss whether all short-term crime reduction activities are effective rather than if responses to individual patterns are effective. That is, the discussion is focused on the combined responses to all patterns to determine if crime is going down and/or are there fewer patterns emerging. The meetings are also used to discuss whether long-term problems are emerging from unresolved short-term problems (e.g., residential burglary patterns are occurring in a neighborhood month after month) and to monitor the progress of ongoing long-term crime reduction strategies (e.g., determining whether implementing crime prevention through environmental design (CPTED) in an apartment community has reduced crime and disorder incidents). In addition, every 12 months the monthly meeting is used for evaluation-oriented accountability for all types of activity at the broadest level. That is, long-term trends of crime and disorder based on the crime reduction goals are examined to determine if all the efforts are making a difference, whether adjustments need to be made, and/or if new crime reduction goals need to be defined.

Crime Reduction Goal Development

Before accountability can be carried out, the police department must have a common purpose and goals for its crime reduction activities so that individuals know what they are expected to do. Instead of a police chief just saying, "We will reduce crime," formalized crime reduction goals are used to guide personnel and to provide specific measures to assess the agency's success in reducing crime and disorder. These goals are different than goals and objectives traditionally formulated in police organizations for a 3-to-5-year strategic plan that address the overall growth of the organization, how many officers will be needed, new units and/or divisions, and equipment needs.

To make sure that crime reduction goals are actionable and relevant in the day-to-day operations of the police department, each goal's outcome is specified, along with its success indicators, baseline and target measurements, strategies, and measurements of performance. Importantly, the outcomes, strategies, and outputs are differentiated in order to assess both the process (i.e., whether strategies were implemented correctly) and impact (i.e., whether the strategies decreased crime), as discussed in Chapter 12.

While crime analysts should not be responsible for developing crime reduction goals on their own, they will serve an important role by providing the department's leaders analysis results that help them to decide which crimes and types of disorder to select as goals, what the indicators and targets should be, and what level of reduction the agency should try to achieve. The following are descriptions of each component and the role of the crime analyst:

- **Crime reduction goal**: This is the desired outcome and is generally stated. It denotes a specific type of activity (e.g., violent crime, burglary, disorder) as well as the geographic area (e.g., countywide, citywide, district, beat). Most likely, very large and/or diverse jurisdictions will develop goals for geographic regions separately. The crime analyst would provide trend analysis for several years of different types and subtypes of crime and disorder for the entire jurisdiction and by geographic area to support initial goal development.

- **Success indicator (i.e., outcome)**: This component specifies the type of activity that is used to measure the impact of the crime reduction strategies. The purpose of this component is to denote the specific measurement relevant to the crime reduction goal. The crime analysts would make suggestions for these measures as the "data expert" of the police department, knowing that using general measurements such as Uniform Crime Report (UCR) Part I Crime categories can mask changes in the specific crimes that are being addressed. For example, instead of using all UCR Part I violent crime (homicide, rape, robbery, and aggravated assault) to measure a goal to reduce violent crime, the success indicator measures specific types of violent crime that the agency has identified as concerns, such as non-domestic aggravated assault and street robbery. Similarly, instead of using data for all burglaries to measure a goal pertaining to property crime and burglary, the success indicator can measure residential or commercial burglary separately, or even more specifically, it can measure residential burglary at single-family homes versus multi-family homes (i.e., apartments).

The success indicator also specifies the level of desired success. This is normally depicted as the percentage of decrease in the type of activity (e.g., a 10% decrease). The percentage of value is developed based on historical trends of the activity, the number of police resources available, and a qualitative decision by the police department's leaders based on their knowledge and experience about what is a realistic crime reduction goal. The trend analysis conducted by the crime analyst would provide insight to what is a realistic goal for the coming year. Lastly, in some cases, geographic areas might be specified within the success indicator, which is different than specifying the geographic area in the entire goal statement. The geographic area within a success indicator means that even though the overall goal may be for the entire jurisdiction, the responses are to be prioritized in a particular area. Or it can mean that even though the goal may be for one precinct within a large jurisdiction, the responses will be prioritized in a particular beat. This too would be informed by crime analysis that identifies which area has the highest number of a specific crime or is at highest risk for a potential increase.

- **Baseline**: This is the initial measurement of the success indicator. The actual value is listed, as well as the time period under consideration and the method of computation. The measurement can reflect frequency or counts of a year of data, or it can reflect a rate or an average over several years. This would depend on the data that is available and the nature of the activity. The crime analyst leads the development of the baseline measure and identifies these numbers through the trend analysis conducted for the previous components.

- **Target**: This is the desired level of success (i.e., reduction of crime) and is computed based on the percentage indicated in the success indicator and the baseline measurement. It is typically computed for 1 year, which is the evaluation period of the crime reduction goal. The crime analyst very easily computes the target once the previous components are designated.

- **Strategies**: The strategies listed here for each crime reduction goal address crime reduction efforts that the police department will implement simultaneously at each level of the organization. That is, a crime reduction goal is selected because it is important to the police department and the jurisdiction; thus, the crime or disorder is addressed at immediate, short-term, and long-term levels. Because there are different strategies that are effective at different levels, this component designates what specific responses will be systematically implemented at each level. The crime analysts have a small role in choosing the strategies, but they may assist by providing insight about evidence-based policing research—for example, the information provided in Chapter 3.

- **Performance indicators (i.e., outputs)**: These elements specify the activity to be measured and are developed based on the strategies outlined in the previous component. Examples include patrol officer activity, such as hours of directed patrol, as well as the number of arrests and cleared cases, which are measures of strategies used to address crime patterns. They also include rate of success in addressing specific types of problems, such as percentage of patterns and problem locations that were resolved successfully, and an analysis of the operational costs of implementing particular responses, such as overtime pay for officers and equipment purchases. The crime analyst would work with the leadership to decide the best measures for each strategy and data availability. That is, some things may not be currently tracked, and new data may need to be collected. Recall the "data modification subcycle" described in Chapter 4.

Table 16.1 is an example of a crime reduction goal and its components. Because crime reduction goals are broad in nature and may be broken down to multiple categories within the success indicator, an agency should have between three and five goals a year, but not many more.

When crime reduction goals are formulated, resulting in the implementation of crime reduction strategies, the crime analyst conducts tactical and strategic crime analysis to guide and support the department, using the techniques and products discussed in the book thus far. The rest of the chapter covers additional crime analysis products created specifically for accountability in weekly and monthly meetings; they are based on the same techniques just discussed but have different uses.

Crime Analysis for Weekly Action-Oriented Accountability Meetings

Crime analysts should not spend time creating products for weekly meetings that show weekly or monthly crime or disorder counts. Because accountability in weekly meetings is action oriented, weekly statistics are not necessary because they do not direct short-term responses. Thus, most of the crime analysis results that are discussed in weekly meetings have already been produced as part of tactical crime analysis (i.e., repeat incident reports and crime pattern bulletins)—another reason why weekly statistics are not necessary.

For example, the weekly repeat incident reports discussed in Chapter 8 are used to identify locations for response. These same weekly products are also used to determine whether responses are effective since the product always includes the last 28 days of calls for service. Thus, if a location was responded

Table 16.1 Example of Crime Reduction Goal Components

Parameter	Goal: Violent Crime
Goal	Reduce violent crime throughout the jurisdiction
Success indicator (outcomes)	Reduce non-domestic aggravated assault and street robbery by 10% (focus on District 1 and District 2)
Baseline	Non-domestic aggravated assaults: 550 Street robbery: 450 Baseline time period: Jan–Dec 2016
Target	Non-domestic aggravated assault: [550 * .90 =] 495 Street robbery: [450 * .90 =] 445 Target date: Jan–Dec 2017
Strategies	Identify and respond to patterns (short-term) Identify and respond to problem areas (long-term) Identify and address repeat offenders
Performance indicator (outputs)	Number of patterns responded to and number resolved Number of problem areas responded to and crime reduced Number of repeat burglary offenders responded to Number of directed patrol hours in patterns and problem areas Number of arrests and clearances Number of known offenders contacted Cost analysis of responses deployed

to one week, the next week's product would be used to determine if the response was effective (i.e., no more calls at that location in 2 weeks). So a separate accountability product is not necessary for repeat incidents because the information from the original product can be used for responding as well as for accountability.

In addition, because crime analysts are constantly updating crime pattern bulletins as new crimes happen, the bulletins themselves tell police leaders whether the responses are being effective (e.g., no more crime in the pattern for 2 weeks would be considered a success). Recall the process of numbering and dating crime pattern bulletins from Chapter 11. Thus, no new statistics are needed to determine whether responses to a particular pattern are working. However, the crime analyst would create a weekly product for pattern accountability that includes statistics on the listed performance measures for the pattern responses to be discussed. This information would be gathered both by the crime analyst and individual patrol managers or with software that tracks crime reduction responses (e.g., an agency management system as discussed in Chapter 11). Table 16.2 shows responses implemented for four active patterns to be discussed in the weekly meeting.

Looking at the table, we can see that pattern 35E has been updated five times (see Chapter 11 for a review of bulletin numbering) with 11 additional crimes and that it has been active for 45 days. We also see that there have been significant resources (e.g., 200 directed patrol hours) expended in response to the pattern. Because crime is still occurring, the action-oriented accountability would likely be to continue the response. Pattern 36, on the other hand, has had no more crimes in 14 days. Typically, 2 or 3 weeks without additional crimes is recommended as a successful response to patterns, so a decision to discontinue response and note it as a success would likely be made by police leaders. Lastly, Pattern 38B has been updated twice and has had five additional crimes in 20 days. It has the fewest responses of any of the four patterns, which would likely prompt the patrol bureau commander to ask the district captain responsible for the pattern why more resources have not been expended since crime is continuing. There might be a good reason for the discrepancy, but by creating this table and comparing the response levels of the active patterns, the police leaders can ensure that resources are being used wisely and appropriately, make changes immediately, if necessary, and recognize successful efforts.

A similar type of product may be created for repeat incidents; however, the responses to those problems tend to be more varied, so a more creative way of measuring the level of response would need to be developed based on the nature of the repeat incidents addressed. For example, domestic violence repeat incident response data might include hours of contact with the family, types and number of referrals made for social services, arrests, restraining orders, and so on. In summary, because crime analysts are conducting action-oriented products every day, there are only a handful of products that would be created specifically for a weekly accountability meeting and would focus on response,

Table 16.2 Response Statistics by Pattern									
Bulletin #	**Days Active**	**Additional Crimes**	**Directed Patrol Hours**	**FI Cards Taken**	**Known Offenders Contacted**	**Reverse 911**	**Potential Victim Contacts**	**Arrests**	**Clearances**
2017-35E	45	11	200	15	4	1	25	0	0
2017-36	14	0	65	3	3	1	12	2	5
2017-37A	17	3	84	10	5	1	0	0	0
2017-38B	20	5	21	0	1	0	0	0	0

not on weekly crime or calls-for-service counts and statistics. Lastly, because long-term problems require long-term responses, weekly discussions of crime analysis for accountability are not effective or realistic.

Crime Analysis for Monthly Evaluation-Oriented Accountability Meetings

On a monthly basis, accountability meetings are evaluation oriented so crime analysts examine long-term trends by month to monitor the effectiveness of responses for repeat incidents, crime patterns, and long-term problems. The purpose of a monthly evaluation is to ensure that crime reduction efforts are being consistently applied and appear to be working at all levels. For short-term activity, monthly meetings are used to monitor the overall levels of specific types of calls for service and crime addressed. Similar to how pattern bulletins that have already been created are discussed at weekly meetings, strategic analysis products previously produced that support the problem-solving process (as described in Part VI) would be discussed in monthly meetings. Monthly meetings are used to monitor short-term problems until the crime reduction goals are evaluated and long-term problems until it is decided that a full evaluation of the responses to that particular problem should take place.

Because crime counts can vary widely from month to month, crime analysis for monthly accountability focuses on examining trends instead of numerical differences or changes in percentage from month to month, year to date, or from year to year. The goal for the crime analyst is to create monthly crime analysis products that are standard, relevant, straightforward, and not unnecessarily complex or statistical. Consequently, this section provides examples of a set of products and explains how each one was created and its specific purpose in the monthly accountability process. Each product could be used to examine any number of crime and disorder types.

Crime and Disorder Monthly Trend Charts

A crime and disorder monthly trend chart is a bar chart that is created each month for the most recent 6 months compared to the same 6 months of the previous year. It contains a trend line for each time period and the percentage of change from the first to second 6-month period. The purpose of this product is to *monitor* crime reduction efforts for one type of activity over the last 6 months in comparison to the same time last year, as well as to account for seasonal changes (i.e., more crime in the summer). A police leader would use it to address any possible deficiencies with the implemented responses and to determine if further discussion and/or action was required during the following month. Working with many different police departments, I have found that 6 months is the appropriate amount of time to use for monitoring monthly trends. Longer time periods are more appropriate to evaluate crime reduction activities more fully, as will be discussed later in the chapter.

The same chart would be created for each monthly meeting, with the months changing to include the most recent 6 months (i.e., **rolling time period**). In addition, the same chart might be created for different geographic areas and for different crime and disorder activity designated in the crime reduction goals. Thus, a crime analyst may produce multiple versions of this single product for each monthly meeting.

Figure 16.1 shows a bar chart with the counts and trend lines for a "selected" crime type. We can see that while the crime counts increase and decrease each month, which is normal, the overall trends show that the 2016 6-month trend was both higher in frequency (i.e., between 150 and 200) and flat across the 6 months, while the 2017 6-month trend is lower (i.e., ranging from about 130 to 85) and is decreasing. The overall percentage of change shows that there are 39% fewer crimes in June through November 2017.

In an accountability meeting, a police leader would look on this as a positive result. However, looking at the individual bars, he or she might point out that after a decrease in each month from July to October 2017, November is higher. Leaders may hold individuals responsible for making sure this increase does not continue in the subsequent months.

A monthly trend chart is also useful to monitor on a monthly basis different types of calls for service and crime activity for each problem level and for the crime reduction goals. See the following examples:

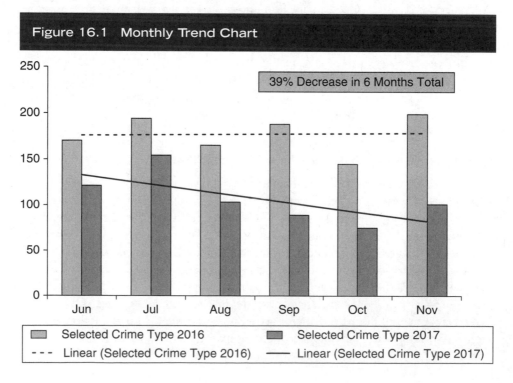

Figure 16.1 Monthly Trend Chart

- Repeat incidents: Charts for domestic violence calls for service in the entire jurisdiction and by geographic area (e.g., district) could be created to monitor the effect of the responses to domestic violence repeat incidents by district and across the jurisdiction.

- Patterns: Charts for street robbery in the entire jurisdiction and/or by geographic area could be created to monitor the effect of the response to street robbery crime patterns and incidents, as well as compare progress across geographic areas.

- Problems: A chart for apartment complex burglaries could be created to monitor the effect of responses to a specifically selected problem of burglaries in apartment complexes.

- Crime reduction goals: Using the crime reduction goal example from the beginning of the chapter, charts would be made for non-domestic, aggravated assault, and street robbery separately to monitor the goal's success indicators. These products could also be broken down into geographic areas to determine if one area was doing better or worse than the others.

The next product is a combination bar and line chart that is created each month for the most recent 6 months and includes a selected crime or disorder activity by month for the current 6 months, the previous 12 months, and an average per month for the last 5 years. The purpose of this product is to anticipate what level of activity to expect over the next 6 months based on the current 6 months, the last 12 months, and the last several years. Including an average can be helpful if the previous 12 months were unusually high or low.

Figure 16.2 includes the same data as Figure 16.1, as well as the counts of crime for June through May of the previous year and the average for each month for the previous 5 years. The chart indicates that current crime counts are lower than last year and the last 5 years. However, based on figures for the coming 6 months, the department might expect an increase in crime (i.e., note how the 2016 and 5-year averages start to increase in December), even if the overall numbers are lower than in past years. As with the previous chart, the purpose is to create a product with a straightforward interpretation to monitor trends. It is not created to systematically predict future crimes, so a complex predictive analysis is not necessary.

Problem Comparison Chart

The strategies listed for a crime reduction goal often designate long-term responses to problem locations, areas, and offenders. Analysis and progress reports for selected problems that have already been created will be discussed in the monthly meeting, so the purpose of a problem comparison chart is for police leaders to compare multiple locations, areas, and offenders at the same

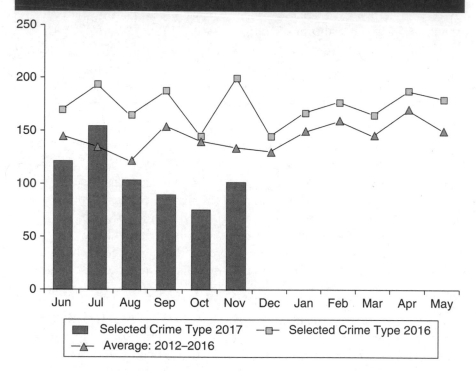

Figure 16.2 Average Trend Analysis for 6 Months, 1 Year, and 5 Years

Legend: Selected Crime Type 2017 ■ | Selected Crime Type 2016 —■— | Average: 2012–2016 —▲—

time in order to get a broader view. The product allows police leaders to both monitor the targeted crime counts individually and compare the problems by placing them side by side.

This product is a bar chart with multiple locations, areas, offenders, and their counts for the most current 6 months compared to the same 6 months in the previous year. Similar to the previous products, each month a new chart would be created with the most recent 6 months (i.e., rolling time period). A trend line is not used in this product because it reflects problems and not sequential months, but a percentage of change is depicted for the difference between the 6-month totals.

Figure 16.3 depicts 10 problem areas that have been identified through an 80/20 analysis and selected for long-term crime reduction. It shows that eight problem areas have seen reductions in crime, that Problem Areas (PA) 2 and 5 have seen increases, and that the overall reduction for the 6-month period for all the problem areas is 20%. These results indicate that the current crime reduction strategies implemented in a majority of the problem areas seem to be working, but the efforts in PA 2 and PA 5 need improvement.

This product is used to monitor different types of calls for service and crime activity as well as different types of problems. It can also be created using rates instead of counts of crime. Some examples follow:

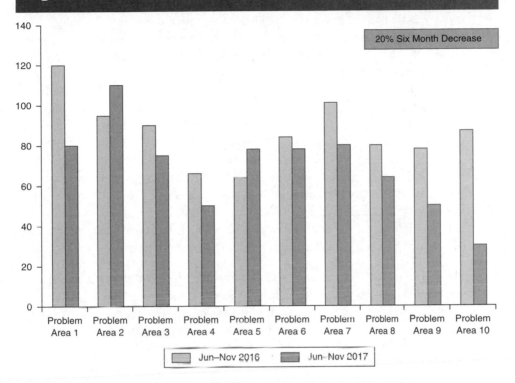

Figure 16.3 Problem Areas: 6-Month Comparison

20% Six Month Decrease

Jun–Nov 2016   Jun–Nov 2017

- Problem locations: Charts might be created for assaults at selected bars, loud parties at apartment communities, and disorder activity at budget motels.

- Problem areas: Charts might be created for problem areas of robbery, aggravated assault, and disorder calls for service. Remember that problem areas may be defined at different scales, so a chart could be created by street block, by a cluster of blocks, or by various-sized areas. The most important aspect of creating this product for problem areas is to have areas with predefined and static boundaries so the crime and disorder activity can be counted accurately and consistently over time.

- Problem offenders: This chart might include the number of arrests and/or police contacts for problem offenders. Note that this product would primarily be used and reviewed monthly for offenders that were being contacted and not for all offenders on a particular problem offender list.

- Rates: Charts might be created using crime per population of the problem area, loud parties per apartment unit, and assaults per occupancy of the bar.

Crime Pattern Trend Map

In addition to charts, maps can be used to monitor short-term and long-term activity, as well as the police department's crime reduction goals. The crime pattern trend map is used to determine whether patterns themselves are clustering over several months and becoming long-term problem areas. It is a single-symbol map depicting all crime incidents of one type over a particular time period. On the map, ellipses mark crimes that are part of pattern bulletins. The important distinction between this and a basic single-symbol or density map is that the crimes within specific patterns are marked. A crime analyst that does not do pattern analysis will not be able to create this product. As with all the previous products, the time period for the monthly map is rolling and includes 6 months of both crime incident and pattern data. Note that these maps make the most sense for crime patterns that cluster in space, such as street robbery, residential burglary, and residential theft from vehicle. Additional information (not shown here for clarity) that might also be included on the map for each pattern includes the pattern number, date of bulletin publication, and whether there was an arrest.

Figure 16.4 shows that there were 11 patterns during this time period and that five seem to have reoccurred in the same area. Based on their own judgment, police leaders would decide whether to continue to monitor this cluster of patterns over the next several months or to begin treating it as a long-term problem area since it appears that the current short-term responses are not working.

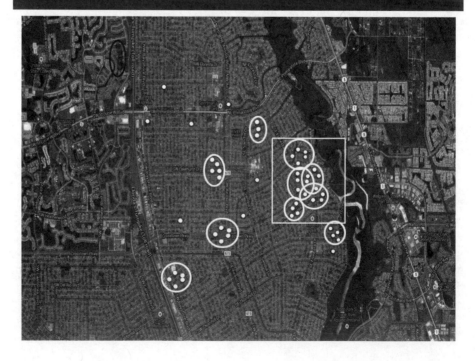

Figure 16.4   Selected Crime Incidents and Patterns: June–November 2017

Crime Analysis for Assessment of Crime Reduction Goals

Because the crime reduction goals are developed for 12-month periods, every 12 months a crime analyst will create additional products in order to assess the performance indicators (i.e., outputs) and their impact on the success indicators (i.e., outcomes) of the crime reduction goals. The data used for assessment come from a variety of sources, including documentation of crime reduction strategies, operational data on costs for implementing responses such as personnel time and equipment; crime and disorder data from the police department; and comparison data from neighboring jurisdictions, the state, and national sources.

Performance Indicator (Output) Products

There are many types of products that could be created to assess whether crime reduction strategies have been implemented successfully and have been cost effective. They would represent both the content analysis of crime reduction activities (e.g., arrests, patrol responses, clearances) and a cost analysis of the strategies implemented. Figure 16.5 is one example of a performance indicator product that is created for yearly accountability. It includes data for the performance indicators of one crime reduction goal and covers responses to repeat incidents, patterns, and problems. Crime reduction activities are discussed in more detail on a weekly and monthly basis, so at this level of accountability, the activities are aggregated and represent totals for the entire year under examination. A separate product would be created for each crime reduction goal. Depending on the nature of the goal, a separate product for each patrol geographic area or division (e.g., patrol vs. investigations) might also be created.

From top to bottom, Figure 16.5 shows outputs for the 12-month period:

- The number of individual patterns of crime responded to
- The average number of hours of directed patrol expended by pattern
- The number of arrests made, based on pattern response
- The number of cases cleared, based on pattern response
- The number of individual problem areas responded to
- The average amount of directed patrol in each problem area per week
- The total number of arrests made in the problem areas
- The number of problem offenders that were contacted

The values depicted in Figure 16.5 may not make much sense here in this textbook, but in practice, the police agency's leadership would have an idea what these numbers mean in the context of their resources and expectations for the crime reduction activities throughout the year. If the police department continues the same crime reduction goal for the following year, the crime analyst would create a product that compares the values for the current and previous year.

To complement the analysis of responses, it is also important to examine how much the crime reduction activities cost since the responses are implemented in addition to the normal police business of answering calls for service and investigating crimes. A cost analysis would examine the number of personnel hours (both scheduled and overtime) and other costs required for crime reduction activities at each level (e.g., deployment of bait vehicles, purchase of additional equipment). These cost analyses may be conducted for one crime reduction goal at a time or for all short-term strategies generally (e.g., pattern responses) within the time period of the goal. The role of the crime analyst in the cost analysis is significant in determining the appropriate data and statistics to use, as well as how the information would be presented. The crime analyst would not conduct the cost analysis alone but would work collaboratively with sworn administrative, administrative data, and budget personnel.

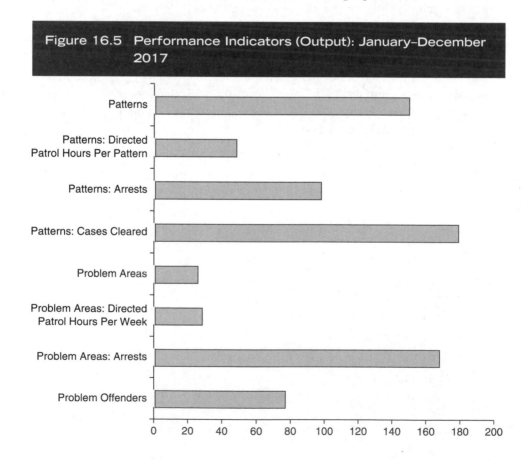

Figure 16.5 Performance Indicators (Output): January–December 2017

Success Indicator (Outcome) Products

To assess each crime reduction goal, the first step is determining whether the police department has met the percentage of reduction it designated as the success indicator by computing the actual percentage of change between the baseline and current counts. Whether or not the agency meets its crime reduction goal, additional analysis is required to help understand the context of the results. That is, just because a police department sees a 10% decrease in violent crime does not mean it was due to its own crime reduction efforts. It could be that neighboring police departments are seeing the same reduction in violent crime because it was a particularly cold and rainy year and people were not outside offending as much. Similarly, the agency may have seen a reduction in all types of crimes, even those that were not specifically targeted. Thus, the purpose of the products presented in this section is to assist the crime analyst in telling the "story" behind the statistics by making comparisons with previous years, other crime types, and other jurisdictions in order to have confidence in the overall results.

Crime and Disorder Long-Term Trend Charts The first crime and disorder long-term trend product is a line chart that depicts the frequency of crimes by month for 3 years of data, the linear trend line for that entire period, and the percentage of change between each year and the next. The purpose of this chart is to evaluate the impact of all the police department's strategies for a particular crime reduction goal beyond 2 years. Three years of data are used to see how the most recent year is related to the previous 2 years by month to provide context. Between 3 and 5 years are typically used for this product, but no fewer than 3 years should be used.

The same chart would be created separately for each type of crime or other activity identified as a crime reduction goal (i.e., separate charts for non-domestic aggravated assault and street robbery). Separate charts could also be created for different geographic areas in order to make long-term comparisons among areas, especially those noted in the success indicator component. Figure 16.6 shows that in 2017 when the police department began responding to residential burglary, there was a drop in crime that continued throughout the year. The percentage of change from 2015 to 2016 showed an 8% decrease, but from 2016 to 2017, there was a 27% decrease. A visual inspection of the chart as well as the results of the differences in percentage seem to indicate that there was an impact that coincided with the police department's response.

The next product is a chart using the same residential burglary data as Figure 16.6, but it overlays the years on the 12-month calendar, which allows for an assessment of the seasonal differences. It is recommended to have no more than 3 years on a single chart, as the lines become confusing and cluttered. If the crime analyst wants to consider more that 3 years, averages might also be used, similar to those in Figure 16.2.

Figure 16.6   Long-Term Residential Burglary Trend Chart for 3 Years

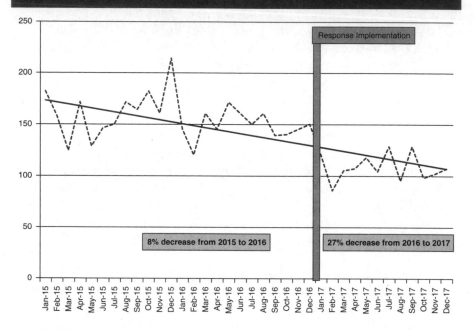

Response Implementation

8% decrease from 2015 to 2016

27% decrease from 2016 to 2017

Figure 16.7 shows that while the current year has the lowest counts, the seasonal patterns appear similar to previous years. Each year, there is a drop from January to February, and the activity increases through May with a decrease in June. What this chart shows is that even though crime reduction activities were implemented in 2017 and crime was lower, the seasonal patterns were not affected. Police leaders may consider adjusting and improving their response during those months in 2018 because even though crime is lower overall, improvement can still be made in the summer months, when there is an increase every year.

Crime Trend Comparison Charts To assist with determining whether decreases are occurring because of the police department's own crime reduction activities and not for other reasons (e.g., spatial displacement, population growth, economy, or natural disasters), it is important to compare the crime reduction goal's baseline and target data to other data, such as data from similar crime types that were not selected as crime reduction goals and data from other jurisdictions. These trend charts typically include 2 to 3 years of data and will depend on what the goal is and what data are available to the analyst. It is the crime analyst's responsibility to determine the best comparison and obtain the data necessary to create the product.

For example, consider a police department that saw a 20% reduction after responding to residential burglary as its crime reduction goal. In comparison, the department saw only a 5% reduction in residential thefts from vehicles,

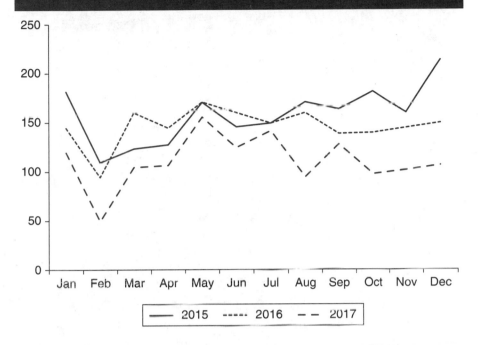

Figure 16.7   Seasonal Residential Burglary Trend Chart for 3 Years

and a neighboring jurisdiction saw a 7% increase in residential burglary over the same time period. Based on these results, police leaders might conclude that the reduction in residential burglary was, in fact, meaningful and due to the police department's responses. The fact that other property crime occurring in residential areas that was not addressed as a crime reduction goal had a much smaller reduction and a neighboring jurisdiction saw an increase implies that something different facilitated the 20% decrease in residential burglary. While these results do not absolutely prove the police department caused the reduction, the additional analysis makes reporting the 20% reduction much stronger than making it without any other comparisons.

Figure 16.8 is a chart that depicts monthly counts for residential and commercial burglary for the current year in comparison to the previous year. The crime reduction goal was to reduce residential burglaries, and the police department did not address commercial burglaries except to answer calls for service and investigate crime incidents (i.e., basic police services). The chart shows the percentage of increase and decrease for each type in the legend. A visual inspection of the chart shows that the monthly counts seem to have gone down for residential burglary when the responses began. The legend tells us that this was, in fact, true overall, in that residential burglary saw a 36% decrease from 2016 to 2017, while commercial burglary saw a 9% increase.

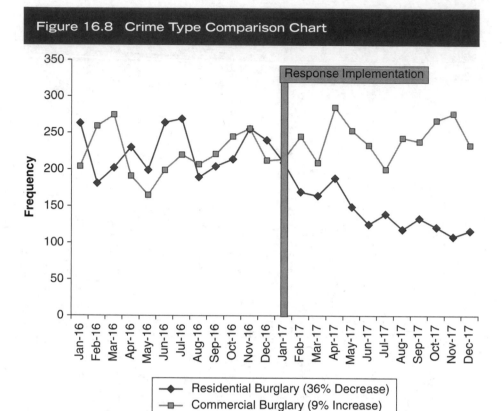

Figure 16.8   Crime Type Comparison Chart

Figure 16.9 is a similar chart that compares the crime analyst's jurisdiction with data from another jurisdiction. As discussed in Chapter 12, to compare jurisdictions with different populations, a rate is used instead of monthly counts because it is unlikely that crime analysts will find a jurisdiction almost identical in size and population to their own. Figure 16.9 shows the monthly rates of residential burglary for the two jurisdictions. In 2016, the crime analyst's jurisdiction rate per 100,000 population has a similar trend as the comparison jurisdiction, but in 2017 when crime reduction strategies for residential burglary were implemented, there was a 23% decrease in the crime rate, while the other jurisdiction saw a 15% increase. Other charts with additional jurisdictions could also be created to strengthen the argument even more. It is important that the crime analyst selects other jurisdictions that—while maybe not similar in population—are similar in zoning (e.g., residential vs. commercial) and other characteristics (e.g., rural/suburban vs. urban/college town/vacation location).

Notably, population is not always the best for comparison of certain types of crime (e.g., commercial burglary). Unfortunately, it is difficult to get comparison measures from other jurisdictions, so population is often the most realistic and practical comparison measure. It may also be difficult to obtain

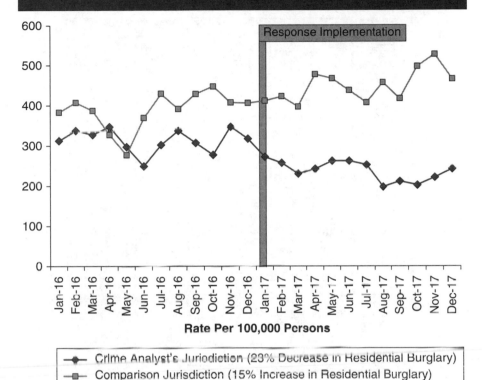

Figure 16.9 Jurisdiction Comparison Chart

Response Implementation

Rate Per 100,000 Persons

—♦— Crime Analyst's Jurisdiction (23% Decrease in Residential Burglary)
—■— Comparison Jurisdiction (15% Increase in Residential Burglary)

specific crime (e.g., residential burglaries at apartment communities) and calls-for-service information (e.g., disorder calls only) from other jurisdictions, so these products may sometimes have to be created by year with more general categories (e.g., all citizen-generated calls or all burglaries). Lastly, an analyst should be cautious when a jurisdiction's population changes within the year (e.g., a college town where students leave in the summer) or is increasing or decreasing over several years (e.g., growth with new industry or decline because a large factory has closed). Because of these considerations, conducting the analysis and making conclusions based on more general data should be done very cautiously.

Yearly Comparison Maps It is also helpful for police leaders to use yearly comparison maps to visualize long-term changes in activity for accountability purposes. In order to see changes from year to year, the analyst creates separate maps for each year. Often in an annual accountability meeting, crime analysis products are presented with presentation software, so maps can be animated and changes over time can be seen more easily than in static form. Analysts might create quarterly or monthly maps; however, making 12 or 24 maps for animation instead of two is a lot of work for the analyst, so it should be done only when the results are meaningful.

Figure 16.10   Density Map of Crime Reduction Goal: 2016

Figures 16.10 and 16.11 are density maps of a selected crime for 2016 and 2017, respectively. The same products could also be created using a graduated-area map. The legends are not shown here, but remember from Chapter 6 that when comparing across time periods, "custom" legends should be created by the analyst so that each color category represents the same values in each map and the years can be compared. While the maps are shown here in black and white, they were originally created in color where the differences are more easily discernable. Looking at the two maps together, we can see a change in the density of the problem areas in the large circled area from 2016 to 2017; it shows the density of crime is lower, meaning there have been improvements in these areas. Additional yearly maps would be created to animate changes over time.

Figure 16.11 Density Map of Crime Reduction Goal: 2017

SUMMARY POINTS

This chapter presents an overview of accountability processes implemented for crime reduction in a police department, how crime reduction goals are developed, and specific crime analysis products that are created for weekly and monthly accountability meetings, as well as for evaluating crime reduction goals. The following are the key points addressed in this chapter:

- Administrative crime analysis is analysis directed toward the administrative needs of the police department, its government, and its community. It supports the internal operations of the organization as well as a police department's interactions with the community and other government entities.

- Crime analysts assist with the development and measurement of crime reduction goals, provide regular products to monitor the success of short- and long-term crime reduction activities, assess whether the crime reduction efforts are effective, and determine whether the crime reduction goals are being met.

- Regularly scheduled daily, weekly, and monthly meetings make up the formal structure that police departments create to facilitate their accountability process.

- Daily and weekly meetings are action oriented because they are used to ensure that police personnel are responding (i.e., the "action") immediately, collaboratively, and appropriately.

- Monthly meetings are evaluation oriented because they are used to assess the overall effectiveness of short-term crime reduction as well as the progress and effectiveness of long-term crime reduction efforts.

- To make sure that a crime reduction goal is actionable and relevant in the day-to-day operations of the police department, the outcome of the crime reduction goal is specified, along with the success indicators, baseline and target measurements, strategies, and measurements of performance.

- The crime reduction goal is the desired outcome and is generally stated.

- A success indicator (i.e., outcome) specifies the type of activity that is used to measure the impact of the crime reduction strategies.

- The baseline is the initial measurement of the success indicator.

- The target is the desired level of success (i.e., reduction of crime) and is computed based on the percentage indicated in the success indicator and the baseline measurement.

- Strategies list the crime reduction responses that the police department will implement simultaneously for each level of activity. They are selected based on the particular type of crime or disorder problem outlined in the crime reduction goal.

- Performance indicators (i.e., outputs) are a list of the activity produced in the crime reduction work of the police department.

- The crime analyst creates a weekly product for pattern accountability that includes information about the implemented pattern responses to be discussed in the meeting. A similar type of product may be created for repeat incidents.

- On a monthly basis, accountability meetings are evaluation oriented so crime analysts examine 6-month trends by month to monitor the effectiveness of responses for repeat incidents, crime patterns, and long-term problems. Because crime counts can vary widely from month to month, crime analysis for monthly accountability focuses on identifying trends instead of numerical differences or percentage of change from month to month, year to date, or from year to year.

- The crime and disorder monthly trend charts are bar charts that compare the most recent 6 months to the same 6 months of the previous year or that compare the current 6 months, the previous 12 months, and an average per month for the last 5 years. The problem comparison chart is a bar chart of each location, area, or offender, with crime counts for the most current 6 months compared to the same 6 months in the previous year. It allows for police leaders to compare multiple selected problems at once for 6 months.

- The crime pattern trend map is used to determine whether patterns themselves are clustering over time and becoming long-term problem areas. It contains crime incidents of one type over a particular time period. Ellipses mark those patterns of crime.

- Performance indicator products are created to assess whether crime reduction strategies have been implemented successfully and have been cost effective. They represent both the content analysis of crime reduction activities as well as a cost analysis of the strategies implemented.

- Success indicator products help determine whether the police department has met the percentage of reduction it established at initial goal development, as well as help understand the context of the results.

- Crime and disorder long-term trend charts evaluate the impact of all the agency's strategies for a particular crime reduction goal. They either depict the frequency by month for 3 years of data or overlay 3 years of data on the 12-month calendar to determine seasonal differences.

- Crime trend comparison charts are used to help determine whether increases or decreases are occurring because of the agency's own crime reduction activities or some other reason. These products typically include 2 to 3 years of data that compare monthly counts or rates of the goal's success indicators to a relevant comparison (e.g., by crime type or other jurisdiction).

- Yearly comparison maps help police leaders visualize long-term changes in activity by geographic area.

DISCUSSION EXERCISES* ─────────────

Develop a goal with the following info.

Exercise 1

For the last 5 years, your police department has seen between a 5% and 10% increase in property crimes, particularly vehicle crimes (theft of and from vehicles). The problem is occurring across the entire city but especially in District 2 and District 4. You have unlimited resources to address this issue. Complete the crime reduction goal chart to the best of your abilities using this chapter as well as what you have learned in the entire book. Following each component, write a short sentence or two to explain your reasoning for each component.

Exercise 2

Over the past 3 years, your police department has seen a 40% total increase in burglaries, particularly those at single-family homes and retail establishments. The problem is occurring across the entire city. You have unlimited resources to address this issue. Complete the crime reduction goal chart to the best of your abilities using this chapter as well as what you have learned in the entire book. Following each component, write a short sentence or two to explain your reasoning for each component.

Exercise 3

Over the past 2 years, your police department has seen a 20% increase in robberies, particularly those occurring on the street (50% of all robberies) and at commercial places (30% of all robberies). Street robberies are predominant on the north side of the city, and commercial robberies mostly occur on the south side. You have very limited resources to address these crimes. Complete the crime reduction goal chart to the best of your abilities using this chapter as well as what you have learned in the entire book. Following each component, write a short sentence or two to explain your reasoning for each component.

Glossary

80/20 rule: A concept that comes from the common observation that 80% of some kinds of outcomes are the results of only 20% of the related causes.

Accountability: In this book, accountability refers to the process by which police personnel are held responsible for implementing strategies to reduce crime and disorder in the community.

Agency management system (AMS): An intranet web-based hardware and software system that facilitates communication and transparency within the police agency and streamlines internal police business. It is used to manage official communications, administration, and business functions in an agency.

Analysis, commodity flow: The analysis of the "flow" of money and other financial information; it is particularly used in cases involving drug trafficking, illicit weapons sales, human trafficking, and money laundering.

Analysis, communication: The focus of this analysis is on the relationships and "flow" of communication through different types of media, including personal interactions, phone calls, e-mail, Internet, intranet, and social media communication.

Analysis, community-focused: Making tactical and strategic criminal analysis results suitable for the public and creating products specifically for the community and neighborhood groups.

Analysis, cost-benefit: An assessment of the relative cost of a particular program or initiative in the police department in comparison with the benefit or impact of that program or initiative

Analysis, crime intelligence: The analysis of data about people involved in crimes, particularly repeat offenders, repeat victims, and criminal organizations and networks.

Analysis, criminal history: The analysis of an individual that includes their personal identification information, aliases, financial information, criminal and arrest activity, correctional status, social media activity. Also known as a *criminal résumé*.

Analysis, districting and redistricting: An infrequent type of analysis that determines the most efficient way to patrol specific geographic boundaries of districts and beats within an jurisdiction.

Analysis, hot spot: This analysis identifies areas within a jurisdiction that have a disproportionate amount of crime compared to other areas both temporally and spatially.

Analysis, link: A type of analysis that presents a visual representation of individuals, their relationships with others, and addresses and personal information relevant to a case.

Analysis, patrol staffing: This is usually done annually of calls-for-service and CAD unit history data to evaluate deployment of officer patrol shifts.

Analysis, problem: This is analysis done to evaluate crime and disorder problems through criminal justice theory, research methods, and comprehensive data collection and analysis.

Analysis, repeat incident: Analysis that uses calls-for-service data to identify locations where similar types of calls have occurred over a short period of time.

Analysis, repeat offender: Using data to identify and prioritize (i.e., put in a rank order) individual offenders by the number, type, and seriousness of their crimes.

Analysis, repeat victim: Using data to identify and prioritize (i.e., put in rank order) individual victims why by the number, type, and seriousness of their victimizations.

Analysis, social media: Using social media sources to identify suspects and potential crimes as well as possible terrorism activity.

Analysis, trend: This analysis identifies long-term increases or decreases in crime by aggregating data, usually by time period and geographic area.

Analysis step: The second step in the SARA process, which includes researching what is known about the specific problem type and potential responses, understanding the local context of the problem, and determining how the problem is currently being addressed in that particular jurisdiction. This is followed by the analysis of data, in which hypotheses are developed that speculate on why the problem is occurring. Next, data are collected to test these hypotheses, and statistical analysis is conducted, from which conclusions are made about the immediate causes of the problem.

Anticipatory benefit: The idea that crime reduction may occur before a strategy is implemented because the work being done before implementation may actually change offenders' perceptions of risk and victims' awareness.

Assessment step: The final step of the SARA process, which determines whether the responses were implemented as intended and whether they worked at reducing the problem.

Baseline: The initial measurement of a crime reduction success indicator.

Beat: A geographic area designated by the police department for patrol officer deployment.

Buffer: An area around a feature on a map that represents a specified distance from that feature in all directions.

Calls for service: Calls about activity (criminal or noncriminal) to which an officer responds.

Calls for service, citizen-generated: Calls for service initiated by a citizen request for police response.

Calls for service, officer-generated: Calls for service initiated by a police officer, such as a traffic or subject stop.

Center for Problem-Oriented Policing (POP Center): A virtual center that contains a wealth of information and resources about problem solving and problem-oriented policing. The website is www.popcenter.org.

Chart mapping: A method of mapping that allows the visualization of several values within a particular variable at the same time.

Chart mapping, bar chart: A type of mapping in which the relative frequencies (represented by bars) of values within a variable are displayed.

Chart mapping, pie chart: A type of mapping in which the relative percentages (represented by slices of a pie) of values within a variable are displayed.

Chronic victims: These are individuals who are repeatedly victimized over time by various offenders for various types of crimes. Also called *multiple victimization*.

Classification, equal interval: A mapping classification for graduation that uses a statistical formula to divide the difference between the highest and lowest values into equal-sized ranges.

Classification, manual method: A mapping classification in which the ranges displayed in the legend are not determined by the values of a variable or a statistical formula, but by the creator of the map. Also known as *custom* mapping.

Classification, natural breaks: A mapping classification for graduation that uses a statistical formula to identify the natural gaps in the distribution of the data.

Classification, quantile: A mapping classification for graduation in which the categories in the range are created by dividing the number of records in the database by the number of categories (selected by the user), which results in categories with equal numbers of records.

Classification, standard deviation: A mapping classification for graduation that uses mean and standard deviation of the selected variable to determine the break points of the categories, which are shown in the legend not as whole numbers, but as standard deviations (e.g., +1, −1 standard deviation from the mean).

Clearance rate: The number of crimes cleared divided by the number of crimes reported. The Uniform Crime Report program acknowledges two ways in which crimes are cleared: by arrest and by exceptional means.

Clearing cases: The process of linking unsolved cases to a recently solved case in order to close them and link them to enhance the prosecution of an individual suspect.

Command personnel: Police personnel who serve as the leadership of the organization, such as the chief or sheriff, deputy chiefs, majors, and in some cases captains.

Commission on Accreditation for Law Enforcement Agencies (CALEA): An independent accrediting authority whose purpose is to improve delivery of police service by offering a body of standards, developed by police practitioners, covering a wide range of up to-date police topics.

Community policing: A philosophy that promotes organizational strategies that support the systematic use of partnerships and problem-solving techniques to proactively address the immediate conditions that give rise to public safety issues such as crime, social disorder, and fear of crime.

Compound problem: A problem that encompasses various locations, offenders, and victims and, in most cases, exists throughout an entire jurisdiction.

Compstat: A data-driven and mapping-driven police management strategy implemented by the New York City Police Department in 1994. A core component of the program is the use of crime mapping software and analysis in weekly meetings of police officials to improve understanding of local crime and disorder incidents.

Computer-aided dispatch (CAD) system: A highly specialized system that uses telecommunications and geographic display to support police dispatch and response functions (as well as those of public safety agencies, such as fire and ambulance services).

Coordinate systems: Values used to locate data on maps.

Crime analysis: A profession and process in which a set of quantitative and qualitative techniques are used to analyze data valuable to police agencies and their communities. It includes the analysis of crime and criminals, crime victims, disorder, quality of life issues, traffic issues, and internal police operations. Its results support criminal investigation and prosecution, patrol activities, crime prevention and reduction strategies, problem solving, and the evaluation of police efforts.

Crime analysis, administrative: The analysis directed toward the administrative needs of the police agency, its government, and its community.

Crime analysis, strategic: The analysis of data directed toward development and evaluation of long-term strategies, policies, and prevention techniques. Its subjects include long-term statistical trends, hot spots, and problems.

Crime analysis, tactical: This is analysis of police data directed toward the short-term development of patrol and investigative priorities and deployment of resources. Its subject areas include the analysis of space, time, offender, victim, and modus operandi for individual high-profile crimes, repeat incidents, and crime patterns, with a specific focus on crime series [sic].

Crime analysis assistant/ technician: An administrative support person who answers the phone, conducts data entry, makes copies, keeps files, produces simple standardized reports, and does anything else that arises administratively in a crime analysis unit.

Crime analysis information: The details about individual incidents (e.g., crime, calls for service, arrests, collisions) or aggregate counts of incidents by different time periods.

Crime analysis process: The general way that crime analysis is practiced, including data collection, data collation, analysis, dissemination of results, and incorporation of feedback from users of the information.

Crime analysis supervisor: A person with substantial crime analysis knowledge and experience who supervises a crime analysis unit.

Crime analysis typology: A classification system of crime analysis results that are broken down by three important factors—type of problem, purpose of crime analysis results, and type of audience.

Crime analysis unit (CAU): A police agency unit responsible for conducting crime analysis.

Crime analysis unit (CAU) strategic plan: A plan specifically written for a CAU that outlines strategies and direction, lays out expectations, and helps guide decisions about how work is done and how to allocate resources.

Crime analyst, entry-level: A person who conducts relatively routine crime analysis duties; this person is likely to be new to the field and to have had limited crime analysis experience.

Crime analyst, experienced: A person who (compared with an entry-level crime analyst) holds more responsibility and is expected to conduct more advanced crime analysis.

Crime analyst, specialty: An analyst who is hired to conduct a particular type of crime analysis. Types of specialty crime analysts include tactical crime analysts, problem analysts, sex crime analysts, school safety analysts, and GIS analysts.

Crime mapping: The process of using a geographic information system to conduct spatial analysis of crime and disorder problems, as well as other police-related issues.

Crime pattern theory: A theory that addresses the nature of the immediate situations in which crimes occur. According to this theory, criminal events are most likely to occur in areas where the activity space of offenders overlaps with the activity space of potential victims/targets.

Crime prevention through environmental design (CPTED): A set of principles based on the theory that the physical environment can be designed in such a way as to reduce or eliminate opportunities for crime.

Crime rate: In the scanning and analysis steps, crime analysts use three rates regularly to compare local crime problems with national crime problems and to describe particular general problems: crime rate, clearance rate, and recovery rate. Typically, it is the number of Part I crimes per 100,000 persons (number of crimes divided by population and the result multiplied by 100,000), but it can also be depicted as crimes per 1,000 or 10,000.

Crime reduction goal: The generally stated desired outcome, which denotes a specific type of activity to reduce and the geographic area it targets.

Criminal Justice Information Services (CJIS): The largest division of the Federal Bureau of Investigation and the central division of its crime services and programs. It is also the criminal justice agency within a district, state, territory, or federal agency that has administrative responsibility for the use of NCIC.

Cross-tabulation: A process in which frequencies are computed for one variable separated into categories of another variable and vice versa.

Daily roll calls: An element of stratified policing that facilitates action-oriented accountability at the line level for evidence-based strategies implemented for immediate and short-term problems.

Data: A collection of organized information that has been collected or gleaned from experience, observation, or experiment, or a set of ideas.

Data matrix: A rectangular table of variables and units from which data have been collected.

Data modification subcycle: A subprocess within the crime analysis process in which the analyst makes changes in data collection and collation procedures based on insights gained during the analysis. The subcycle illustrates that crime analysis is not linear; rather, it moves from collection to collation to analysis, but each of these steps informs the next.

Database: A collection of data that have been organized for the purposes of retrieval, searching, and analysis through a computer.

Database, arrests: A database containing information about arrests gleaned from arrest reports.

Database, calls for service: A database containing information about officer- and citizen-generated calls for service obtained from a computer-aided dispatch system.

Database, crime incidents: A database containing information about crime incidents (including how, when, and where the incidents occurred) gleaned from crime reports taken by police officers or other police personnel. (Also called a *crime report database*.)

Database, field information: A database containing information collected by patrol officers about suspicious behavior and unique features of individuals.

Database, gang: A database that contains information collected and validated by patrol officers and detectives about individuals who are both members and associates of gangs.

Database, pawn: A database that contains information about property received by pawnbrokers, as well as the personal information of the person who pawned the property.

Database, persons: A database containing information about all individuals involved in criminal incidents, including witnesses, victims, investigative leads, suspects (some police agencies have suspect databases that are separate from their persons and arrest databases), and arrestees.

Database, property: A database containing information about individual pieces of property that have been stolen, found, or used in the commission of crimes.

Database, registered sex offender: A database containing information on individuals convicted of sex crimes and who have registered with authorities.

Database, relational: See relational database.

Database, traffic: A database containing data on traffic citations and vehicle stops.

Database, traffic crash or collision: A database containing police report information about incidents when vehicles collide with people, property, or other vehicles.

Deduction: The process of examining a phenomenon by starting with general ideas about it and moving to specific facts supporting those general ideas.

Density mapping: A type of mapping in which analysts use point data to shade surfaces that are not limited to area boundaries (as is the case in graduated-color mapping).

Diffusion of benefits: A phenomenon in which the elimination of a targeted problem results in the reduction of other types of problems in the area as well.

Disorder policing: Also known as *broken windows policing*. A police strategy that focuses on the strict enforcement of laws against disorderly behavior and minor offenses to prevent more serious crimes from happening.

Displacement: A phenomenon in which crime problems change by shifting to other forms, times, and/or locales instead of being eliminated.

Displacement, spatial: Displacement that consists of a shift from targets in one area to those in another area.

Displacement, tactical: Displacement that consists of a shift in the tactics of the offender.

Displacement, target: Displacement that consists of a shift from one victim/target to a more vulnerable one.

Displacement, temporal: Displacement that consists of a shift of activity from one time to another.

Ellipse: A closed curve that is formed from two foci or points in which the sum of the distances from any point on the curve to the two foci is a constant. Crime analysts use ellipses to determine hot spots or geographic concentrations of activity in data distributions (i.e., points that are closer to one another than to any other point).

Embedded criminologist: A person with a doctorate degree and/or a researcher who is not working *with* the police agency but is working *within* the police agency as an independent, unbiased full-time employee. This person has expertise in criminology, criminal justice practices, analysis, statistics, research methodology, and evaluation.

Evidence-based policing: Crime reduction strategies that have been proven effective by researchers and have been implemented by police.

Environmental criminology: A perspective in criminology containing several theories that is different from others in that it focuses on offenders' patterns of motivation, opportunities that exist for crime, levels of protection for victims within the criminal events, and the environments in which criminal events occur.

Exact time series analysis: The examination of incidents that have exact times of occurrence, such as robbery and sexual assault.

Facilitators, chemical: Chemical factors that increase offenders' abilities to ignore risks or moral prohibitions.

Facilitators, physical: Physical factors that can augment offenders' behavior or help overcome prevention measures. Some physical facilitators are tools, but others are part of the physical environment.

Facilitators, social: Social processes that can stimulate crime or disorder by enhancing rewards, legitimating excuses to offend, or encouraging offending.

Feature, line: A real-world element that can be represented on a map by a line or set of lines.

Feature, point: A discrete location that is usually depicted on a map by a symbol or label.

Feature, polygon: A geographic area represented on a map by a multisided figure with a closed set of lines.

FI card: A small card completed by an officer in the field; designed for the collection of information on noncriminal incidents. (FI stands for *field information* or *field interview*.)

Field information: Information collected by a patrol officer when there is not enough probable cause to take a police report, but some information about the incident, the person, or a vehicle is worth collecting.

Focused deterrence: Also known as the *"pulling levers" strategy*. It is essentially a specific problem-solving approach to address serious violent offenders in high-crime areas of a city using certain, sever, and swift responses.

Frequency: The number (count) of all categories of a variable.

Geocoding: The process of linking an address with its map coordinates so that (a) the address can be displayed on a map, and (b) the geographic information system can recognize that address in the future.

Geocoding match rate: The number of addresses in the database that have been successfully geocoded or matched to the geographic data.

Geographic data system: A system that creates, maintains, and stores geographic data.

Geographic information system (GIS): A set of computer-based tools that allows the user to modify, visualize, query, and analyze geographic and tabular data.

Geographic profiling: A subset of criminal investigative analysis in which the analyst uses the geographic locations of an offender's crimes (e.g., body dump sites, encounter sites) to identify and prioritize areas the offender is likely to live.

Global positioning system (GPS): A combination of hardware and software that uses satellite technology to provide the latitude and longitude of particular locations.

Graduated maps: Maps in which different sizes or colors of features represent particular values of variables.

Grid mapping: A method for resolving an unequal area in which a standard-sized grid is used for analysis. The analyst begins by placing an artificial grid (generated by the GIS) on top of the area of interest and then uses graduated-color shading classifications to show different levels of crime.

Hot place: A location in which similar crimes are committed by one or more individuals.

Hot prey: Victims, who share similar physical characteristics and/or engage in similar behavior, of a group of crimes committed by one or more individuals.

Hot product: Unique type of property targeted for theft by one or more individuals.

Hot setting: A type of place that is frequently victimized; common hot settings include beauty salons, schools, and convenience stores.

Hot spot: A type of pattern where similar crimes committed by one or more individuals occur at locations within close proximity to one another in a short period of time.

Hot spot, micro-time: The emergence of several closely related crimes within a few minutes' travel distance from one another (i.e., micro-place) that occur within a relatively short period of time (i.e., micro-time)—a crime "flare-up."

Hot spots policing: A police strategy in which police systematically identify areas within a city that have disproportionate amounts of crime over a long-term period (i.e., 1 to 3 years) and employ responses in those specific areas.

Hypothesis: A statement about a problem that can be true or false; it is the answer to a question posed about the problem that is based on theory and experience.

Incidents: Individual events that an officer typically responds to or discovers while on patrol. They can result in either citizen- or officer-generated calls for service and include crime, disorder, or service-related tasks such as disturbances, robbery in progress, traffic crashes, subject stops, and traffic citations, all of which usually occur and are resolved within minutes or hours—most of the time within one shift.

Incidents, serious: Individual events that arise from calls for service that are deemed serious by laws and policies of the police department and require additional investigation and/or a more extensive immediate response; these include rapes, hostage negotiations, homicides, traffic fatalities, or armed robbery. They occur within minutes or hours but may take days, weeks, or in some cases, months to resolve.

Induction: The process of examining a phenomenon by beginning with individual facts or specific ideas about it and relating them back to general concepts.

Information: The knowledge that is communicated about a particular fact or circumstance.

Intelligence-led policing: A contemporary police management model in which the intelligence or analysis function is the key to a police agency's crime reduction and prevention efforts that are primarily offender-based strategies.

Interactive crime mapping: Crime mapping conducted using simplified geographic information systems made available to novice users over the Internet.

Intern: An undergraduate or graduate student who works in a police department to obtain practical work experience and college credit.

International Association of Crime Analysts (IACA): A nonprofit member organization formed in 1990 to help crime analysts around the world improve their skills and make valuable contacts, to help law enforcement agencies make the best use of crime analysis, and to advocate for standards of performance and technique within the profession of crime analysis.

Intranet: A network that functions much like the Internet but connects only a limited number of users, usually people associated with a particular organization.

Investigative lead: A person who is a potential suspect for a crime.

Jail management system (JMS): A computer-based system that stores a detention facility's information pertaining to the people who have been booked into the facility, including the current population as well as those already released.

Known offender: A person who has been convicted, *not just arrested,* for any crime other than a sex offense.

Legend: An element of a map in which the map's tabular and geographic data sources are displayed, and the symbols used to represent each data source are indicated.

Linear trend line: Created by a statistical equation (linear regression), which produces a line that best estimates the direction of the month-to-month figures and is most often used in crime analysis.

Management personnel: Police personnel who are midlevel managers, such as lieutenants and in some cases captains.

Mean: Also known as an *average.* The sum of the values of a variable divided by the number of values.

Median: The value within a data distribution at which 50% of the data are higher and 50% are lower.

Mention: A person mentioned in a police report who might be a possible investigative lead or suspect in the crime.

Mode: The most frequent value within a data distribution.

Modus operandi (MO): The method of the crime; that is, the key elements of the crime incident itself, such as what the crime entailed and how, where, and when the crime was committed. (*Modus operandi* is a Latin term meaning literally "method of procedure.")

Monthly accountability meetings: These are accountability meetings that are held every month and facilitate evaluation-oriented accountability within patrol districts and investigations, as well as across the entire police department.

National Crime Information Center (NCIC): The National Crime Information Center is a computerized index of criminal justice information pertaining to individual criminal record histories, fugitives, stolen property, and missing persons within the entire United States.

Near victims: These are victims or targets that are physically close to the original victim and share characteristics with the original victim.

Normalizing: A term used in geographic information systems software to refer to a rate—when one variable (the denominator) is used to determine the relative difference between values of another variable (the numerator).

North directional: The element on a map that indicates the geographic orientation of the map.

Operational personnel: Police personnel who are line-level officers (e.g., officers, corporals) and first-line supervisors (e.g., corporals, sergeants).

Pattern: A group of two or more crimes reported to or discovered by the police that is treated as one unit of analysis because they share one or more key commonalities that make them notable and distinct; there is no known relationship between victim and offender; and the criminal activity is typically of limited duration.

Pattern finalization: The process of refining the list of cases thought to be related by determining which cases have key characteristics in common.

Pattern identification, ad hoc linking: The linking of cases by memory in the course of the analyst's everyday work.

Pattern identification, query method: The linking of cases through an iterative process in which the analyst manipulates, searches, and sorts characteristics of crimes using a database matrix.

Pattern identification, weights and thresholds method: The linking of cases through a process in which various characteristics of crimes are weighted and the weights summed up for each case. This process highlights cases that meet a particular threshold indicating they have similar characteristics.

Pattern identification, initial: The first step in a two-step process, during which the analyst links together all of the cases that might make up a pattern.

Percentage of change: The amount of relative increase or decrease between two values over two time periods; expressed as a proportion of the value at the first time period (Time 1), or the difference between a measurement at Time 1 and a measurement at Time 2, divided by the measurement at Time 1, and then multiplied by 100 (to arrive at a percentage).

Percentage: The count of one category divided by the count of all categories of a variable multiplied by 100.

Percentile: A value above and below which a certain percentage of cases lie.

Performance indicators: Also known as *outputs*. These elements of a crime reduction goal specify the activity to be measured and are developed based on the outlined strategies of the goal.

Persons crime: Crime (such as robbery, sexual assault, indecent exposure, public sexual indecency, and kidnapping) in which a person is the target.

Predictive policing: An "advanced" analytical approach used to deploy patrol officers in the immediate and short term.

Primary data: Data collected specifically for the purposes of the analysis at hand.

Primary data collection: The collection of information directly from individuals or locations for purposes of the analysis at hand through methods such as interviews, surveys (individual and focus group), and observation.

Principal case: The case within a pattern that best represents the characteristics of the pattern and is used to determine the other key cases in the pattern.

Problem: A set of related crimes or harmful activities that occur over several months, seasons, or years and that the public expects the police to address.

Problem, immediate: An incident that occurs and is resolved within minutes, hours, or in some cases, days and is responded to by patrol officers and detectives who use the investigative skills learned in basic police training and more intensive investigative training.

Problem, long-term: A set of related activity that occurs over several months, seasons, or years that stems from systematic opportunities created by everyday behavior and environment.

Problem, short-term: A problem that occurs over a limited amount of time and is considered acute. Two types discussed in the book are repeat incidents and patterns.

Problem analysis triangle: The concept at the core of environmental criminological theory, which asserts that a crime occurs only when a motivated offender and a victim/target come together at a particular place, with the likelihood of occurrence affected by several controls (known as handlers, guardians, and managers).

Problem area: It is a relatively small geographic area with a disproportionate amount of crime or disorder activity of one or several types over a long period of time (i.e., at least 1 year).

Problem location: An individual address or a type of place at which there is a concentration of crime or problematic activity over a long period of time.

Problem offender: See *repeat offender*.

Problem-oriented policing: A systematic approach to crime reduction in which problems are identified, analyzed, and addressed and the resulting efforts evaluated.

Problem property: See *hot product*.

Problem victim: Individual people or groups of victims who share characteristics as victims of crime over a long period of time, also called *repeat victim(s)*.

Projections: Adjustments made to data files as they are incorporated into the software and used for analysis.

Property crime: Crime in which property is the target of an offender, such as residential and commercial burglary, criminal trespass, and criminal damage.

Qualitative data and methods: Nonnumerical data and the methods used to examine them (e.g., field research, content analysis). Crime analysts use qualitative data and methods to discover the underlying causes of crime.

Quantitative data and methods: Numerical or categorical data and the methods used to examine them (e.g., statistical analysis). Among other things, crime analysts use quantitative data and methods to determine the prevalence, make comparisons, and examine historical and future trends of crime and disorder activity.

Raster data: A type of geographic data used to display features on the earth's surface. Raster data are an arrangement of grid cells or pixels that overlay the surface and are assigned attribute data (typically a numeric value). Raster files are typically used to store satellite images or remote sensing pictures and are often displayed in color.

Rate: A statistic that uses one variable (the denominator) to determine the relative difference between values of another variable (the numerator).

Rational choice theory: A theory that asserts that all people make choices about the actions they take based on the opportunities and rewards they anticipate receiving as a result. This theory suggests that, if given a chance or the right "opportunity," any person will commit a crime.

Records management system (RMS): A data entry and storage system designed especially for police records.

Recovery rate: The percentage of vehicles that have been stolen in a jurisdiction and subsequently recovered.

Relational database: A database that contains seemingly infinite numbers of records or cases and allows users to examine complex relationships among various tables through software such as Microsoft Access, SQL Server, and Oracle.

Repeat incidents: Repeat incidents are two or more incidents that are similar in nature and have happened at the same place (typically) or to the same person.

Repeat offenders: Individuals or types of individuals who commit multiple crimes over long periods of time.

Repeat victimization: The recurrence of crime in the same places and/or against the same people.

Response step: The third step of the SARA process; it includes identifying realistic responses from the POP guides, from the situational crime prevention techniques, from what other communities have done successfully, and by brainstorming for new responses.

Risky facilities: Individual locations that attract or generate a disproportionate amount of crime.

Rolling time period: When conducting ongoing daily, weekly, or monthly analysis, the time period of a chart or table may change to include the most recent days (i.e., last 7 days), weeks (i.e., last 4 weeks), or months (i.e., last 6 months) instead of a static time period (i.e., January through December) or year to date (i.e., January until the most recent month).

Routine activities theory: A theory that focuses on how opportunities for crime change based on changes in behavior on a societal level.

SARA model: The 4-step process used in problem solving: scanning, analysis, response, and assessment.

Scale: Depicts the ratio of the map distance and the distance on the ground.

Scale bar: An element in a map that illustrates the distance units used in the map.

Scanning step: The first step in the SARA process; it includes identifying recurring problems of concern to both the public and the police, prioritizing those problems, and selecting problems for closer examination. It also includes confirming that the problem exists, determining how frequently the problem occurs and how long it has been taking place, and identifying the consequences of the problem.

Search radius: In density mapping, the distance set by the user that determines the breadth of the calculations of concentration of incidents.

Seasonality: When a problem occurs every year at the same time of year (e.g., assaults and burglaries are up in the summer months).

Secondary data: Data that have been collected previously; such data are typically housed in electronic databases.

Series: A group of similar crimes thought to be committed by the same individual or group of individuals acting in concert.

Sex offender: A person who has been convicted, *not just arrested,* for a sex offense.

Single-symbol maps: Maps in which individual, uniform symbols represent features such as the locations of stores, streets or roads, or states.

Situational awareness: The development of a perception of the environment in which an officer of any rank works.

Situational crime prevention: A practice initiated in England in the 1980s, based on the concepts of environmental criminology, that addresses why crime occurs in specific settings and seeks solutions that reflect the nature of those settings.

Sociodemographic information: Information on the personal characteristics of individuals and groups, such as sex, race, income, age, and education.

Software, database management (DBMS): Software that allows the user to enter and store data in a database and to modify and extract information from a database.

Software, geographic information systems (GIS): Software that allows the user to modify, visualize, query, and analyze geographic and tabular data.

Software, graphics: Software that allows the user to create and manipulate pictures and images.

Software, presentation: Software that allows the user to create slide shows to enhance the presentation of information.

Software, publication: Software that allows the user to create professional-looking printed or electronic products such as reports, brochures, and newsletters.

Software, spreadsheet: Software that allows the user to create and change spreadsheets easily.

Software, statistical: Software that accesses databases obtained from spreadsheets and DBMS and facilitates working with data. The core purposes of statistical software are statistical computation and data manipulation, and these applications are designed to handle large numbers of records.

Software, word processing: Software that primarily supports the creation and manipulation of text but also may include functionality for incorporating tables, charts, and pictures into a document.

Spatial information: Information on geographic features.

Spreadsheet: A table that displays information in rows and columns of cells.

Spree: A specific type of series characterized by high frequency of criminal activity within a remarkably short time frame, to the extent that the activity appears almost continuous.

Standard deviation: In simple terms, the standardized average variation of the values from the mean. The standard deviation indicates the shape of a data distribution.

Standard model of policing: The common general strategy for policing that entails enforcing the law in a broad and reactive way, primarily using police resources.

Strategic plan: A plan for any type of organization, division, or unit that outlines strategies and direction, lays out expectations, and helps guide decisions about how work is done and how to allocate resources. It is a formal mechanism that describes the function and purpose of the CAU within the specific agency.

Strategies: The specific responses of a crime reduction goal that will be implemented at the immediate, short-term, and long-term levels.

Stratified policing: This is a method in which a police department can organize its crime analysis and crime reduction activities. It is the only policing approach that seeks to implement crime analysis into the daily operations of the police department and to present a specific stratified structure for crime analysis products, crime reduction responses, and accountability.

Success indicator: Also known as an *outcome*. A component of a crime reduction goal that specifies the type of activity that is to be used to measure the impact of the reduction strategies.

Suspect: A person who was seen committing a crime or about whom there is enough evidence to "suspect" he or she committed the crime.

Tabular data: Data that describe events that are not inherently geographic but that may contain geographic variables.

Target: The desired level of success in a crime reduction goal. It is computed based on the percentage indicated in the success indicator and the baseline measurement.

Temporal analysis: The analysis of data in relation to units of time. Also known as *time series analysis*.

Temporal information: Information about time, days, dates, and the like.

Time series analysis: See temporal analysis.

True repeat victims: Previously victimized individuals and/or places that were victimized again.

Uncommitted patrol time: The time that patrol officers have for proactive activity between dispatched calls for service and writing reports.

Uniform Crime Reporting (UCR) program: A nationally based classification system developed by the federal government in 1930 in order to keep consistent counts of crime across the United States.

Vector data: Type of geographic data in which a GIS uses three types of features to represent objects and locations in the real world.

Virtual repeats: These are victims or targets that are virtually identical to the original victim and share some of the same characteristics.

Volunteer: A person who works for a police department without pay. Many volunteers are students or retired persons.

Weekly accountability meetings: These are accountability meetings that are held every week and facilitate action-oriented accountability within and/or among divisions so that police employees can come together to develop, coordinate, and assess strategies implemented for short-term activity.

Weighted time span analysis: Analysis of time span data in which each time span is assigned a value of 1, and each hour within the time span is a proportion of the time span.

Witness: A person who is able to provide information about a crime.

References

Austin, R., Cooper, G., Gagnon, D., Hodges, J., Martensen, K., & O'Neal, M. (1973). *Police crime analysis unit handbook.* Washington, DC: U.S. Department of Justice, National Institute of Law Enforcement and Criminal Justice.

Baltaci, H. (2010). *Crime analysis: An empirical analysis of its effectiveness as a crime fighting tool* (Doctoral Dissertation). The University of Texas at Dallas, Richardson.

Baker, T. E. (2004). *Introductory criminal analysis: Crime prevention and intervention strategies.* Upper Saddle River, NJ: Prentice-Hall.

Barthe, E. (2006). *Crime prevention publicity campaigns* [Monograph]. Washington, DC: Office of Community Oriented Policing Services.

Beck, C., & McCue, C. (2009, November). Predictive policing: What can we learn from Wal-Mart and Amazon about fighting crime in a recession? *Police Chief Magazine, 76,* 18–20, 22–24.

Bernasco, W. (2010). A sentimental journey to crime: Effects of residential history on crime location choice. *Criminology, 48*(2), 389–416.

Bichler, G., & Gaines, L. (2005). An examination of police officers' insights into problem identification and problem solving. *Crime & Delinquency, 51*(1), 53–74.

Block, R. C., Dabdoub, M., & Fregly, S. (Eds.). (1995). *Crime analysis through computer mapping.* Washington, DC: Police Executive Research Forum.

Boba, R. (2003). *Problem analysis in policing.* Washington, DC: Police Foundation.

Boba, R. (2010). A practice-based evidence approach in Florida. *Police Practice and Research,11*(2), 122–128.

Boba, R., & Crank, J. (2008). Institutionalizing problem-oriented policing: Rethinking problem identification, analysis, and accountability. *Police Practice and Research, 9*(5), 379–393.

Boba, R., & Santos, R. G. (2007). Single-family home construction site theft: A crime prevention case study. *International Journal of Construction Education and Research, 3,* 217–236.

Boba, R., & Santos, R.G. (2011). *A police organizational model for crime reduction: Institutionalizing problem solving, analysis, and accountability.* Washington DC: Office of Community Oriented Policing Services.

Booth, W. L. (1979). Management function of a crime analysis unit. *Law and Order, 27*(5), 28–33.

Bowers, K. J., & Johnson, S. D. (2005). Domestic burglary repeats and space–time clusters: The dimensions of risk. *European Journal of Criminology, 2,* 67–92.

Braga, A. (2013). *Ideas in American policing: Embedded criminologists in police departments.* Washington DC: Police Foundation.

Braga, A. A., Papachristos, A. V., & Hureau, D. M. (2014). The effects of hot spots policing on crime: An updated systematic review and meta-analysis. *Justice Quarterly, 31*(4), 633–663.

Braga, A., & Weisburd, D. L. (2006). Problem-oriented policing: The disconnect between principles and practice. In D. L. Weisburd & A. Braga (Eds.), *Police innovation: Contrasting perspectives* (pp. 133–154). Cambridge, UK: Cambridge University Press.

Braga, A. A., & Weisburd, D. (2010). *Policing problem places: Crime hot spots and effective prevention.* New York, NY: Oxford University Press.

Braga, A., & Weisburd, D. (2012). The effects of focused deterrence strategies on crime: A systematic review and meta-analysis of the empirical evidence. *Journal of Research in Crime and Delinquency, 49*(3), 323–358.

Brantingham, P. J., & Brantingham, P. L. (1981). *Environmental criminology.* Thousand Oaks, CA: Sage.

Brantingham, P. L., & Brantingham, P. J. (1990). Situational crime prevention in practice. *Canadian Journal of Criminology, 32,* 17–40.

Brantingham, P. L., & Brantingham, P. J. (1993). Nodes, paths and edges: Considerations on the complexity of crime and the physical environment. *Journal of Environmental Psychology, 13*(1), 3–28.

Bruce, C. (2008a). Fundamentals of crime analysis. In S. Gwinn, C. Bruce, J. Cooper, & S. Hick (Eds.), *Exploring crime analysis: Readings on essential skills* (2nd ed., pp. 11–36). Charleston, SC: BookSurge.

Bruce, C. (2008b). *Police strategies and tactics: What every analyst should know.* Retrieved July 21, 2011, from http://www.iaca.net/Resources/Articles/Police StrategiesTactics.pdf.

Bureau of Justice Assistance (BJA). (2005). *Why law enforcement agencies need an analytical function.* Washington DC: United States Department of Justice, Author.

Bureau of Justice Statistics. (2016). *Law Enforcement Management and Administrative Statistics (LEMAS), 2013.* Retrieved June 21, 2016, from http://www.icpsr.umich .edu/icpsrweb/NACJD/studies/36164

Burrell, A., & Bull, R. (2011). A preliminary examination of crime analysts' views and experiences of comparative case analysis. *International Journal of Police Science and Management, 13,* 2–15.

Center for Problem-Oriented Policing. (2016). Retrieved June 21, 2016, from http://www.pop center.org

Chainey, S., & Ratcliffe, J. (2005). *GIS and crime mapping.* Hoboken, NJ: John Wiley & Sons.

Chamard, S. E. (2003). *Innovation-diffusion networks and the adoption and discontinuance of computerized crime mapping by municipal police departments in New Jersey* (Doctoral Dissertation). Rutgers, The State University of New Jersey, Newark.

Chammah, M. (n.d.). Policing the future: In the aftermath of Ferguson, St. Louis cops embrace crime-predicting software. *The Verge, 2*(3). Retrieved August 18, 2016, from http://www.theverge.com/2016/ 2/3/10895804/st-louis-police

Chang, S. K., Simms, W. H., Makres, C. M., & Bodnar, A. (1979). *Crime analysis system support: Descriptive report of manual and automated crime analysis functions.* Washington, DC: National Criminal Justice Information and Statistics Service.

Chula Vista (California) Police Department. (2009). *Reducing crime and disorder at motels and hotels in Chula Vista, California.* Submission for the 2009 Herman Goldstein Problem-Oriented Policing Award. Retrieved July 19, 2016, from http://www.popcenter.org

Clarke, R. V. (1980). "Situational" crime prevention: Theory and practice. *British Journal of Criminology, 20,* 136–147.

Clarke, R. V. (1983). Situational crime prevention: Its theoretical basis and practical scope. In M. Tonry & N. Morris (Eds.), *Crime and justice: An annual review of research* (Vol. 4, pp. 225–256). Chicago, IL: University of Chicago Press.

Clarke, R. V. (Ed.). (1992). *Situational crime prevention: Successful case studies.* Albany, NY: Harrow & Heston.

Clarke, R. V. (1999). *Hot products: Understanding, anticipating, and reducing demand for stolen goods* (Police Research Series Paper 112). London, UK: Home Office, Research, Development and Statistics Directorate, Policing and Reducing Crime Unit.

Clarke, R. V., & Eck, J. (2005). *Crime analysis for problem solvers: In 60 small steps.* Washington, DC: Office of Community Oriented Policing Services.

Clarke, R. V., & Schultze, P. A. (2005). *Researching a problem.* Washington, DC: Office of Community Oriented Policing Services.

Clarke, R. V., & Weisburd, D. (1994). Diffusion of crime control benefits: Observations on the reverse of displacement. In R. V. Clarke (Ed.), *Crime prevention studies* (Vol. 2, pp. 165–183). Monsey, NY: Criminal Justice Press.

Commission on Accreditation for Law Enforcement Agencies. (2016). *About CALEA*. Retrieved February 21, 2016, from http://www.calea.org/content/commission

Cope, N. (2004). Intelligence-led policing or policing led intelligence? *The British Journal of Criminology, 44,* 188–203.

Cornish, D. B., & Clarke, R. V. (1986). *The reasoning criminal.* New York, NY: Springer-Verlag.

Cornish, D. B., & Clarke, R. V. (2003). Opportunities, precipitators, and criminal decisions: A reply to Wortley's critique of situational crime prevention. In M. J. Smith & D. B. Cornish (Eds.), *Theory for practice in situational crime prevention* (pp. 41–96). Monsey, NY: Criminal Justice Press.

Coupe, T., & Blake, L. (2006). Daylight and darkness targeting strategies and the risks of being seen at residential burglaries. *Criminology, 44,* 431–464.

Dabney, D. (2010). Observations regarding key operational realities in a Compstat model of policing. *Justice Quarterly, 27,* 28–51.

Darroch, S., & Mazerolle, L. (2012). Intelligence-led policing: A comparative analysis of organizational factors influencing innovation uptake. *Police Quarterly, 16*(1), 3–37.

Demir, S. (2009). *Diffusion of police technology across time and space and the impact of technology use on police effectiveness and its contribution to decision-making* (Doctoral Dissertation). Kent State University, OH.

Eck, J. (2002). *Assessing responses to problems: An introductory guide for police problem-solvers.* Washington, DC: Office of Community Oriented Policing Services.

Eck, J., Chainey, S., Cameron, J., Leitner, M., & Wilson, R. (2005). *Mapping crime: Understanding hot spots.* Washington, DC: National Institute of Justice.

Eck, J., Clarke, R. V., & Guerette, R. T. (2007). Risky facilities: Crime concentration in homogeneous sets of establishments and facilities. In G. Farrell, K. J. Bowers, S. D. Johnson, & M. Townsley (Eds.), *Imagination for crime prevention: Essays in honour of Ken Pease* (pp. 225–264). Portland, OR: Willan.

Eck, J., & Spelman, W. (1987). *Problem solving. Problem-oriented policing in Newport News.* Washington, DC: Police Executive Research Forum.

Eck, J., & Weisburd, D. (1995). Crime places in crime theory. In J. Eck & D. Weisburd (Eds.), *Crime and place* (pp. 1–34). Monsey, NY: Criminal Justice Press.

Emig, M., Heck, R., & Kravitz, M. (1980). *Crime analysis: A selected bibliography.* Washington, DC: U.S. National Criminal Justice Reference Service.

Farrell, G., & Pease, K. (1993). *Once bitten, twice bitten: Repeat victimization and its implications for crime prevention* (Crime Prevention Unit Series Paper 46). London, UK: Home Office, Police Research Group.

Federal Bureau of Investigation (FBI). (2004). *UCR: Uniform crime reporting— Handbook.* Washington, DC: US Department of Justice.

Federal Bureau of Investigation (FBI). (2016). *2014 Crime in the United States.* Retrieved June 21, 2016, from https://www.fbi.gov/about-us/cjis/ucr/crime-in-the-u.s/2014/crime-in-the-u.s.-2014/resource-pages/fbi-releases-2014-crime-statistics

Felson, M. (2006). *Crime and nature.* Thousand Oaks, CA: Sage.

Felson, M., & Boba, R. (2010). *Crime and everyday life.* Thousand Oaks, CA: Sage.

Felson, M., & Clarke, R. V. (1998). *Opportunity makes the thief: Practical theory for crime prevention* (Police Research Series Paper 98). London, UK: Home Office, Research, Development and Statistics Directorate, Policing and Reducing Crime Unit.

Giblin, M. J. (2006). Structural elaboration and institutional isomorphism: The case of crime analysis units. *Policing: An International Journal of Police Strategies & Management, 29*(4), 643–664.

Gill, C., Weisburd, D., Telep, C., Vitter, Z., & Bennett, T. (2014). Community-oriented policing to reduce crime, disorder and fear and increase satisfaction and legitimacy among citizens: A systematic review. *Journal of Experimental Criminology, 10,* 399–428.

Goldstein, H. (1979). Improving policing: A problem-oriented approach. *Crime & Delinquency, 24,* 236–258.

Goldstein, H. (1990). *Problem-oriented policing.* New York, NY: McGraw-Hill.

Gottlieb, S., Arenberg, S., & Singh, R. (1994). *Crime analysis: From first report to final arrest.* Montclair, CA: Alpha.

Groff, E. R., & La Vigne, N. G. (2002). Forecasting the future of predictive crime mapping. In N. Tilley (Ed.), *Analysis for crime prevention* (pp. 29–58). Monsey, NY: Criminal Justice Press.

Grove, L., Farrell, G., Farrington, D. P., & Johnson, S. D. (2012). *Preventing repeat victimization: A systematic review.* Stockholm, Sweden: Swedish National Council for Crime Prevention.

Guerette, R. T., & Bowers, K. J. (2009). Assessing the extent of crime displacement and diffusion of benefits: a review of situational crime prevention evaluations. *Criminology, 47*(4), 1331–1368.

Gwinn, S., Bruce, D., Cooper, J., & Hick, S. (2008). *Exploring crime analysis: Readings on essential skills* (2nd ed.). Charleston, SC: BookSurge.

Haberman, C., & Ratcliffe, J. (2012). The predictive policing challenges of near repeat armed street robberies. *Policing,* 6(2),151–166.

Harries, K. D. (1980). *Crime and the environment.* Springfield, IL: Charles C Thomas.

Harries, K. D. (1999). *Crime mapping: Principles and practice.* Washington, DC: National Institute of Justice.

Harris, S. (2014). Product feature: Predictive policing helps law enforcement: See around the corners. *The Police Chief, LXXXI* (11). Retrieved from http://www.policechiefmagazine.org/magazine/index.cfm?fuseaction=display_arch&article_id=3539&issue_id=112014

Helms, D. (2004). Temporal analysis. In C. Bruce, S. Hick, & J. Cooper (Eds.), *Exploring crime analysis: Readings on essential skills* (pp. 220–262). Charleston, SC: BookSurge.

Henry, V. (2002). *The COMPSTAT paradigm.* Flushing, NY: Looseleaf Law.

Hesseling, R. (1994). Displacement: A review of the empirical literature. In R. V. Clarke (Ed.), *Crime prevention studies* (Vol. 3, pp. 197–230). Monsey, NY: Criminal Justice Press.

Hick, S., Bair, S., Fritz, N., & Helms, D. (2004). Crime mapping. In C. Bruce, S. Hick, & J. Cooper (Eds.), *Exploring crime analysis: Readings on essential skills* (pp. 314–339). Charleston, SC: BookSurge.

Hollywood, J., Smith, S., Price, C., McInnis, B., & Perry, W. (2012). Predictive policing: *What it is, what it isn't, and where it can be useful* (PowerPoint Presentation). Washington, DC: RAND.

Hollywood, J., & Winkelman, Z. (2015). *Improving information-sharing across law enforcement: Why we can't know.* Washington DC: RAND.

Hunt, P., Saunders, J., & Hollywood, J. (2014). *Evaluation of the Shreveport predictive policing experiment.* Washington, DC: RAND.

INTERPOL. (2014). *Intelligence analysis.* Retrieved May 10, 2014, from http://www.interpol.int/INTERPOLexpertise/Intelligence-analysis

International Association of Crime Analysts (IACA). (2011a). *Certified Law Enforcement Analyst program (CLEA).* Retrieved from http://www.iaca.net/certification.asp

International Association of Crime Analysts (IACA). (2011b). *Crime pattern definitions for tactical analysis* (White Paper 2011–01). Overland Park, KS: Author.

International Association of Crime Analysts. (2013). *RMS technical requirements of crime analysis* (White Paper 2013-01). Overland Park, KS: Author.

International Association of Crime Analysts. (2014a). *Information-sharing platforms* (White Paper 2014-01). Overland Park, KS: Author.

International Association of Crime Analysts. (2014b). *Definition and types of crime analysis* [White Paper 2014-02]. Overland Park, KS: Author.

Jang, H., Hoover, L., & Joo, H. (2010). An evaluation of Compstat's effect on crime: The Fort Worth experience. *Police Quarterly, 13,* 387–412.

Johnson, S., & Bowers, K. (2003). Opportunity is in the eye of the beholder: The role of publicity in crime prevention. *Criminology & Public Policy, 2*(3), 497–524.

Johnson, S. D., & Bowers, K. J. (2004). The burglary as a clue to the future: The beginnings of prospective hot-spotting. *European Journal of Criminology, 1,* 237–255.

Johnson, S. D., Guerette, R. T., & Bowers, K. (2014). Crime displacement: What we know, what we don't know, and what it means for crime reduction. *Journal of Experimental Criminology, 10*(4), 549–571.

Johnson, S. D., Lab, S., & Bowers, K. J. (2008). Stable and fluid hot spots of crime: Differentiation and identification. *Built Environment, 34*(1), 32–46.

Johnson, S. D., Summers, L., & Pease, K. (2007). *Vehicle crime: Communicating spatial and temporal patterns.* London, United Kingdom: Jill Dando Institute of Crime Science.

Johnson, S. D., Summers, L., & Pease, K. (2009). Offenders as forager: A direct test of the boost account of victimization. *Journal of Quantitative Criminology, 25,* 181–200.

Kelling, G. L. (2015). An author's brief history of an idea. *Journal of Research in Crime and Delinquency, 52,* 626–629.

Kennedy, D. M., Braga, A. A., & Piehl, A. M. (1998). The (un)known universe: Mapping gangs and gang violence in Boston. In D. Weisburd & T. McEwen (Eds.), *Crime mapping and crime prevention* (Crime Prevention Studies, Vol. 8, pp. 219–262). Monsey. NY: Criminal Justice Press.

Kennedy, D. M., Braga, A. A., & Piehl, A. M. (2001). *Reducing gun violence: The Boston Gun Project's Operation Ceasefire.* Washington, DC: National Institute of Justice.

Koper, C. S., Lum, C., Willis, J. J., Woods, D. J., & Hibdon, J. (2015). *Realizing the potential of technology in policing.* Arlington, VA: George Mason University and Washington, DC Police Executive Research Forum.

Laub, J., & Sampson, R. (2003). *Shared beginnings, divergent lives: Delinquent boys to age 70.* Cambridge, MA: Harvard University Press.

LeBeau, J. L. (1987). The methods and measures of centrography and the spatial dynamics of rape. *Journal of Quantitative Criminology, 3,* 125–141.

Lynch, J. P., & Jarvis, J. P. (2008). Missing data and imputation in the Uniform Crime Reports and the effects on national estimates. *Journal of Contemporary Criminal Justice, 24,* 69–85.

Maltz, M. (1999). *Bridging gaps in police crime data.* Washington, DC: Bureau of Justice Statistics.

McGarrell, E., Freilich, J., & Chermak, S. (2007). Intelligence-led policing as a framework for responding to terrorism. *Journal of Contemporary Criminal Justice, 23,* 142–158.

McLaughlin, L., Johnson, S. D., Bowers, K. J., Birks, D. J., & Pease, K. (2006). Police perceptions of the long- and short-term spatial distribution of residential burglary. *International Journal of Police Science & Management, 9*(2), 99–111.

Metropolitan Police Service. (2016). *Metropolitan Police Service: Timeline 1829–1849.* Retrieved June 21, 2016, from http://content.met.police.uk/Site/historypolicing

Mohler, G., Shorty, M., Malinowskiz, S., Johnson, M., Tita, G., Bertozzik, A., & Brantingham, J. (2015). Randomized controlled field trials of predictive policing, *Journal of the American Statistical Association.* doi:10.1080/01621459.2015.1077710

Newman, G. (2007). *Sting operations* [Monograph]. Washington, DC: Office of Community Oriented Policing Services.

Office of Community Oriented Policing Services. (2014). *Community policing defined.* Washington DC: Author.

Omnibus Crime Control and Safe Streets Act of 1968, Pub. L. No. 90-351, 82 Stat. 197 (codified as amended in scattered sections of 18 U.S.C.A.).

O'Shea, T. C., & Nicholls, K. (2003). Police crime analysis: A survey of U.S. police departments with 100 or more sworn personnel. *Police Practice and Research, 4,* 233–250.

Pace, E. (1972, July 22). Fifty-seven slain in week, a record for city. *The New York Times,* p. 1.

Paulsen, D. J., Bair, S., & Helms, D. (2009). *Tactical crime analysis: Research and investigation.* Boca Raton, FL: CRC Press.

Petersen, M. (1994). *Applications in criminal analysis: A sourcebook.* Westport, CT: Greenwood.

Petersillia, J. (2008). Influencing public policy: An embedded criminologist reflects on California prison reform. *Journal of Experimental Criminology, 4,* 335–356,

Police Executive Research Forum. (2013). *Compstat: Its origins, evolution, and future in law enforcement agencies.* Washington, DC: Author.

Pomrenke, N. E. (1969). *Police selection, training and education action grant programs in 1969: State law enforcement plans submitted under Title I, Omnibus Crime Control and Safe Streets Act of 1968–1969 state plan analysis.* Washington, DC: National Sheriffs' Association.

Ratcliffe, J. H. (2002). Aoristic signatures and the spatiotemporal analysis of high-volume crime patterns. *Journal of Quantitative Criminology, 18,* 23–43.

Ratcliffe, J. H. (2004a). Crime mapping and the training needs of law enforcement. *European Journal of Criminal Policy and Research, 10,* 65–83.

Ratcliffe, J. H. (2004b). The hotspot matrix: A framework for the spatiotemporal targeting of crime reduction. *Police Practice and Research, 5*(1), 5–23.

Ratcliffe, J. H. (2008). *Intelligence-led policing.* Cullompton, UK: Willan.

Ratcliffe, J. H. (2011). *Jerry's top ten PowerPoint tips.* Retrieved July 24, 2011, from http://jratcliffe.net

Ratcliffe, J. H., & Guidetti, R. (2008). State police investigative structure and the adoption of intelligence-led policing. *Policing: An International Journal of Police Strategies & Management, 31,* 109–128.

Ratcliffe, J. H., & McCullagh, M. (2001). Chasing ghosts? Police perception of high crime areas. *British Journal of Criminology, 41,* 330–341.

Reiner, G. H., Greenlee, M. R., & Gibbens, M. H. (1976). *Crime analysis in support of patrol: National evaluation program, Phase I summary report.* Washington, DC: Law Enforcement Assistance Administration.

Rengert, G., & Wasilchick, J. (1985). *Suburban burglary: A time and a place for everything.* Springfield, IL: Charles C Thomas.

Rossmo, D. K. (2000). *Geographic profiling.* Boca Raton, FL: CRC Press.

Sampson, R. (2003, October). *Crime analysis in the United States: What it's accomplished, where it's going.* Paper presented at the annual training meeting of the International Association of Crime Analysts, Kansas City, MO.

Sampson, R. (2004). *Theft of and from autos in parking facilities in Chula Vista: A final report on the field applications of the Problem-Oriented Guides for Police project.* Washington, DC: U.S. Department of Justice, Office of Community Oriented Policing Services.

Santos, R. B. (2013). Implementation of a police organizational model for crime reduction. *Policing: An International Journal of Police Strategies and Management, 32*(2), 295–311.

Santos, R. B. (2014). The effectiveness of crime analysis for crime reduction: Cure or diagnosis? *Journal of Contemporary Criminal Justice, 30*(2), 147–168.

Santos, R. B., & Santos, R. G. (2015d). Examination of police dosage in residential burglary and theft from vehicle micro-time hot spots. *Crime Science, 4*(27), 1–12. doi:10.1186/s40163-015-0041-6.

Santos, R. B., & Taylor, B. (2014). The integration of crime analysis into police patrol work. Results from a national survey of law enforcement. *Policing: An International Journal of Police Strategies and Management, 37*(3), 501–520.

Santos, R. G. (2011, February). Systematic pattern response strategy: Protecting the beehive. *FBI Law Enforcement Bulletin.* Retrieved from http://www.fbi.gov/stats-services/publications/law-enforcement-bulletin/february2011/copy_of_notable-speech

Santos, R. G., & Santos, R. B. (2015a). An ex post facto evaluation of tactical police response in residential theft from vehicle micro-time hot spots. *Journal of Quantitative Criminology, 31*(4), 679–698.

Santos, R. G., & Santos, R. B. (2015b). Evidence-based policing, "What works" and stratified policing, "How to make it work." *Translational Criminology, 8*, 20–22.

Santos, R. G., & Santos, R. B. (2015c). Practice-based research: Ex post facto evaluation of evidence-based police practices implemented in residential burglary micro-time hot spots. *Evaluation Review.* doi:10.1177/0193841X15602818.

Schaible, L. M., & Sheffield, J. (2012). Intelligence-led policing and change in state law enforcement agencies. *Policing: An International Journal of Police Strategies and Management, 35*(4), 761–784.

Schmerler, K., & Velasco, M. (2002). Primary data collection: A problem-solving necessity. *Crime Mapping News, 4*(2), 4–8.

Schmerler, K., Wartell, J., & Weisel, D. (2004). Applied research in crime analysis and problem solving. In C. Bruce, S. Hick, & J. Cooper (Eds.), *Exploring crime analysis: Readings on essential skills* (pp. 121–143). Charleston, SC: BookSurge.

Scott, M. (2000). *Problem-oriented policing: Reflections on the first 20 years* [Monograph]. Washington, DC: U.S. Department of Justice, Office of Community Oriented Policing Services.

Scott, M. (2004). *The benefits and consequences of police crackdowns* [Monograph]. Washington, DC: Office of Community Oriented Policing Services.

Sever, B., Garcia, V., & Tsiandi, A. (2008). Municipal police departments' attention to crime analysis: Essential or impractical? *Police Practice & Research, 9*, 323–340.

Shaw, C. R., & McKay, H. D. (1969). *Juvenile delinquency and urban areas* (Rev. ed.). Chicago, IL: University of Chicago Press.

Sherman, L. W. (1998). *Evidence-based policing: American ideas in policing.* Washington, DC: Police Foundation.

Sherman, L. W., Gartin, P. R., & Buerger, M. E. (1989). Hot spots of predatory crime: Routine activities and the criminology of place. *Criminology, 27*, 27–55.

Sherman, L. W., Gottfredson, D., MacKenzie, D. L., Eck, J., Reuter, P., & Bushway, S. (1997). *Preventing crime: What works, what doesn't, what's promising: A report to the attorney general of the United States.* Washington, DC: U.S. Department of Justice, Office of Justice Programs.

Silverman, E. (2006). Compstat's innovation. In D. L. Weisburd & A. Braga (Eds.), *Police innovation: Contrasting perspectives* (pp. 267–283). Cambridge, UK: Cambridge University Press.

Skogan, W., & Frydl, K. (2004). *Fairness and effectiveness in policing: The evidence.* Washington, DC: The National Academies Press.

Smith, M. J., Clarke, R. V., & Pease, K. (2002). Anticipatory benefit in crime prevention. In N. Tilley (Ed.), *Analysis for crime prevention: Crime prevention studies* (Vol. 13, pp. 71–88). Monsey, NY: Criminal Justice Press.

Sousa, W., & Kelling, G. (2006). Of "broken windows," criminology, and criminal justice. In D. L. Weisburd & A. Braga (Eds.), *Police innovation: Contrasting perspectives* (pp. 77–97). Cambridge, UK: Cambridge University Press.

Taxman, F. S., & McEwen, T. (1997). Using geographical tools with interagency work groups to develop and implement crime control strategies. In D. Weisburd & T. McEwen (Eds.), *Crime mapping and crime prevention* (pp. 83–111). Monsey, NY: Criminal Justice Press.

Taylor, B., & Boba, R. (2011). *The integration of crime analysis into patrol work: A guidebook.* Washington DC: Office of Community Oriented Policing Services.

Taylor, B., Kowalyk, A., & Boba, R. (2007). The integration of crime analysis into law enforcement agencies: An exploratory study into the perceptions of crime analysts. *Police Quarterly, 10*(2), 154–169.

Telep, C. W., & Weisburd, D. (2012). What is known about the effectiveness police practices in reducing crime and disorder? *Police Quarterly, 15*(4), 331–357.

Theodore, J. (2001). Crime mapping goes Hollywood: CBS's *The District* demonstrates crime mapping to millions of TV viewers. *Crime Mapping News, 3*(3), 7.

The SMT Mission. (n.d.). Standards, Methods and Technology Committee. iaca.net. Retrieved from http://www.iaca.net/committee_smt.asp.

Tompson, L., & Townsley, M. (2010). (Looking) Back to the future: Using space–time patterns to better predict the location of street crime. *International Journal of Police Science and Management, 12*, 23–40.

Townsley, M., Homel, R., & Chaseling, J. (2003). Infectious burglaries: A test of the near repeat hypothesis. *British Journal of Criminology, 43*, 615–633.

Truman, J. L., & Langton, L. (2014). *Criminal victimization, 2013.* Washington DC: Bureau of Justice Statistics.

Uchida, C. (2010). *A national discussion on predictive policing: Defining our terms and mapping successful implementation strategies.* Washington DC: National Institute of Justice.

Weisburd, D. (2015). The 2014 Sutherland Address: The law of crime concentration and the criminology of place. *Criminology, 53*(2), 133–157.

Weisburd, D. L., & Braga, A. (2006a). *Police innovation: Contrasting perspectives.* Cambridge, United Kingdom: Cambridge University Press.

Weisburd, D., & Eck, J. (2004). What can police do to reduce crime, disorder, and fear? *The Annals of the American Academy of Political and Social Science, 593*, 42–65.

Weisburd, D., & Lum, C. (2005.). The diffusion of computerized crime mapping in policing: Linking research and practice. *Police Practice and Research, 6*(5), 419–434.

Weisburd, D., Mastrofski, S. D., McNally, A. M., Greenspan, R., & Willis, J. J. (2003). Reforming to preserve: Compstat and strategic problem solving in American policing. *Criminology and Public Policy, 2*, 421–456.

Weisburd, D., Mastrofski, S., Willis, J., & Greenspan, R. (2006). Changing everything so that everything can remain the same: Compstat and American policing. In D. L. Weisburd & A. Braga (Eds.), *Police innovation: Contrasting perspectives* (pp. 284–304). Cambridge, UK: Cambridge University Press.

Weisburd, D., & McEwen, T. (1997). Crime mapping and crime prevention. In D. Weisburd & T. McEwen (Eds.), *Crime mapping and crime prevention* (pp. 1–26). Monsey, NY: Criminal Justice Press.

Weisburd, D., Telep, C. W., Hinkle, J. C., & Eck, J. (2010). Is problem-oriented policing effective in reducing crime and disorder? Findings from a Campbell systematic review. *Criminology & Public Policy, 9*(1), 139–172.

Weisel, D. L. (2004). *Street prostitution in Raleigh, North Carolina: A final report for the field applications of Problem-Oriented Guides for Police project.* Washington, DC: Office of Community Oriented Policing Services.

Weisel, D. L. (2005). *Analyzing repeat victimization.* Washington, DC: Office of Community Oriented Policing Services.

Welsh, B., Braga, A., & Bruinsma, G. (2015). Reimagining broken windows: From theory to policy, *Journal of Research in Crime and Delinquency, 52*(4), 447-463.

Willis, J. J. (2011). Enhancing police legitimacy by integrating Compstat with community policing. *Policing: An International Journal of Police Strategies & Management, 34,* 654–673.

Willis, J. J., Mastrofski, S. D., & Kochel, T. R. (2010). The co-implementation of Compstat and community policing. *Journal of Criminal Justice, 38,* 969–980.

Willis, J. J., Mastrofski, S. D., & Weisburd, D. (2007). Making sense of COMPSTAT: A theory-based analysis of organizational change in three police departments. *Law & Society Review, 41*(1), 147–188.

Wilson, J., & Kelling, G. (1982). Broken windows: The police and neighborhood safety. *Atlantic Monthly, 24*(9), 29–38.

Wilson, O. W. (1957). *Police planning* (2nd ed.). Springfield, IL: Charles C Thomas.

Wilson, O. W. (1963). *Police administration* (2nd ed.). New York, NY: McGraw-Hill.

Wilson, O. W., & McLaren, R. C. (1977). *Police administration* (4th ed.). New York, NY: McGraw-Hill.

Wright, R., & Decker, S. (1997). *Armed robbers in action: Stickups and street culture.* Boston, MA: Northeastern University Press.

Index

Graduated-symbol maps, 163–175
Grant work, support for, 105
Graphics software, 144
Grid mapping, 368
Guardians, 41, 45
Guerry, André-Michel, 13

Handlers, 40
Heck, R., 11
Histogram, 332
Hot places, 231, 246, 247, 265–266. *See also* Patterns
Hot prey, 230, 246, 255–256, 257–259. *See also* Patterns
Hot products, 49, 231, 247, 266–267, 272, 273–275. *See also* Patterns
Hot setting, 230, 246, 247, 256, 264, 269–270, 271, 273. *See also* Patterns
Hot spot analysis, 102
Hot spots, 48, 81, 230, 253, 256, 258–259, 268, 272
   micro-time hot spot, 230, 247, 263, 268, 294–295, 295 (figure), 357
   policing, 69–70
   See also Patterns
Hypotheses, 313–314, 329–330, 374

IACA (International Association of Crime Analysts). *See* International Association of Crime Analysts
IAFIS (Integrated Automated Fingerprint Identification System), 116
Illinois Criminal Justice Information Authority, 15
ILP (intelligence-led policing), 73
Immediate problems, 78–79, 93, 183, 189–190, 196–198
Impact evaluation, 314–315
"Improving Policing" (Goldstein), 67
Incidents, 118–119, 328. *See also* Events
Incidents, repeat, 79, 100, 190–191, 211–215, 328
Incidents, "reported," 131–132, 143
Incidents, serious, 79
Induction, 231, 232–233, 234 (figure), 241
Information, 184, 251, 252. *See also* Dissemination of results; Results
Information-sharing platforms, 115
Integrated Automated Fingerprint Identification System (IAFIS), 116
Intelligence, 4, 97–100, 107
Intelligence-led policing (ILP), 73

Interactive crime mapping, 163
International Association of Crime Analysts (IACA)
   categories rejected by, 106
   categorization of crime patterns, 229–231
   creation of, 12
   on criminal intelligence analysis, 4, 99–100
   on criminal investigative analysis, 101
   Definition and Types of Crime Analysis, 97
   definition of crime analysis, 4
   definition of crime intelligence analysis, 4
   recommendations for RMS, 114–115
   Standards, Methods, and Technology Committee (SMT), 3, 33, 97
Interns, 21–22
Intervals between events, 287, 289 (table)
Interviews, 128, 370
Intranets, 144, 298, 387
Investigative leads, 220, 238–240
Investigative support, 65, 106

Jail management systems (JMS), 116
Johnson, S., 346
Journals, 33

Kelling, G., 70–71
Known-offender database, 127
Kravitz, M., 11

Latitude, 154, 155
Law, criminological, 46
Law Enforcement Management and Administrative Statistics (LEMAS), 17
Law of crime concentration, 47, 49
Laws, changes in, 143
Leads, identifying, 223–224
Levers, pulling, 70
Line charts, 332, 341, 342
Line features, 150, 151 (table), 152, 166, 167 (figure)
Linear trend line, 343
Link analysis, 98
London, 9
Long-term problems, 78, 80–83, 101, 183, 192–193, 195, 203–206, 411. *See also* Strategic crime analysis
Longitude, 154, 155
Loyola University Chicago, 15

Operations analysis, 103, 107
Opportunity, for crime, 55, 347
    and crime prevention, 50–53
    and problem analysis triangle, 41–42
    and rational choice theory, 43–44
    reducing, 42, 51
    routine activities theory, 45–46
    and settings, 40
Organizational procedures, 13
O'Shea, T. C., 61

Parents, 42. *See also* Guardians; Handlers
Pareto principle (80/20 rule), 50, 320,
    358, 361, 371
Patrol, directed, 249, 251, 252, 253,
    257, 258, 259
Patrol staffing analysis, 104–105
Patrol time, uncommitted, 196
Patrol work, integration of crime analysis
    in, 17
Pattern analysis, 80, 223
Pattern finalization, 237–238, 254
Pattern identification
    data for, 215–225
    deduction, 231–232, 232 (figure),
        233
    identifying meaningful patterns,
        253–275
    induction, 231, 232–233, 234 (figure)
    initial pattern identification, 233–237
    methodology, 229–238
    pattern finalization, 237–238, 254
    and persons crimes, 254–262
    preparing for, 245
    and property crimes, 262–275
Patterns, 42, 80, 192
    analysis of, 100
    commercial burglary patterns,
        270–272
    investigating, 250
    of persons crimes, 245–246, 248
    of persons crimes, responding to,
        251–252
    vs. problems, 80
    of property crimes, 246–247, 248
    of property crimes, responding to,
        252–253
    residential burglary patterns, 267–270
    robbery patterns, 255–260
    sexual crime-related patterns,
        260–262
    types of, 229–231
Patterns, describing
    modus operandi summary, 279–280

spatial analysis of, 294–295
    suspect descriptions, 281
    time series analysis, 281–291
    vehicle descriptions, 281
Patterns, short-term, 100
Pawn database, 127
Pease, K., 346
Percentage, 316–317, 330, 333–334
Percentage of change, 344–346
Percentile, 319–320
Performance indicators, 407–408,
    417–418
Personnel
    and crime reduction strategies,
        195–206
    and immediate problems, 196–198
    and long-term problems, 192–193,
        195, 203–206
    and short-term problems, 190, 192,
        198, 200–202
    and situational awareness, 189–195
Persons crimes
    described, 245
    and identifying patterns, 254–262
    MO summary, 280
    patterns of, 245–246, 248, 254–262
    rate of, 337
    responding to patterns of, 251–252
    robbery patterns, 255–260
    sexual crime-related patterns,
        260–262
Persons database, 126
Phenomena, crime, 53
Physical facilitators, 375–376
Pie chart mapping, 162, 162 (figure)
Pie charts, 333–334
Place, 46, 47. *See also* Geographic
    analysis; Problem area; Problem
    location
Place, hot. *See* Hot places
Point features, 149–150, 151 (table),
    152, 164, 166
Police
    focus of, 11
    goals of, 13
    See also Personnel; Police agencies
Police Administration (Wilson and
    McLaren), 10
Police agencies
    administrative crime analysis,
        103–105, 108, 399
    benefits of crime analysis to, 6–7
    decision-making, 104
    federal funding, 15

London Metropolitan Police Service, 9
planning, 104, 107
and problem analysis, 312–313
in United States, 10
use of crime analysis, 18
use of term, 4
Police Executive Research Forum, 16–17
Police Planning (Wilson), 10
Policies, changes in, 143
Policing, standard model of, 64–65
Policing, stratified. *See* Stratified policing
Policing approaches. *See* Crime
reduction strategies
Polygon features, 150, 152 (figure), 153,
153 (table), 164, 166, 168 (figure)
Polygon maps, 168, 169 (figure), 170
(figure), 172 (figure), 173 (figure),
174 (figure)
POP (problem-oriented policing), 11,
12, 67–69
POP Center. *See* Center for Problem-
Oriented Policing
Population, in comparisons, 422–423
Predictive analysis, 107
Predictive policing, 73–74
Prelude, 328
Presentation software, 144
Prevention
and crime reduction strategies, 75
effectiveness of, and crime analysis, 61
and 80/20 rule, 50
and opportunity, 50–53
and repeat victimization, 48
Prey, hot. *See* Hot prey
Primary data, 113, 128–130, 131 (table)
Principal case, 237
Probation/parole database, 239
Problem, compound, 82
Problem, defining, 78
Problem analysis, 17, 102
Problem analysis triangle, 40–42,
47, 53
Problem analyst, 23
Problem area, 81, 357, 364–368, 370
(table)
Problem comparison charts, 413–415,
415 (figure)
Problem location, 81, 357, 358–364
Problem offender, 81
Problem-oriented policing (POP), 11,
12, 67–69. *See also* Center for
Problem-Oriented Policing
Problem-Oriented Policing (Goldstein), 12
Problem property, 82

Problem solving, 11, 66, 68, 72. *See also*
Problem-solving process; SARA
process
Problem-solving process, 15, 72
analysis in, 312–314, 337, 381,
382–384
assessment, 314–315, 330, 341,
346–347
determining change in problem,
340–347
determining nature of problem,
328–330
determining offenders/repeat
offenders, 371–374
determining prevalence of problem,
330–340
determining temporal nature of
problem, 347–352
determining victims/repeat
victimization, 369–371
determining why problem is
occurring, 374–376
geographic analysis, 357–369
hypotheses, 313–314, 329–330
response to, 314, 330. *See also*
Response, Police
scanning, 308–311, 330, 336–337,
341, 362, 381–382
See also SARA process
Problem stratification, 78–83
Problem victim, 82
Problems
identifying, 308
local context of, 312–313
vs. patterns, 80
See also Immediate problems; Long-
term problems; Short-term
problems
Process, of crime analysis, 91–96, 92
(figure)
Process evaluation, 314
Products, hot. *See* Hot products
Profiling, criminal, 101
Projections, 154
Property, problem, 82
Property crimes
and clearing cases, 253
described, 246
geographic proximity of incidents,
295
hot product patterns, 273–275
MO summary, 280
patterns of, 246–247, 248, 262–275
rate of, 337